DAVID MILNE

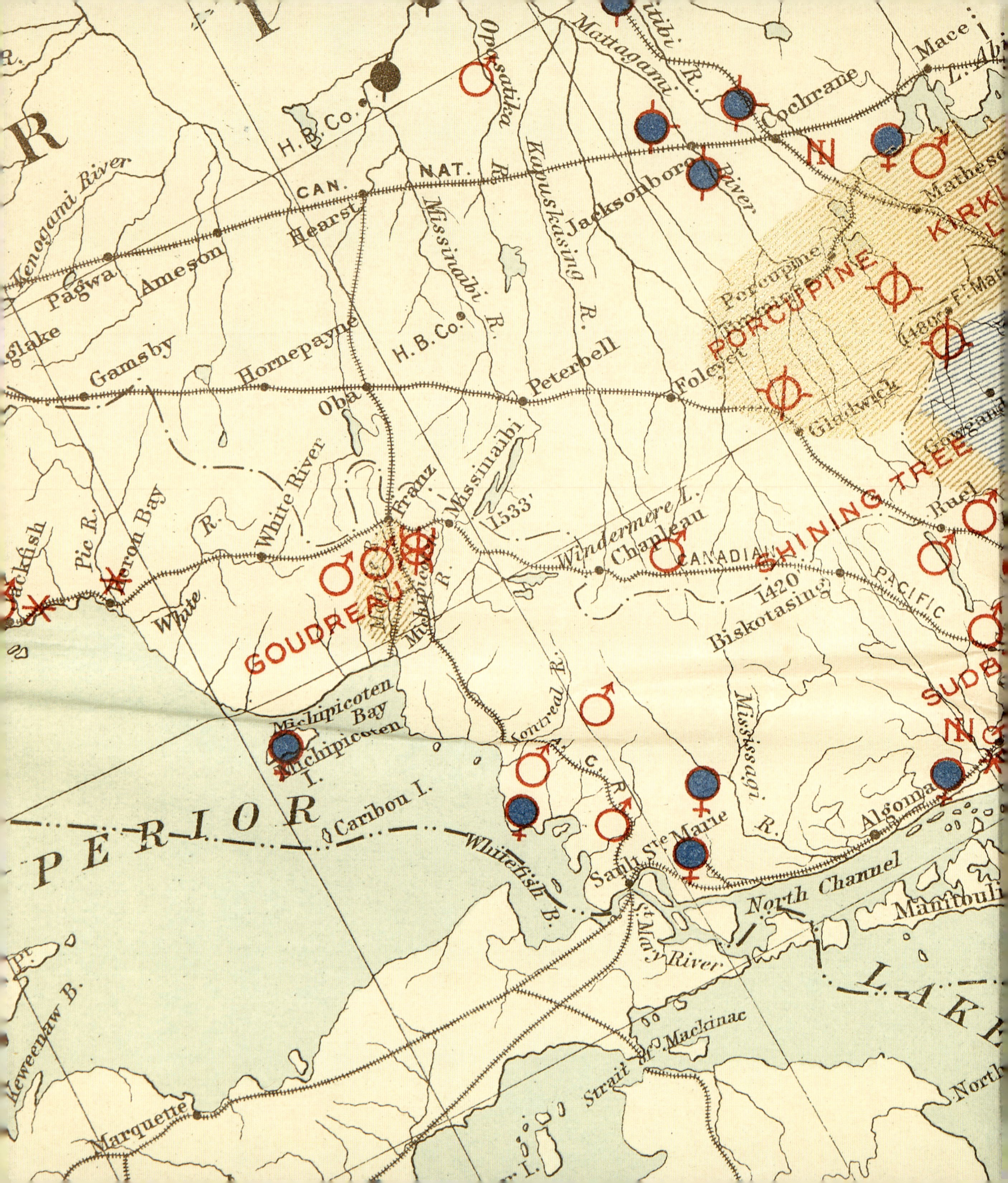

Mattagami R.
Opasatika R.
Kenogami River
H.B.Co.
CAN. NAT.
Hearst
Cochrane
Mace
Jacksonboro
River
Kapuskasing R.
Missinaibi R.
Pagwa
Ameson
glake
Gamsby
Hornepayne
H.B.Co.
Peterbell
Foleyet
Porcupine
PORCUPINE
KIRKL
Matheso
Gladwick
Oba
White River
Franz
Missinaibi
1533'
Windermere L.
Chapleau
CANADIAN
PACIFIC
SHINING TREE
Ruel
1420
Biskotasing
Pic R.
Heron Bay
Jackfish
White R.
White
GOUDREAU
Michipicoten R.
Michipicoten Bay
Michipicoten I.
Caribou I.
PERIOR
Montreal R.
A. C. R.
Mississagi R.
Algoma
SUDB
Sault Ste Marie
Whitefish B.
North Channel
Manitouli
St Mary River
LAKE
Strait of Mackinac
Keweenaw B.
Marquette
North

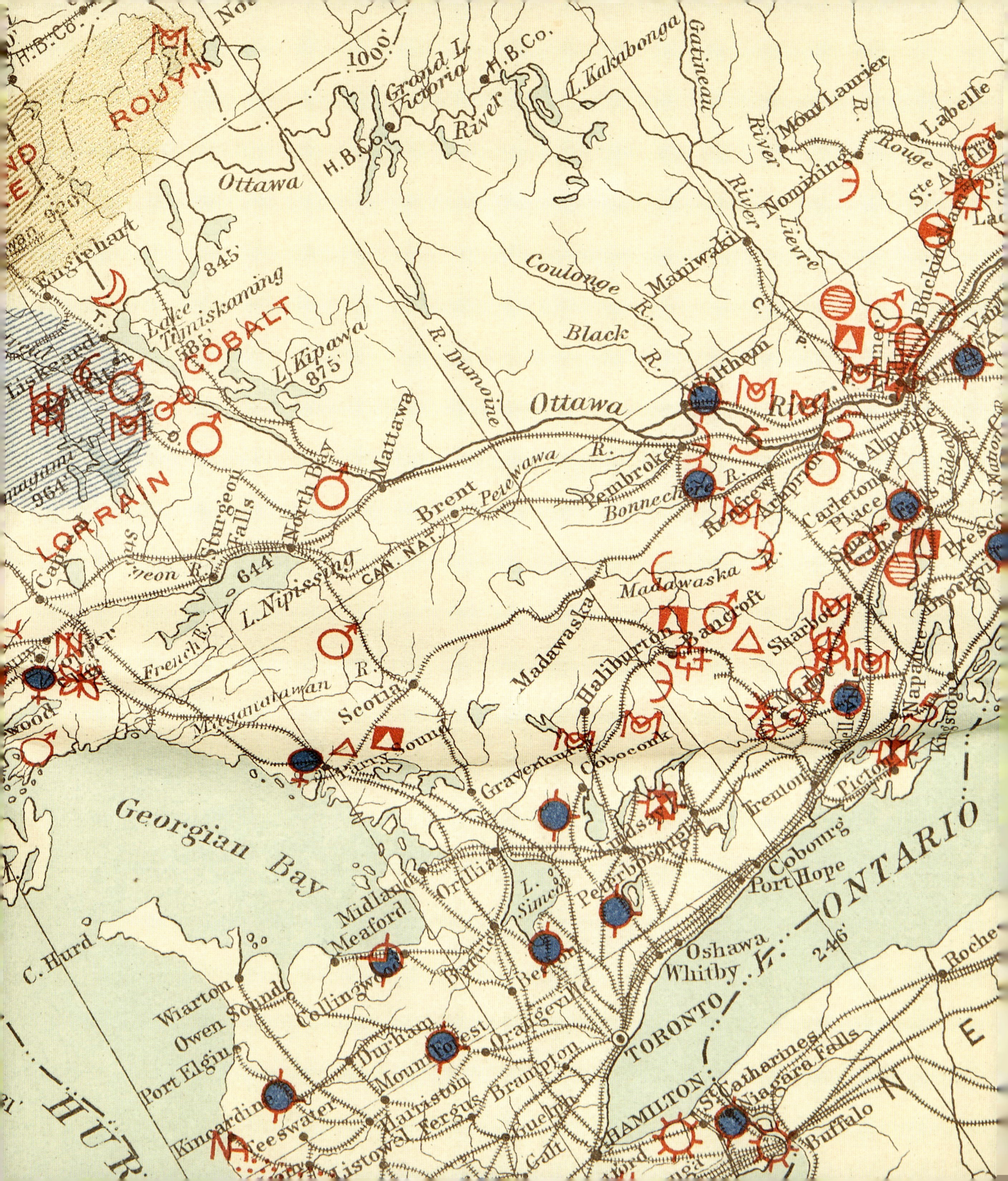
ROUYN
H.B.Co.
1000'
Grand L. Victoria
H.B.Co.
L. Kakabonga
Gatineau
Mont Laurier
Labelle
Rouge
Ste Agathe
River
Nominingue
Lievre
Ottawa
Englehart
845
Lake Timiskaming
585
COBALT
L. Kipawa
875
Liskeard
964
LORRAIN
Coulonge R.
Maniwaki
Black R.
R. Dumoine
Ottawa
River
Mattawa
North Bay
Brent
Petewawa R.
Pembroke
Bonnechère R.
Renfrew
Arnprior
Almonte
Carleton Place
Perth
Sturgeon Falls
644
L. Nipissing
CAN. NAT.
French R.
Madawaska
Madawaska
Haliburton
Bancroft
Sharbot L.
Napanee
Kingston
Magnetawan R.
Scotia
Gravenhurst
Coboconk
Trenton
Picton
Georgian Bay
Lindsay
Peterborough
Cobourg
Port Hope
ONTARIO
246'
Midland
Orillia
L. Simcoe
Meaford
C. Hurd
Collingwood
Barrie
Oshawa
Whitby
Wiarton
Owen Sound
Orangeville
TORONTO
Port Elgin
Durham
Mount Forest
Brampton
Harriston
Kincardine
Teeswater
Listowel
Fergus
Guelph
Galt
HAMILTON
St Catharines
Niagara Falls
Buffalo

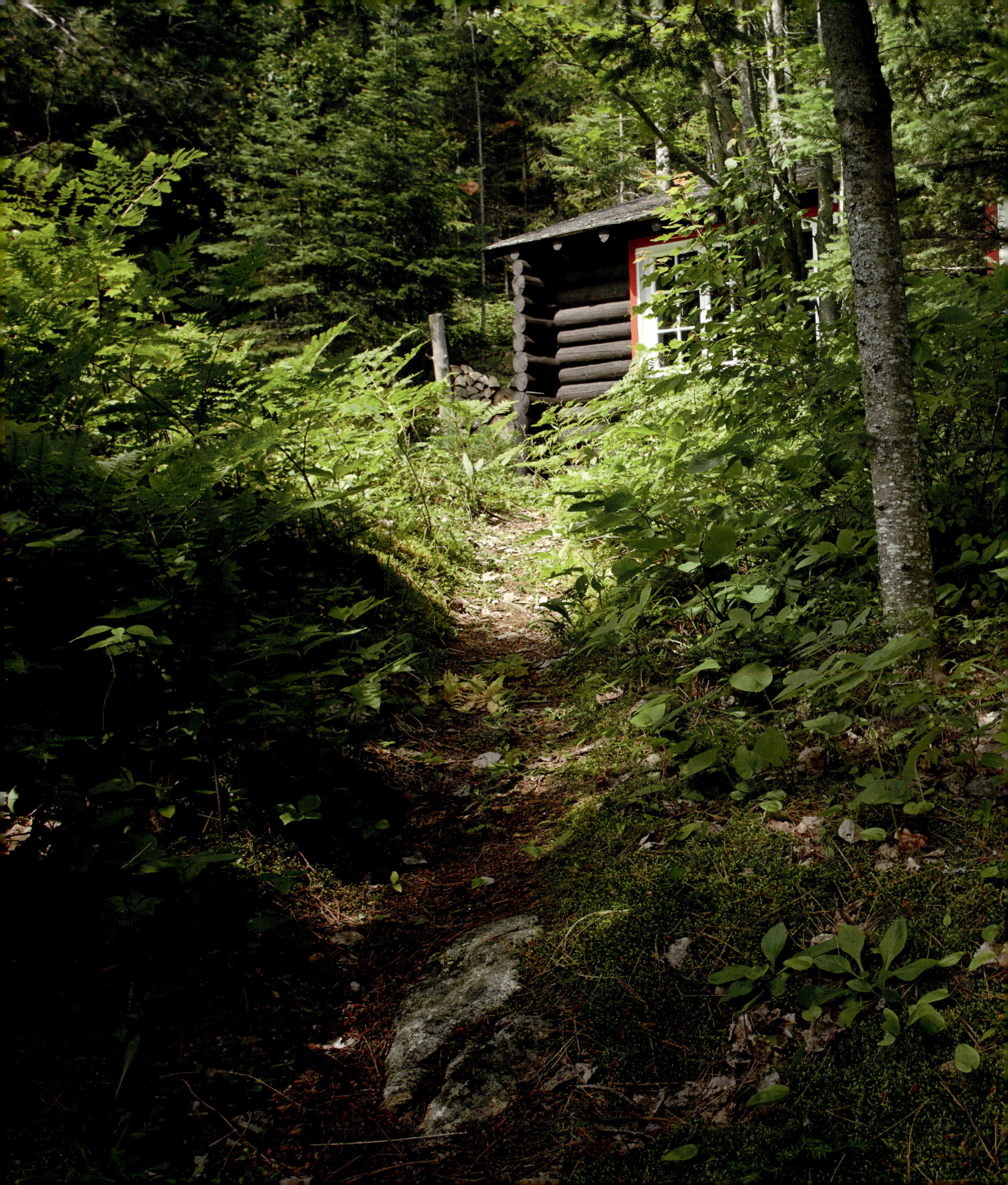

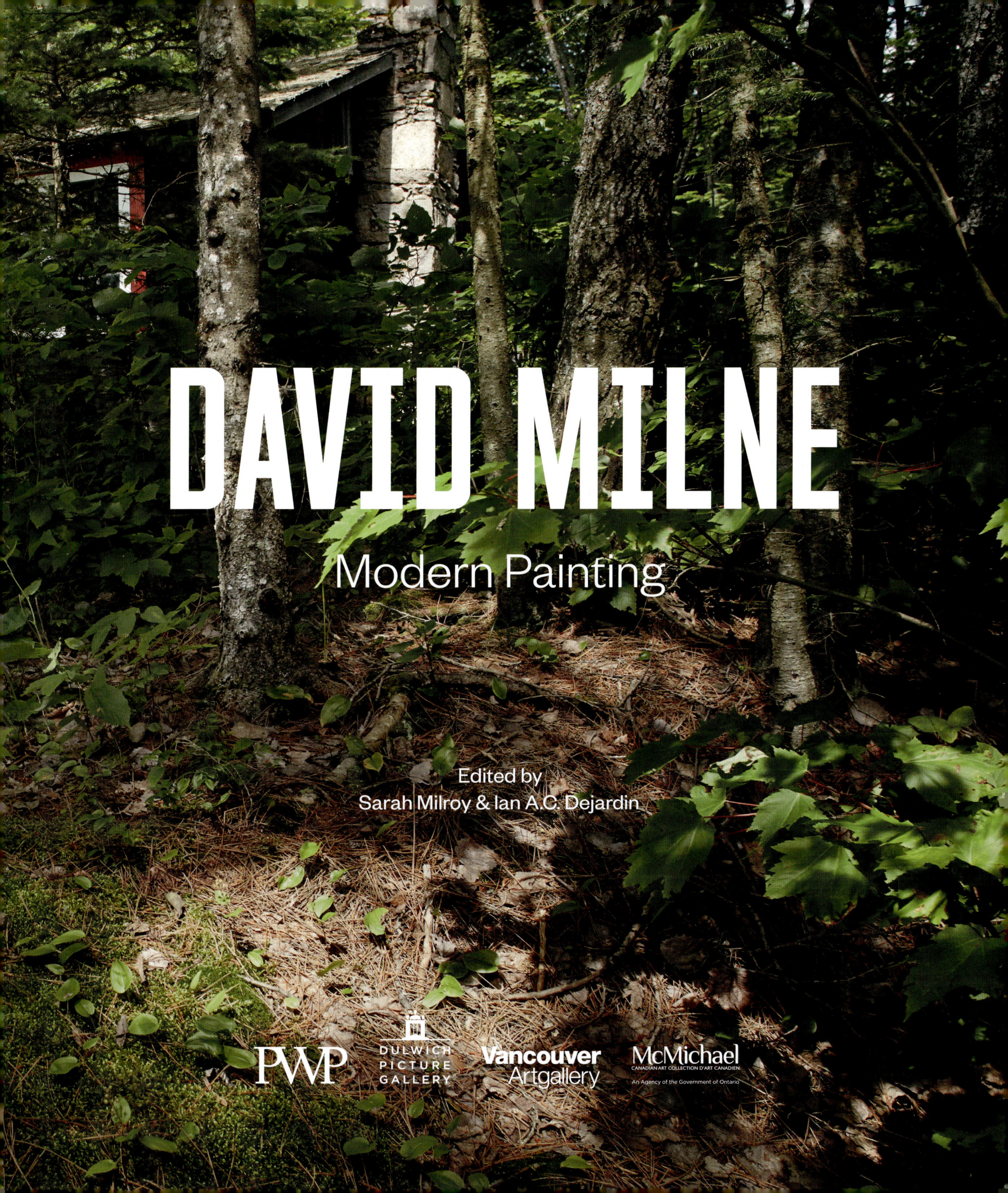

DAVID MILNE

Modern Painting

Edited by
Sarah Milroy & Ian A.C. Dejardin

PWP
DULWICH PICTURE GALLERY
Vancouver Artgallery
McMichael CANADIAN ART COLLECTION D'ART CANADIEN
An Agency of the Government of Ontario

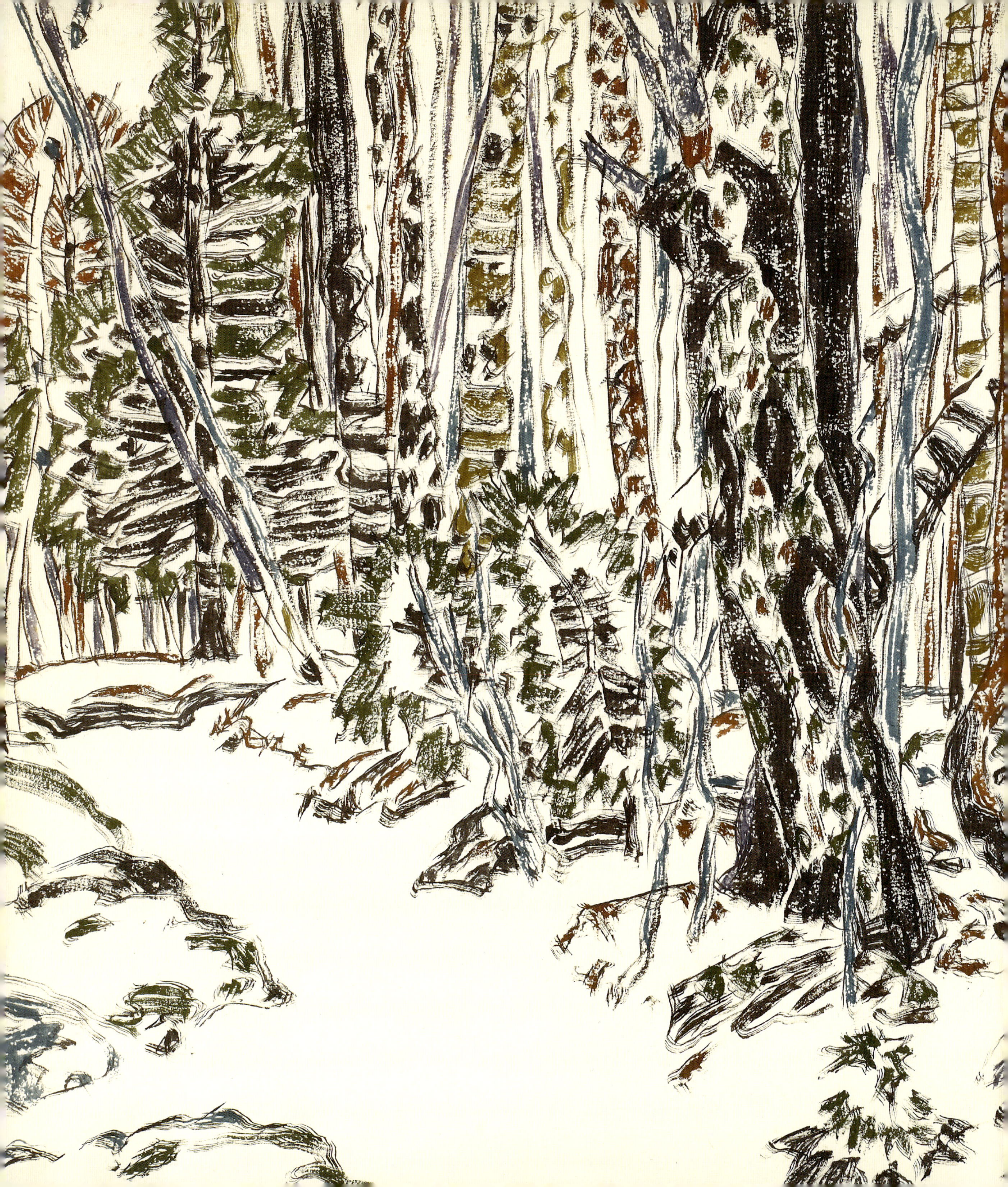

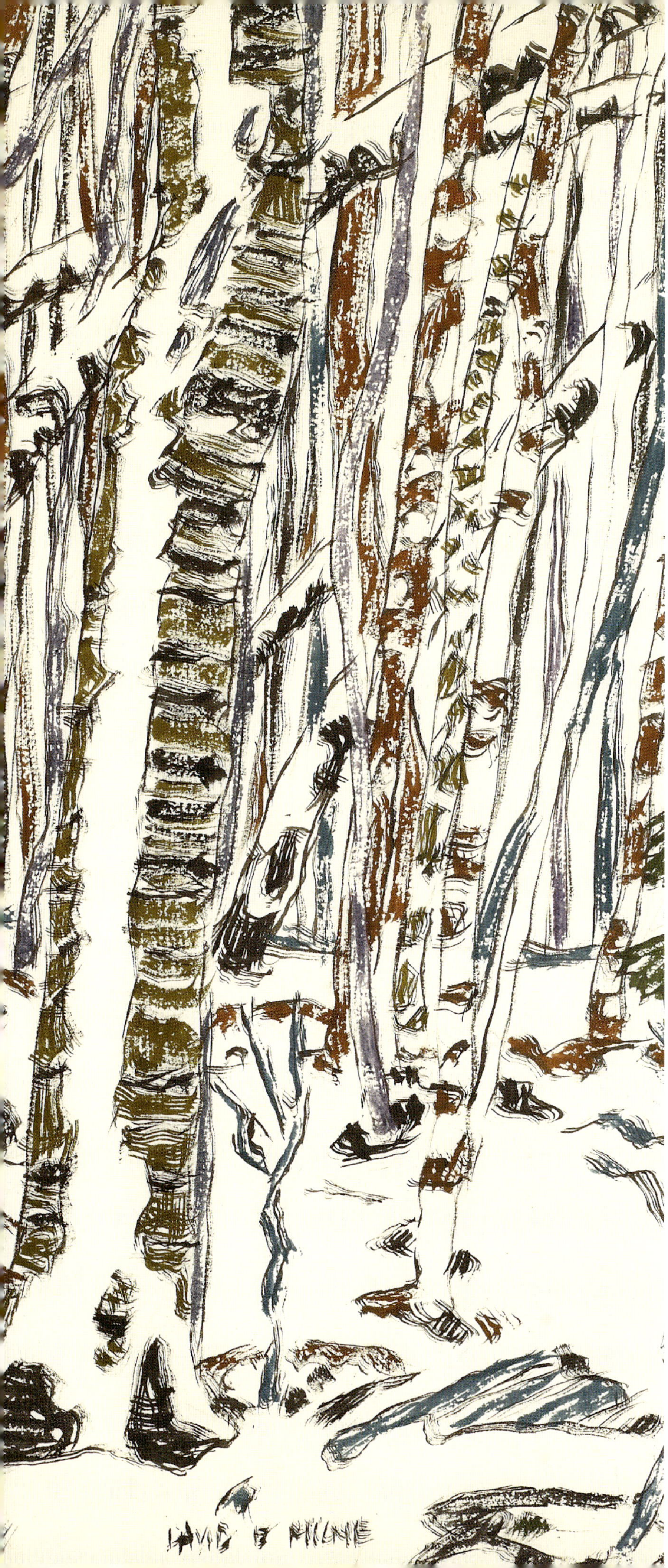

A book has a beginning and an end—
so have paintings. And we read them
very much as we read a book, but faster ...
A picture seen while walking past an open
door might be grasped completely enough
to be remembered for life—if it is a good
enough picture.

David Milne, from 'Pictures Have
Beginnings and Endings', *c.* 1942

Published on the occasion of the exhibition
David Milne: Modern Painting

Dulwich Picture Gallery London 14 February–7 May 2018
Vancouver Art Gallery 16 June–16 September 2018
McMichael Collection of Canadian Art 4 October 2018–13 January 2019

Published by Philip Wilson Publishers
an imprint of I.B.Tauris & Co. Ltd
London • New York
www.philip-wilson.co.uk

Dimensions, height preceding width, are given where possible for all works illustrated.

ISBN (hardback): 978 1 78130 072 5
ISBN (paperback): 978 1 78130 061 9

A full CIP record is available from the British Library, Library and Archives Canada and the Library of Congress

Library of Congress Catalog Card Number: available

Designed and typeset in Lyon Text and MFred by
Myfanwy Vernon-Hunt, This-Side.co.uk

Printed and bound in Wales by Gomer Press Limited

FSC www.fsc.org MIX Paper from responsible sources FSC® C114687

pp. 2–3: Department of Mines, Mineral map of Canada, 1925, collected by David Milne
pp. 4–5: Milne cabin at Baptiste Lake, Ontario, 2017
pp. 6–7: David Milne, *Path in the Woods* (detail), 1921, watercolour on paper
pp. 10 and 15: Interior of the Milne cabin, Baptiste Lake, Ontario, 2017
p. 16: David Milne, Self-portrait, Black Lake, Quebec, 1918
p. 28: David Milne at Six Mile Lake, *c.* 1934, photographed by Douglas Duncan
p. 84: Postcards acquired by David Milne in France or Belgium in 1919
pp. 190–1: Baptiste Lake, Ontario, 2017
pp. 206–7: David Milne, *Sparkle of Glass* (detail), 1926 or 1927, oil on canvas
p. 208: David Milne at Six Mile Lake, *c.* 1933

Principal Sponsor

BMO

Presenting Sponsor

AIMIA

Catalogue Supporter

The Elizabeth Cayzer Charitable Trust

Visionary Partner for
Scholarship and Publications
at the Vancouver Art Gallery

The Richardson Family

Generously supported by

Carol Gray, The Horne Family Charitable Foundation, Rosamond Ivey, The McLean Foundation, and Dasha Shenkman

POWER CORPORATION
OF CANADA

A Canadian Friends of
Dulwich Picture Gallery exhibition

DULWICH
PICTURE
GALLERY
CANADIAN
FRIENDS

Official Paint Partner

MYLANDS
ESTABLISHED LONDON 1884

An exhibition organised by Dulwich Picture Gallery and the McMichael Canadian Art Collection in collaboration with the Vancouver Art Gallery, with the exceptional support of the National Gallery of Canada

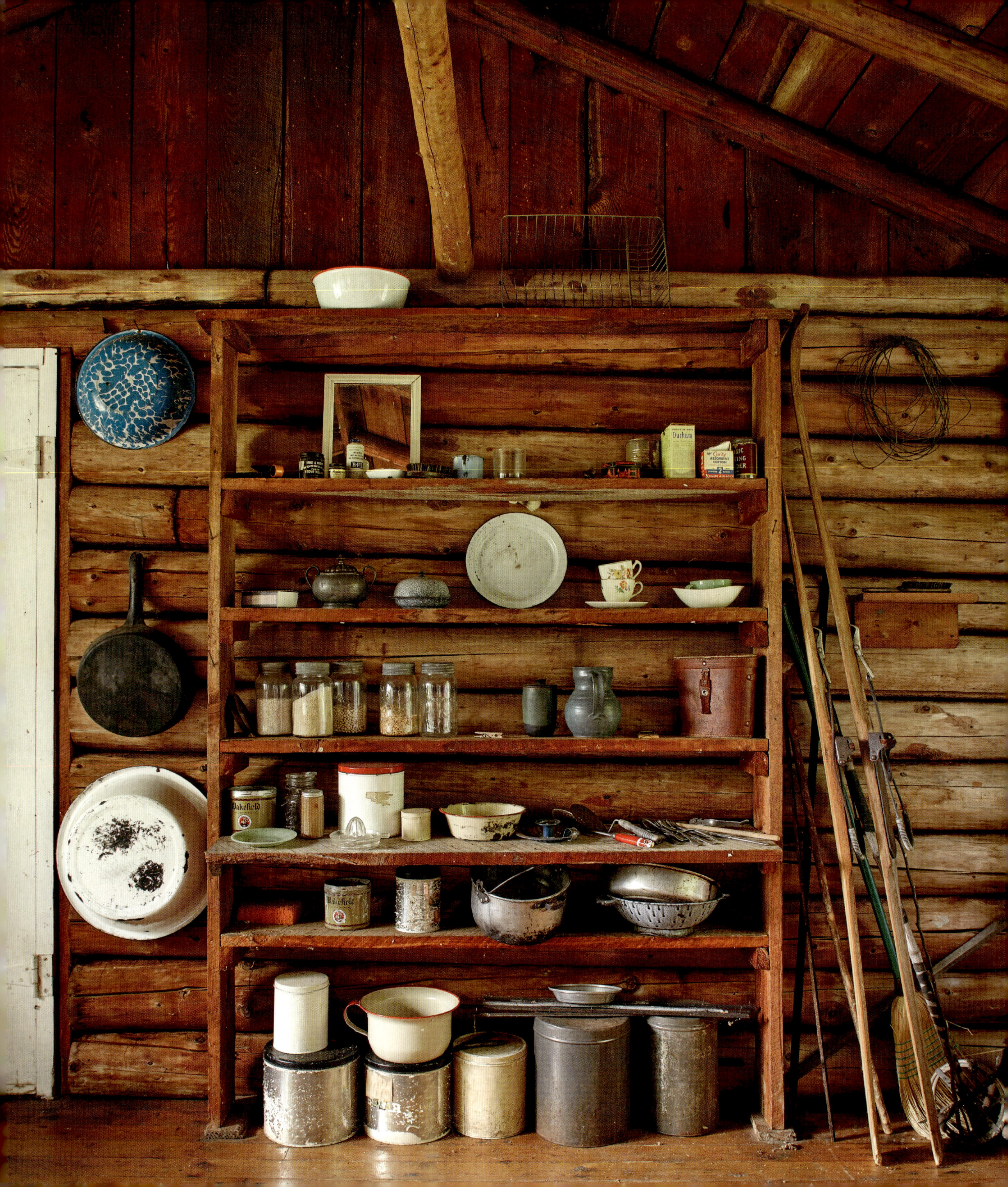
Durham
Curity
ABSORBENT
COTTON
2
BAUER & BLACK
Wakefield
Wakefield

CONTENTS

DIRECTOR'S FOREWORD

The scholar John Gage once described art as 'the most vivid surviving manifestation of general attitudes towards colour expressed in visual form'. When discussing and contemplating artworks we can easily overlook the role of colour. It seems so simple, but form and meaning can dominate to such an extent that we can find ourselves unable to recall whether Leonardo's *Mona Lisa* wears blue or red or whether Van Gogh's *Sunflowers* sit in a yellow or a brown vase. But we know instinctively that colour has a seminal function in the visual power of these masterpieces.

I recently watched an online video of a man seeing colour for the first time thanks to a pair of innovative glasses. His face lit up with understanding and joy as the world around him came to life. Rather than running towards his friends and family to share the moment, it became something purely for him—a deeply personal unravelling of the explosion of colour which made sense of places and things that he previously thought he knew.

In bringing David Milne to the UK in this major exhibition at Dulwich Picture Gallery, the Canadian curator Sarah Milroy and Ian Dejardin, my distinguished predecessor at Dulwich, have allowed us the privilege of seeing through David Milne's eyes. With both the exhibition and this stylish publication they present an artist who used colour as a tool to convey the essence of place and time. Colour is an artist's choice. Red, orange, white, yellow, blue, green, brown or black each have the potential to create energy and to lead the viewer's imagination into the wilderness of the artist's intensely private experience of the world. The Dulwich Picture Gallery team and I are tremendously grateful to Ian and Sarah for sharing with us these visions which irrevocably alter our perception of art.

The exhibition would not have been possible without the generosity of David Milne Jr, who could not have been more helpful over the course of the project with his early enthusiasm for the idea of staging an exhibition, by allowing us access to his father's archive and in granting us permission to reproduce works from the Milne estate.

As always we are deeply indebted to the great many lenders to the exhibition—too numerous to list here—and to the private lenders and directors and trustees of museums who have agreed to part with major works from their collections for the duration of our exhibition and subsequent tour.

Special thanks to the National Gallery of Canada for granting us a particularly significant loan request. Director Marc Mayer and Deputy Director Anne Eschapasse worked hard with their staff to support the exhibition in a substantial and transformative way. We are grateful to the Art Gallery of Ontario for facilitating the loan of key works from their collection, including rarely seen archive material. Works on loan from the Milne Family Collection are a revelation. The Mira Godard Gallery, which represents the Milne estate, provided assistance in our process of identifying and securing loans.

Our thanks to Anne Jackson and Clare Martelli at Philip Wilson Publishers for producing this ambitions publication, and Myfanwy Vernon-Hunt for the beautiful design—it has been a great pleasure to work with them. In this book we have been incredibly fortunate in obtaining contributions from a number of authoritative voices. In addition to the excellent opening essays by Ian and Sarah, curators Katerina Atanassova and Katharine Lochnan, novelist Jane Urquhart, photographer Edward Burtynsky, and art historians John O'Brian and David P. Silcox have provided fascinating insights into Milne's life and work. Our gratitude to them all for their thoughtful and illuminating commentaries.

The team at the McMichael Canadian Art Collection has collaborated with us to achieve another successful international partnership. Our thanks to Sarah Stanners, Director, Curatorial and Collections, and to Janine Butler and Jennifer Withrow for their confidence in the project and expertise. We are indebted to the Vancouver Art Gallery for coming on board as tour partners and grateful to Kathleen Bartels, Director, Ian Thom, Senior Curator, and Emmy Lee Wall, Bruce Wiedrick and Jenny Wilson for their invaluable support. At Dulwich Picture Gallery I would like to extend my thanks to all my colleagues for their dedication, passion and creativity.

The Vancouver Art Gallery would like to acknowledge the important contribution of its Visionary Partner for Scholarship and Publications, the Richardson Family, who play such an important role in helping to inform and inspire readers for decades to come.

For Dulwich Picture Gallery, the exhibition and publication would not have been possible without generous support. Special thanks must go, above all, to our Principal Sponsor, BMO Financial Group. We are also very grateful to our Presenting Sponsor, AIMIA. Support from The Elizabeth Cayzer Charitable Trust made this publication possible. Assistance from The McLean Foundation, Rosamond Ivey, Carol Gray, and Dasha Shenkman was vital to the project. I would like to thank the Canadian Friends of Dulwich Picture Gallery for this exhibition, another important and successful strand of our programming, and to give a special mention to David P. Silcox for his enthusiasm, wisdom and guidance throughout the course of this extraordinary project.

Jennifer Scott
The Sackler Director, Dulwich Picture Gallery

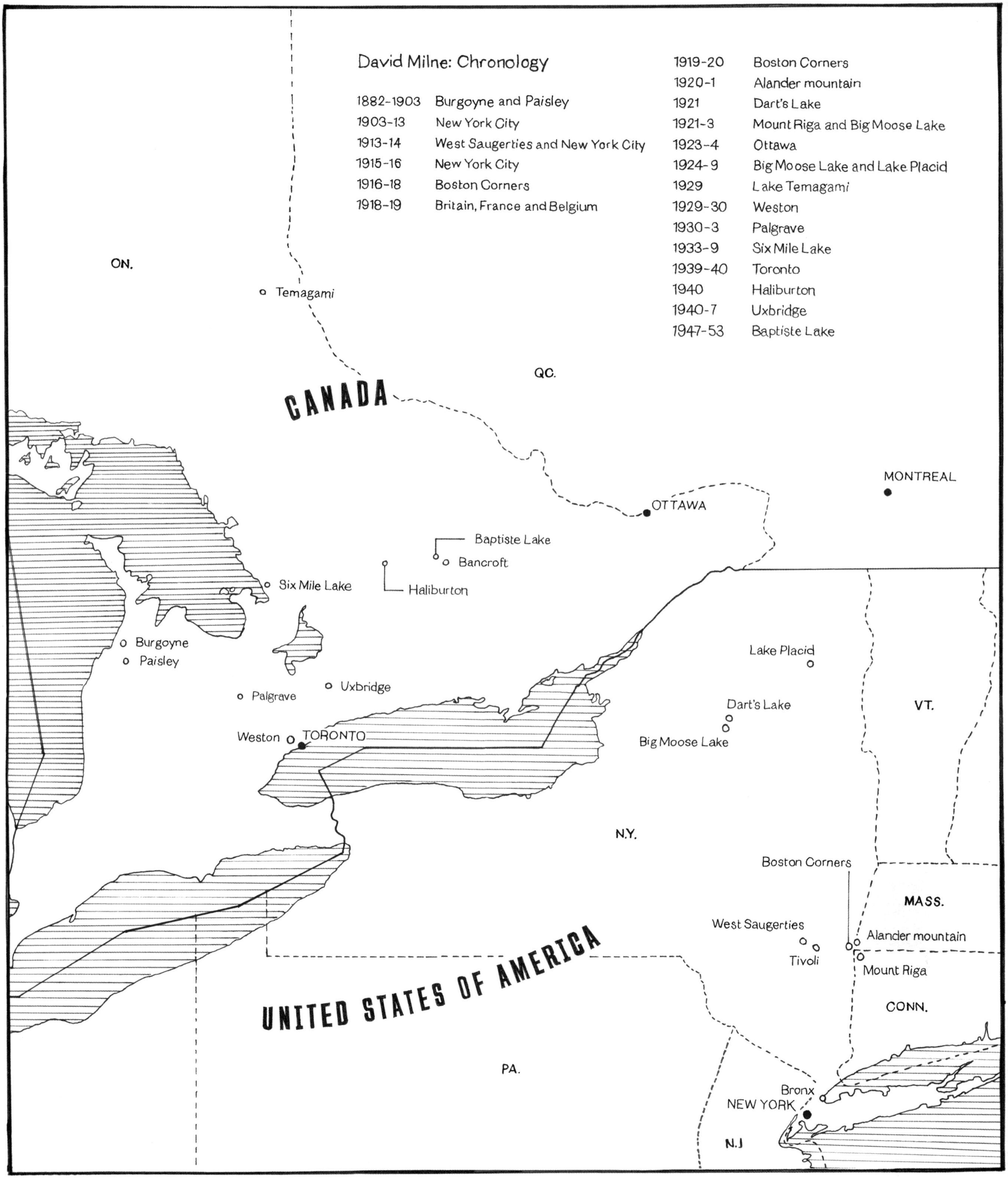
David Milne: Chronology
1882-1903 Burgoyne and Paisley
1903-13 New York City
1913-14 West Saugerties and New York City
1915-16 New York City
1916-18 Boston Corners
1918-19 Britain, France and Belgium
1919-20 Boston Corners
1920-1 Alander mountain
1921 Dart's Lake
1921-3 Mount Riga and Big Moose Lake
1923-4 Ottawa
1924-9 Big Moose Lake and Lake Placid
1929 Lake Temagami
1929-30 Weston
1930-3 Palgrave
1933-9 Six Mile Lake
1939-40 Toronto
1940 Haliburton
1940-7 Uxbridge
1947-53 Baptiste Lake
ON.
Temagami
QC.
CANADA
MONTREAL
OTTAWA
Baptiste Lake
Bancroft
Haliburton
Six Mile Lake
Burgoyne
Paisley
Uxbridge
Palgrave
Weston
TORONTO
Lake Placid
Dart's Lake
Big Moose Lake
VT.
N.Y.
Boston Corners
MASS.
West Saugerties
Alander mountain
Tivoli
Mount Riga
CONN.
UNITED STATES OF AMERICA
PA.
Bronx
NEW YORK
N.J

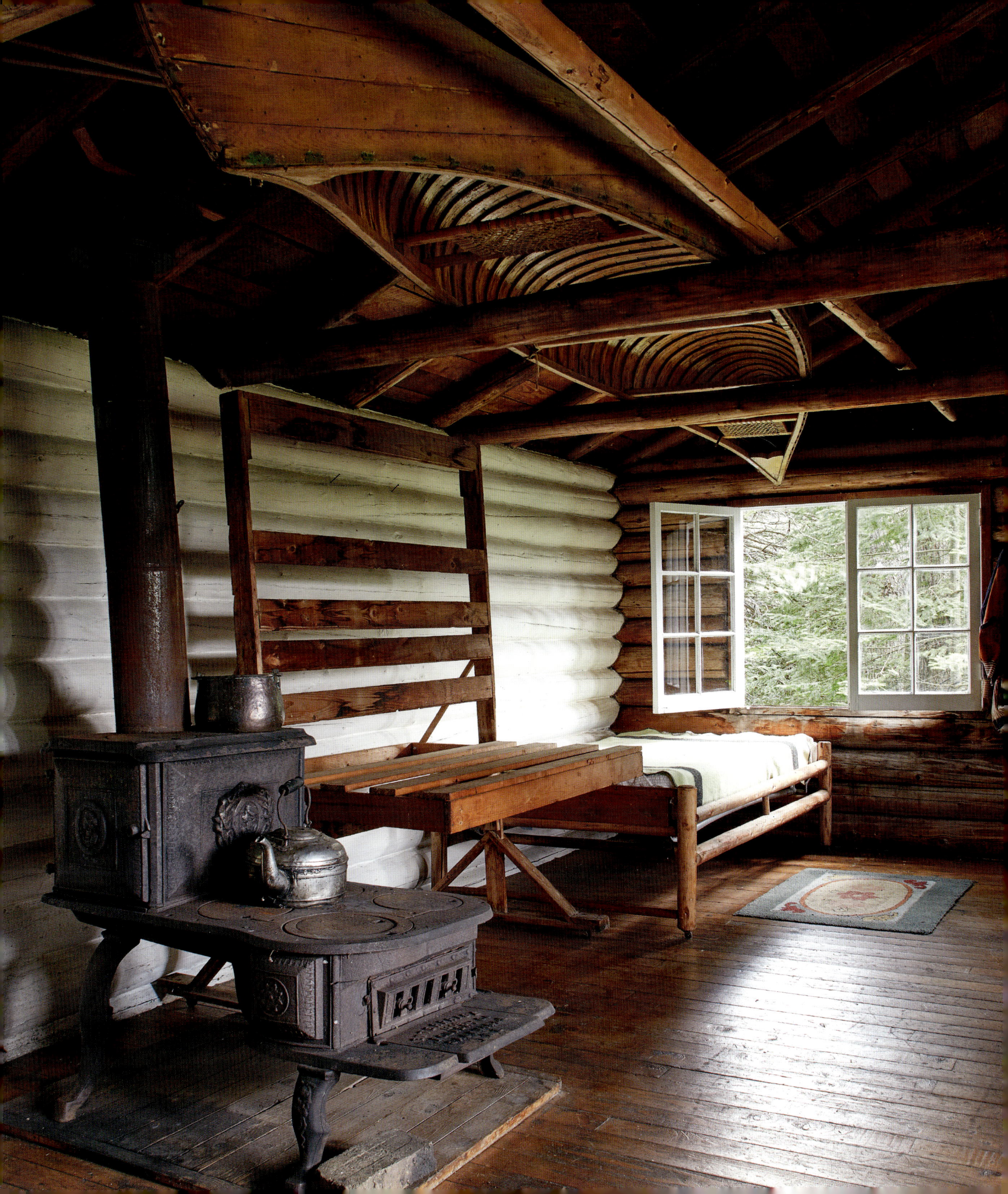

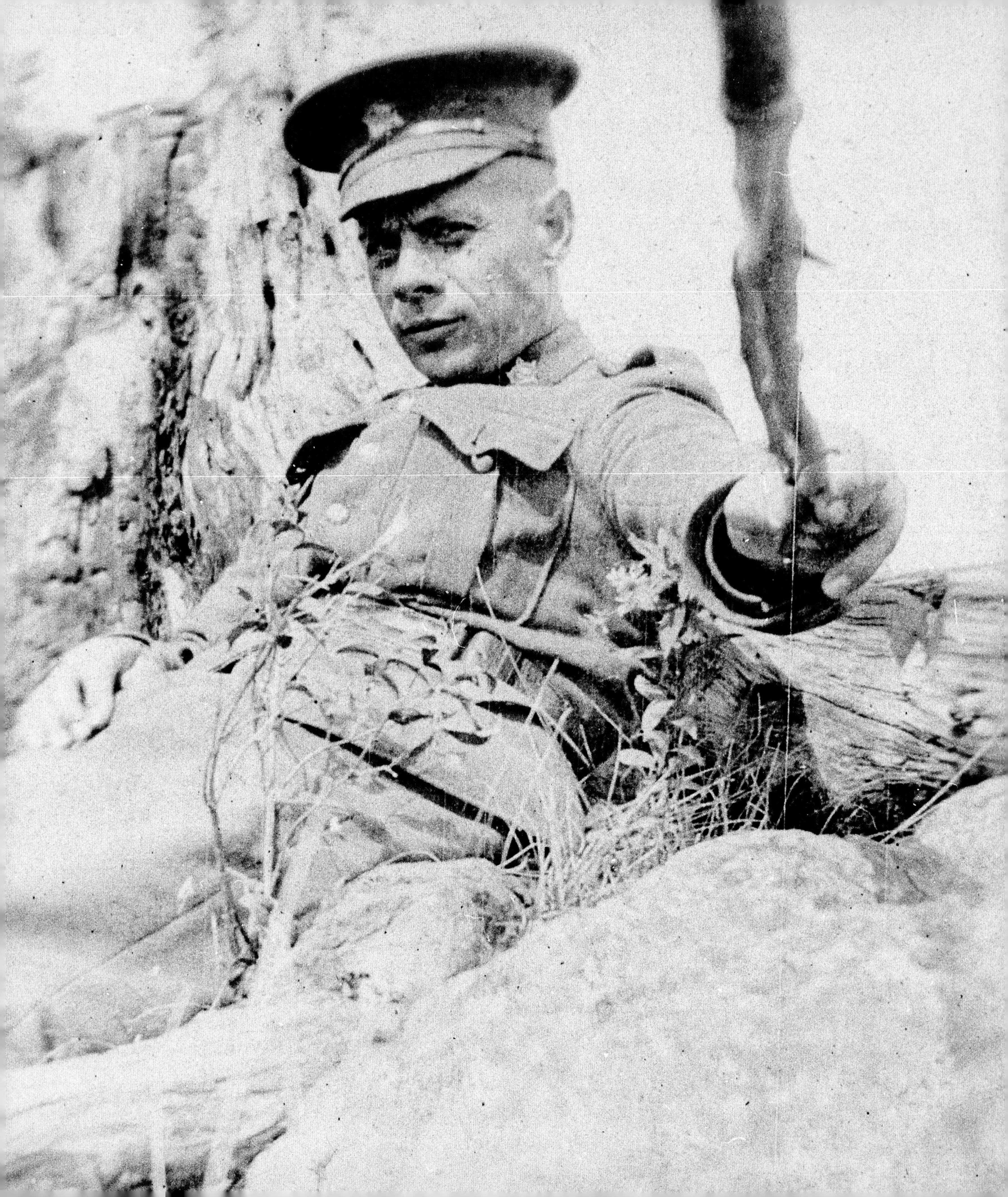

DAZZLE AND KICK: THE LIFE OF DAVID MILNE

Ian A.C. Dejardin

David Milne (1882–1953) once declared that Tom Thomson, the Canadian painter who died in a tragic canoeing accident in Ontario's Algonquin Park in 1917, had taken Canadian painting with him to the bottom of Canoe Lake.[1] His admiration was no doubt for Thomson's painterly brilliance, the seemingly magical ability to suggest atmospheric conditions and light that he developed over his short career. But the artists were kindred spirits in other ways. Both of Scottish stock, they shared a characteristic solitariness, seemingly happiest left to themselves roughing it in the remote wilderness. Yet, more than that, they shared a belief that process outweighed subject. They painted what caught their eye, and that could be a stump in a clearing (p. 119) or a patch of undistinguished undergrowth in snow.

The sense of spontaneity in Milne's work is as strong as in Thomson's but very differently achieved. Milne forensically analysed what he was doing with every brushstroke, every colour choice, every balance of space and composition—that sounds like a recipe for a laboured result but this is not the case. He was always on the lookout for the moment when a work lost its 'kick', as he liked to say, destroying pictures that did not meet his high standards. In fact, he found that Thomson's practice—working up the best of his oil sketches done in front of the motif into finished paintings back in the studio—did not suit him (though he often worked from pencil sketches in his later career). It was as if the painting 'died' in the process. That vivacity—that kick—was a fragile flower that wilted all too easily.

Every artist has his or her own visual language, but few artists' languages reveal such obvious delight in painterly grammar and punctuation as that of David Milne. This is what makes him so definitively a modernist: the precision of thought and heightened awareness of exactly what he was doing make his personal language not only unique but also unmistakable—no other artist's works look like Milne's. And this in spite of his apparently simple, figurative and often superficially conventional subject matter: landscapes, still lifes, interiors.

Born in a log cabin in Bruce County, Ontario, to Scottish immigrant parents, Milne excelled at school. His first job was as the teacher in a single-

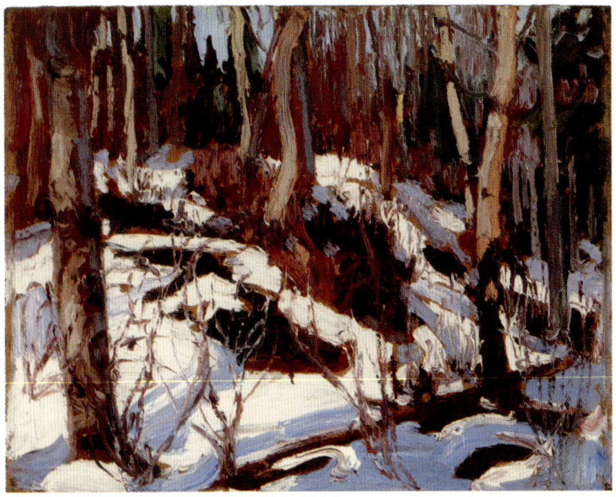

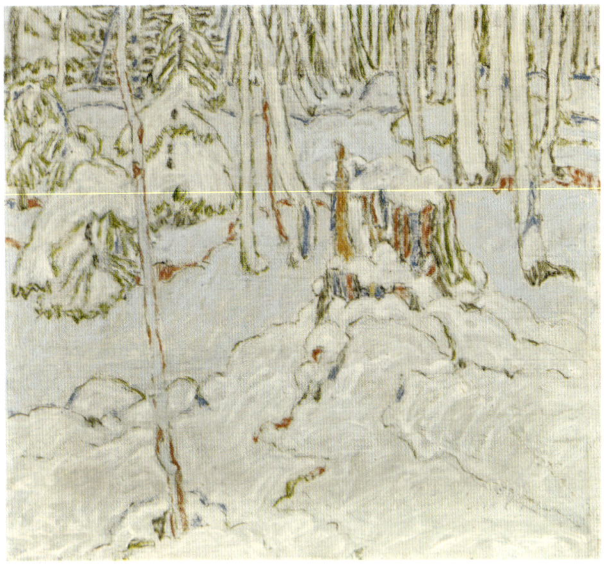

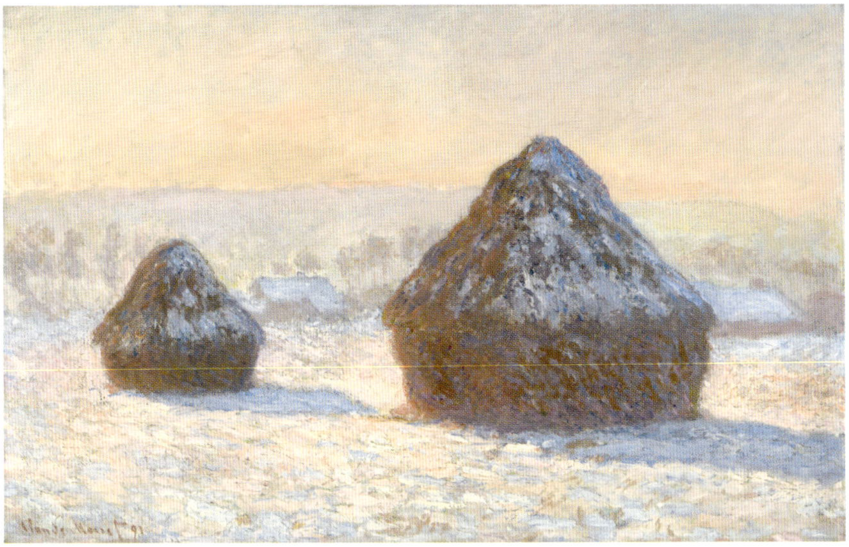

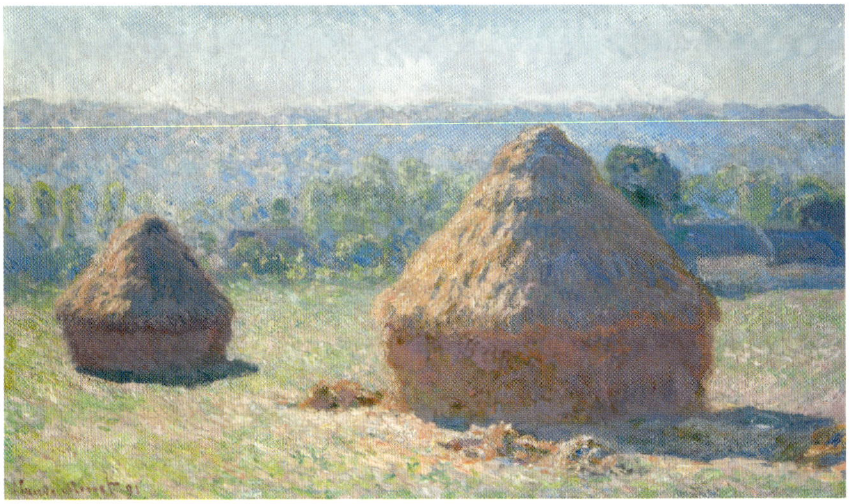

Top
Tom Thomson
Winter Thaw in the Woods
1917, oil on board

Above
David Milne
Snowy Hemlocks
1921, oil on canvas

Top right
Claude Monet
Wheatstacks, Snow Effect, Morning
1891, oil on canvas

Below right
Claude Monet, *Haystack, End of Summer, Morning*
1891, oil on canvas

room rural school, and he was good at it. Intellect and the drive to communicate were there from the start. But when he caught the bug for drawing, he headed not for Toronto but for the dazzling modernity of New York City, intent on becoming an illustrator—and in one, non-commercial, sense, an illustrator he remained throughout his life; he needed a subject, however straightforward.

The elements of his visual language were present from very early on. Though Milne started his career in art as a commercial illustrator, it was the painting that mattered, particularly after 1909. Arriving in New York in September 1903, he was there at the birth of the modernist revolution as that liberating tsunami hit North America. His paintings from these years show the influence of European Post-Impressionism and an immediate interest in mark making; there are experiments with dots and dabs somewhat akin to pointillism.

He himself acknowledged a great debt to the Impressionist Claude Monet, while recognising that an observer would struggle to perceive that debt in his own work.[2] (It is traceable, perhaps, in his interest in serial subjects and his fascination with light, though his means of achieving his effects were very different.) Taking classes at the Art Students League from 1903 to 1905, and in the evenings in 1906, Milne was among the first generation of North American artists to encounter and engage with other current French art—the Fauves, the Nabis and Cubism—in commercial venues such as the Montross Gallery, the Daniel Gallery, the Macbeth Gallery, the Durand-Ruel Galleries (where he saw a selection of Haystack paintings by Monet)

Right
David Milne
City Rain
1911–12, oil on canvas

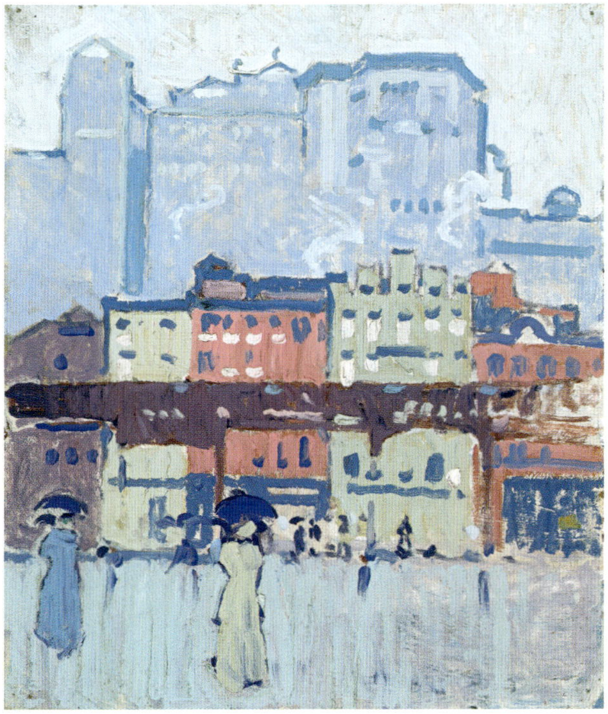

Right
David Milne and his pupils, Walkerton, Ontario
c. 1900–3

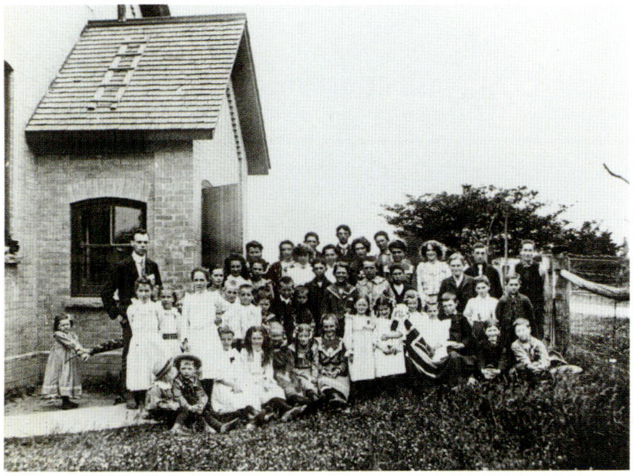

Bottom right
Life class at the Art Students League
1906

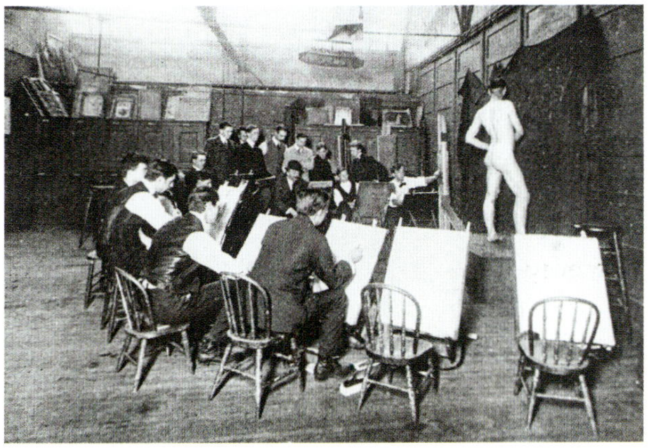

and Alfred Stieglitz's 291 gallery. In 1911 alone, for instance, at 291 he viewed the Cézanne, Matisse and Brancusi exhibitions. By the time of the famous Armory Show of 1913—the landmark exhibition that signalled the arrival of modernism in North America for good and all—he was clearly seen as one of the brightest of New York's contemporary artists since five of his works were included in that exhibition, alongside the latest and best of Europe's modern masters. While the outraged reactionary press fulminated over Matisse and Duchamp, Milne's works made a quieter, but positive, impact.

Milne's New York paintings are vibrant images of metropolitan bustle, but for all their attractiveness they are bold and experimental, particularly with regard to choice of colour as 'value', a seminal concept of Milne's, and the dramatic exploitation of the bare surface as a positive and dynamic compositional element. His fondness for street scenes featuring colourful advertising billboards—subject matter that indicates his awareness of the Ashcan School of American painting—also demonstrates another favourite compositional concept: achieving spatial clarity out of a bright mosaic of colour diffused across the entire sheet or canvas—a challenge he loved. This was something he was to explore in many different ways, both in interior and exterior scenes, throughout his early career, notably in a series of figures in a landscape, where the figure is effectively camouflaged against the background, emerging only on closer inspection (pp. 64-5). Also present more or less from the outset, and growing out of the idea of colour as value, was his fascination with black and white used as positive stand-ins for colour.

Milne was distinctive in his colour sense and in how he used the colours that he chose. Although the sunny yellow of a billboard (*Billboards*, *c.* 1912 [p. 46]) may be an intensification of the actual colour of the object in the manner of Van Gogh painting his bedroom chair, the very same yellow is used across the composition to outline trees, carriage wheels or street furniture. The complementary pale blue that traces the shadowed side of a tree against that yellow is the same blue that delineates the buildings, that outlines the figures on the streets, and that comes to rest in another of those

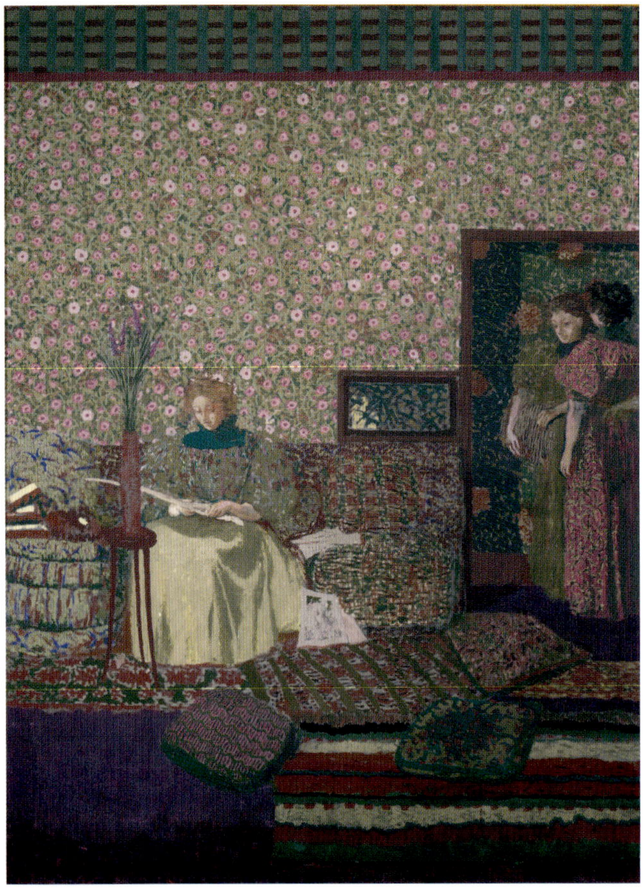

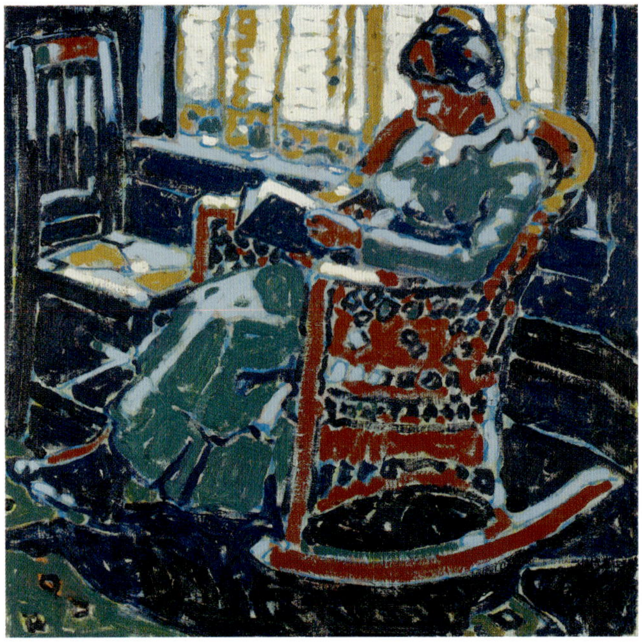

Top
Édouard Vuillard
Figures in an Interior
1896, oil on canvas

Above
David Milne
The Blue Rocker
1914, oil on canvas

billboards. Sunshine, whether illuminating a horse or the dresses of the promenading women, bouncing off the road surface, or reflecting off the wall on which the billboards are hung, is suggested, conversely, through *absence* of paint. The bare canvas performs a positive role equivalent to the applied colours, a lesson he could have learned from the watercolours of Cézanne, seen at 291.

Matisse and the Nabis, particularly Vuillard and Bonnard, are clearly the inspirations behind his interior scenes of the period after the Armory Show, as Milne explored the phenomenon of all-over decorative patterning; figure and ground appear stitched together into a continuous visual field. His painting *Red*, 1914 (p. 58), illustrates perfectly what he had learned. Red (actually a reddish-brown), used as a value, denotes *inside*, while outside, in this case a dazzle of light through the window, is applied white (a different effect from the passive white of the untouched surface). The deliberate incorporation of a 'dazzle spot', as he called such flat, bright passages, was another of Milne's seminal compositional discoveries, discernible throughout his work.

Red in this painting does not (only) denote shadow. Milne's wife Patsy's blue dress (rendered in blue, but of course there is no guarantee that it was actually blue) is also outlined in red, and the chair she is leaning on is drawn in exactly the same two colours. The same red defines a plant pot and, most surprisingly, Patsy's silhouetted head. Colour does not primarily express mood here; but neither is it entirely divorced from representation. Milne's limited palette, the colours once chosen and codified as a sequence of tonal values, is spread across the surface in a masterclass of economical rigour.[3] He recognised this tendency in himself and referred to it (self-deprecatingly) as the 'Scotch motive', defined in a letter to his friend James Clarke as 'getting the result with the slightest possible means'.[4]

As an exercise in making red suggest light, air and space, the picture *Red* is a tour de force, ultimately indebted to the revelation of Matisse's famous painting *The Red Studio*, 1911. Milne uses a very limited palette of black, white, yellow ochre, burnt umber, dark red, green and blue in a series of pictures like this, many of them also strongly reminiscent of Vuillard, most particularly when Milne chooses to focus on complicated pattern and

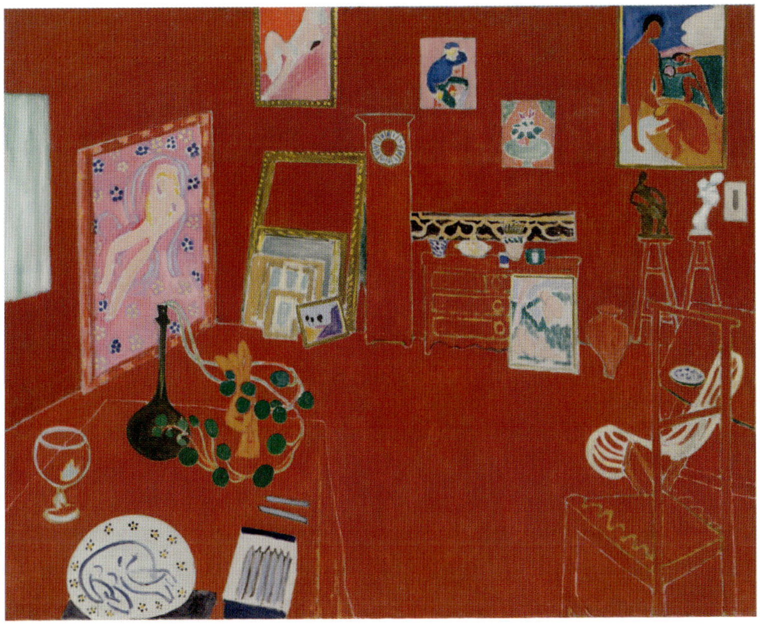

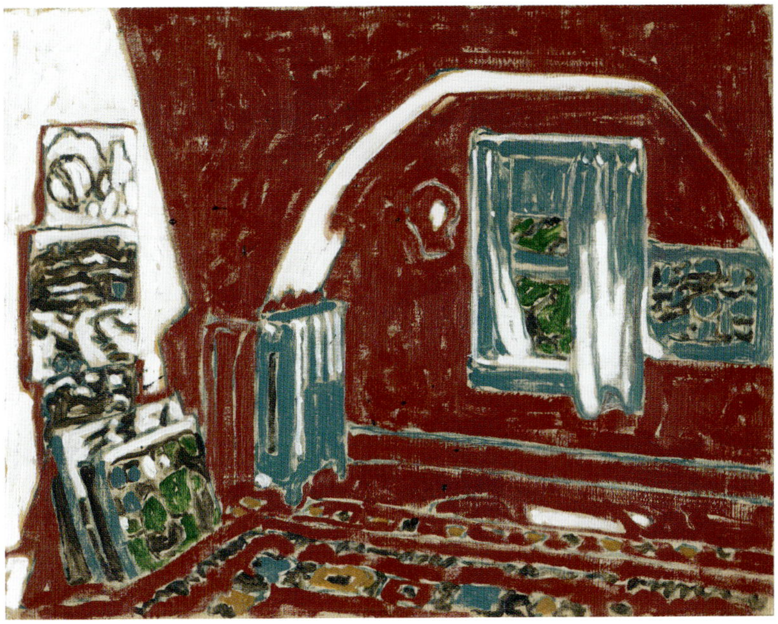

Above
Henri Matisse
The Red Studio
1911, oil on canvas

Above right
David Milne
Alcove
1914, oil on canvas

detail surrounding and encompassing a figure (pp. 55–7). In these interiors, he makes the eye work to discern the figurative matter—it is usually Patsy—emerging from the patchwork of colour values in a sophisticated deconstruction of the act of seeing.

By 1916, Milne was tired of New York, and the stress of life there had been bad for his nerves. He had married, on a shoestring, his long-time American fiancée, May Frances Hegarty, known as Patsy—but the flattering notices he had received in the Armory Show and elsewhere had not translated into sales. It was time for a change, and another step along Milne's personal modernist path, away from the city. In May 1916, he and Patsy moved to Boston Corners, a village in New York State that answered several needs. It was, as he described it, 'within a reasonable distance of New York City, yet beyond commuting range and it had to be suitable for painting, preferably with hills to sit on while painting other hills'.[5] The idea was to be able to paint full-time; but he still needed to do some commercial work, such as showcards for clients in New York. Ever a practical person, though no businessman, he even tried his hand at some limited market gardening (celery, then onions), without much success. However, Boston Corners was to inspire some of his most distinctive works, particularly the view over the valley to the hills beyond, the foreground and middle ground marked by strings of trees and buildings (pp. 72–3). For Canadians, these are among his most iconic paintings.

Milne had not been oblivious to the outbreak of war in Europe in 1914. He had followed its progress, and after the United States finally joined the conflict in April 1917, he felt an increased patriotic urgency. When Canada introduced conscription, he enlisted in the Royal Canadian Army at the British Recruiting Office in New York in late December 1917. Turning up in Toronto on 1 March 1918 for training, he had any gung-ho expectation of heading immediately for Europe dashed by an outbreak of conscription riots in Quebec, and instead he found himself there rounding up deserters. He embarked for England finally on 10 September 1918. Based at Kinmel Park Training Camp in Wales, and poised for action, Milne must have received news of the declaration of Armistice on 11 November with a mixture of joy and some frustration. Demobilisation did not instantly follow, however; a boring wait was relieved by a period of leave in London in December 1918, and there he stumbled upon the existence of the Canadian War Memorials Fund, set up by Max Aitken, Lord Beaverbrook, the Canadian-born British politician and newspaper publisher. The

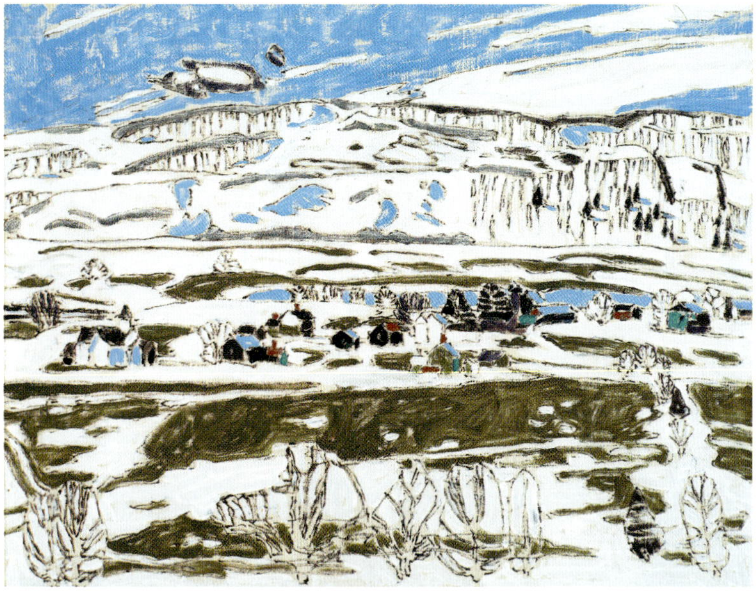

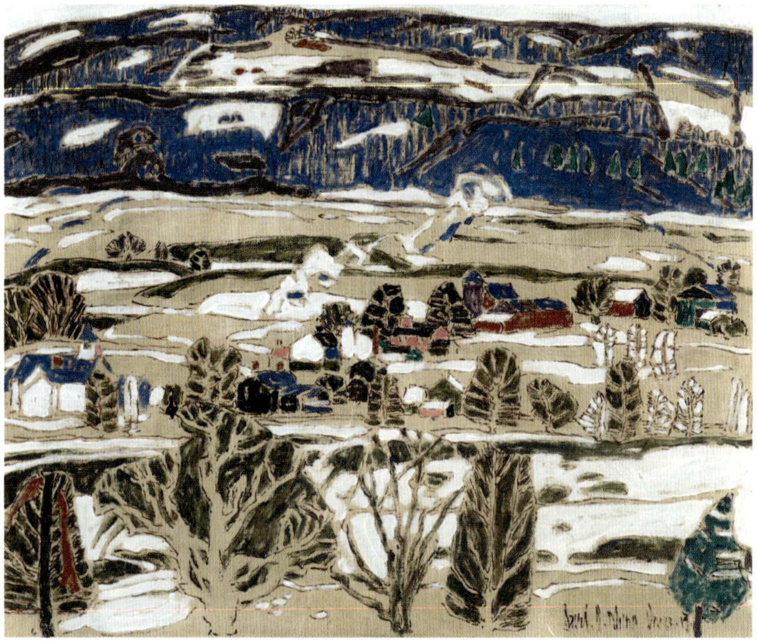

Top
David Milne
White Cloud, Boston Corners
1918, oil on canvas

Above
David Milne
Snow Patches
1917, oil on canvas

fund employed artists to document the war, thus accomplishing two worthwhile ends—a proper record of the conflict and the survival of a generation of artists. Milne rushed to put himself forward.

Once he had satisfied the criteria—his friend James Clarke back in New York sent over a box full of his work[6]—his first assignment was to record the training camps associated with the Canadian troops. He began with Kinmel Park; then on to Ripon in February 1919; then to Bramshott in Hampshire on 20 March; and finally to Seaford in Surrey in late April. Never having had subject matter dictated to him before, he nonetheless quickly found that his hard-won and carefully honed technique was fully adaptable to the task at hand, and some very distinctive watercolours of Kinmel Park and Ripon High Street awash in khaki (p. 83) were produced. His first nine watercolours were added to the great 1919 Canadian War Memorials exhibition at the Royal Academy of Arts, London (where he would have encountered works by A.Y. Jackson and Frederick Varley, Canadians who were future Group of Seven members).

What Milne really wanted, however, was to be sent to record the now-deserted battlefields of Flanders and France, and for that he had to wait until May 1919. From having been a lowly private, and in sharp contrast to his struggles to earn a living through art in New York and Boston Corners, he found that as a war artist he had status—he was effectively treated like an officer, assigned a car and driver and even special quarters for a studio. From 17 May to 30 August 1919, he toured the battlefields as a curious amalgam of soldier, artist and tourist, recording his impressions of Arras, Vimy Ridge, Courcelette, Lens, Monchy-le-Preux, Ypres and Passchendaele. By the end of his stint with the Canadian War Memorials Fund he had produced 109 watercolours in all—42 in the United Kingdom and 67 on the Continent.

Other artists and photographers recorded the devastation of those battlefields, both under bombardment on the front line and after the war had ended, but Milne's war pieces have a special quality: he took the technical discoveries of his previous output—the rigorous control of colour as value, the positive use of the bare paper, the overall mosaic effect, the dazzle spot, the dry brush—and honed them to a razor's edge. Controlled and quiet, the war watercolours pack a punch simply through the contrast of subject matter with the objective language in which they are expressed. With the same analytical and dispassionate eye that he used to record Patsy in their New York apartment, he depicted the vast craters, the abandoned detritus of war, the graves, the ruined churches, the shattered trees—a nightmare landscape over which, he noted, the smell of death still lingered.[7]

Right
David Milne in
northern France
1919

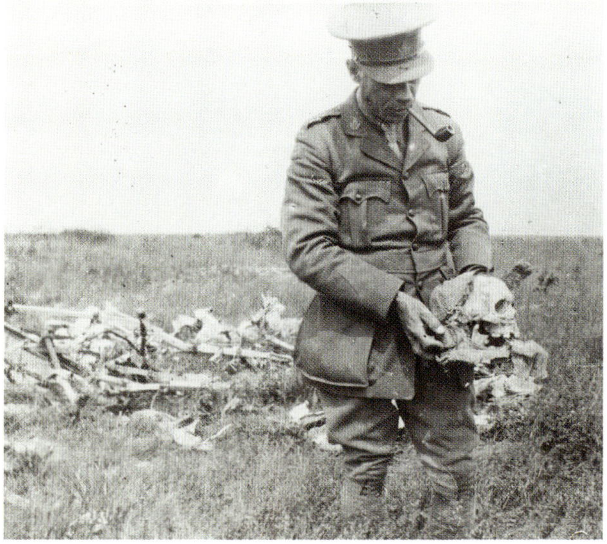

In one of the most extreme environments of the twentieth century, David Milne reaffirmed his awareness that for him the act of painting had an emotional truth that was separate from subject matter, having nothing to do with romanticism, melodrama or sentiment. His unique technique could record anything at all, rendering even that blighted landscape with dispassionate objectivity. In fact, it tightened his process: his habit of leaving the surface untouched acquired a new compositional impact when deployed to record the battlefields (pp. 104–5); his touch became more austere as he applied paint more sparingly with a dry brush. The lessons of this period would be observable in his output thereafter, perhaps notably in the stark landscapes of Dart's Lake, in the Adirondacks, and in his Temagami subjects—a remarkable series of images of flooded mineshafts that it is impossible to imagine having been made without his battlefield experiences (pp. 148, 154–5). These are effectively post-industrial craters. But restraint is also evident in some of Milne's paintings of the Big Moose Lake tea house, in which drybrush technique is so pared back that the distinction between painting and drawing is blurred.

With his war service over, Milne was back in Boston Corners by November 1919, having stopped off in Aberdeenshire to visit his parents' place of origin, before demobilisation in Toronto. He started painting again in December, and over the next three or four months was prolific—ninety pictures, half in oil, half in watercolour, flowed from his brush. From August to October 1920, he worked on another series—a group of reflection paintings at Weed Iron Mines, Kelly Ore Bed and Bishop's Pond—that embodied one of his most distinctive personal technical discoveries. He found that in watercolour a wash of clear water could be used to suggest reflection; it became one of his signature effects—a simple and economical technique that packed a powerful visual punch. The result was most magical in watercolour, but he would also explore the concept of reflection in oils (pp. 133, 136).

Always a rather solitary figure, his mind racing continually with thoughts about painting (his son, David Milne Jr, remembers him in later years sitting for hours in the evening contemplating his day's work, thinking it through), he was never going to be

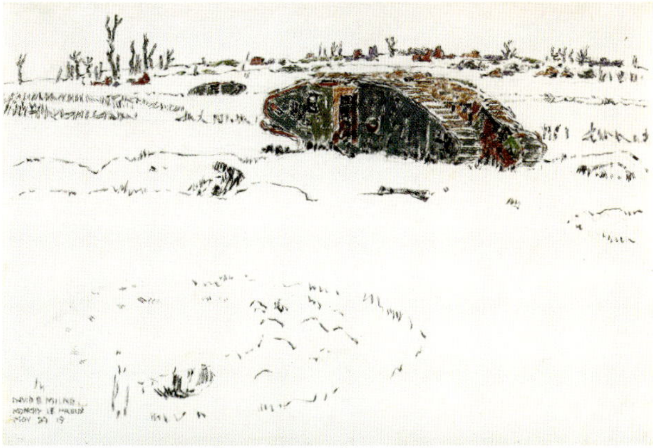

Right
David Milne
Wrecked Tanks outside Monchy-le-Preux
1919, watercolour over graphite on wove paper

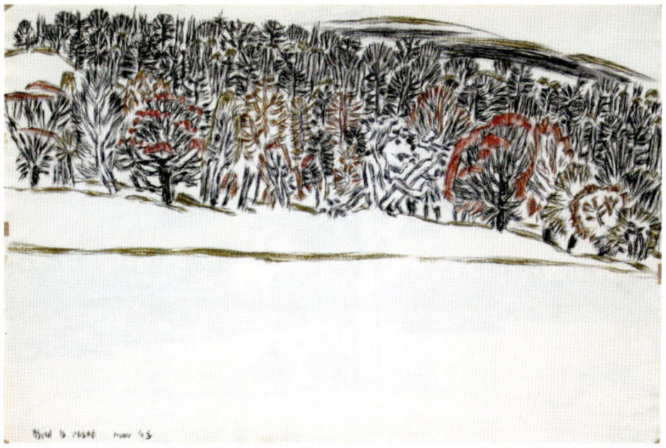

Below right
David Milne
Beginning of Spring I
c. 1923, drybrush watercolour on paper

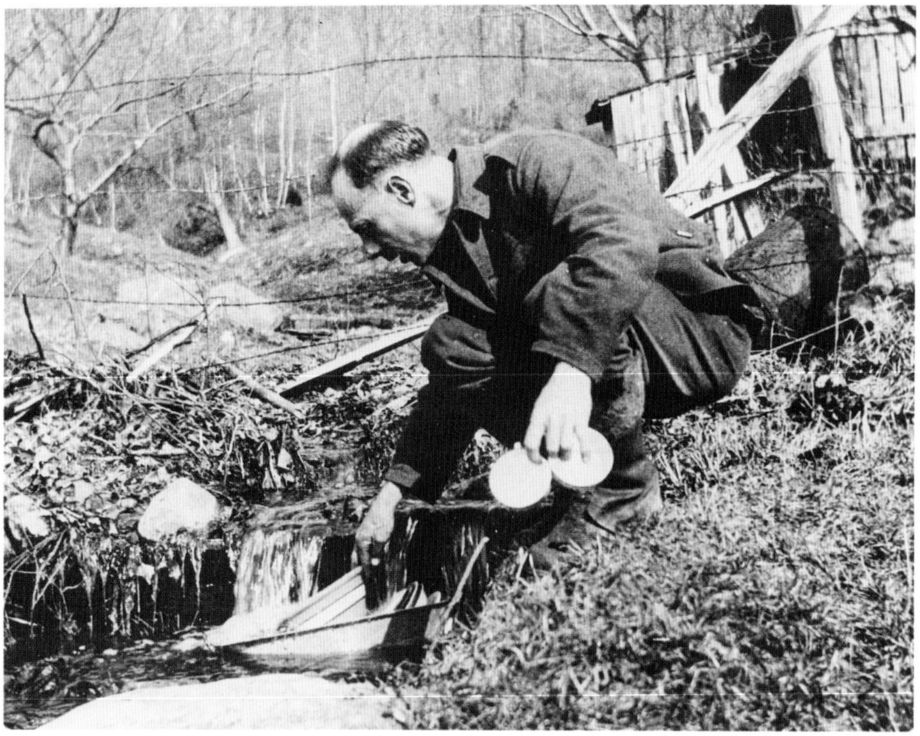

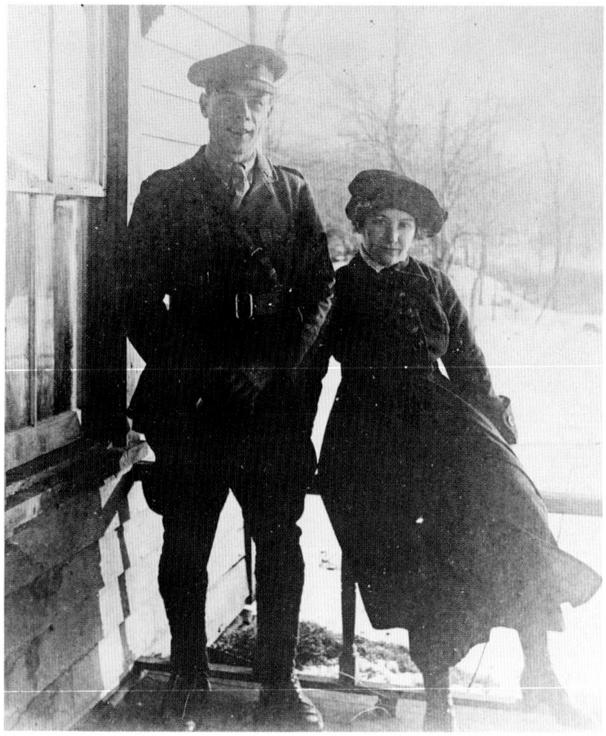

Above
David Milne near his Alander cabin
c. 1920

Above right
David and Patsy Milne, Boston Corners
1918

ideal husband material—and in the years following his war experience, the cracks in his relationship with Patsy began to show. Money was always a problem, exacerbating the tension, and in the winter of 1920–1 Patsy was obliged to leave for New York to find work. Milne, meanwhile, built himself a cabin, on the model of a wartime Nissen hut, on the flank of nearby Alander mountain, surrounded by trees.

He endured a freezing winter there, virtually cut off from the world, painting just thirty works. These include some of his greatest paintings, but the interlude was a strange one of self-imposed isolation, marked by an almost obsessive recording in writing of every detail of every day: an inner monologue. When it was too cold to step outside, he painted the stump in front of the cabin from the doorway, recording it with a cape of snow, or with the snow melting from it (pp. 120, 125). From this period also comes a characteristic experimental masterpiece, titled *White, the Waterfall*, 1921 (pp. 25, 118), which takes the notion of white as value to an extreme, leaving the mind's eye to read the colours in a dazzle of light. Typically, he then tried the same subject in darker tones of blue and black.

The period from May 1921, when he abandoned his Alander hut, to 1923 was a frustrating time, with Milne on the move between various types of cheap accommodation, including a friend's summer house during winter at Mount Riga. Throughout the summers of 1922 and 1923, he and Patsy ran the Little Tea House at Big Moose Lake, but by 1923, the money situation became urgent. Milne briefly moved back to Canada, to Ottawa, in an attempt to earn some money teaching, and tried also to interest the National Gallery of Canada there in buying some work. The contact was not entirely without success: two watercolours were put into the great British Empire Exhibition at Wembley in 1924 (where his contemporaries the Group of Seven and the now-deceased Tom Thomson made their first international impact) and three more into the 1925 iteration of that show. In that year Milne was also given a large monographic exhibition at the Art Association of Montreal (now the Montreal Museum of Fine Arts)—95 works, but none sold. The only bright spot came in March, when the National Gallery finally bought six watercolours, at $25 each. He returned to Big Moose Lake.

The five years from 1924 saw Milne trying out various moneymaking ventures. His friend Clarke, an advertising executive from New York,

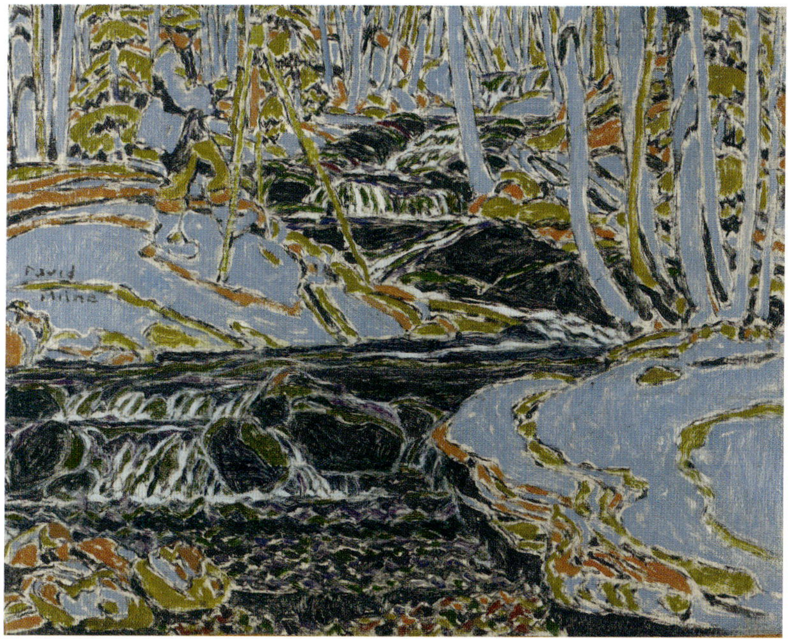

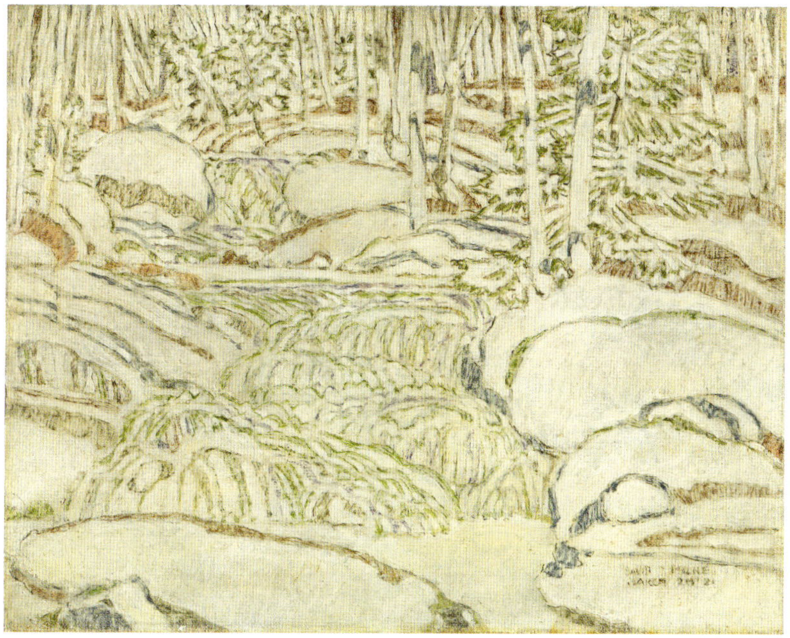

Top
David Milne
Black Waterfall
1921, oil on canvas

Above
David Milne
White, the Waterfall
1921, oil on canvas

financed the building of a house for the Milnes at Big Moose Lake. The plan was for the couple to run it as a tea house in the summer, but Milne's construction work, mostly undertaken on his own, dragged on over the next four years. In 1924 and 1928, he and Patsy ran the tea house at a local hotel; in winter, it was the tea house at the foot of the ski jump at Lake Placid. Opportunities to paint were few, and from 1925 he stopped painting watercolours, and his production dropped. However, 1927 marked an important development, in that Clarke bought him a small etching press. Milne experimented imaginatively with colour drypoint, a printmaking variation he had invented in 1922; his drybrush technique and colour theories translated well to drypoint, a medium suited to his established fascination with serial repetition. He was to become one of the most innovative printmakers of his time, though the prints lie outside the scope of this exhibition.

The house at Big Moose Lake finally sold in 1928 after several attempts to unload it (though due to the stock market crash of October 1929, Milne would receive only partial payment in instalments from the cash-strapped buyers). By then he had returned to Canada on his own, settling for the summer of 1929 near the northern Ontario mining town of Temagami, where he painted one of his most experimental series of works, depicting the abandoned flooded mineshafts he found in the nearby woods. As the Depression began to bite deeper in 1930, however, he moved farther south to Palgrave, Ontario, some 60 kilometres northwest of Toronto, where he and Patsy rented an unfurnished house. Here Milne began to paint seriously again—possibly, it has to be said, to escape Patsy, from whom Milne was increasingly disengaging, and whose tendency to cling and complain he now resented. He was perfectly happy painting clouds and houses—particularly his neighbour Ollie Matson's house, whose pleasing combination of proportions and angled planes anchored sky to land in *Ollie Matson's House in Snow*, 1932 (p. 165). The whimsical title *Ollie Matson's House Is Just a Square Red Cloud*, 1931 (p. 164), gives an insight into how Milne thought of his subject matter. The subject of the painting is the great pile-up of clouds in the sky, seen as outline, shape and colour—Matson's house

Below
David Milne
Stream in the Woods
1929, colour drypoint
on wove paper

Bottom
David Milne
Stream in the Woods
1929, colour drypoint
on wove paper

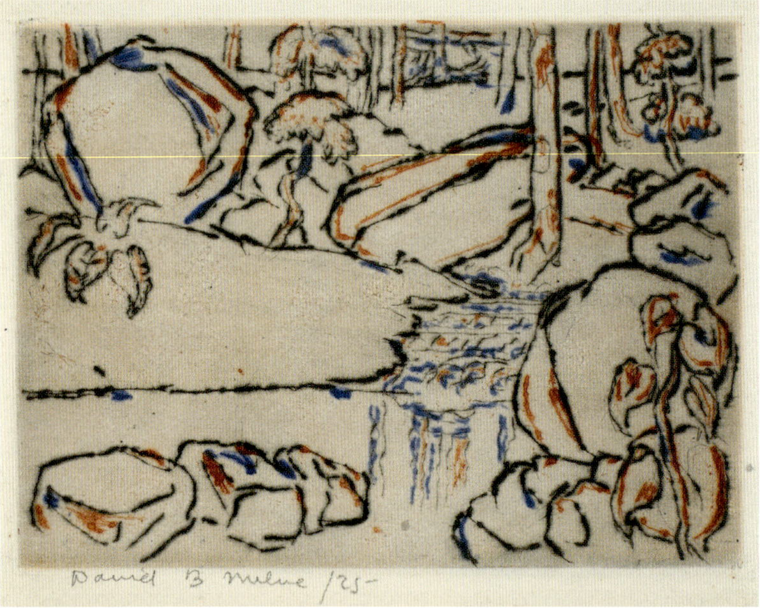

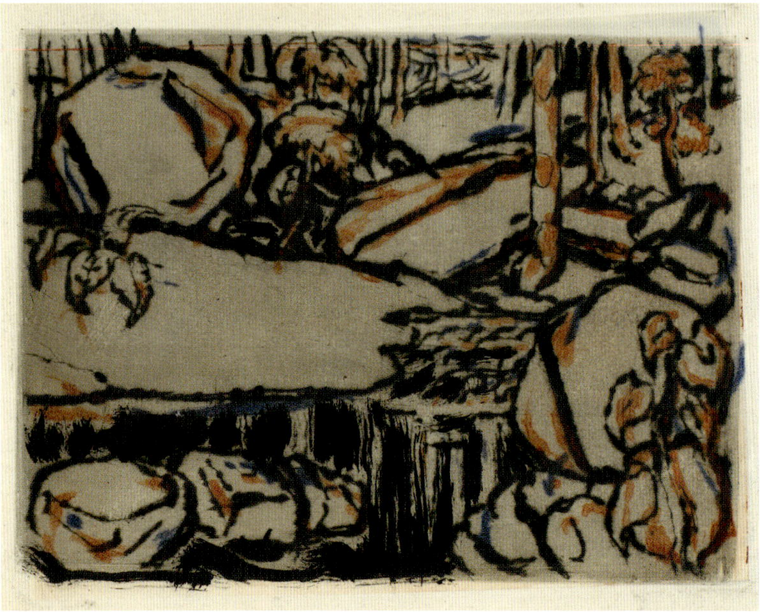

is just another shape but earthbound, geometric and red. The fact that it shelters people is neither here nor there.

By April 1933, the Milne marriage had broken down completely (at least as far as David Milne was concerned) and on 24 April he and Patsy signed a separation agreement, although Patsy never seems to have accepted the split and had an irritating—to Milne—habit of turning up to 'look after' him without notice. The next month Milne left Palgrave and settled at Six Mile Lake in Ontario's Muskoka district, alone. This was an extremely isolated place, accessible in winter only on foot or on skis. Following a by-now-familiar pattern, Milne built his own cabin on a promontory. He was to stay there for the next six years.

His period at Six Mile Lake also saw a focus on still-life subjects, and these oils are among his masterpieces. Pictures such as the exquisite *Flour Bag*, 1935 (p. 170), or *Moccasin Flower*, 1935 (p. 174), sum up this group. Subject matter was chosen from whatever was close at hand—picked flowers, glass jars, a paper bag, a flour bag—and a fiercely pared-back colour range of burnt orange and dirty grey with black outlines emerged, the burnt orange often seemingly bleeding out from the black to bring vibrancy to the drawing.

Outside, the low horizons over the vast expanse of water brought a concentration on skies, cloud formations and weather systems. Finally, in the isolation of Six Mile Lake, Milne discovered his own communion with the kind of landscape that the Group of Seven had chosen to depict in the previous decade. However, the astonishing, almost abstract, simplicity of *Lightning*, 1936 (p. 183), takes Milne into territory very far from the Group's visual language. *Across the Still Lake*, 1936 (p. 176), and its night-time equivalent *Setting Stars*, 1935 (p. 182), shows him grappling with cosmic effects, and the results are some of the most remarkable works of his career. His austere palette and economical technique were even up to the capturing of *Northern Lights*, 1935 (p. 189), or the sparks in the smoke of a bonfire in *Smoke*, 1935 (p. 188).

In the meantime, a source of income, albeit by curious and unsatisfactory means, had been achieved. In August 1934, Milne had made a pitch to two major collectors, the wealthy lawyer and diplomat (and future Governor General of Canada) Vincent Massey and his wife, Alice. His idea was that they should buy all his extant paintings (there were about a thousand of them) for $5 each. This they were not prepared to do, astonishing bargain though it was. Instead, they bought about three hundred. Milne's objective had been to keep his work together, but the Masseys promptly held an exhibition of selected works in a Toronto commercial gallery and sold some of them, promising to share the profits with him after they had recouped their $1,500 original payment to the artist. But the gallerist's steep 50 per cent commission meant that no such profit was ever realised. To make matters worse, the Masseys then continued to acquire his current production but refused to pay a reasonable market price, simply choosing to think that the $5-a-painting deal still applied. Milne's letters to them on the subject were ignored.

Yet income was income. All that Milne really cared about was being able to paint without having to worry about money, and his lifestyle was anything but expensive. Eventually, he extricated himself from the Masseys and their gallerist. Their activities had at least put his works on display through several exhibitions, and in 1937 he entrusted boxes of his work to the American-born Canadian art advocate and collector Douglas Duncan, who was to become his agent and dealer until his death. Duncan would organise almost annual exhibitions in Toronto of Milne's work at his Picture Loan Society. Milne had again taken up watercolour as a medium, after several years concentrating exclusively on oils and drypoint. Duncan and the meat-packing industrialist and philanthropist J.S. McLean bought many of his early watercolours, and through one purchase of 22 watercolours for $1,600, McLean became Milne's most generous patron.

About the same time, life took a surprising turn for the artist on his lonely promontory on Six Mile Lake with the arrival, by accident, in a canoe, of a young woman, Kathleen Pavey. One thing led to another, and in 1939, Milne moved to Toronto with Kathleen, who took his name. They lived as man and wife. Patsy, who still refused to accept that David had moved on, would not agree to a divorce, even when Kathleen became pregnant. This was scandalous according to the mores of the day; the couple soon moved to Uxbridge, Ontario, to deliver their son, David Jr, on 4 May 1941. Milne delegated Duncan to act as intermediary with Patsy, but she declined the arrangement and even sent back cheques in unopened envelopes.

Apart from these domestic disturbances, the 1940s brought some stability and increased income, largely through the championship of Duncan. Milne even managed to build one final cabin for himself in 1948 at Baptiste Lake, Bancroft, south of Ontario's Algonquin Provincial Park, although his health was already beginning to fail. In 1951, he survived an operation for cancer of the lower intestine. Painting on his own at Baptiste Lake, returning to Kathleen and David Jr in Uxbridge for birthdays and holidays, he finally achieved the recognition of representing Canada at the Venice Biennale in 1952, but suffered four strokes between November of that year and July 1953.

David Milne died on 26 December 1953, at age 71, leaving behind a vast body of work of remarkably consistent high quality. He stands as one of the most distinctive of twentieth-century artists anywhere in the world, but he is rightly revered in Canada as one of the country's greatest visual poets.

Ian A.C. Dejardin *became Executive Director of the McMichael Canadian Art Collection in 2017 after 12 years as the Sackler Director of Dulwich Picture Gallery. He has organised countless exhibitions over the years and has previously curated* Painting Canada: Tom Thomson and the Group of Seven *(2011) and co-curated* Vanessa Bell *(2017) and* From the Forest to the Sea: Emily Carr in British Columbia *(2014–15) with Sarah Milroy.*

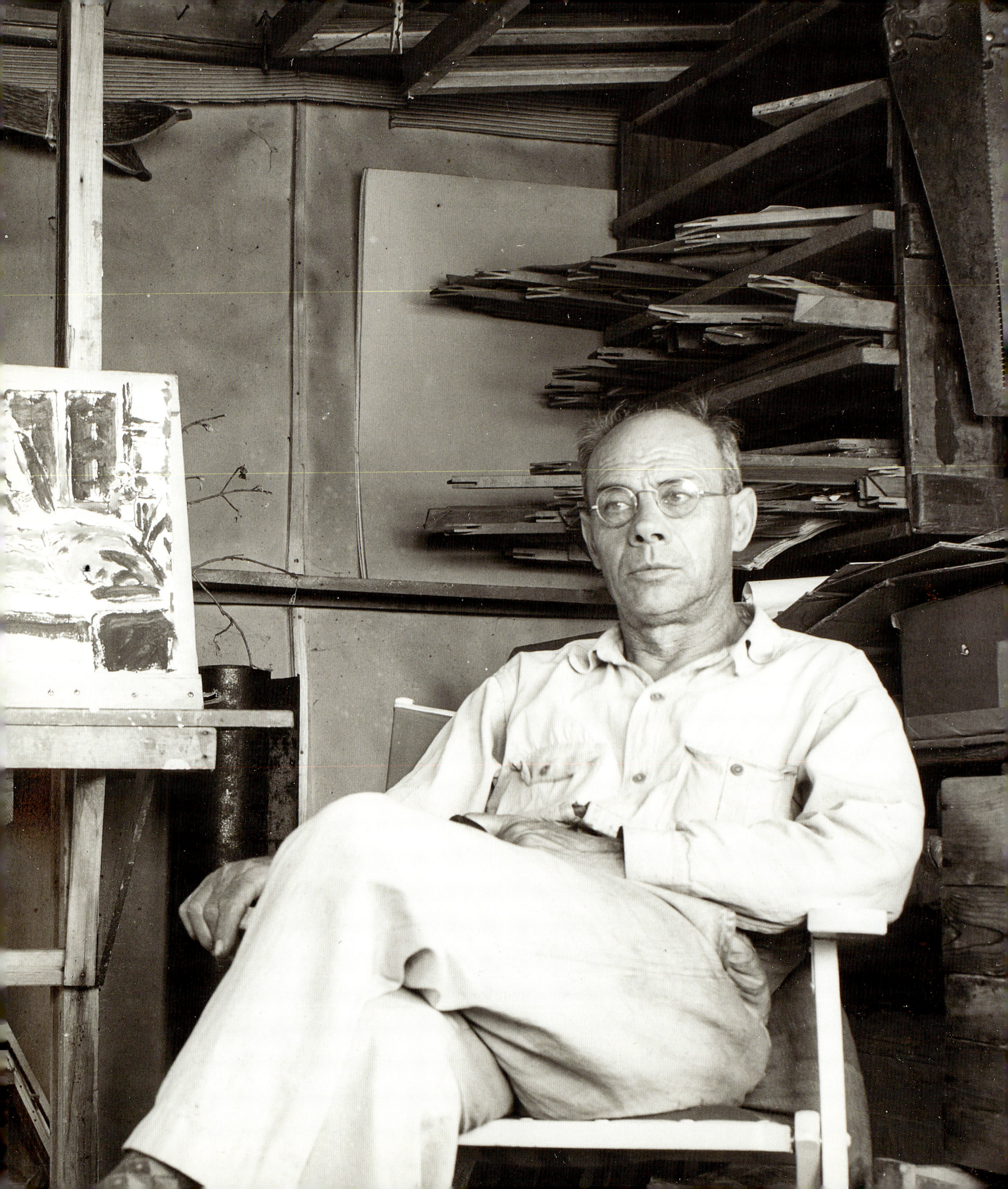

A MIND OF HIS OWN

Sarah Milroy

At the tail-end of a transatlantic flight from London to Toronto, we were slowly making our southbound descent from 35,000 feet, and I was playing with the map function on the small screen in front of me. There, the North American continent slowly rolled towards me: first the rocky, glacier-scoured brow of northern Ontario—Timmins, North Bay, then Huntsville, Toronto, Windsor, Kingston—then, seamlessly, the greener land beyond it: Buffalo, Schenectady, Syracuse, Albany, the Adirondacks, the Berkshires, Boston, New York, their place names popping up on the screen as we continued down. The world on this screen was one without borders, a world that is just topography—that far-reaching swath of north-eastern territory that Milne traversed during his five decades of making art.

The screen map allowed me to look at the world from new angles, from upside down, from above, disembodied from any particular point of view, with my destination always approaching—a green disc whirling in the distance, the holding pattern over Toronto, where I live.

David Milne loved maps, and he would have loved this one. During his time at Alander mountain in New York State, in March 1921, he even wrote a quirky essay titled 'Touring on a Topographic Map', about walking in a world of dotted lines and elevations.[1] Yet, his own art defies the kinds of distinctions that conventional maps impose (Canadian versus American, North American versus European). Milne is one of Canada's most treasured visual artists, his mindful and disciplined devotion to painting and printmaking leading him to become a beloved model for generations of Canadian artists; but his sensibility was honed by experiences on both sides of the border, informed equally by his understanding of the artistic conventions of the United States and Europe. He is, in this sense, an artist beyond nationality.[2]

For this reason, it has always seemed to me that Milne's true context is not that of his Canadian contemporaries such as the Group of Seven—to whom he is sometimes hitched as a kind of sidecar in our national narrative of art—but rather that of

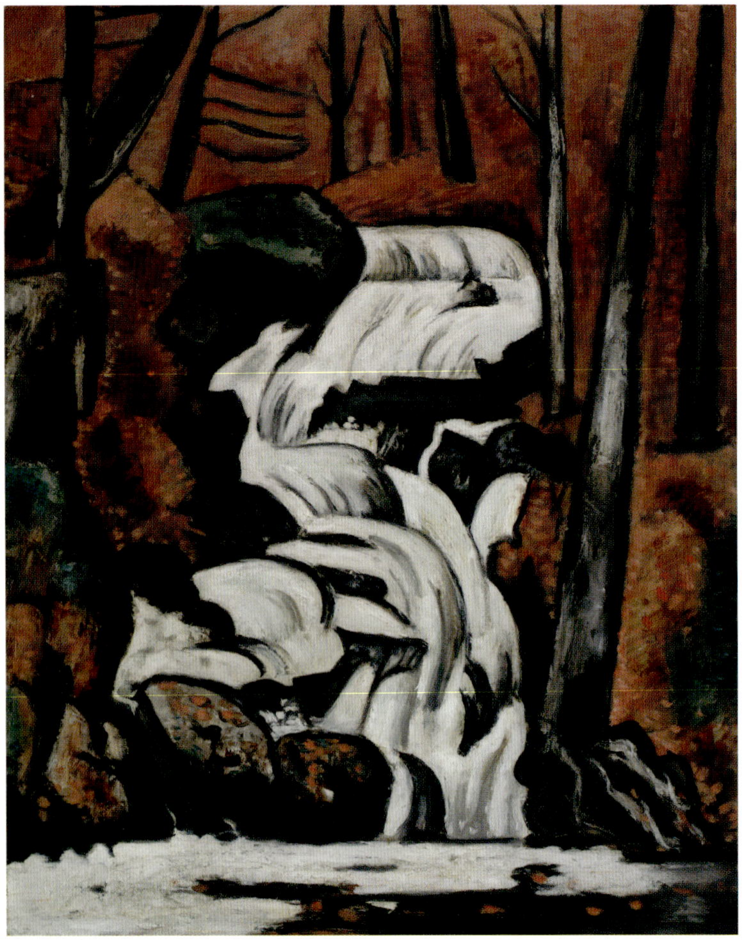

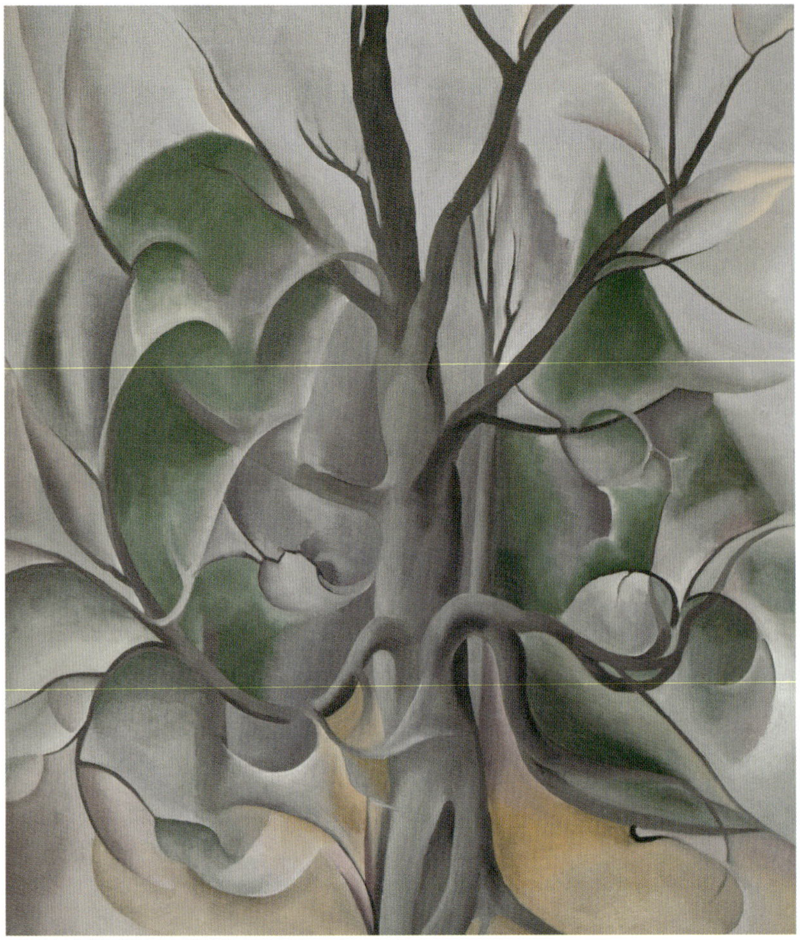

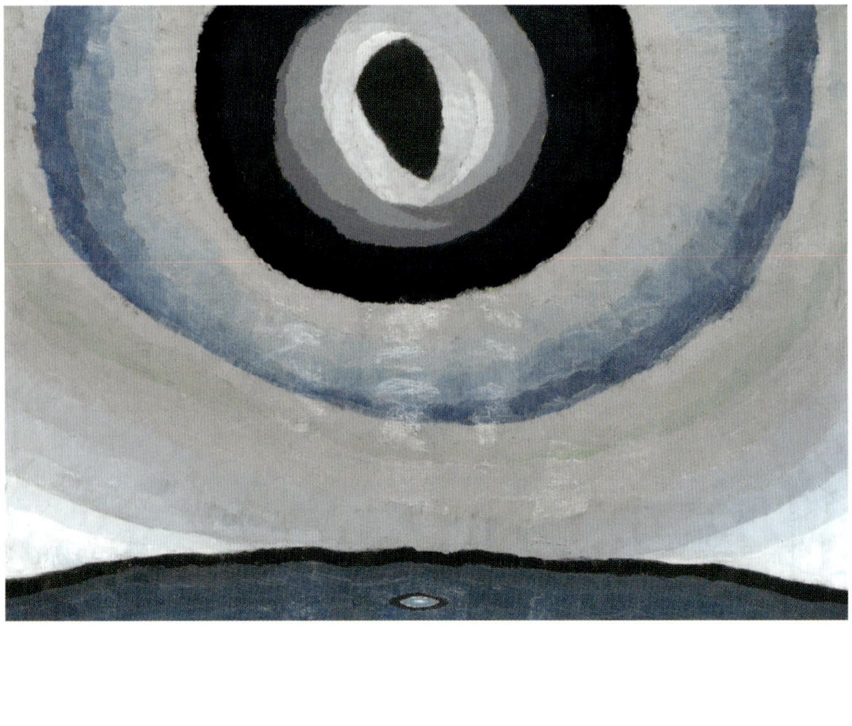

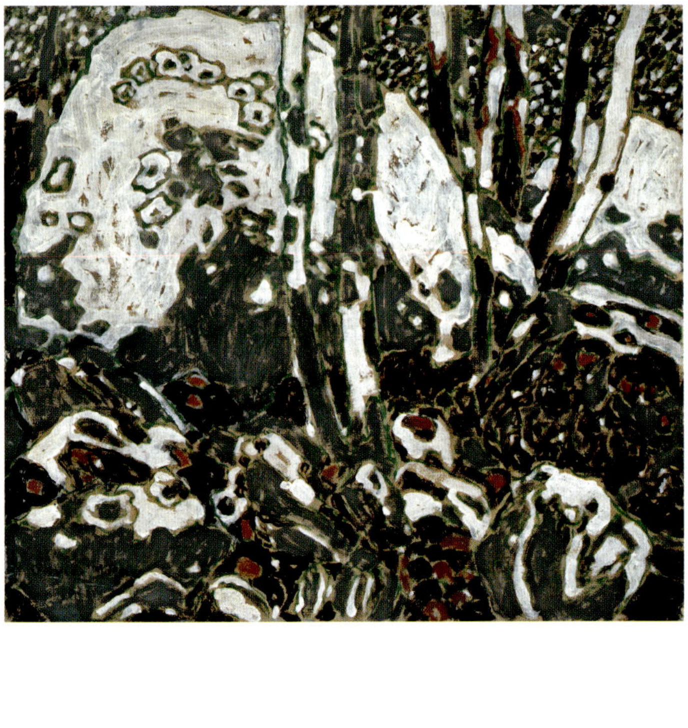

his American contemporaries Marsden Hartley, John Marin (whom he met in New York), Georgia O'Keeffe and Arthur Dove. These artists largely began their lives in small-town settings, like Milne, and were drawn by their artistic ambition to the flame of New York City, eventually exhibiting their paintings at Alfred Stieglitz's gallery 291, on Fifth Avenue, where Milne was a frequent visitor. As Milne remembered in a letter to Vincent and Alice Massey decades later, he would seldom miss an exhibition at 291 during his years in the city,[3] and he was doubtless deluged by Stieglitz's endless spontaneous lectures on modern art, to which all comers were subjected.[4] (By one account, the artist was once considered so much a part of the furniture there that he was asked to help shift a Brancusi sculpture when a young back was needed.)[5] Like Milne, his American contemporaries painted the city in daring new ways, but like him they also returned to nature, forging a revitalised modern landscape charged by that cosmopolitan experience, under the continent's eastern skies.

These artists shared with Milne a vivid and solitary connection to that natural world—a connection extolled in the writings of Emerson, Whitman and Thoreau, to whom they had all been heirs—as well as the drive to develop their own idiosyncratic pictorial language. Milne's most kindred Canadian artist was arguably the British Columbian painter Emily Carr, whose accomplishment Milne singled out when he encountered her painting *Indian Church*, 1929, in a 1930 exhibition in Toronto.[6] Like Milne, Carr was born of British immigrant parents and developed an amalgamated transatlantic sensibility, informed by the USA (including the galleries and museums of New York City) and Europe, where she received her artistic training. Like Milne, too, she sought sources far from the wellsprings of Canadian art, her paintings eventually having more to do with the ecstatic landscapes of Van Gogh and the writings of Whitman—and with the strength she sensed in the culture of Canada's Indigenous peoples—than with the output of her much-publicised contemporaries in settler culture. Like Milne, she would go her own way.

The key to understanding Milne's life and art, I think, lies in appreciating this highly informed independence of mind: independence from nationality, from dogma and ideology, from the fashions of his own time, from theories of art history (he would develop his own in dialogue with past and present), and from conventions of all sorts. Showing his work in New York alongside a number of the Ashcan School realist painters such as Robert Henri and William Glackens, Milne took the path of aestheticism instead, dismissing their efforts as the 'Salvation Army in paint'.[7] His independence of mind meant that Matisse's painting *The Red Studio*, 1911 (p. 21), could impress itself upon him as readily as an Egyptian carved relief from the Land of Punt in the Metropolitan Museum of Art,[8] or even a Stieglitz photograph glimpsed on the fly.[9]

Milne's receptivity also meant that he could admire both the writings of Ruskin, whom he described as 'the greatest of art critics',[10] and the work of those who rebelled against him—the British formalists Clive Bell and Roger Fry.[11] Always, he was at pains to hold himself apart from the herd. 'Much obliged for the two Clive Bell articles', he wrote to his friend and patron James Clarke in the fall of 1920, though he went on to describe his scepticism regarding Bell's quasi-devotional relationship to Cézanne. 'The new man is much more apt to develop from the more distant than the immediate past', he wrote, '[from] Holbein not Cézanne, who he has seen copied, developed and carried on by everyone he knows.... He is more apt to delve (so far as he has to borrow at all) in some mine where the exhaustion of the vein is not so apparent as in this.'[12]

More fruitful to look to the art of the past—whether a cave painting at Altamira[13] or a religious work by El Greco.[14] Milne wrote of his admiration of Velázquez, for his dynamic use of the blank space in *Las Meninas*, 1656,[15] and of Whistler, for his daring reduction of surface detail;[16] both would serve as imaginary thought companions as he made his modern journey. 'Very fine morning now indeed', Milne wrote to Clarke on a cold January day in London, during his period of war service overseas. 'The ground is all white frost and the air white mist with sun overhead. Monet would bathe in this.'[17]

Sometimes Milne's influences and affirmations came in literary form, from the writings of Marcel Proust,[18] whom he admired for his ability to capture internal life in language, or of Thoreau, who affirmed his intense connection

Opposite
Clockwise from top left
Marsden Hartley
Smelt Brook Falls
1937, oil on board

Georgia O'Keeffe
Gray Tree, Lake George
1925, oil on canvas

David Milne
The Boulder
1916, oil on canvas

Arthur Dove
Silver Sun
1929, oil, metallic paint and an unidentified material (possibly wax) on canvas

Right
Alfred Stieglitz
From the Back Window, 291, Snow Covered Tree, Back Yard
1915, platinum print

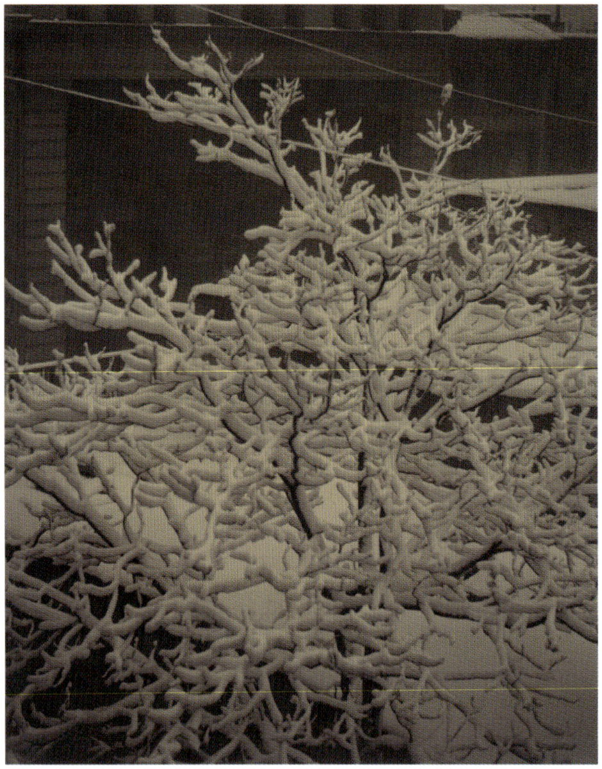

Far right
David Milne
Heavy Snow
1915, watercolour on paper

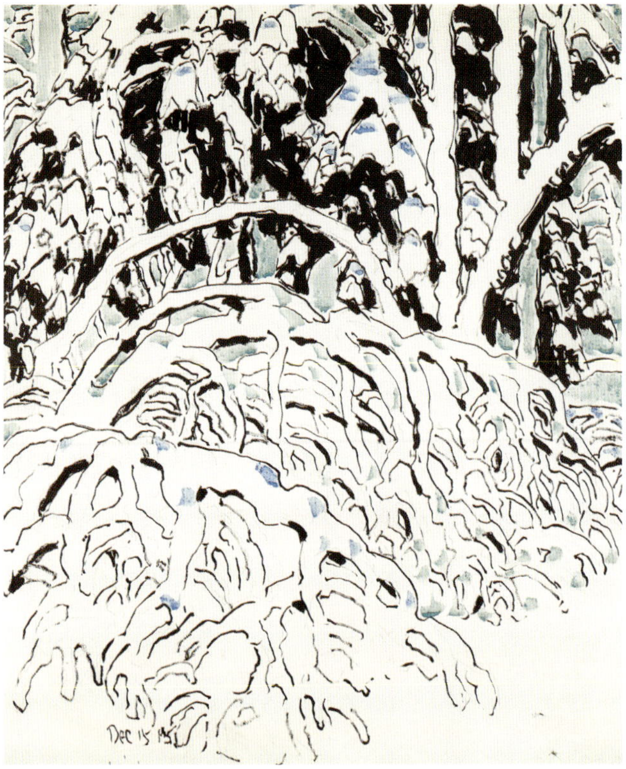

to nature and his choice of an austere and simple life of seclusion. That seclusion enabled a kind of extreme concentration, as Milne ran at pictorial problems again and again in his trademark reiterations of set themes, whether he was making a series of still lifes in the bush at Six Mile Lake (his inventory of subjects as reduced and economical as Giorgio Morandi's—a water jar, a bowl, a plate, a flour bag) or a sequence of stump paintings made from the secluded vantage point of his cabin door on Alander mountain.

If the role of the artist is, as the poet Kenneth Patchen has written, 'to experience only experience',[19] then Milne is the exemplar. He liked to hear his own mind at work. In his scribbled notes to himself at Alander, for example, during one of the periods of most extreme isolation (and one of his most artistically experimental), he mentioned several times his frustrating efforts to observe his own mind at rest while engaged in apparently mindless chores, such as chopping wood or chinking the walls of his cabin with moss. (He kept forgetting to notice, of course.)[20]

In the manner of Thoreau, his diaries record the minutiae of perception in ways that still reverberate a century later. 'A sharp click from a stick in the fire', Milne wrote on a cold December night in 1920, methodically noting down each sensory experience in a kind of inventory. 'Sharper sound of a drop falling into the tea kettle from a pole above.'[21] In an earlier moment that winter, he noted: 'The stove with its rust vermilions, grays, blues & purples is as brilliant as an orchid.'[22] With his attention dilated in the quiet of the woods, he could discover the most unlikely beauty. Paintings like *Thaw in the Woods*, 1921 (p. 125), express that fierce interiority, as he pushes for ever more extreme experiments in describing perception through distinct painterly textures. Watching the stump, he also watches himself watching.

While some pages in Milne's writings expose a loneliness, aloneness—a not-unwelcome solitude—is a much more consistent theme. 'Usually there was no sound except for the fire in the stove', he wrote years later of his time at Alander, describing his life in the cabin with a hermit's euphoria:

> but sometimes I could hear the wind in the tops of the hemlocks or the snow or sleet against the windows and the stove pipes.

> Nearly every night and always about the same time, seven o'clock, the owls started their strange crying and screeching in the trees over my head. I often went to the door to look for them but all I ever saw was a shadow moving without sound among the trees.[23]

Milne's 'inexhaustible source of entertainment' on these long nights was the reading of a 'big Webster's dictionary I have brought up in a red box'.[24] As he observed once in a letter to Clarke, 'if all the workings of one's mind for half an hour could be set down they would fill a book bigger than the Encyclopedia'.[25]

Most often, though, Milne's mind was occupied with the act of painting itself, and he describes in meticulous detail his strategies for composition as well as the varieties of his visual experience. He was clear in declaring a distinction, for example, between his general love of natural beauty and the special aesthetic charge that kindles the work of art, something that could not be forced.[26] Throughout his life, he drafted and redrafted his accounting of the spontaneous flash of perception and creativity that precipitated, he felt, the corresponding flash of perception in the mind of the viewer.

Crucial to this for Milne was the concept of the 'dazzle spot', the use of a dynamic blank area of light that appears as a phenomenon in his art in his New York period and continues throughout his career. It was Milne's strategy for arresting the attention of the viewer. 'The dazzle area is violent', he wrote to Clarke, in 1932, in one of many iterations, 'a sharp contrast in value. It is the first thing to engage the eye, throws you violently and quickly into the middle of things, then, since it has no interest, releases you into the detailed part.'[27] In his essay 'Pictures Have Beginnings and Endings', Milne presented a visceral account of the act of looking at a painting, describing how the artist choreographs the experience of the viewer through his formal composition of the image. Our attention 'may speed at one point', Milne wrote, 'delay at another; one part may gain our attention quickly and release it almost at once; another may not force itself on our attention so readily, but may hold it much longer'. Continuing in a more vernacular vein, he added: 'Our progress is very much like that of a robin on a lawn: we may make a quick dash at some point, find nothing to hold us there; take another step or two, fast or slow, grasp an insect; another movement and we pull up and swallow a very large and satisfactory worm'. A picture, he said, offers a kind of journey. 'Some are like old trails, often used and well worn, some are new paths. None but the great artists get far off the beaten roads.'[28] One thing was for certain: the perception of a work of art was no idle matter but rather a kind of perceptual track-and-field event set up for the engaged viewer, not without its exertions.

Milne found new paths, too, in his rethinking of traditional genres. Never has the theme of a woman by the fire been more unsettling than in his

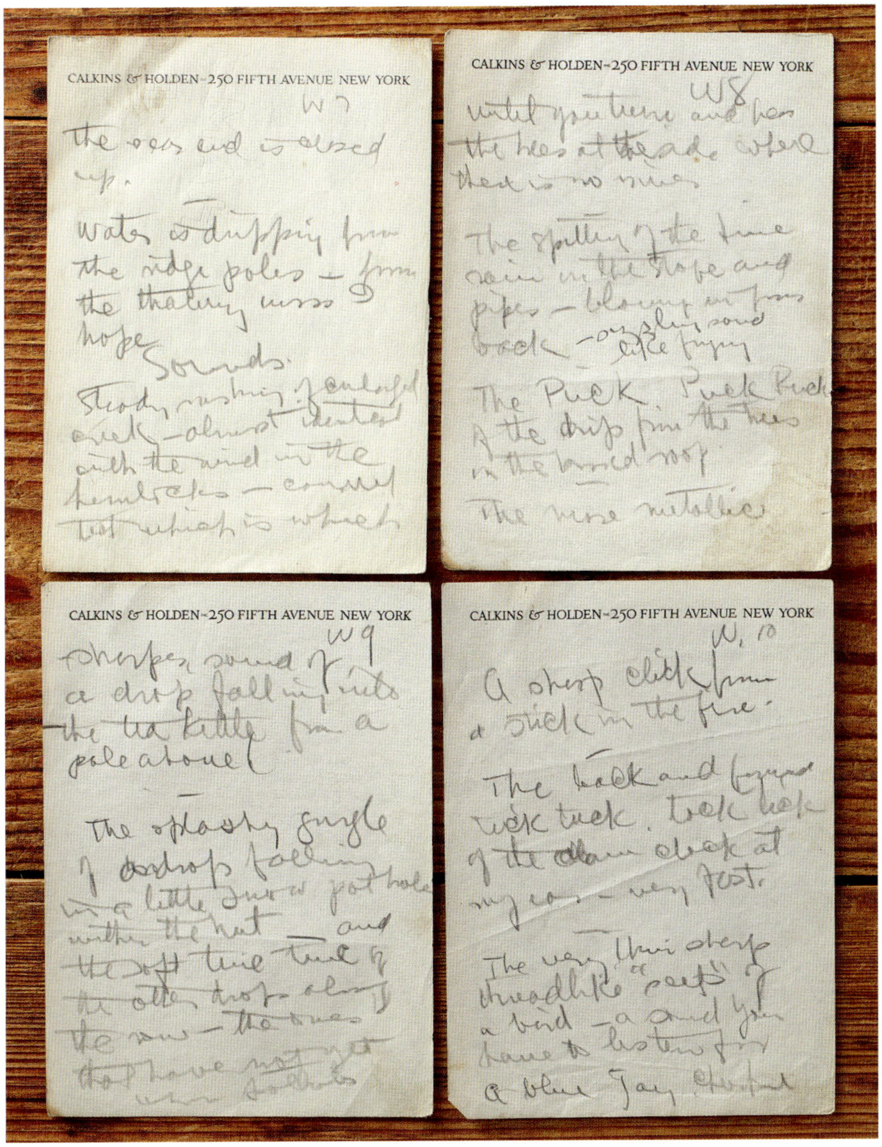

David Milne
Notes from Alander cabin
1 December 1920

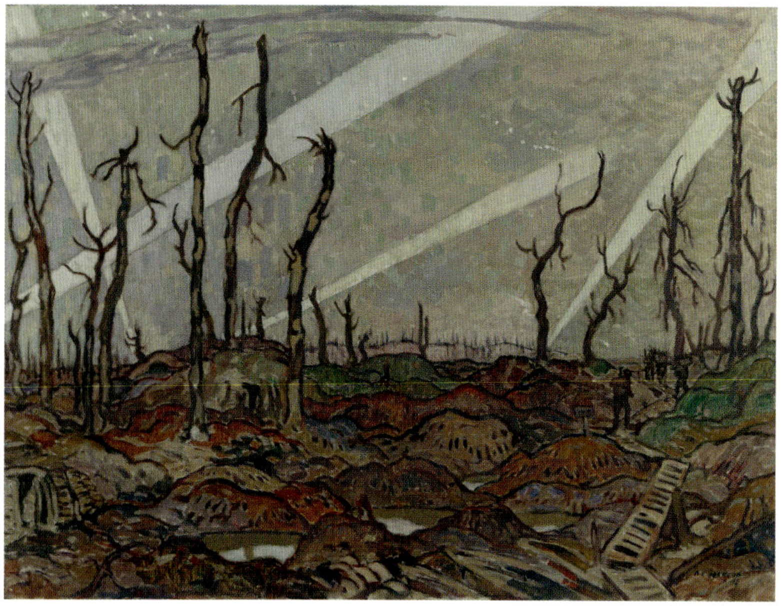

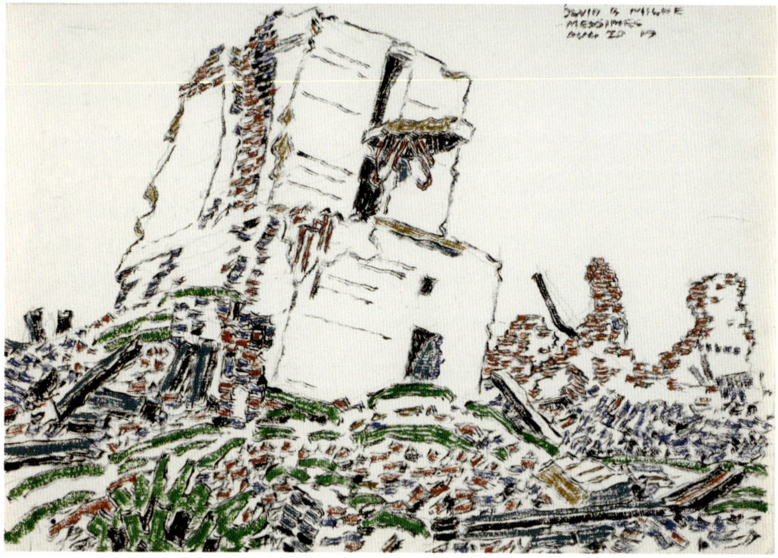

Top
Alexander Young Jackson
A Copse, Evening
1918, oil on canvas

Above
David Milne
Skyscraper Pillbox at Messines
1919, watercolour over graphite on wove paper

Summer Night, Saugerties, 1914 (p. 62), in which the shadow of Patsy looms on the wall like a malevolent poltergeist, a striking contrast to the seated lady herself. Milne's *White Waterlilies in a Prospector's Cabin*, 1929 (p. 156), also challenges the genteel tradition of still life, his charred-seeming pictorial ground emitting colour and light through a web of cracks and fissures. While some of his landscape paintings achieve a serene harmony, such as the still calm of *Pink Reflections, Bishop's Pond*, 1920 (p. 127), others appear positively bloody-minded, as in the inky, edgy near-abstraction of *Reflected Forms*, 1917 (p. 79), another watercolour that defies any conventions of the picturesque. Rather than seeming like a refuge for contemplation, the black surface of the water appears inert, even menacing, surrounded by a standing army of starkly rendered trees. Scholars of Canadian art have long noted that the genre of landscape serves at the pleasure of those who control it, and that landscape can express—as did the paintings of the Group of Seven—both the experience of the artist in nature but also the allure of the frontier as an element of nationalist ideology.[29] Milne's landscapes serve no such overarching agenda. More often than not, the paintings suggest an eerily solitary confrontation with a silent land. Milne bears witness for an audience of one.

The artist went his own way, too, when it came to the subject of war, holding to his view that war propaganda 'has no place in self expression'.[30] His suite of watercolours made in northern France and Belgium in 1919 is the antithesis of the roiling trenches and portentous shafts of light painted by other war artists from both sides of the Atlantic. True, Milne was working in the aftermath of the conflagration, yet his tendency was still to stick to the bleak material facts of the desolate scene before him, stripping away narrative inflection, anecdotal detail and patriotic pathos from his renderings. Instead of a diatribe about the folly of war, or a paean to manly sacrifice, what we find is a clear-eyed encounter with apocalypse, in scenes that shock us still by their refusal to editorialise.

In the years to come, he would use the language of war to describe his experiences, whether it be the 'detonation' of an idea in his mind (his reading of Thoreau) or the sound 'as loud as the bursting of a shell' when the ice formed in the dead of winter at Six Mile Lake.[31] Thinking about painting, he observed: 'The thing that makes a picture is the thing that makes dynamite—compression.'[32] His observations of the natural world, too, often took on a kind of mock-military precision. 'Heard two partridges in the woods, probably the same one at two times—the second time was on it and saw it plainly', he wrote in one typical entry, describing a walk at Boston Corners in the fall after his return from Europe. 'Before I got my pad out of my haversack I had made the following observations. The River Fog bank had changed from Vanilla or Peach to Neapolitan.'[33] A meticulous 'tree census' follows, with a detailed accounting of species and their state of vitality or decay. As a soldier records the details of calamity with cool detachment, so Milne would attempt to lay hold of reality with a kind of forensic rigour.

Milne's solitary ways did not mean, however, that he was a man without professional and personal attachments—his letters make that clear—but he was highly selective. He held close to the relationships that sustained him, whether it was his friend and patron James Clarke or Alice Massey in the 1930s (who sent him a steady supply of art magazines during his early years at Six Mile Lake),[34] or his correspondents Donald W. Buchanan (an art historian, writer and cultural administrator), H.O. McCurry (director of the National Gallery of Canada), the Toronto art critic Graham McInnes or the art dealer Douglas Duncan, who would represent him after 1938. When Kathleen Pavey showed up in his little bay at Six Mile Lake, he was quick to strike up an attachment to the intrepid and well-read young woman and would remain connected to her for the rest of his life. (One of the rites of passage of their early courtship was her insistence that he read James Joyce's *Ulysses*—a task that would have confounded all but the most cerebral suitor.)[35] A handful of artists also won Milne's friendship, among them the painters Carl Schaefer and Paraskeva Clark, the latter of whom bought one of Milne's Alander stump paintings for her own collection.[36] His discussions with these figures ranged far and wide, whether he was defending the autonomy of the National Gallery from the bullying tactics of the Royal Canadian Academy of Arts, conversing on Roger Fry's *Vision and Design*, or describing the pleasures of listening to Dvořák or Stravinsky on a friend's phonograph.[37] The fellowship of likeminded souls was a welcome balm to his own.

Still, one has the sense that for Milne, the company of nature was the best company of all, and an immersion in his writings is a lesson in natural history. Through him, one learns of the habits of freeloading porcupines, of his wolf-in-residence at Six Mile Lake, his surreptitious photography of beavers at work on their dam at Dart's Lake in the Adirondacks, his sad encounter with a mouse at Alander (it fell in the bucket of water and froze to death), or the 'angry and dignified march' of a turtle thwarted in her efforts to lay eggs in Milne's vegetable garden at Six Mile Lake.[38] Always, he was in pursuit of knowledge. In a letter to Pavey, he exults in his reading of J.H. Fabre's 1914 treatise, *Social Life in the Insect World*, which had been supplied to him by a mutual friend. ('I feel like a saint after reading it', he noted.)[39] For Milne, even the sounds of nature were known by heart. 'There must be a pine behind and above me', he wrote to Clarke in August 1924, while sitting outdoors on a breezy summer day: 'The full soft rush of the wind made by the combing of innumerable like sounds is unmistakable. Right! But I had to twist my neck and pivot the end of my spine quite a bit to prove it.'[40] That openness to the minutiae of sensory experience is one of the marvels of his sensibility.

Not surprisingly, an immersion in Milne's art expands our own powers of perception; in fact, this is one of the principal pleasures of these paintings. I can remember the moment when I came to realise the impact of this. It was a freezing cold winter day, the sky a polar blue, and I was walking my old dog in the Winston Churchill ravine in Toronto—the kind of urban respite that Milne and Pavey used to roam in during their spell in this city in the winter of 1939. The light that day was almost blinding in its sheer force. It is the kind of winter light that my eastern-born friends seem to love, though having grown up on Canada's rainy west coast, I have always found it scalding to the eye.

On this day, however, I saw a kind of beauty I had been schooled by Milne to see. The trunks of the bare trees rose from the blanket of snow,

Right
Peter Doig
Windowpane
1993, oil on canvas

Far right
David Milne
Cobalt Forms
c. 1913, watercolour on paper on board

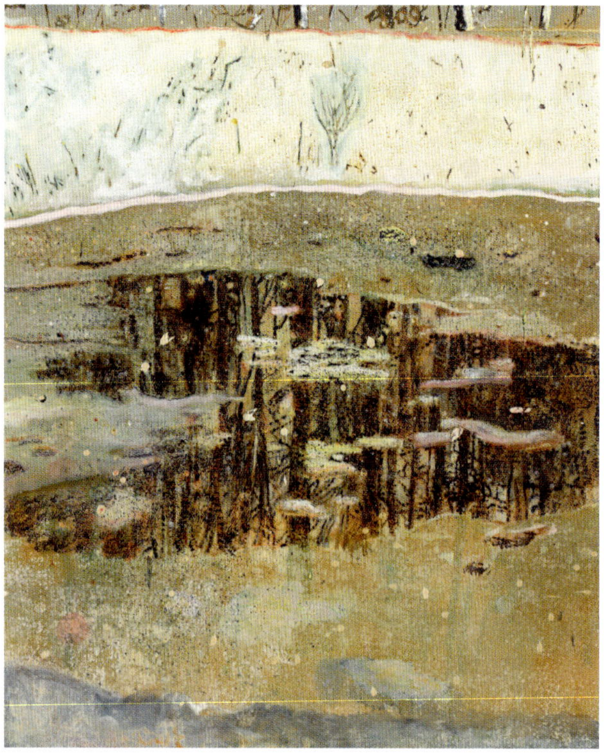

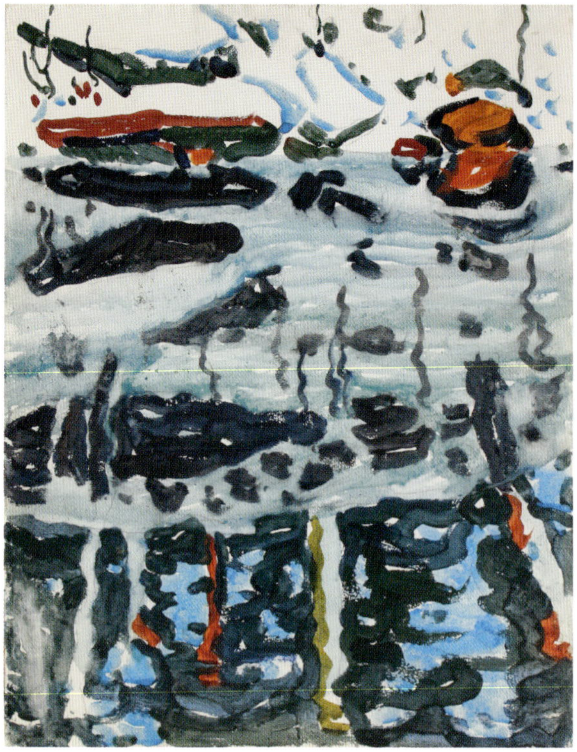

each of their forms with its own colour and texture. Their shadows, lying across the granulated white, were revealed to me as not white but lavender, blue, moleskin grey. The pleasures here were spare and spartan—a simple scene of snow and stumps, rocks and sticks—but in that economy an exquisite balance could be discovered in the shapes, the spacing and the clustering of the forms, in the scintillation of signals to the eye, denoting dazzle. Milne had allowed me to understand the way we know cold by sight. Looking down from the curve of the pathway ahead of me, I had discovered a micro-landscape far more beautiful at ground level, nearer to my footfall. It was a Milne subject, but one I could so easily have walked right by.

Milne has made me that patient watcher in the woods, searching out his quieter epiphanies. Not for Milne the swooning trees and skies of Emily Carr, sweeping us up to the heavens, or the heaving, furrowed fields of the Group of Seven member A.Y. Jackson, both of them artists who strived to do justice to a natural world *out there*, beyond them. Instead, Milne self-consciously sought to record the processes of perception within the confines of his own mind. It is this interest in perception itself that connects him to the contemporary British painter Peter Doig, who has acknowledged his awareness of Milne's art during his own early years of artistic development in Canada, and who has shared Milne's mastery of painting the meditative winter world of ice, snow and reflection.[41]

Milne's art speaks of that interior life, protected from distraction, embodying something closer to the sensibility that Wallace Stevens writes of in 'The Snow Man', when he describes the modern poet who sees 'nothing that is not there and the nothing that is'.[42] Stevens' poet is in pursuit of representation stripped of narrative, without any overarching meaning beyond its own formal elements—elements assembled by the clearest of minds, detached from preconception. That disciplined, most solitary, most sophisticated eye is what we find in Milne. It's what we cherish him for.

***Sarah Milroy** is the former editor and publisher of* Canadian Art *magazine and a co-founder of the Canadian Art Foundation. From 2001 to 2010, she was chief art critic of* The Globe and Mail *and co-curated* From the Forest to the Sea: Emily Carr in British Columbia *(2014) and* Vanessa Bell *(2016).*

David Milne
Winter Shadow
1912, watercolour on paper

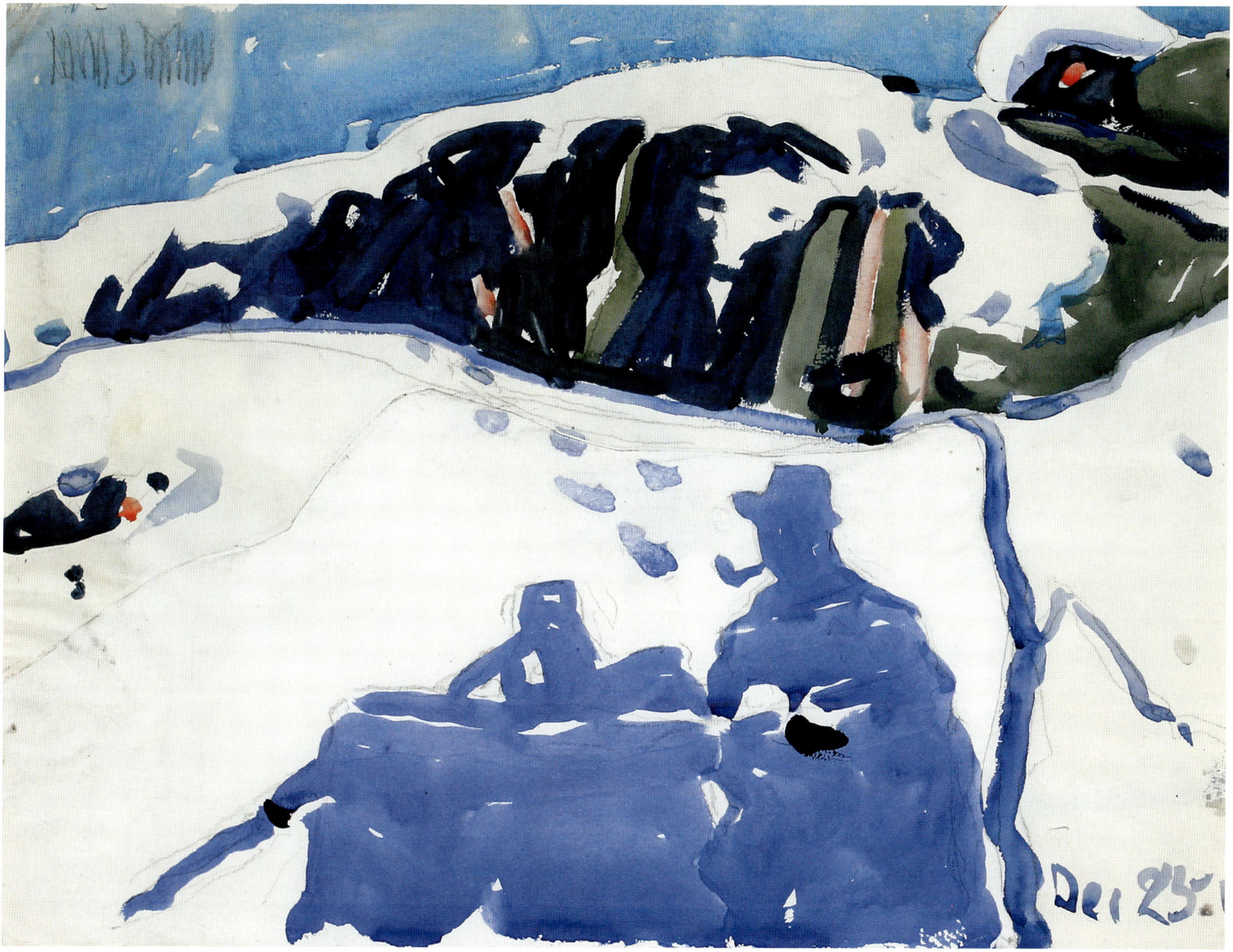

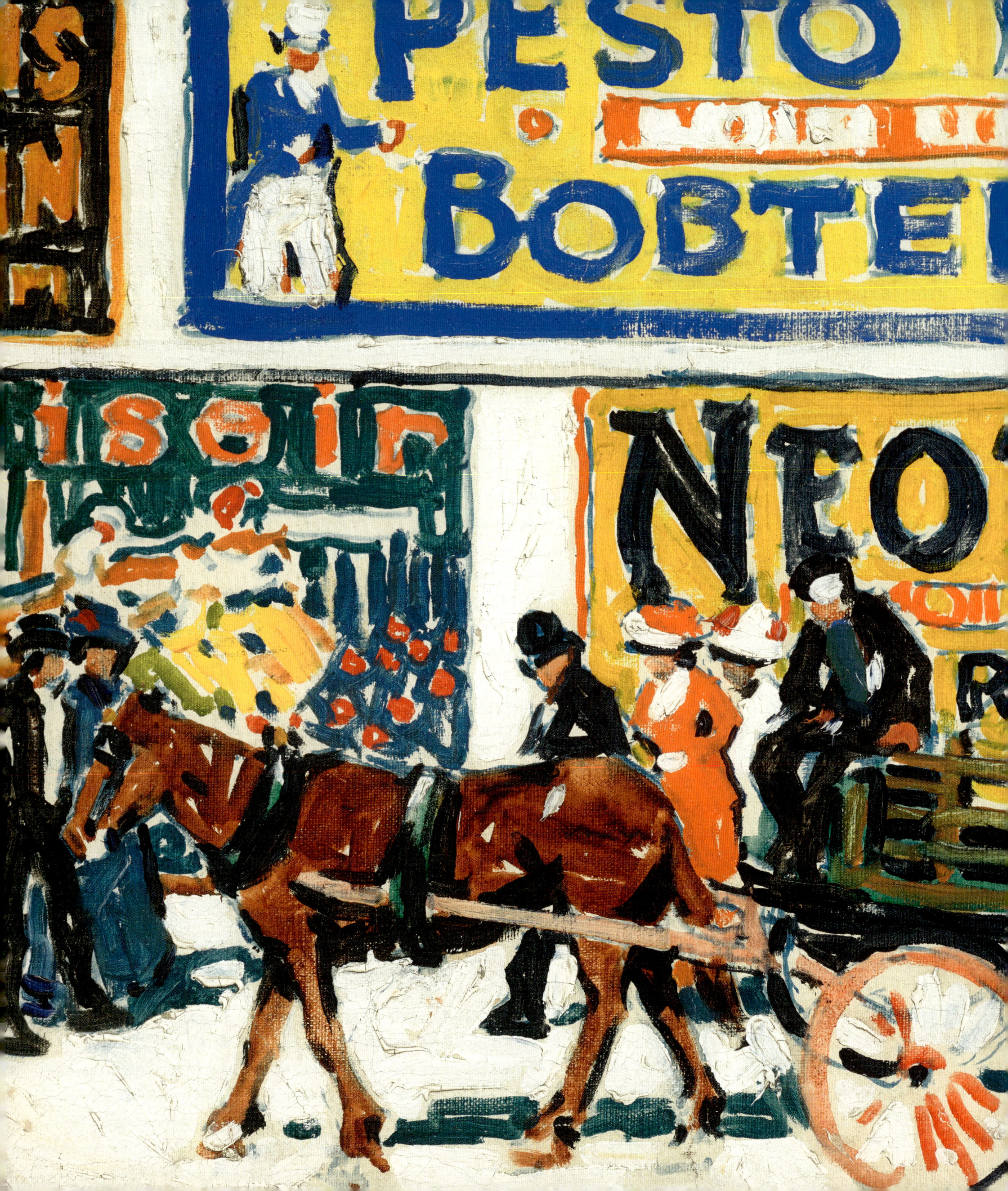
PESTO
BOBTE
NEO

THE NEW YORK YEARS

Milne grew up in a log cabin near the farming community of Burgoyne, Ontario, and in the nearby town of Paisley. His ambitious decision at 21 to move to New York to study art precipitated an immersion in the limitless possibilities of the burgeoning metropolis.

Milne was ferociously industrious there, both in his pursuit of commercial illustration work and in his grappling with current and historic art. Taking in the visual texture of the city, he painted street scenes featuring jazzy billboards and bustling pedestrians.

Milne was a frequent visitor to the leading art galleries of the day, from the Metropolitan Museum of Art (where he feasted on antiquities, Asian art and the paintings of Whistler) to the city's foremost commercial spaces such as Stieglitz's 291, Montross Gallery (where he exhibited alongside members of the Ashcan School) and Durand-Ruel Galleries (where he first saw the paintings of Monet in 1903). In 1913, Milne's work was included in the landmark Armory Show, receiving favourable interest. But increasing episodes of 'nervous heart' prompted a move in 1916 to rural seclusion north of the city. Nonetheless, the lessons of Cézanne, Matisse, Bonnard and Vuillard had by then been fully assimilated. While Milne would henceforth avoid the cosmopolitan life, he was firmly set on his path of modern experimentation.

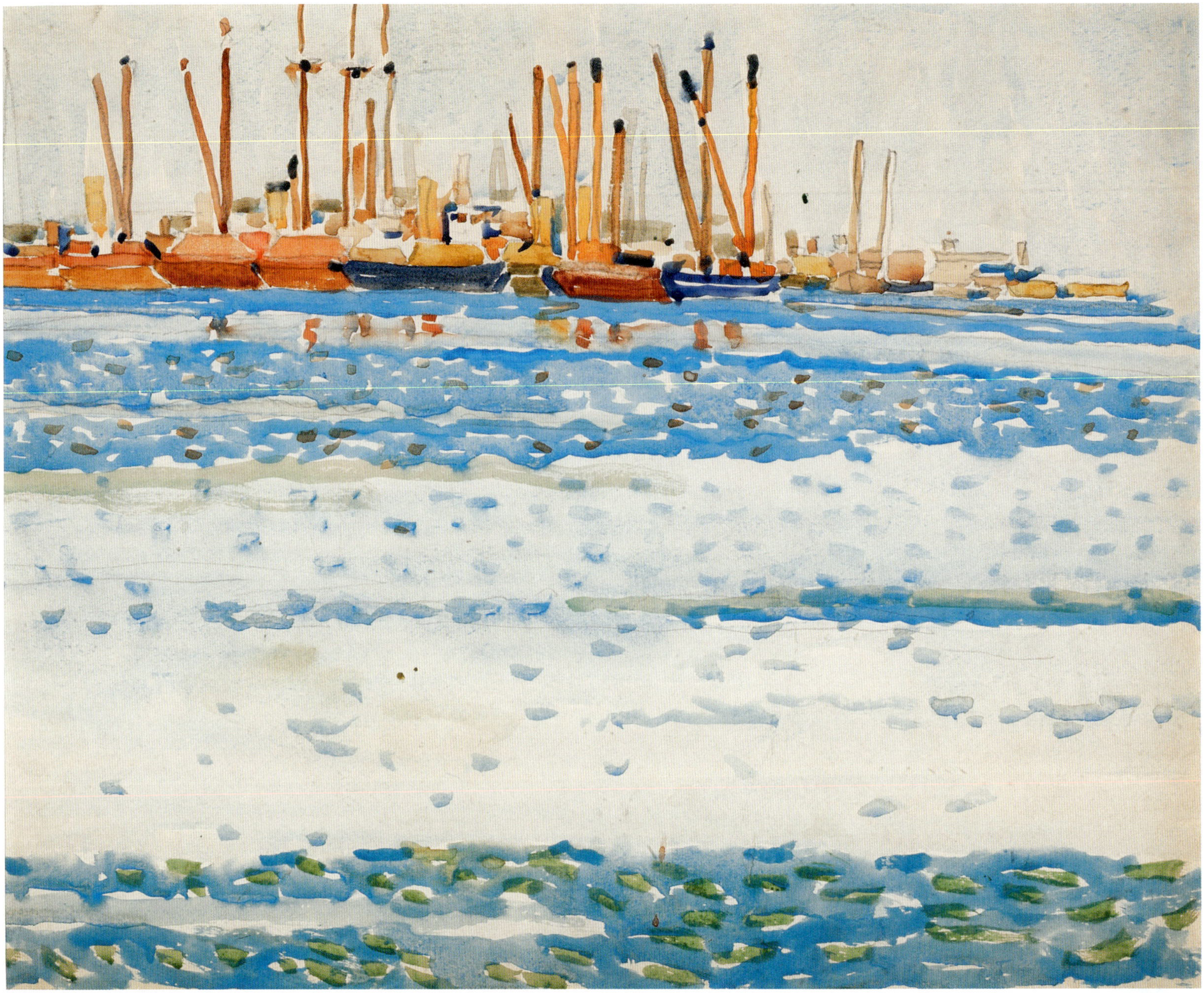

Shimmering Water
1912, watercolour on illustration board

Opposite
Dreamland Tower, Coney Island
1912, watercolour with bodycolour over black chalk on board

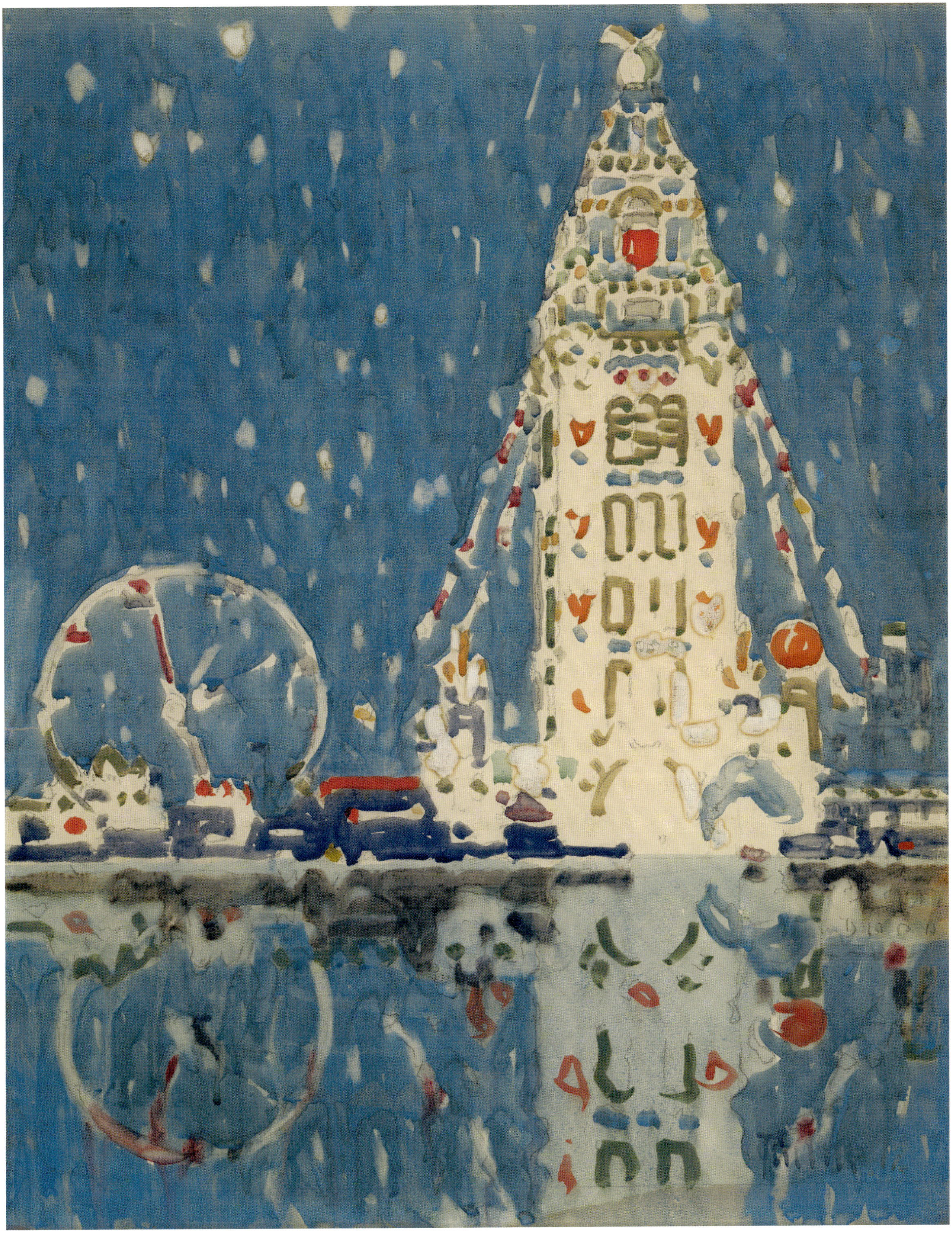

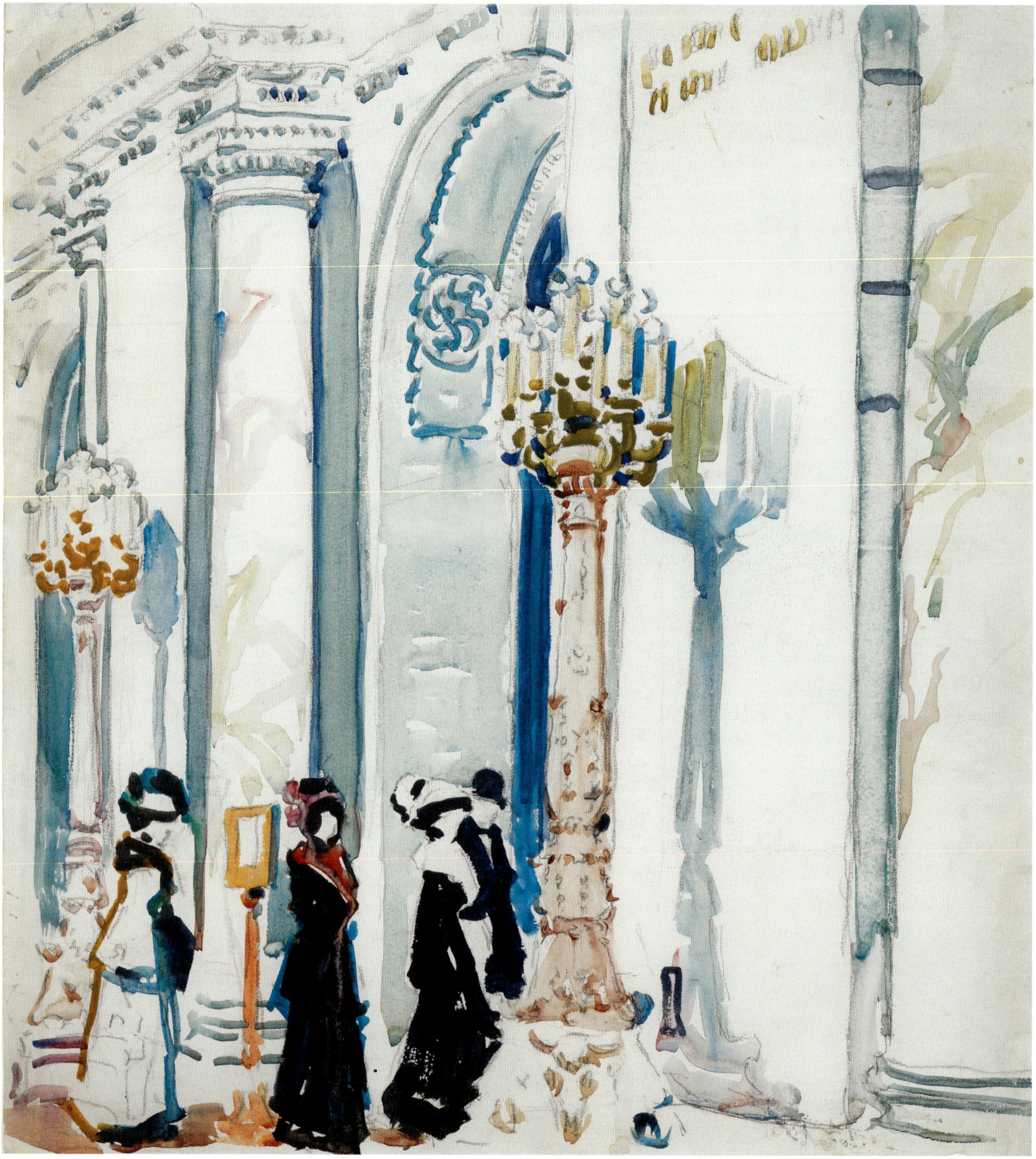

Library Interior
c. 1911–13, watercolour on paper

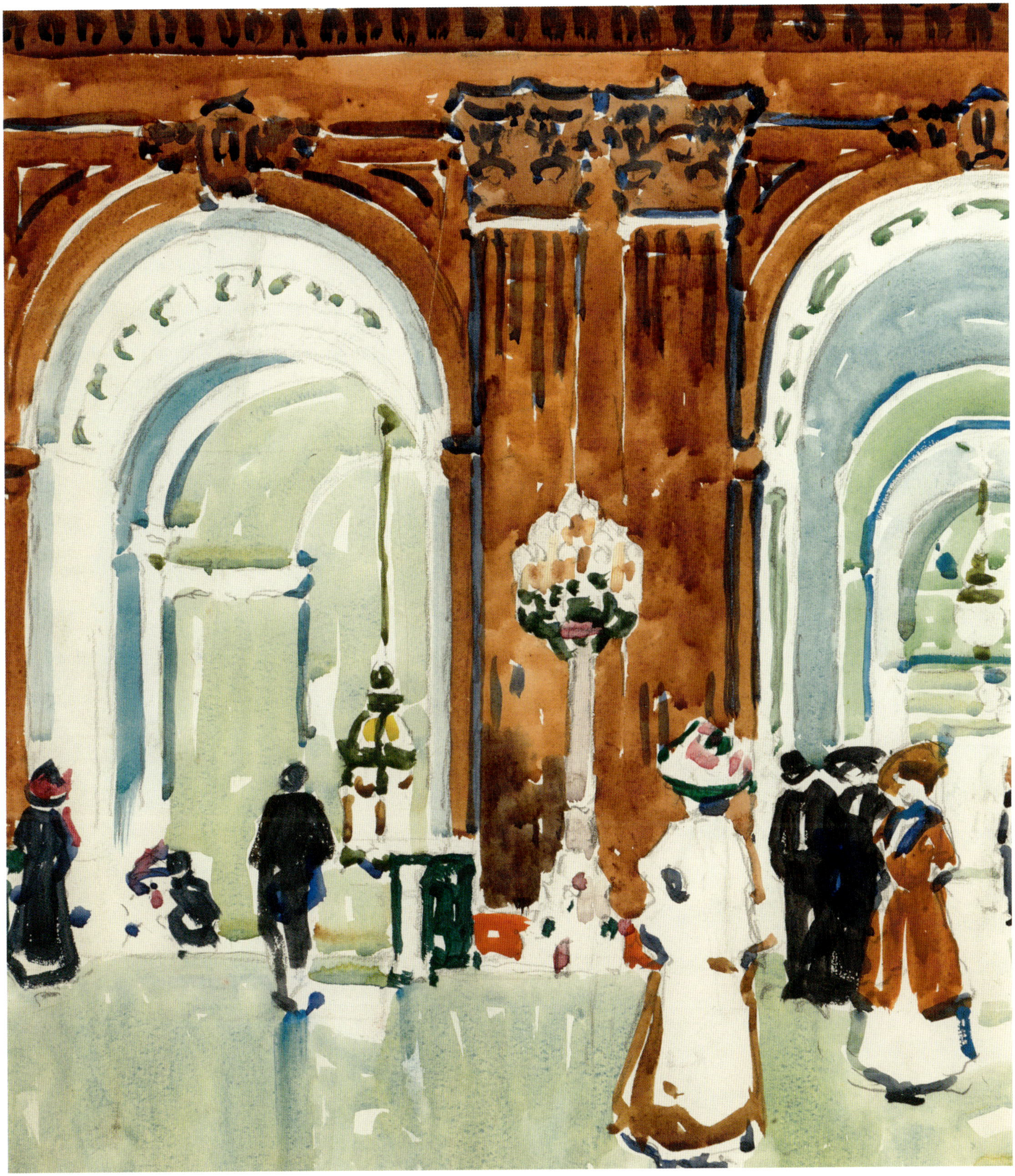

42nd Street Library
1913, watercolour on illustration board

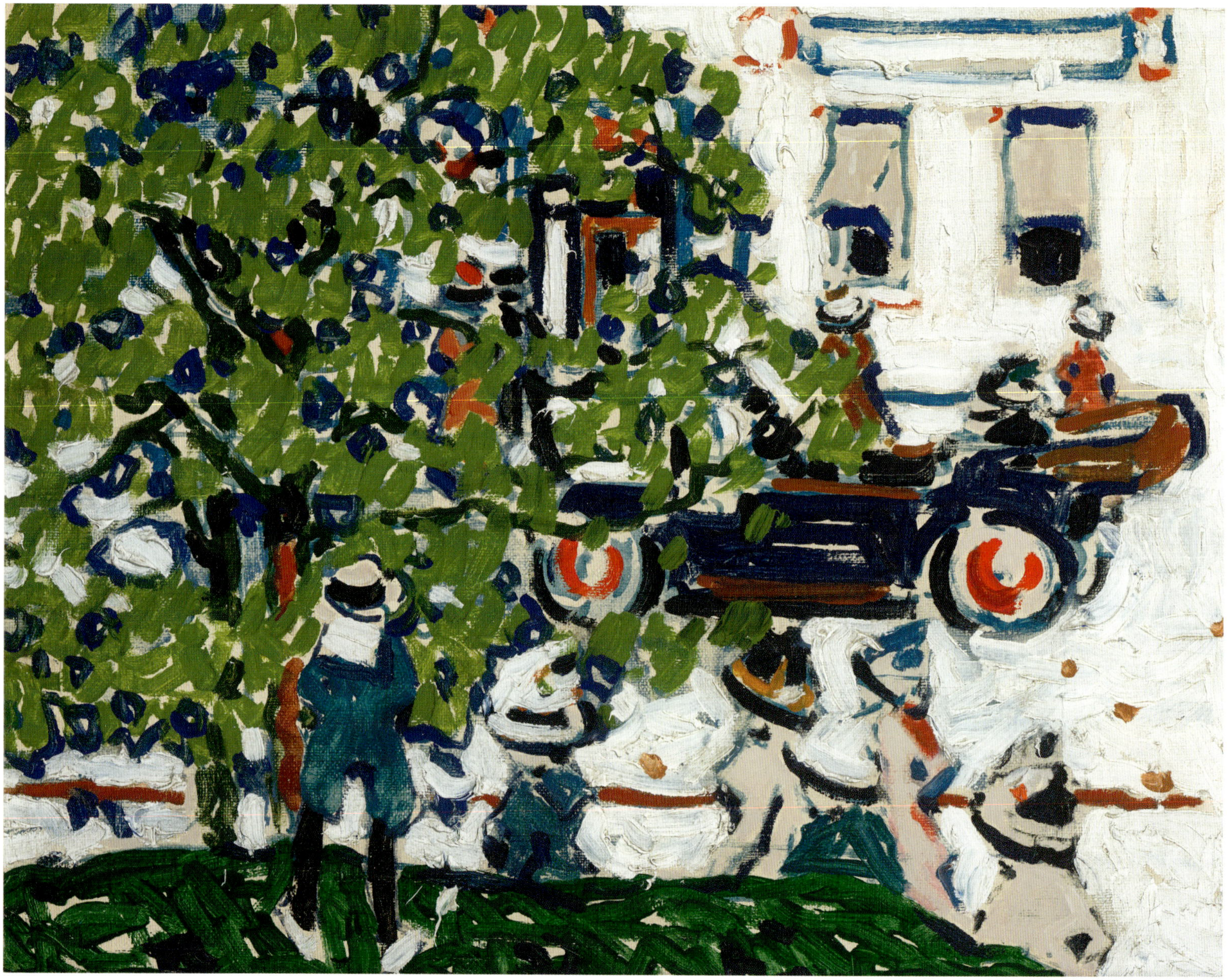

Passing Car
1913, oil on canvas

Opposite
Fifth Avenue, Easter Sunday
1912, watercolour on
illustration board

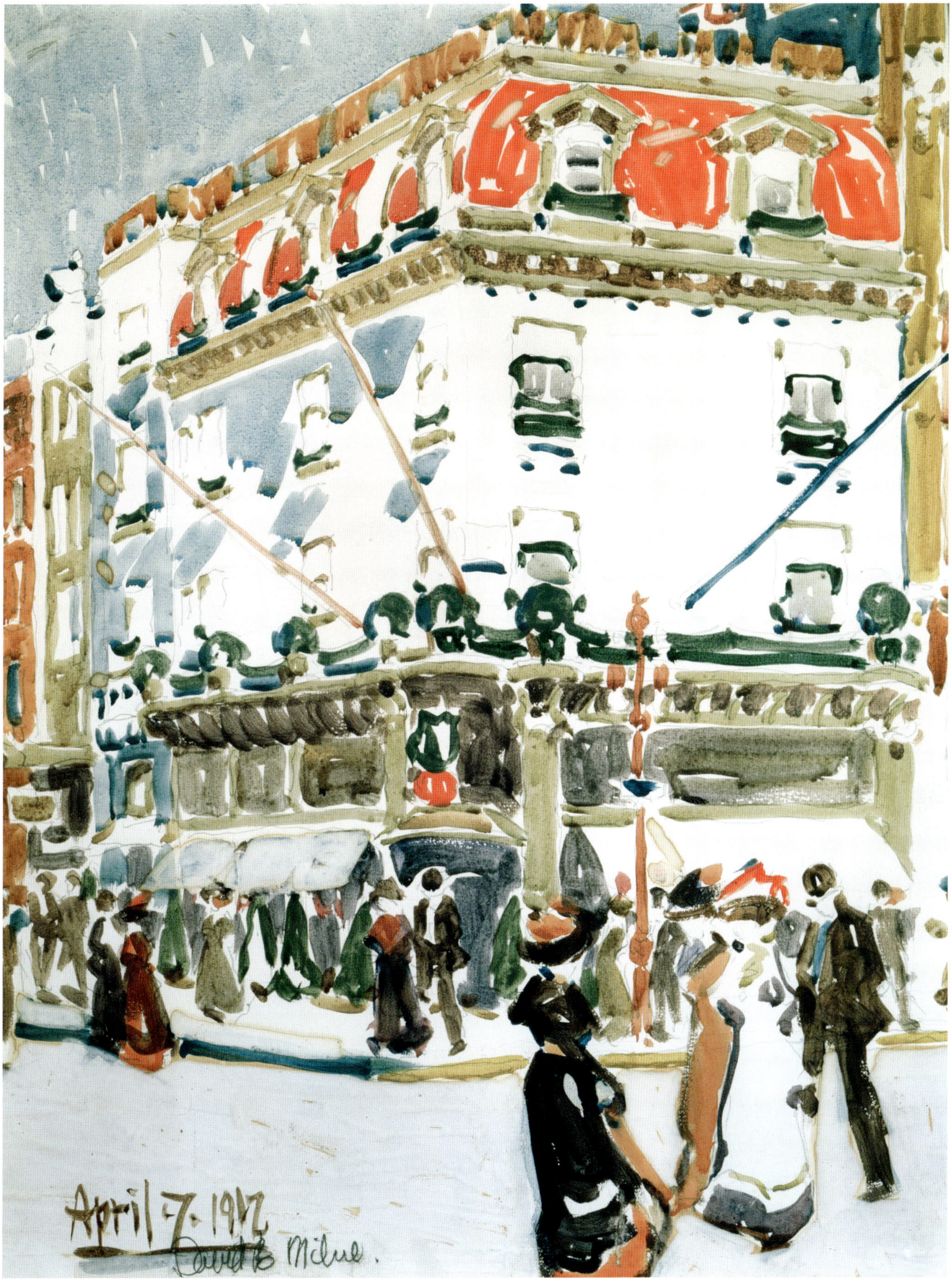
April 7. 1912
David B Milne.

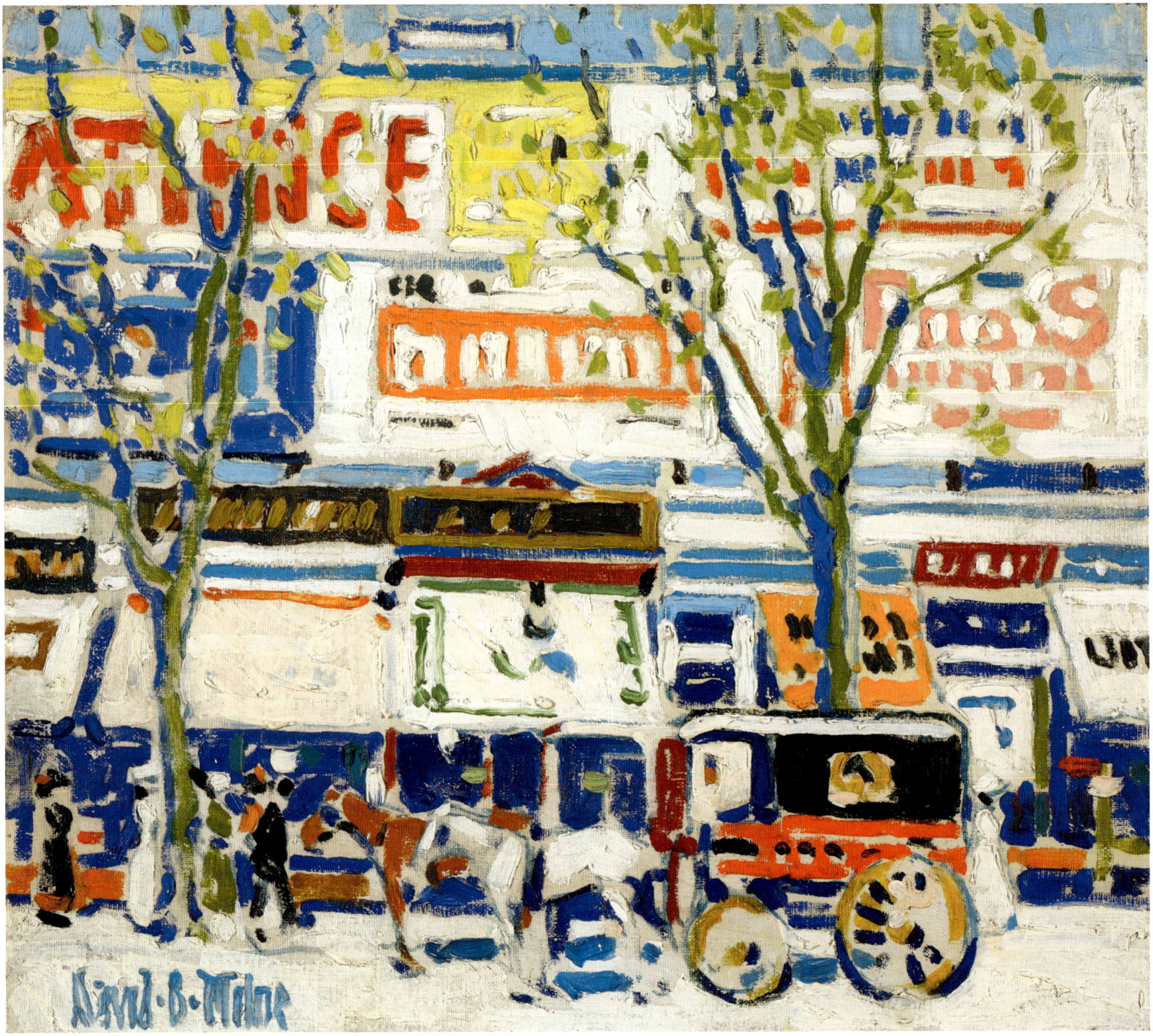

Billboards
c. 1912, oil on canvas

'PLUNGING INTO THE SUN': DAVID MILNE IN NEW YORK CITY

Katerina Atanassova

David Milne's formative years in New York City were conditioned by the modernist movement. Turning from his earlier landscape subjects, he attended now to the world of the city, exploring in paint the patterns and structures of perception. During his earlier attempts at impressionistic painting, in his years at the Art Students League from 1903 to 1906, Milne had explored light and atmosphere, but now he would take a new approach. Line, colour and space were to determine his innovative future search in painting, and the streets of New York would provide the subject matter through which he could explore his ideas about perception and reality. Three unimpeachable principles guided his art: experimentation in rendering line, distillation of colour, and the dynamic employment of negative space. Using these principles, he painted multiple views of the city from about 1911 until his move to Boston Corners in 1916. The distinctive mood of the paintings conveys his exultation in life on the street, ringing a note of gaiety and excitement.

Commenting on his paintings of New York, the art historian David Silcox has observed that by 1911 Milne appears to have found his style.[1] Always experimenting, he struggled to integrate his sense of pattern with his awareness of solid forms. Although the earliest attempts from the period of 1910–11 appear illustrative, by 1912 he had quickly moved to painting in flat planes. *Billboards*, *c.* 1912 (p. 46), epitomises this crucial turning point, when Milne's artistic vision was rapidly evolving and crystallising.

Composed in a nearly square format, one preferred by such American painters as John Twachtman,[2] *Billboards* showcases the life of the modern metropolis. In its immediacy, it emphasises structure. Parallel lines echo rhythmically down the picture plane, as blue sky gives way to billboards, hoardings, shop windows and the street itself in a series of horizontal bands. At the same time, the vertical trees provide a contrasting structure, the energy of the moment evoked in the tension between these two directions.

Urban subject matter had been a favourite among American painters as early as the 1890s, with artists foregrounding the phenomenon of seeing and being seen in urban space. The Ashcan

Opposite, clockwise
from top left:
Street scene, New York City
c. 1909, photograph

John Sloan
The Hairdresser's Window
1907, oil on canvas

Maurice Prendergast
Central Park
c. 1901, watercolour
and pencil on paper

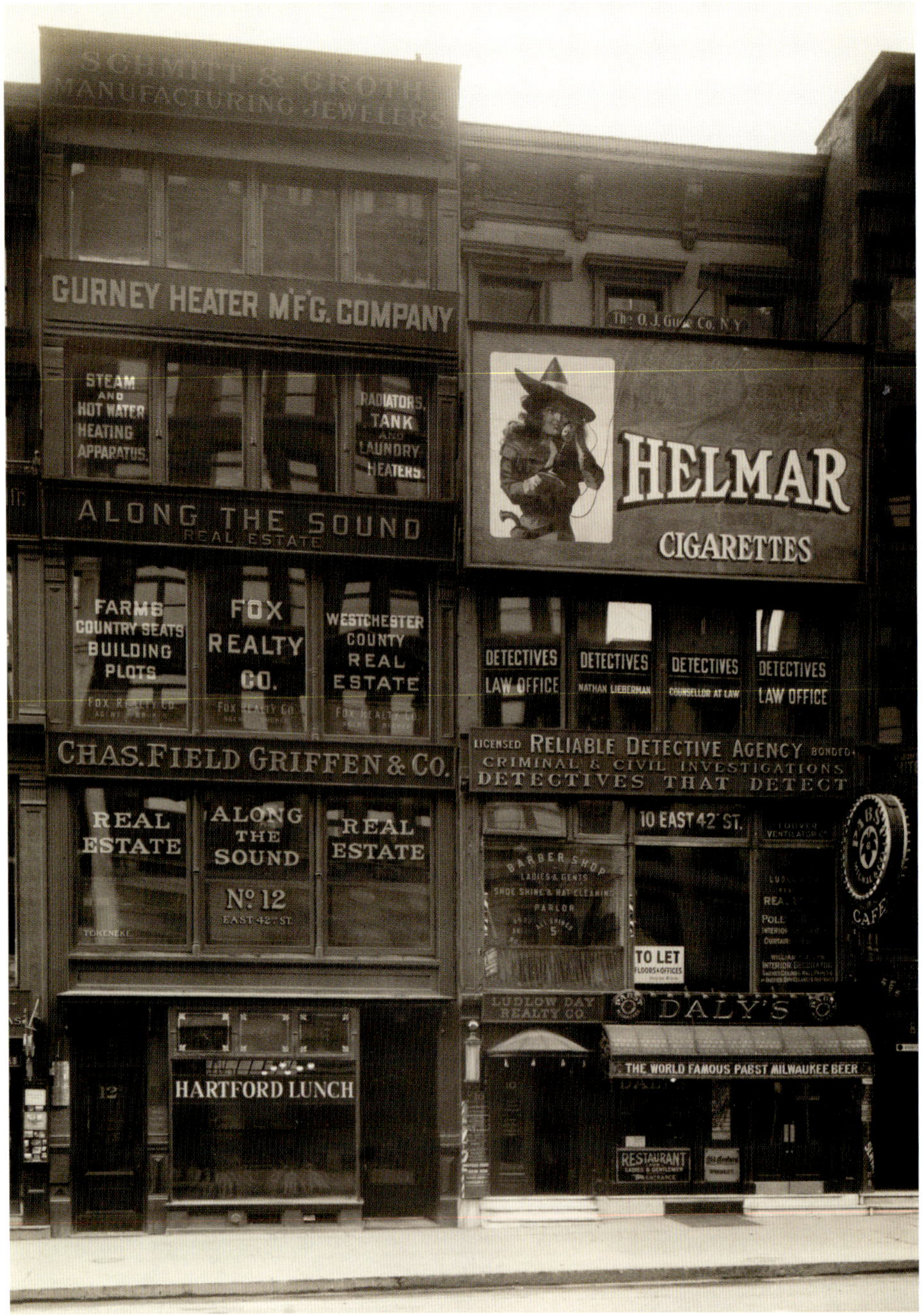

Above
Milne's New York studio
location, above Daly's
restaurant, Wurts Bros,
10–12 East 42nd Street
gelatin silver print

School artist John Sloan, for example, encapsulates this spirit of the modern street as spectacle in his best-known work, *The Hairdresser's Window*, 1907.[3] Like Sloan and many of his contemporaries in New York, Milne soon developed a kindred interest in the spectacle of New Yorkers out and about, yet his paintings avoid any narrative innuendo or anecdotal social commentary. The art historian John O'Brian detects a similarity between Milne's treatment of billboard lettering and the depiction of people by the American Post-Impressionist Maurice Prendergast, describing the results of both initiatives as 'decorative ciphers, whose purpose is to contribute to the overall design of the work'.[4] Milne's urban scenes are akin to Prendergast's paintings such as *Central Park*, *c.* 1901, in which subject matter provides the pretext for formal experimentation.

Milne's early experience as a commercial illustrator contributed to his skill in framing a scene and creating a composition driven by colour and pattern,[5] but that experience no doubt also reinforced his fascination with the increasingly omnipresent advertising on buildings and billboards around the city. Works such as *Gray Billboards*, *c.* 1912 (p. 51), and *Yellow Billboards*,

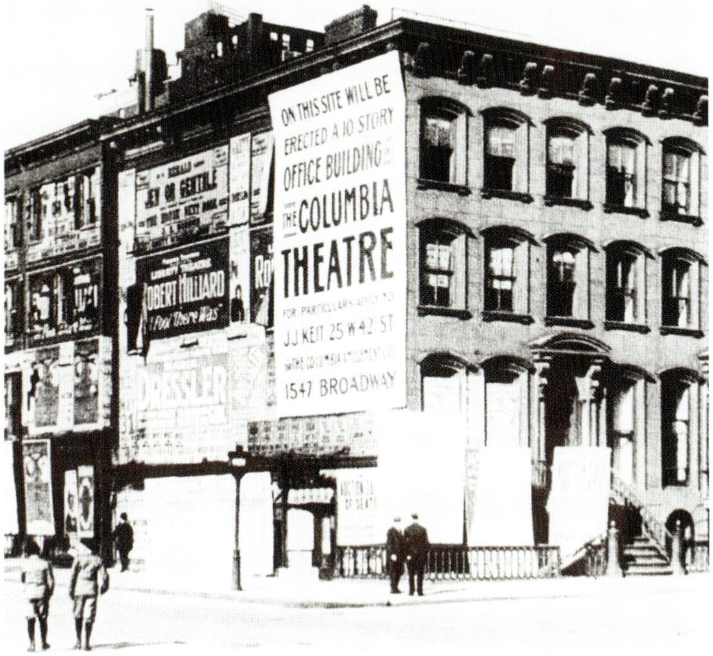
ON THIS SITE WILL BE
ERECTED A 10 STORY
OFFICE BUILDING
COLUMBIA
THEATRE
1547 BROADWAY
JEW OR GENTILE
ROBERT HILLIARD
DRESSLER

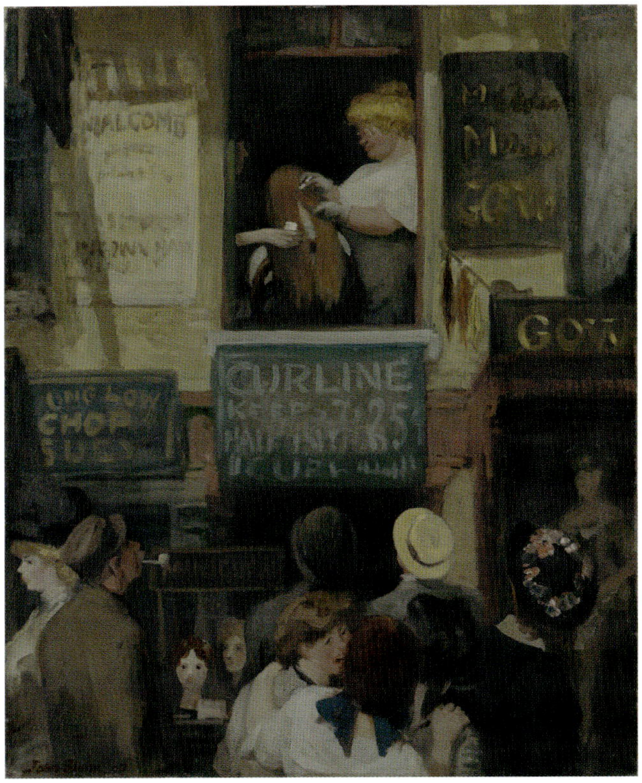
CURLINE
GOW

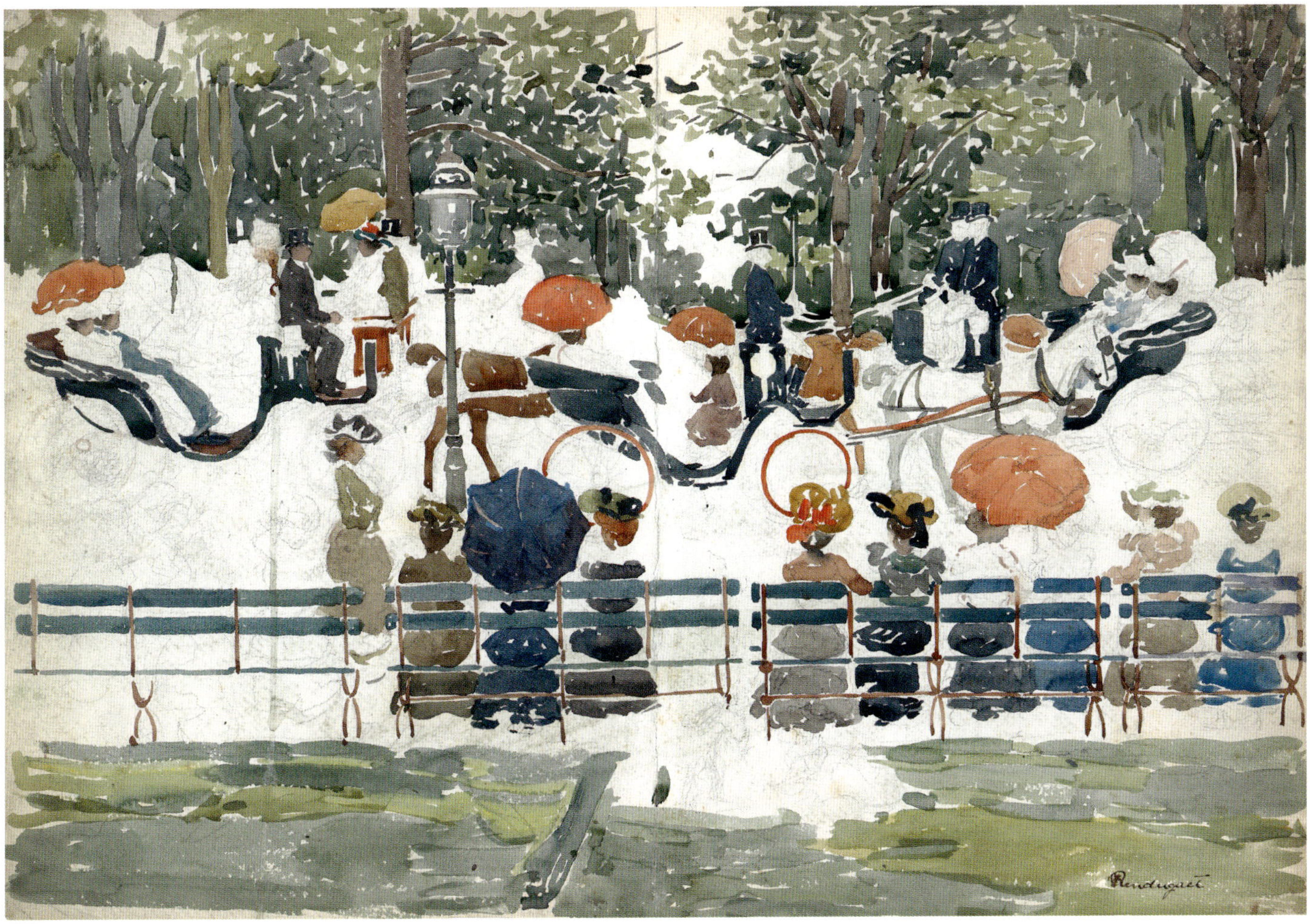

John Marin
Woolworth Building, No. 31
1912, watercolour over graphite

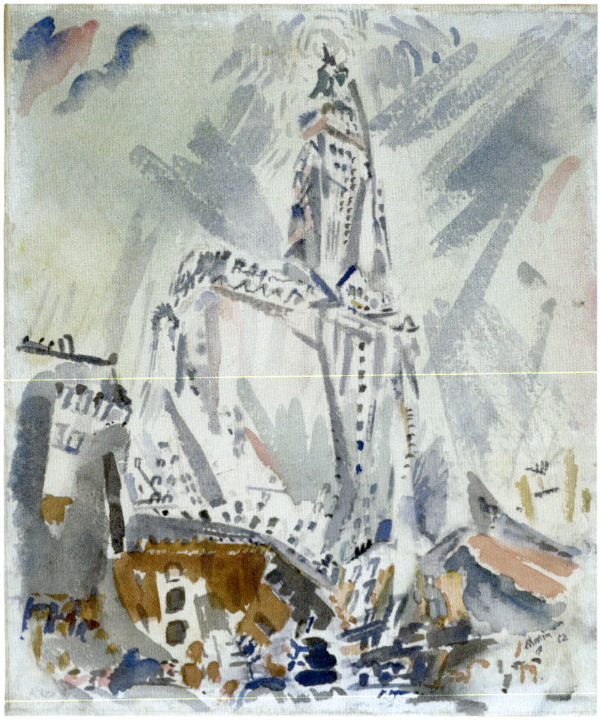

c. 1912 (p. 53), ingeniously represent the new and popular type of outdoor announcement with its colourful appeal to consumerism. They offer not only an important visual record of the early history of commercial outdoor advertising in the biggest city in North America but also a slice-of-life perspective by a Canadian who, although reclusive by nature, was not afraid to step up to confront the visual chaos of the big city.

Milne's work also reflects a change in urban life that was common to all major metropolitan centres across North America. Migration to the cities at the turn of the twentieth century had resulted in urban overcrowding as well as an energised street life, and artists such as Milne seized as material the city residents' new habit of spending more time outside than in the privacy of their own homes.[6] The numerous figures in Milne's compositions from his middle New York period suggest that he saw human presence as at the very core of city life. The actions and interactions of his figures, whether understated or emphasised, express a view of urban life not as static but as a dynamic and constantly changing flow in which human beings are immersed. The integration of figure and ground in a painting like *Billboards* is thus both formal and descriptive of Milne's experience, a distinctive contribution to the development of modern urban iconography.

Looking at the works of the New York period, one can see that the seeds of Milne's later development are sown. In his New York oils and equally in his watercolours, he concentrates on colour, outline and pattern, as he would in the years to come. Here he embarks on his experiment with negative space, often leaving blank areas—as in the unpainted foreground in *Fifth Avenue, Easter Sunday*, 1912 (p. 45)—a compositional device that gradually became a highly expressive and meaningful element in his art. His watercolour *Dreamland Tower, Coney Island*, 1912 (p. 41), shows Milne's characteristic obsession with economy of means, a lifelong concern, and a predilection he shared with a fellow exhibitor at the 1913 Armory Show, the American painter John Marin, an artist similarly drawn to describe the startling visual drama of urban architecture.

But while they look forward stylistically, Milne's paintings also bear witness to the specific historic moment in which he was working. The horses that stand with their carriages in the dappled sunlight of *Billboards* can be seen as near-phantoms of a dying era, soon to be replaced by the streetcars and automobiles that figure in many of the artist's other works from these years. Stranded in modernity, subtly distinct from the jangle of the crowded streets, they strike a note of quiet nostalgia in a world of rapid change.

***Katerina Atanassova** is Senior Curator of Canadian Art at the National Gallery of Canada, where she recently completed* Our Masterpieces, Our Stories, *the reinstallation of the NGC's Canadian and Indigenous Galleries. Atanassova was a co-curator of* Painting Canada: Tom Thomson and the Group of Seven *(2011) at Dulwich Picture Gallery and has recently presented* James Wilson Morrice: The A.K. Prakash Collection in Trust to the Nation *(2017) at the NGC.*

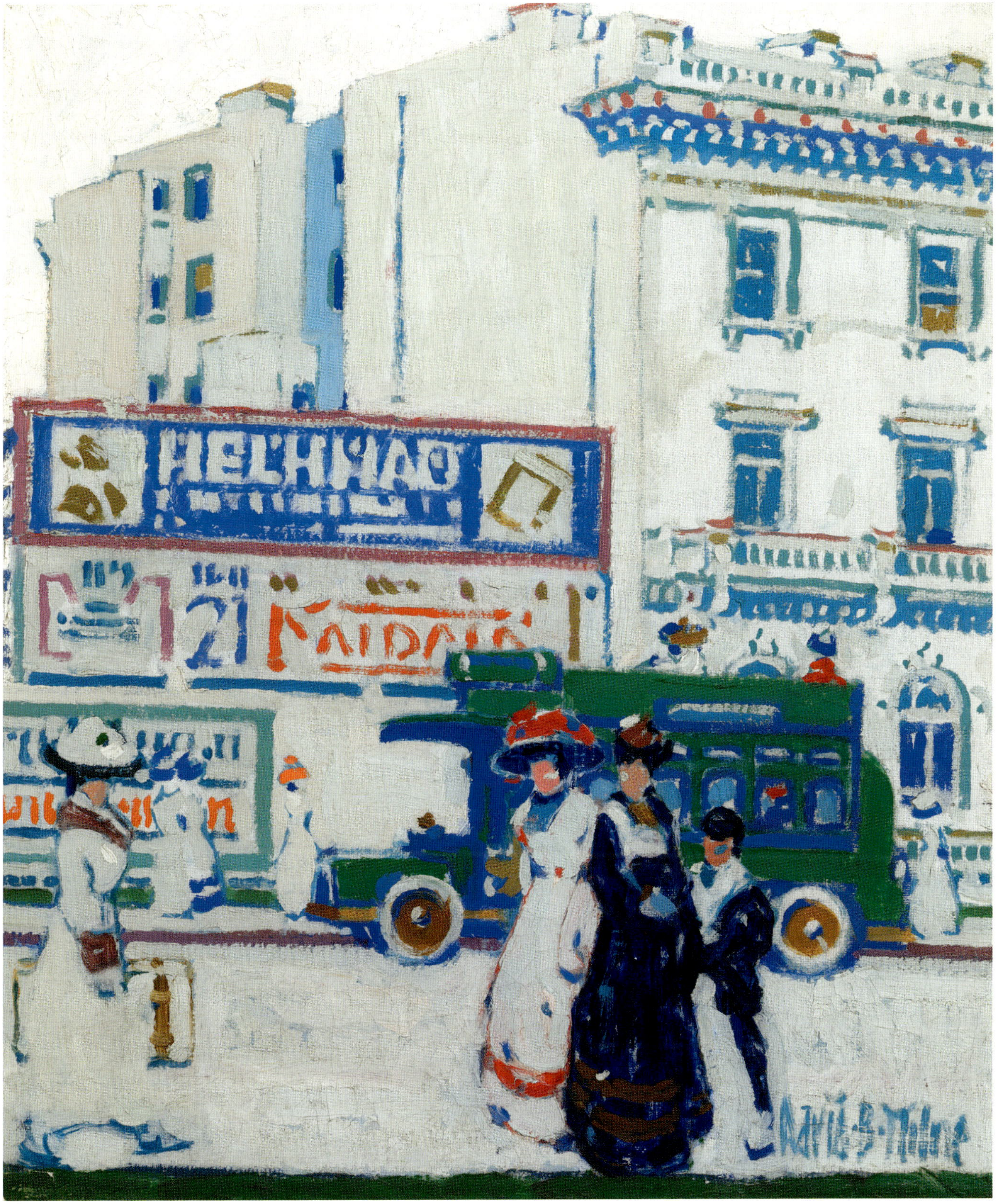

Gray Billboards
c. 1912, oil on canvas

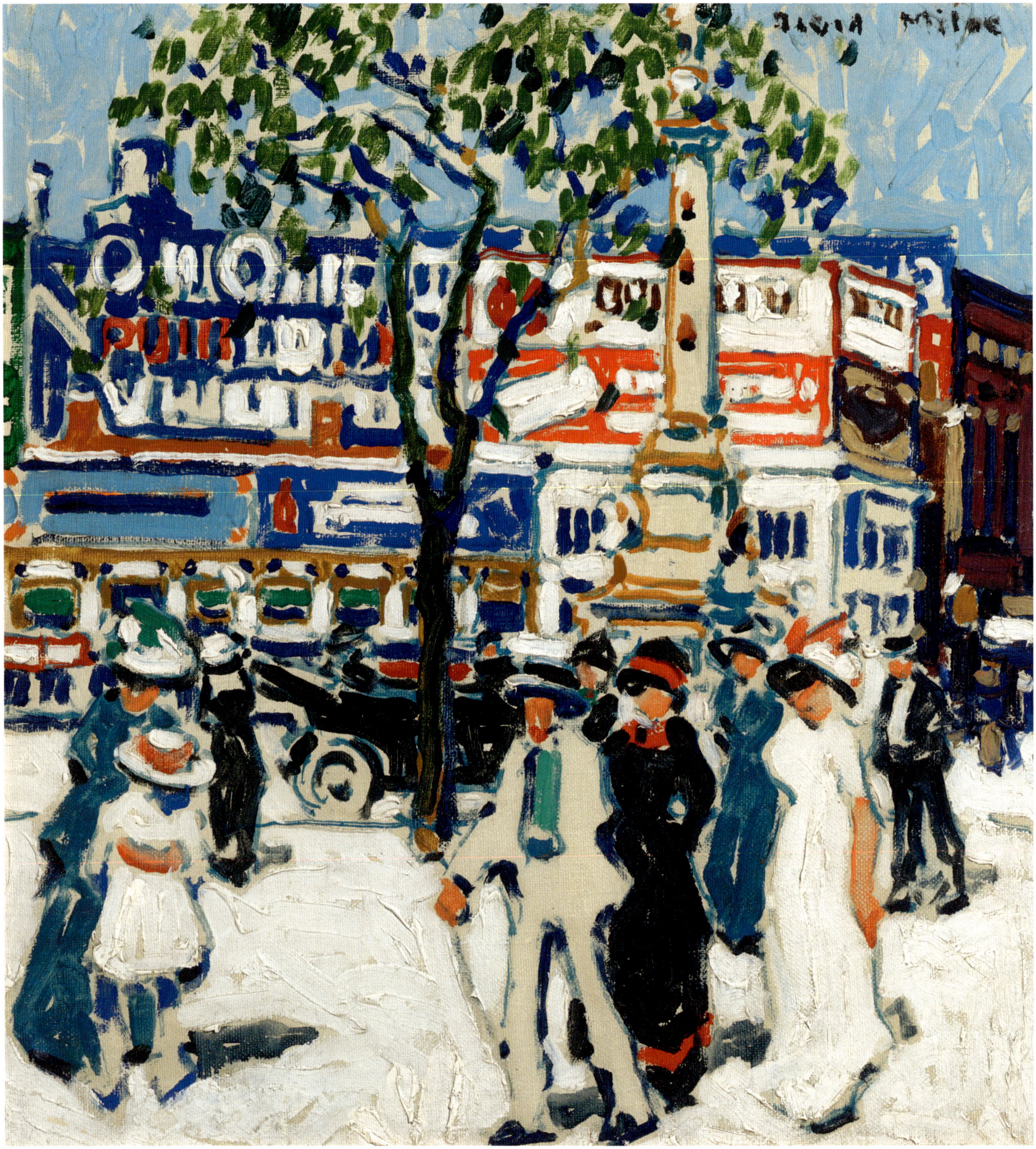

Columbus Monument
1912, oil on canvas

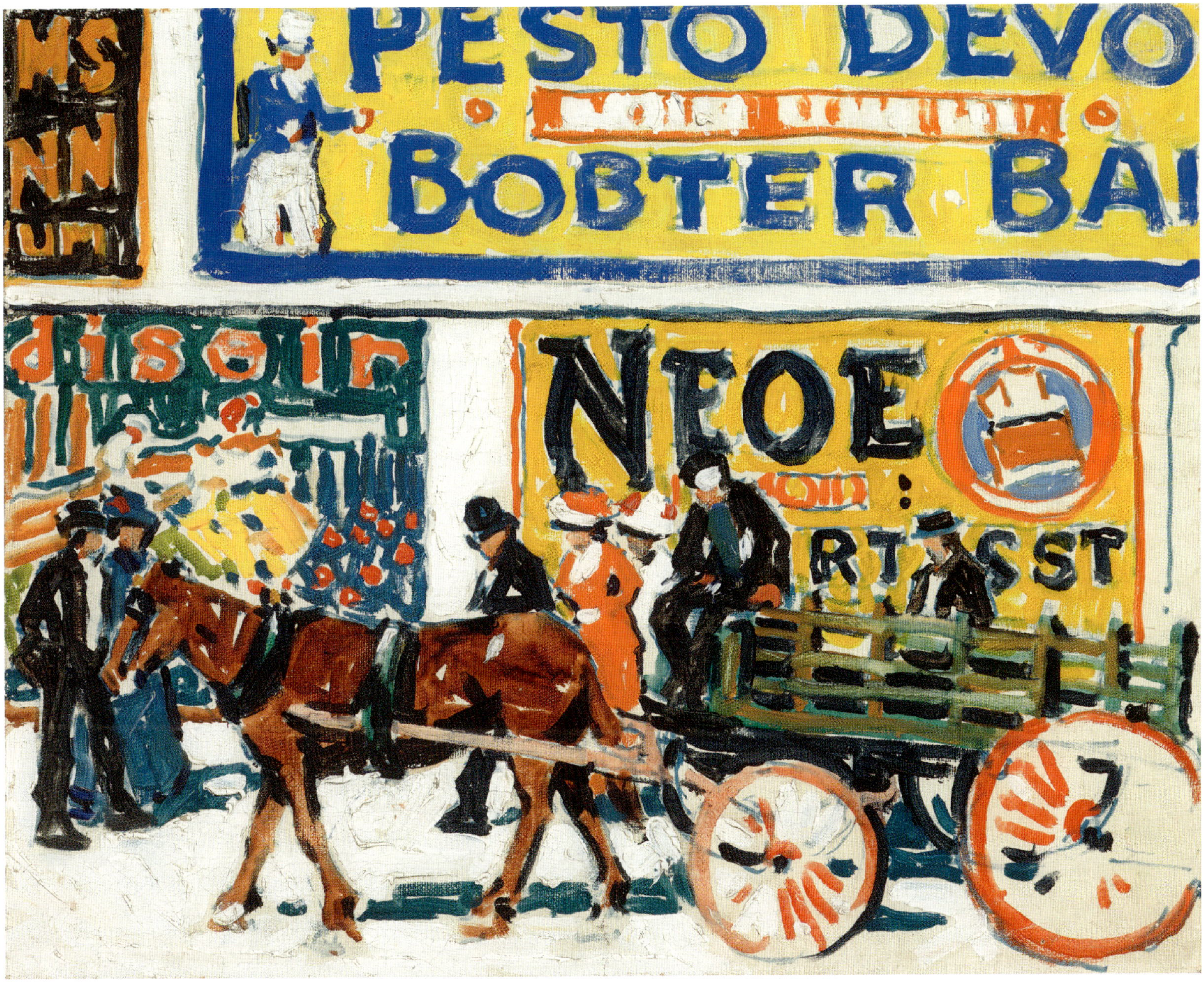

Yellow Billboards
c. 1912, oil on canvas

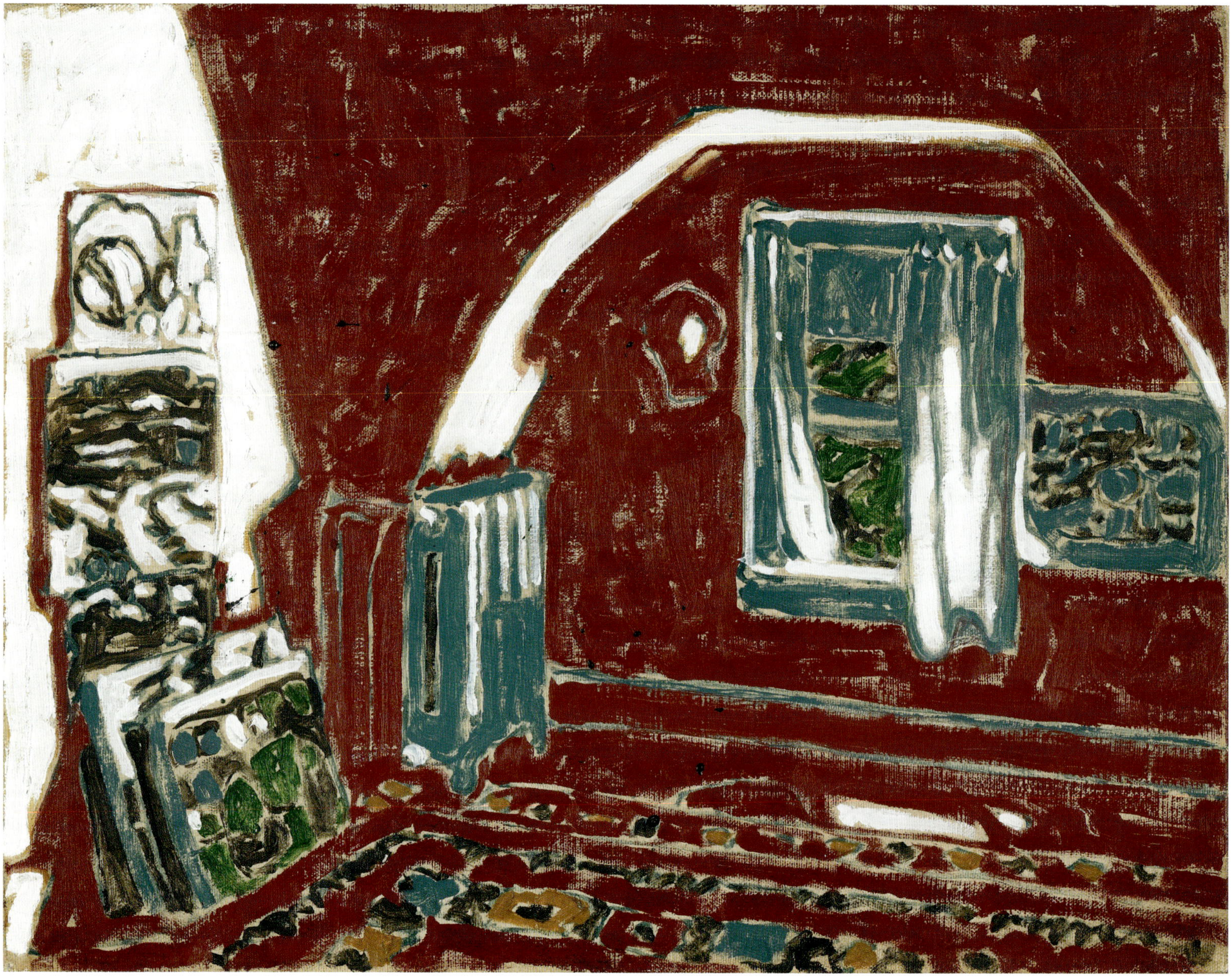

Alcove
1914, oil on canvas

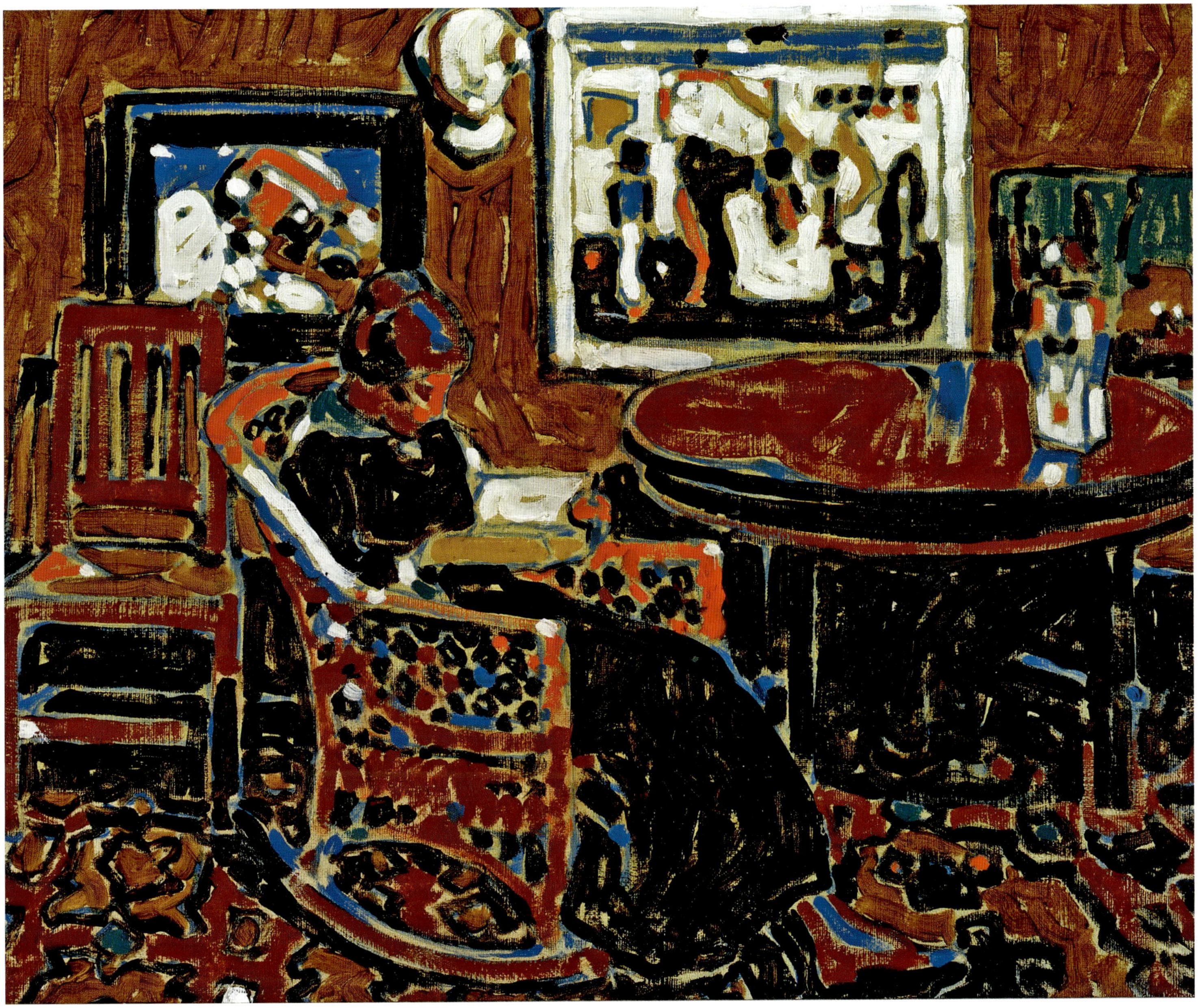

Interior with Paintings
1914, oil on canvas

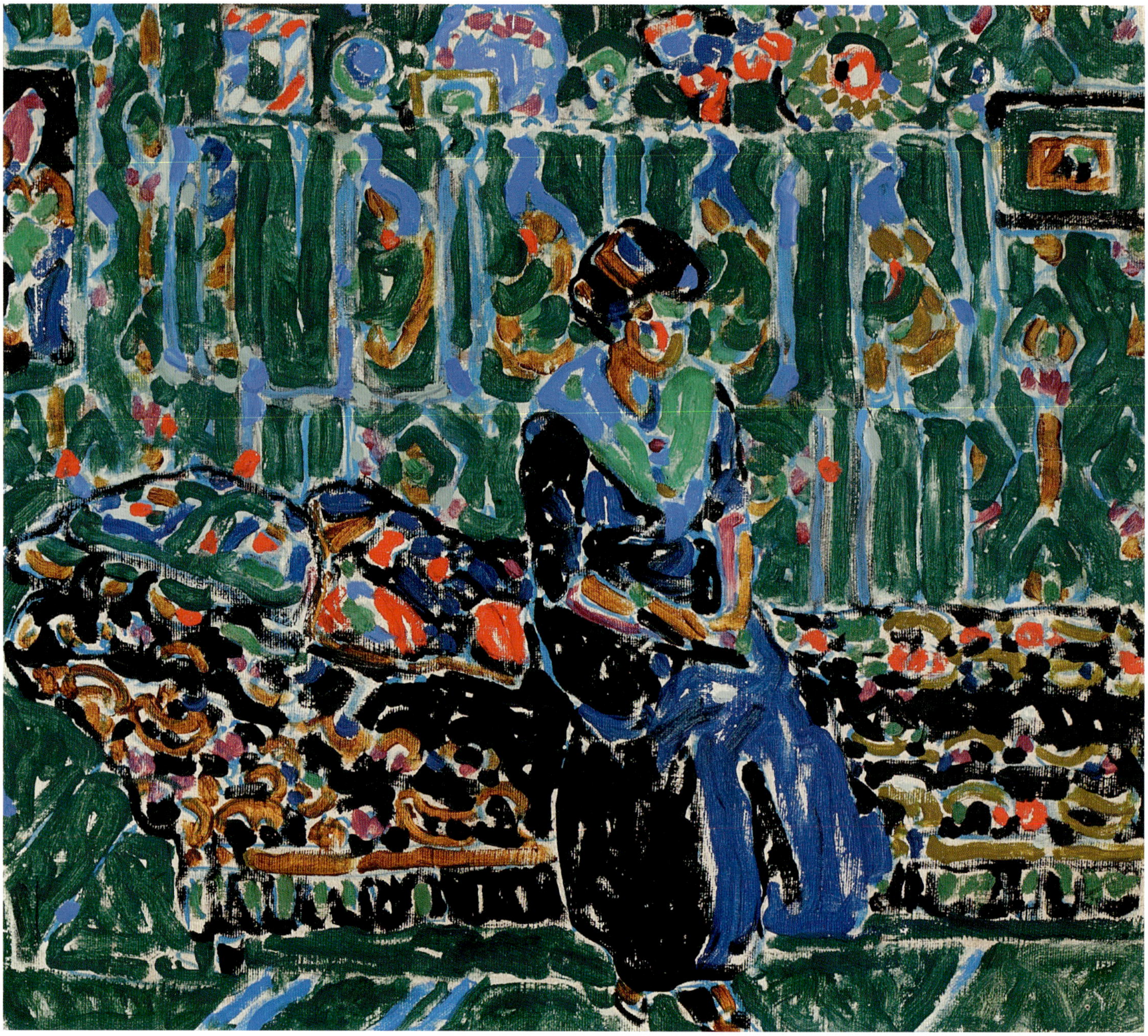

The Black Couch
1914, oil on canvas

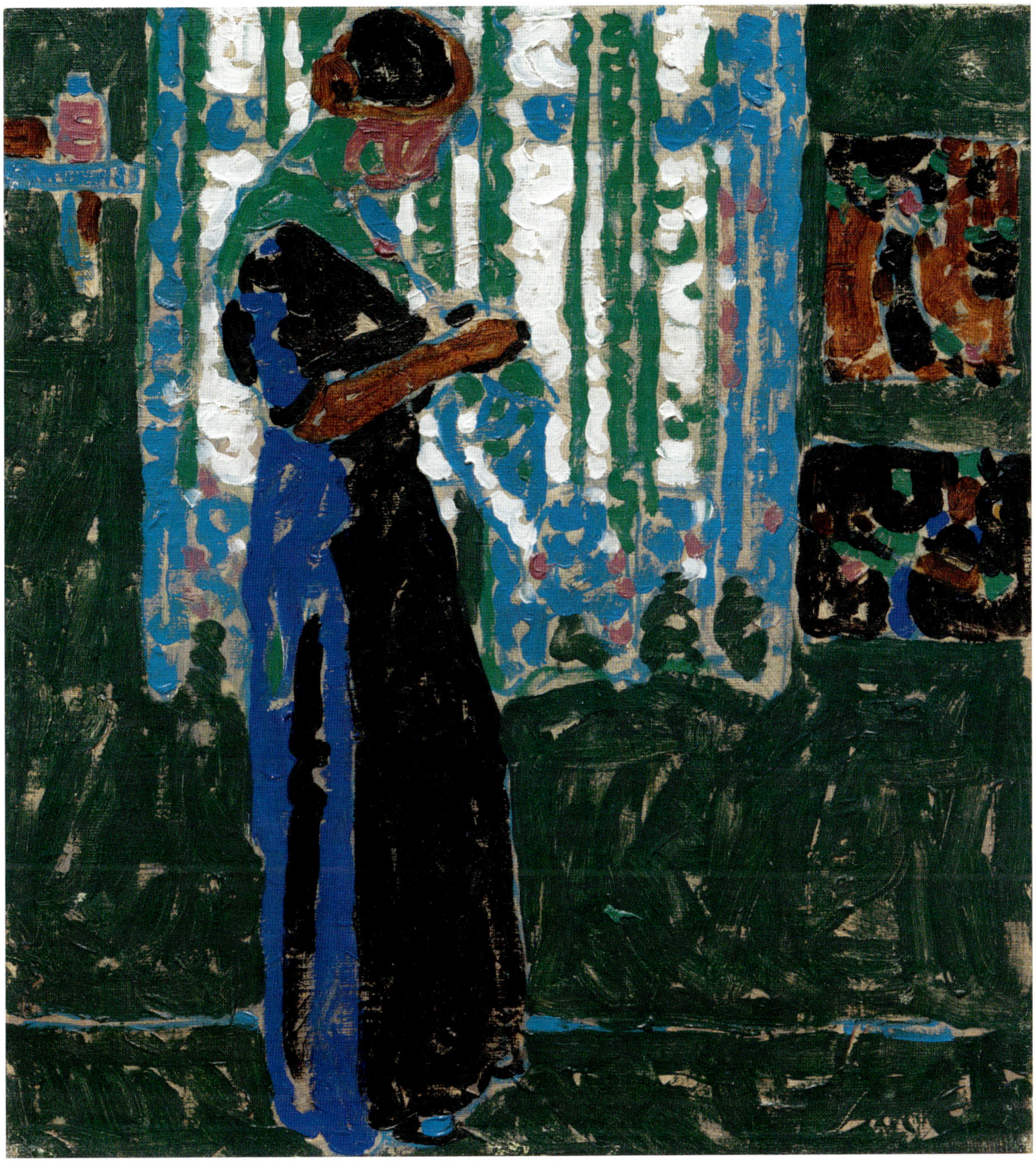

Bright Curtains
1914, oil on canvas

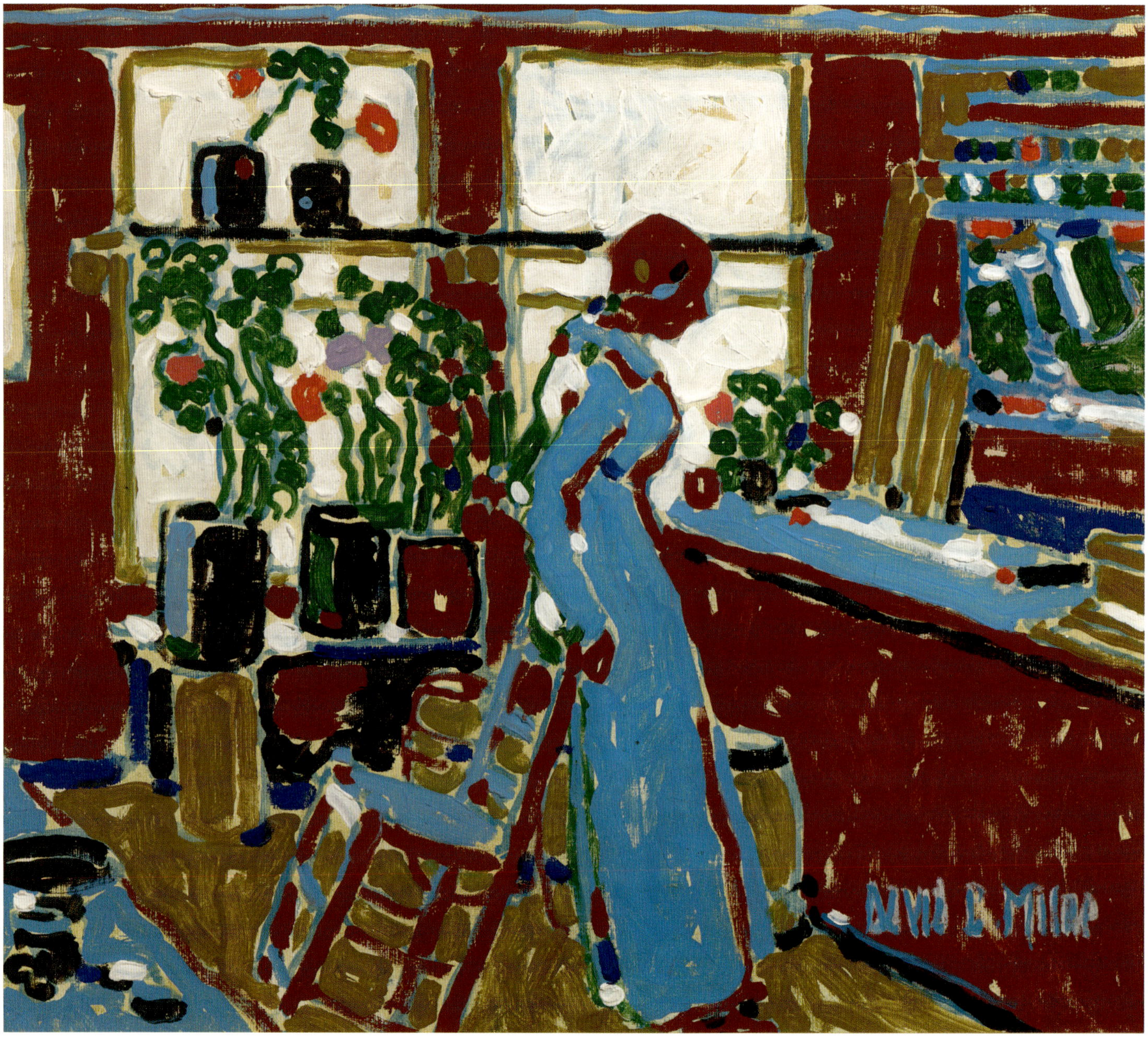

Red
1914, oil on canvas

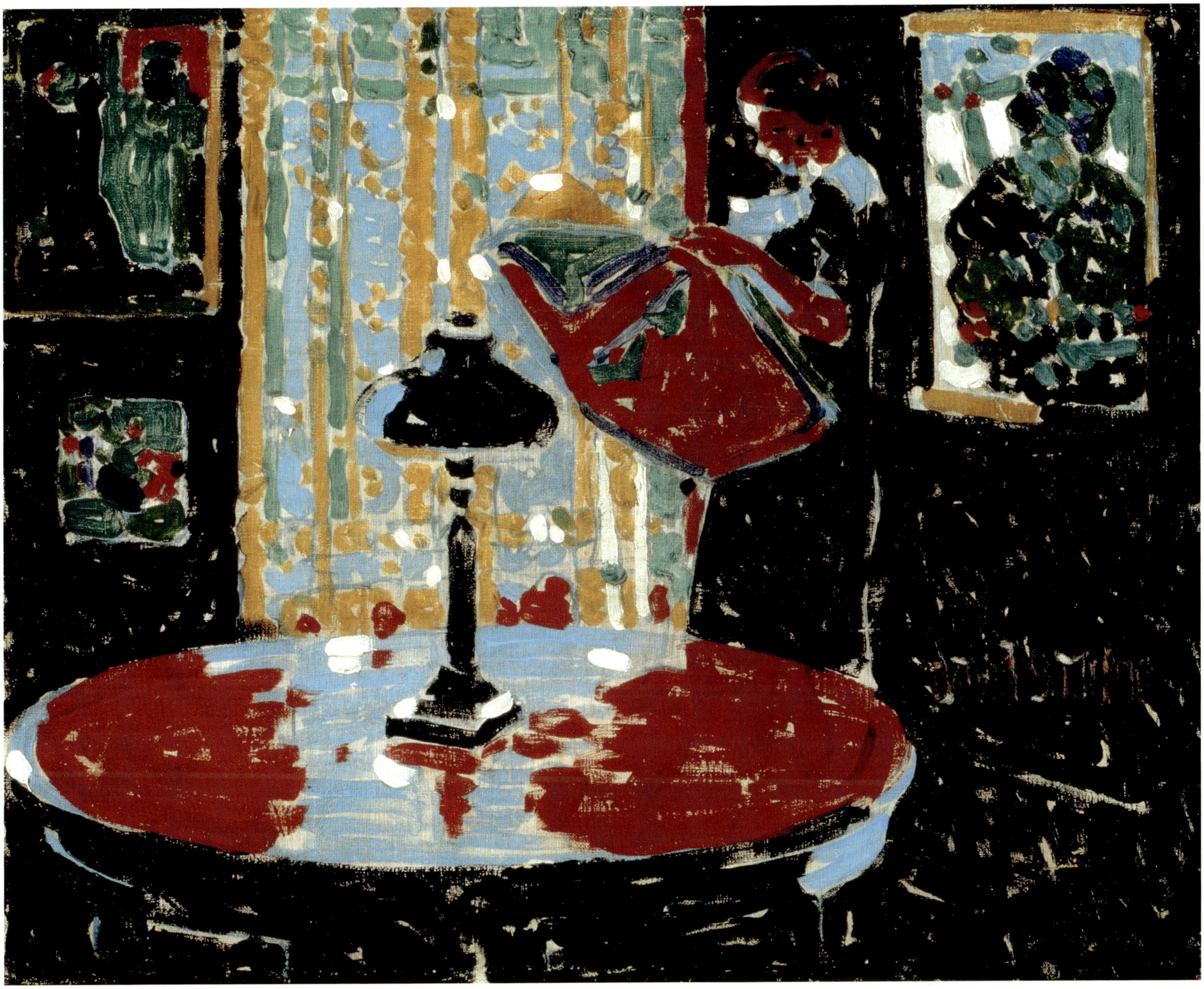

Black
1914, oil on canvas

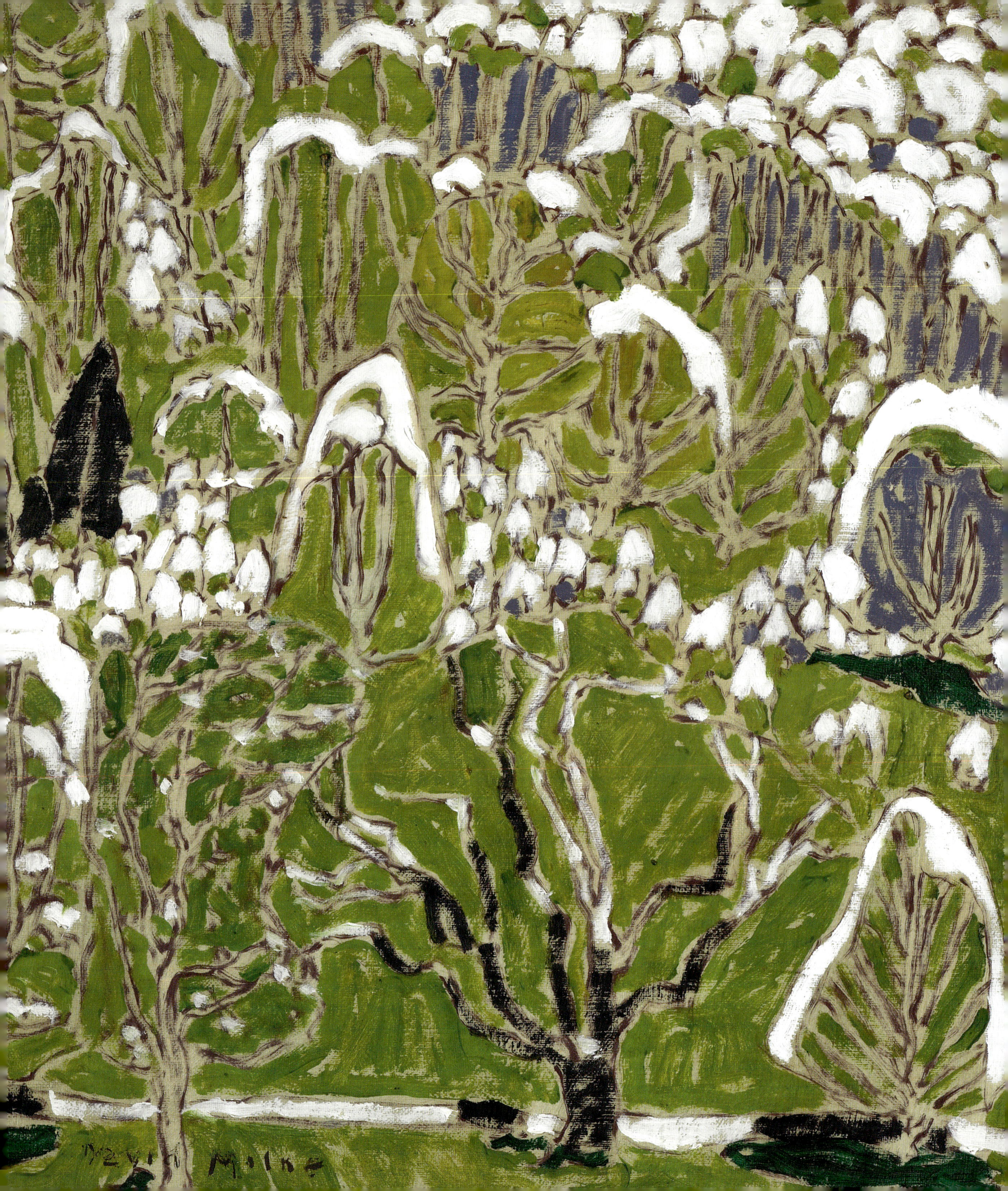
David Milne

INTO THE WOODS

At West Saugerties, and then at Boston Corners in upstate New York in 1916, Milne sought a new way of life, away from the city. A series of paintings of his new bride, Patsy Hegarty, seated in the landscape, explores the phenomenon of camouflage, a feature of contemporary material culture that was ready to hand as World War I gathered steam across the Atlantic. Other works from this period experiment with all-over patterning, as Milne brought landscape to the threshold of abstraction. At Boston Corners, he and Patsy set up an austere sort of life in a largely unfurnished house, with Milne's time being devoted, as far as possible, to his painting. Not surprisingly, such focus and seclusion precipitated major advances in his work, as he experimented with conjuring reflections and other light effects. These latter paintings reveal Milne in a seemingly more meditative mode, painting in a kind of cloisonné style sometimes washed over with a film of water. His oil paintings of the village of Boston Corners seen from a nearby hill are masterpieces of tonal control, each one constituting a perfect world of colour and texture governed by its own internal pictorial logic. These are among Milne's most beloved and canonical works.

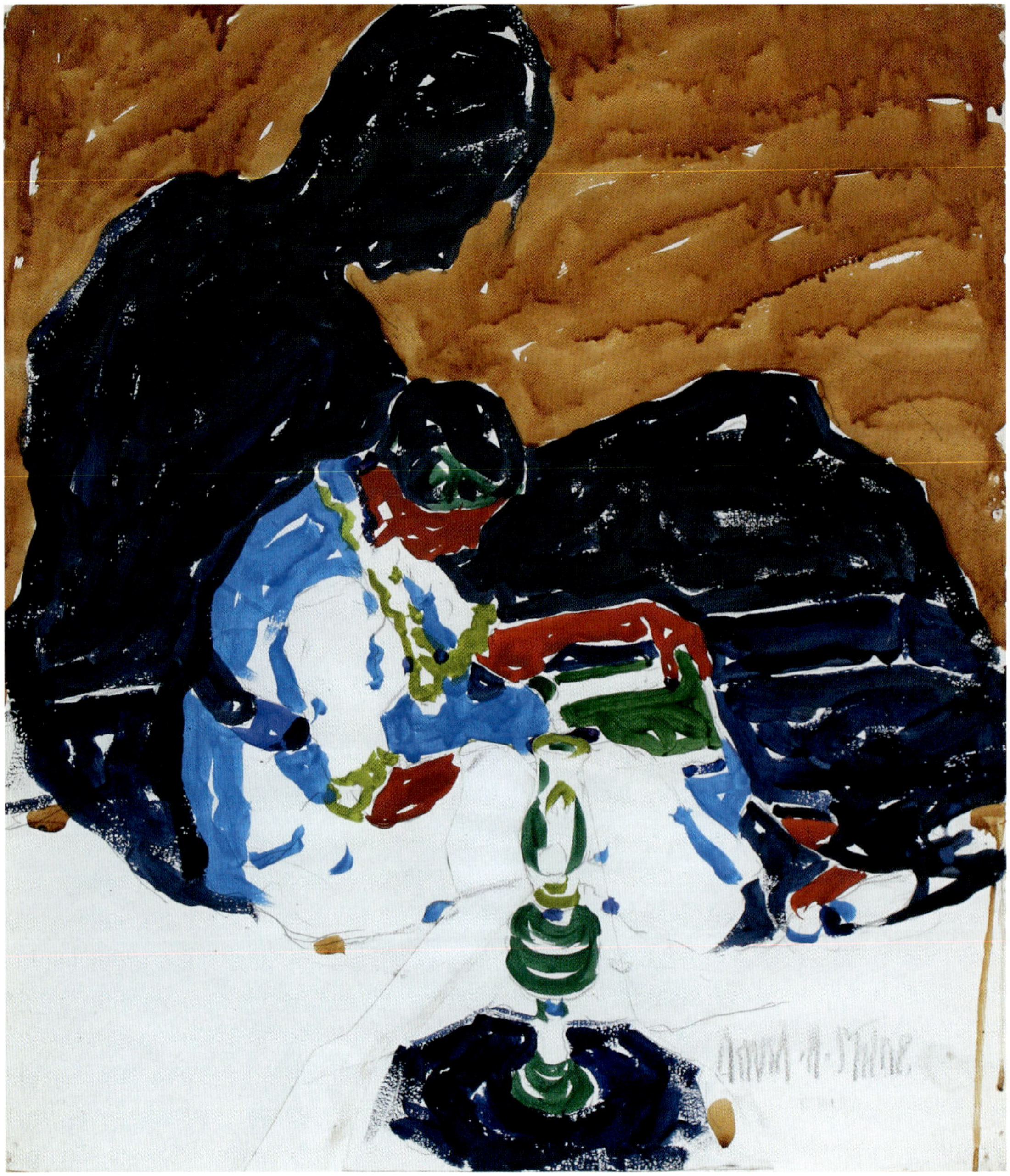

Summer Night, Saugerties
1914, watercolour on paper

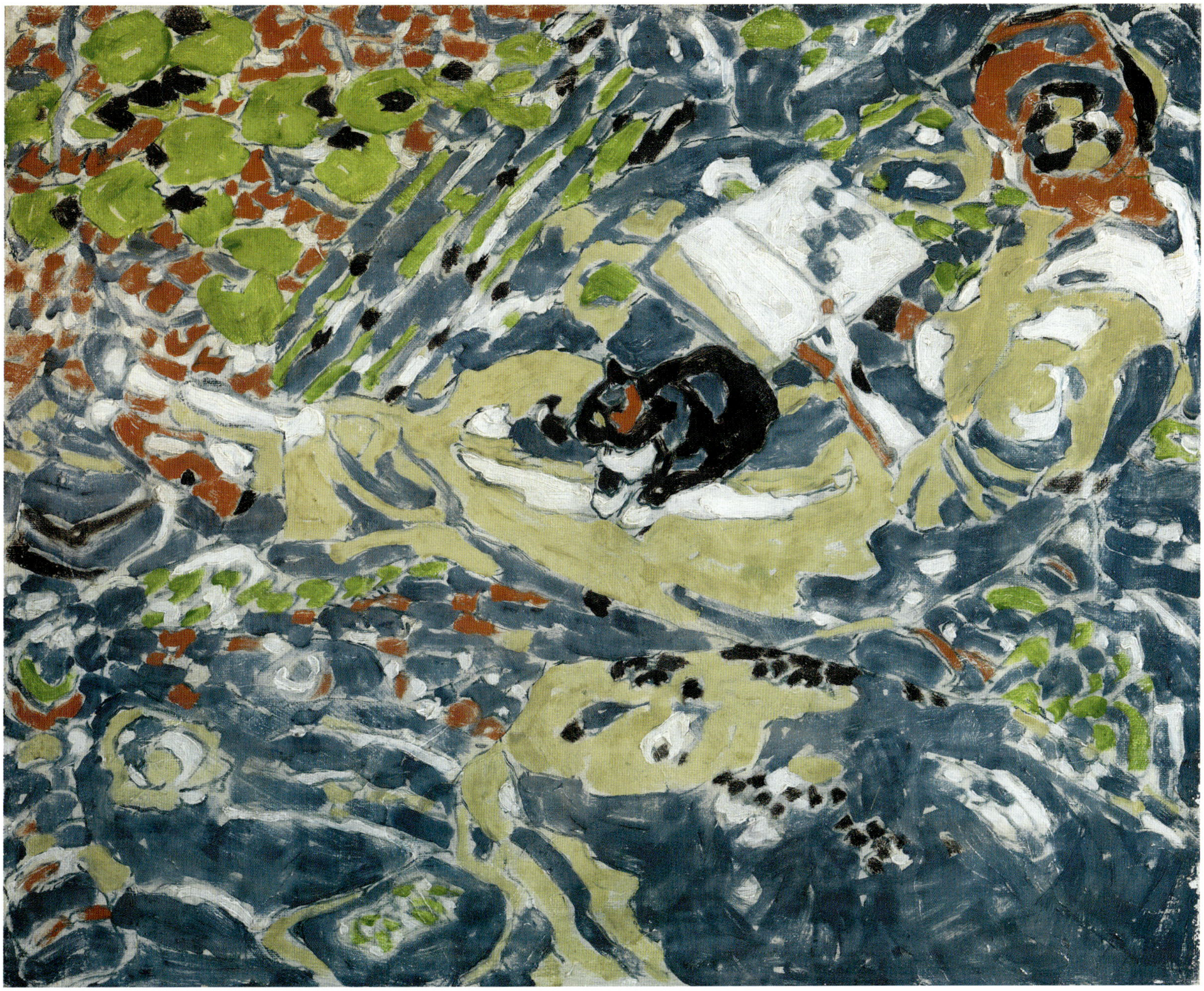

Reader with Cat
1916, oil on canvas

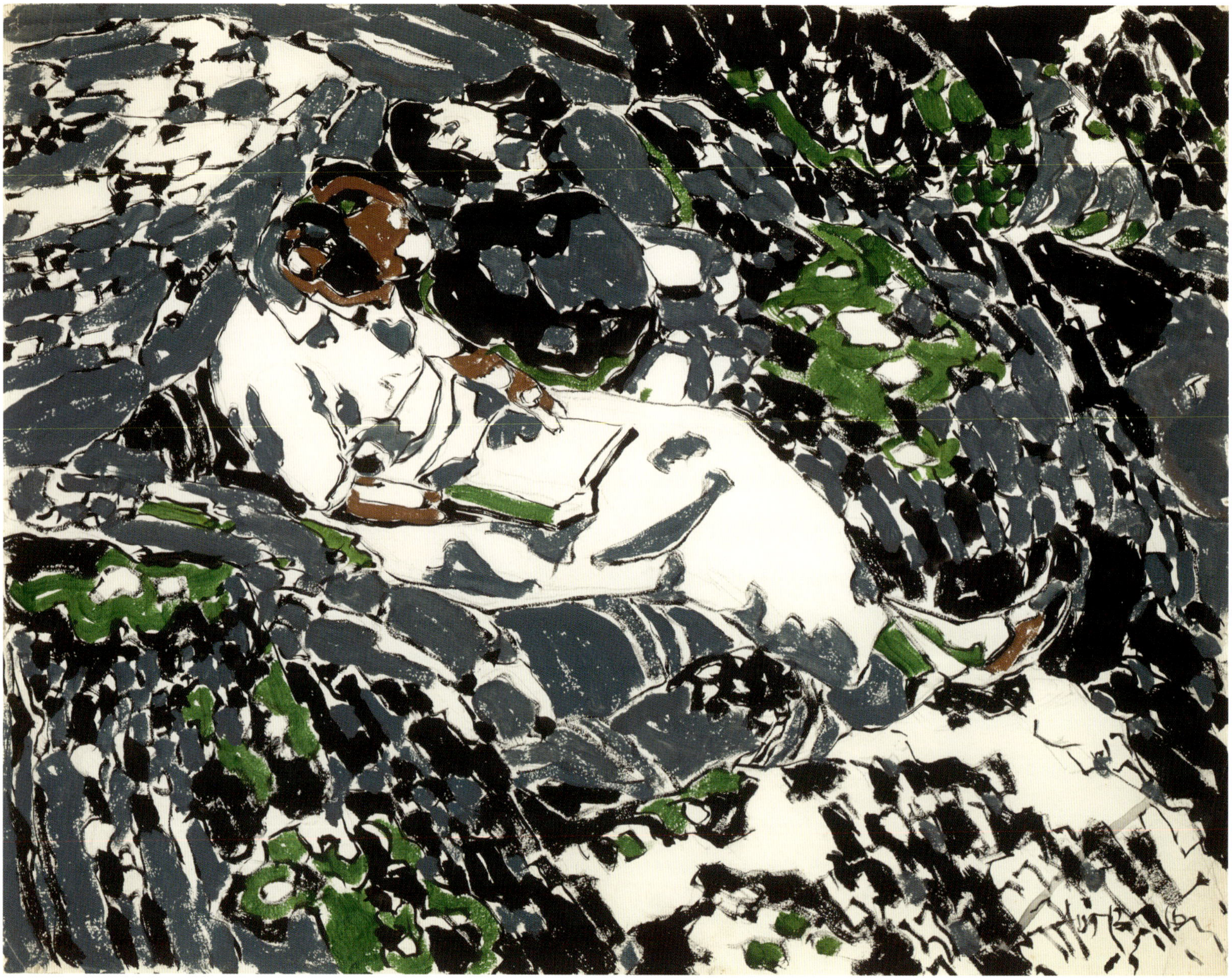

The Waterfall
1916, watercolour on paper

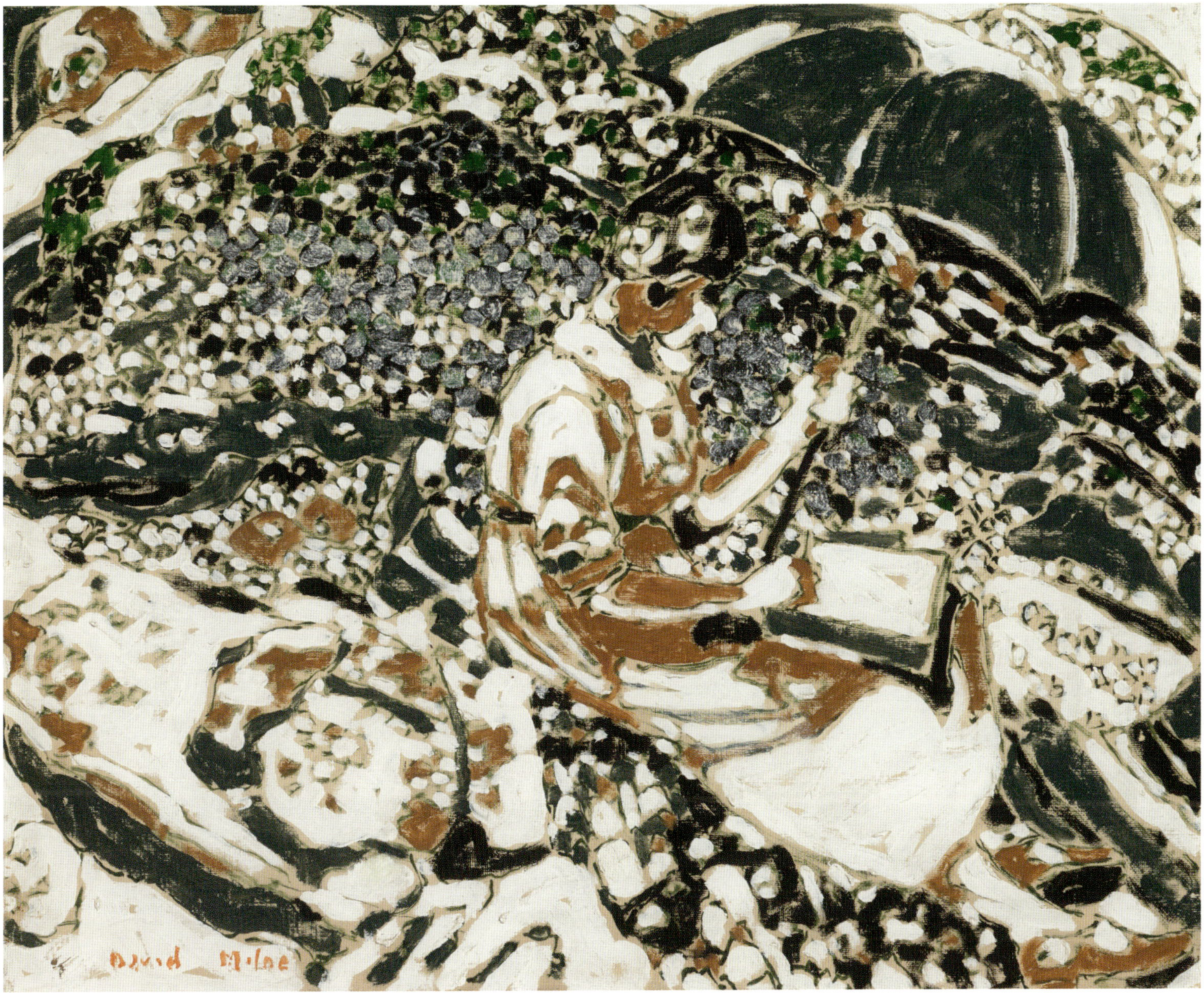

Figure on the Rocks
1916, oil on canvas

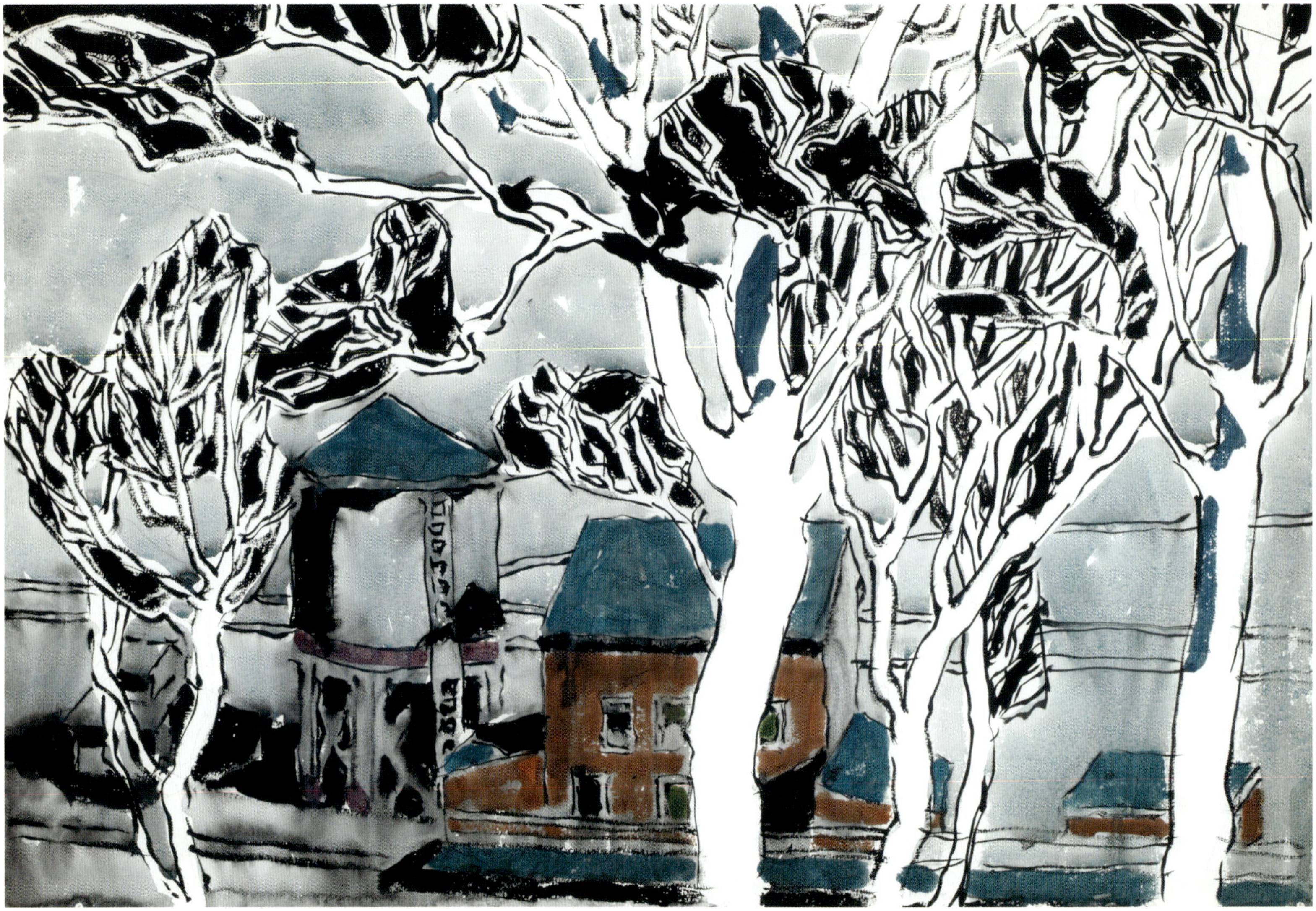

White Trees
c. 1916, watercolour on paper

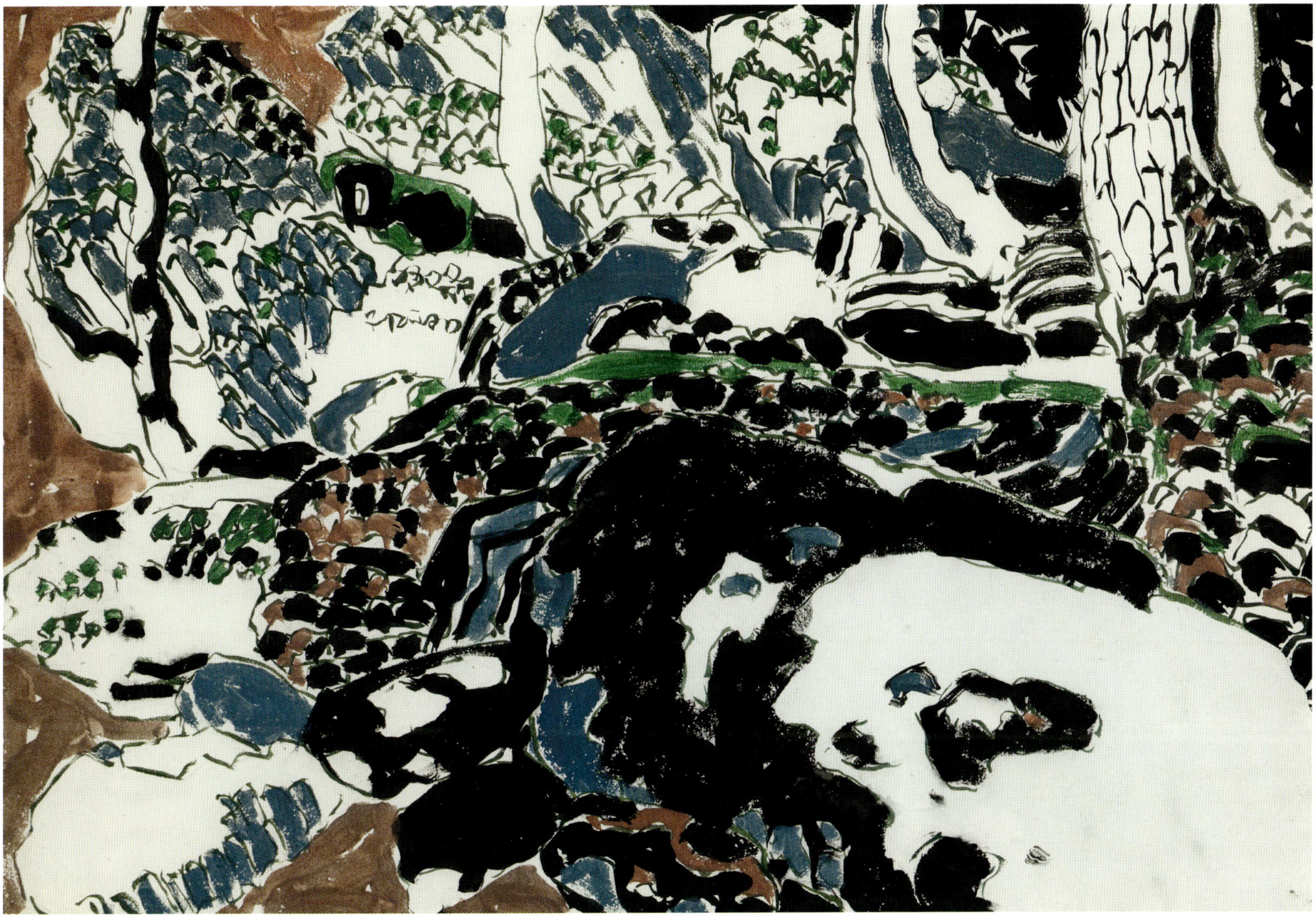

Limestone Rocks
1916, gouache and graphite on paper

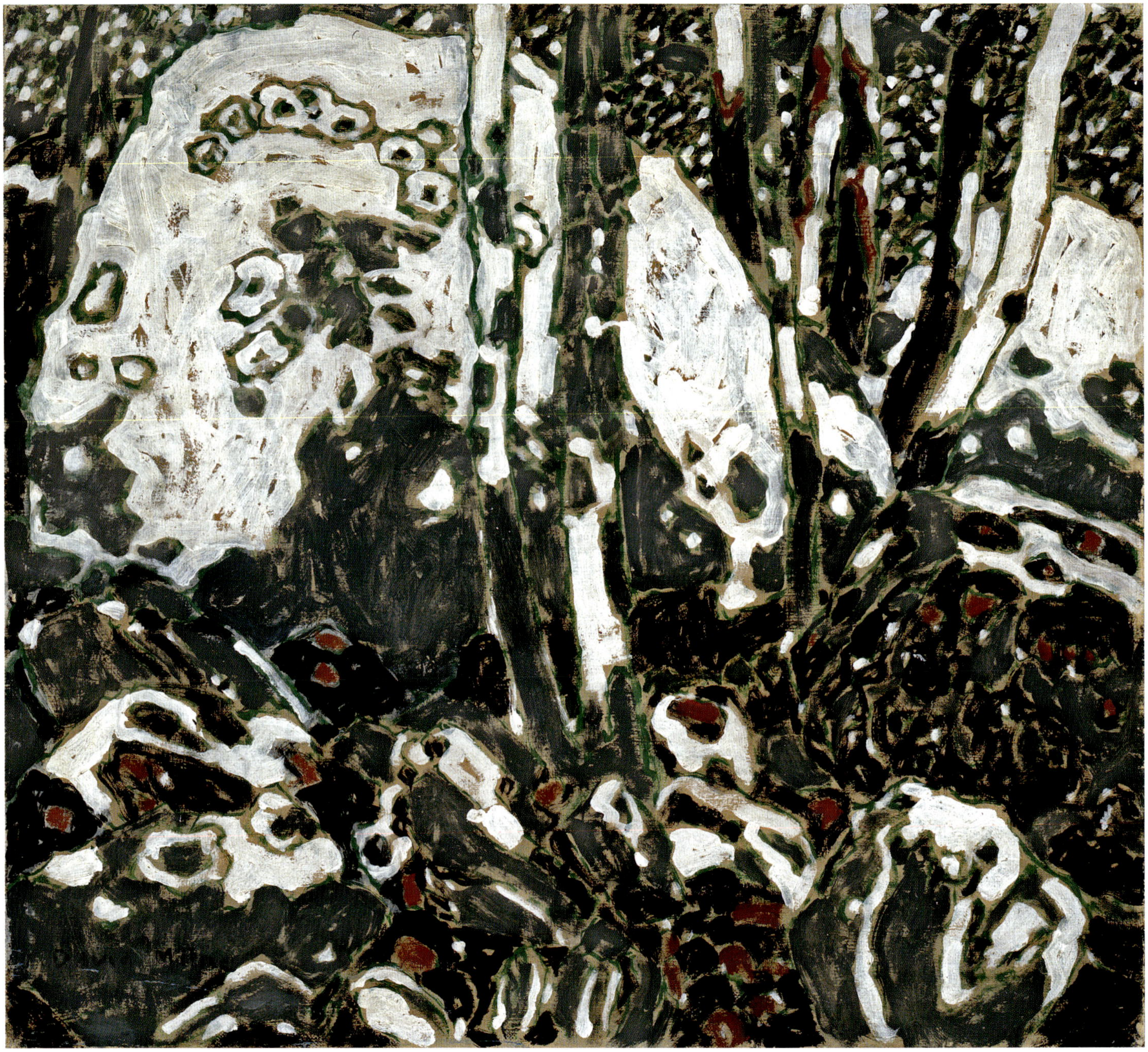

The Boulder
1916, oil on canvas

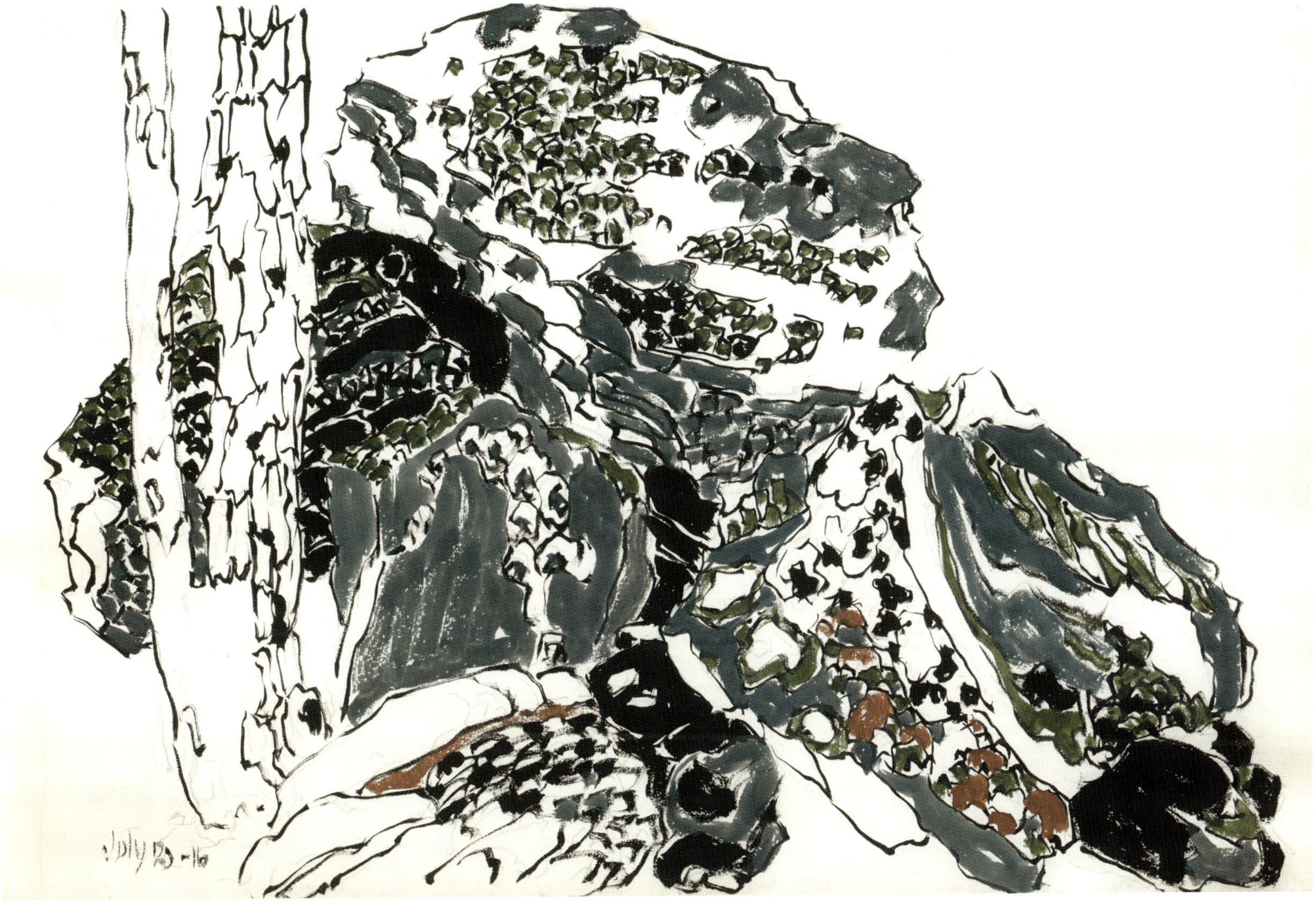

Rock Forms
1916, watercolour on paper

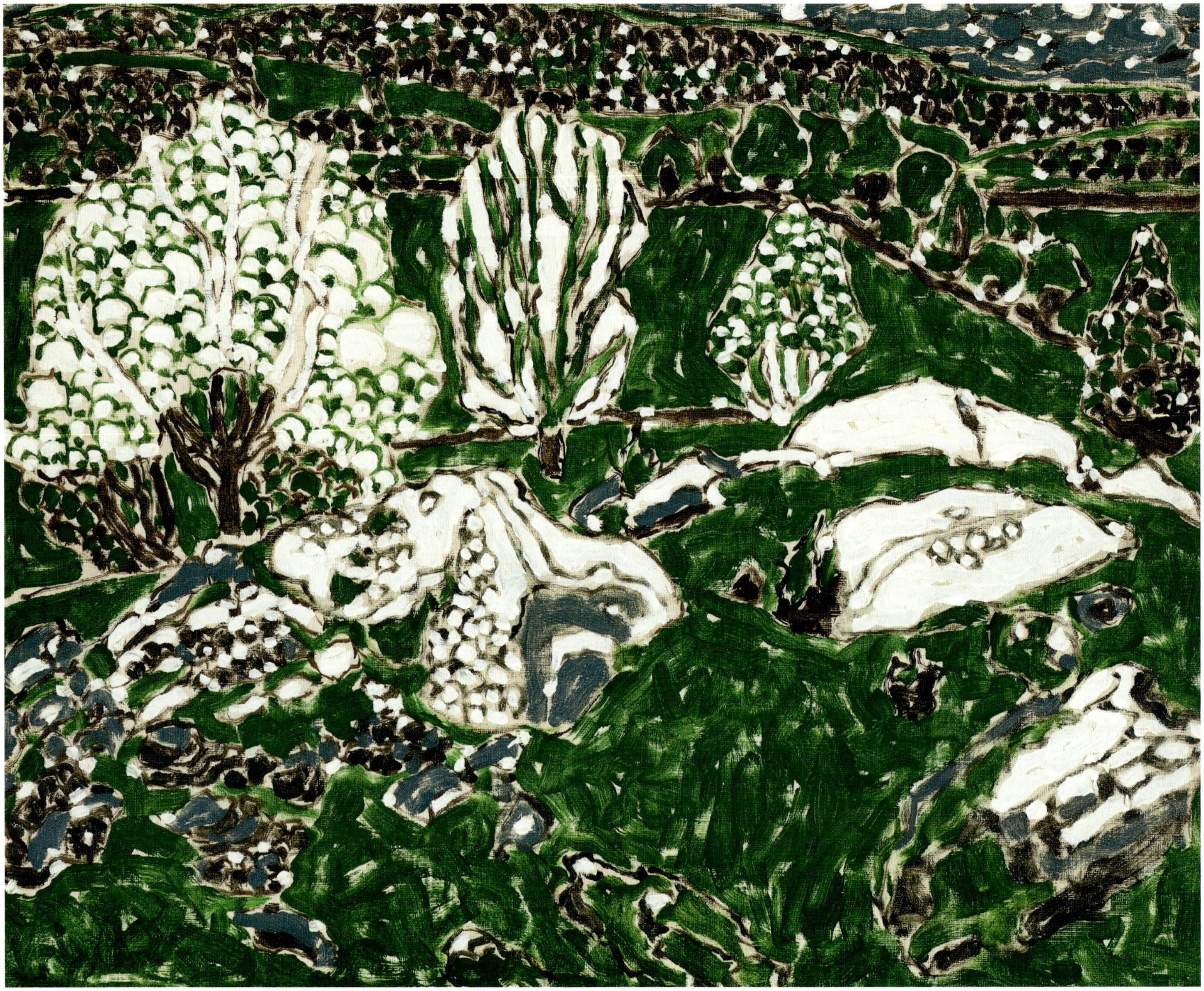

White Trees in a Green Valley
c. 1916, oil on canvas

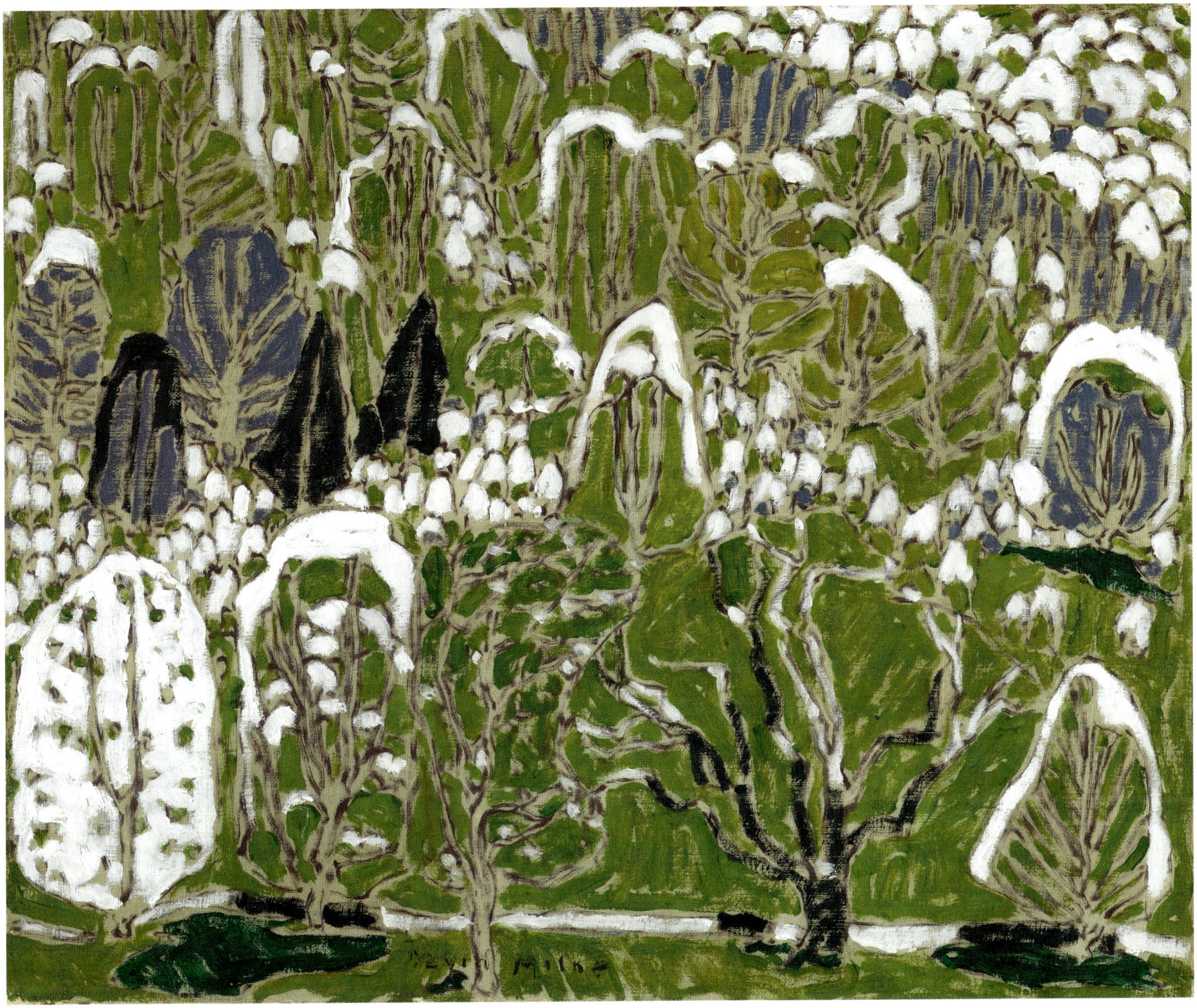

Trees in Spring
c. 1917, oil on canvas

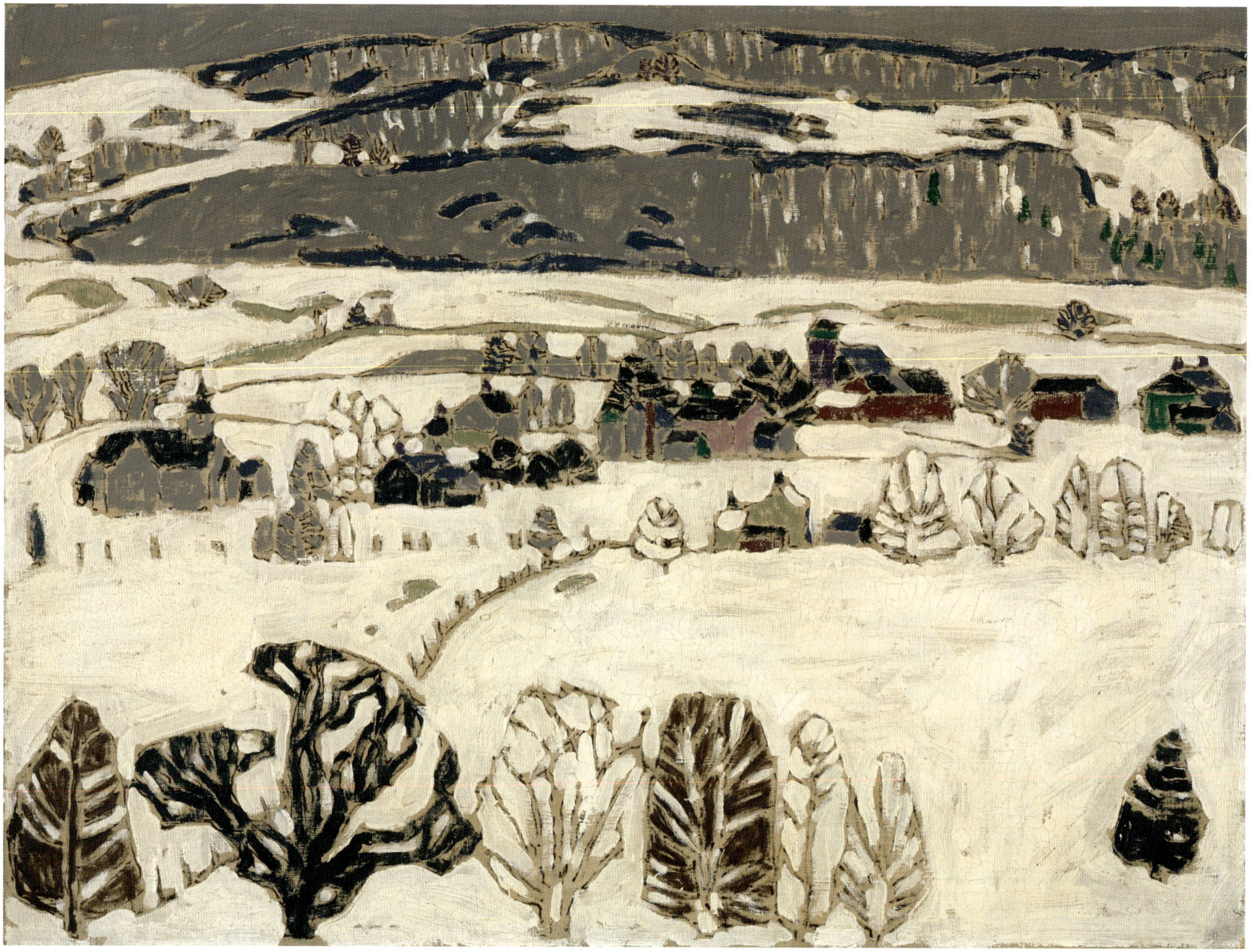

Boston Corners
1917–18, oil on canvas

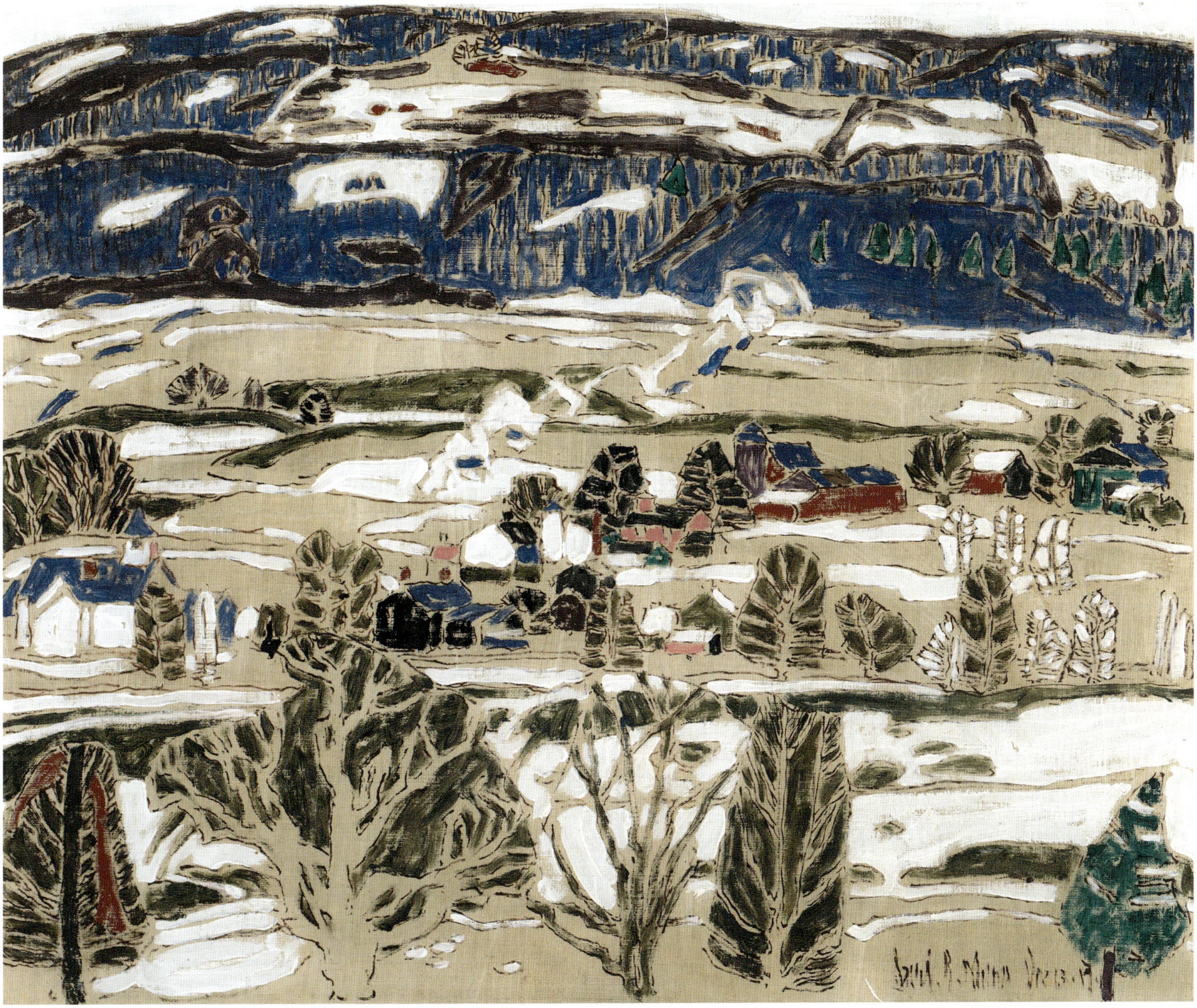

Snow Patches
1917, oil on canvas

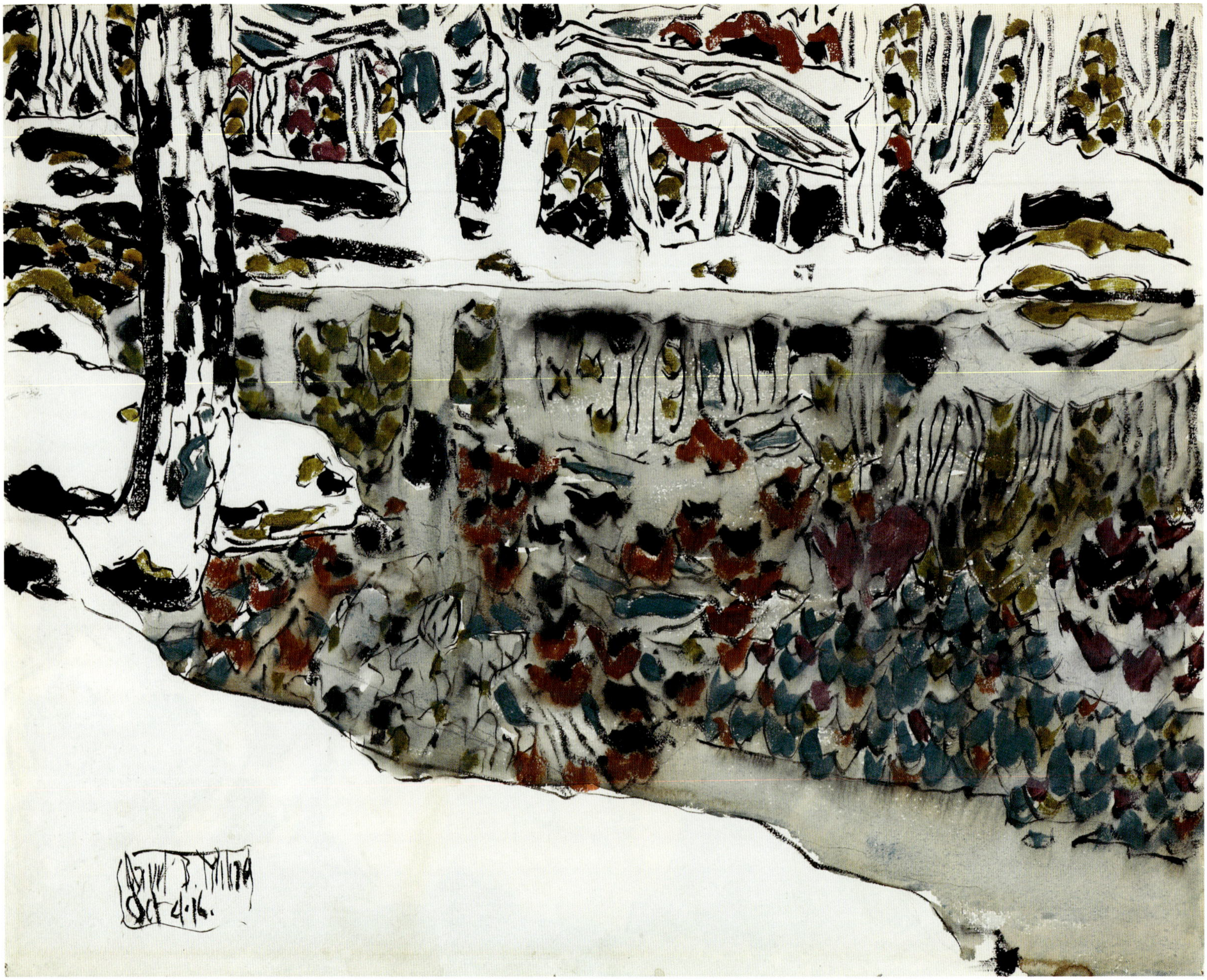

Bishop's Pond (Reflections)
1916, watercolour on paper

'THE MYSTERY THING': DAVID MILNE AND SPIRITUALITY

Katharine Lochnan

As a child, David Milne spent a lot of time with his mother in her garden; Mary Milne, a deeply religious person, was 'a great lover of flowers and her flower garden was her hobby'.[1] The spirituality, asceticism and communion with nature that underpinned his art found their origins in that environment. 'I think we go to flowers as we go to art, because both are useless', Milne later observed. 'We do not reach for either as an aid in our struggle for existence. Our devotion to either or both is a statement of faith, a declaration that for us there is more to life than mere continuance, it is good for itself, without purpose, that heaven is not far away and shadowy and unreal, but here, now and very real.... In our love of art and love of roses we build our own small heavens in our own small gardens or on our own thin canvas, we accept the imperfect world around us, we must, but within it we build our own perfect world.'[2]

Milne believed that we are defined by our roots and our upbringing, and he was very mindful of his family's Scottish heritage and their attachment to nature. 'I have stood in the smooth, green churchyard of St. Peter's Presbyterian Church in Fyvie, Aberdeenshire, Scotland', he would write, 'encompassed by the Milnes of two hundred years, and been thrilled to see how unfailingly they had held to the land'.[3] Following their immigration to Canada, the Milnes lived in a log cabin at Burgoyne, Bruce County, where David was born in 1882. After their move to the nearby town of Paisley nine years later, they became members of Knox Presbyterian Church, which would support the controversial union of the Methodist and Congregational churches as the United Church of Canada in 1925.[4] The family—David was the last of ten children—read the Bible daily and attended services three times on Sunday. It was said of Milne's mother that 'barely did she miss a Sunday morning service as long as she was able. Like many of the old school of staunch Presbyterians, she loved the Word of God—her Bible was her guide and comfort. So familiar was she with its sacred contents that to the last she could quote from memory long passages of the scriptures.'[5] When Milne was seven, one of his brothers gave him the New Testament for Christmas; he drew a dove, symbolic of the Holy Spirit, on the flyleaf. Milne memorised a vast store of scripture in childhood and continued to read

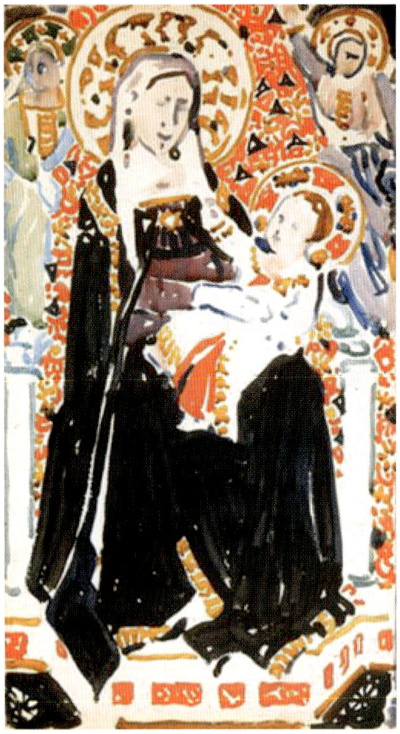

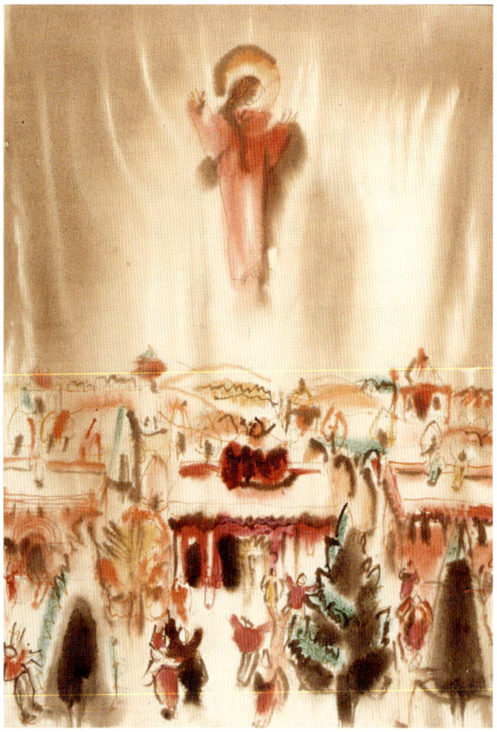

David Milne
Madonna and Child after Taddeo Gaddi's Madonna and Child Enthroned with Saints
c. 1911–12, watercolour on illustration board

David Milne
Ascension XX
c. 1945, watercolour on paper

the Bible regularly as an adult.[6] He saw his life journey through a biblical lens and quoted passages verbatim in interviews, conversations and letters.

His child's view of nature began to expand when he was permitted a glimpse of 'the unknown world' on Sundays when a brother would accompany him to the top of the hill behind the family's home. From this vantage point looking down at the rolling landscape that stretches toward Lake Huron, Milne 'was brought face to face with Infinity where anything might be and anything might happen'.[7] Nature is viewed by Calvinists (including Presbyterians) as 'the Second Book of God', because it is through the Creation that God is made manifest.[8] Milne believed that the painter's 'art is a way of life that in the very highest sense is a "labour to the glory of God"'; however, 'we don't bring God into it, not in words anyway'.[9]

For Milne, it was necessary to be reborn spiritually, to allow himself to be led by the Spirit.[10] He saw creating works of art as a way of fulfilling Christ's commandment to love one another, writing in a letter that 'art is love, but not love of man or child, or love of woman, not love of nature or love of country or of mankind. It is just love, love without an object, a spilling of the oil of love.'[11] He had a strong sense of vocation. As his friend James Clarke said, 'I don't think there was ever a shadow of a doubt [in Milne's mind] that he was put on earth to make paintings and that he would make them and that eventually people would recognise his destiny and his mission.'[12]

After moving to New York in 1903, Milne stopped attending church, but he was drawn to works of art with overtly spiritual content. During a visit to the Metropolitan Museum of Art, he made a pair of watercolours, one of St Lawrence and the other of a Madonna and Child, both based on the museum's newly acquired altarpiece *Madonna and Child Enthroned with Saints*, from around 1340, by the Florentine Taddeo Gaddi. Early Italian gold ground painting, with its two-dimensional spatial construction and stamped ornament, became a source of inspiration for Milne's construction of picture space, his palette and his idiosyncratic calligraphy. It also seems likely that he was drawn to stained glass, as his New York paintings were often compared to stained-glass windows.[13]

It was in New York at the Durand-Ruel Galleries in 1903 that Milne first encountered Claude Monet's paintings from his Haystacks series (p. 18). These works, with their ostensibly secular subjects, were seen as mystical by Evelyn Underhill, author of the widely read book *Mysticism* (1911) who saw the haystacks as 'modes of light'.[14] Underhill pointed out that the highest mystical state is one of unity; perhaps Milne sensed this element in Monet's work when he said that he 'was thrilled by just one thing, his singleness of heart, the unity of his pictures'.[15] In an appreciative essay on the artist, Milne wrote that he believed Monet achieved this unity by 'compression ... by forcing all detail to work to the one end. In all other pictures I was conscious of parts, in these I felt only the whole.'[16]

At that time, Monet was at the height of his international celebrity, and working on his series of *nymphéas* (water lilies), studies of his Japanese-inspired water lily pond at home in Giverny, northwest of Paris (p. 78). By contemplating the pond for prolonged periods, Monet entered into a mystical state that he likened to a hypnotic trance, feeling that he became one with nature.[17] In 1909, the French art critic Roger Marx published an article on the *nymphéas*, in which he quotes Monet's words to him about the pond: 'its image awakens in you a sense of infinity; you can observe, as in a microcosm, the unstable elements of the universe transforming themselves at every moment, under your gaze'. And in the same conversation, Monet said, 'My only virtue resides in submission to instinct; it was through discovering secret, intuitive forces and allowing them to lead me that I have been able to identify myself with the Creation, and become absorbed within it. My art is an outpouring of faith, an act of love and humility.'[18]

Milne found the pace of New York City overwhelming; painting while trying to earn a living proved so stressful that he moved to the country, eventually settling in Boston Corners in upstate New York in 1916. 'We may have life without glorifying God', he said, 'but we cannot glorify God without living'.[19] In Boston Corners, he planted a garden and devoted himself to art making. He was inspired by the American transcendentalist philosophers, especially Henry David Thoreau; *Walden* was his favourite book. He also loved Ralph Waldo Emerson, who believed that those who are in touch with nature 'participate in the Creation ... [and] see God every day, face to face'.[20] Emerson saw the whole of nature as a metaphor for the human condition and the universe as the externalisation of the soul.[21] He believed that the purpose or 'end' of nature is 'ascension', the passage of the soul into higher forms, and that the poet and artist play a pivotal role in this transcendental process.

Clive Bell's influential book *Art*, published in 1914, was also important to Milne's developing artistic theory. Bell writes that the artist, through the contemplation of nature, may be able to perceive the ultimate reality that lies behind appearances and, by capturing the 'significant form' of the subject, may be able to convey to the viewer the 'aesthetic emotion' experienced at the time of creation. In this way, the artist shares his or her glimpse of ultimate reality.[22] Milne tried to incorporate Bell's concepts of 'significant form' and 'aesthetic emotion' into his work. In his chapter 'Art and Religion', Bell describes religion as 'an expression of the individual's sense of the emotional significance of the universe', and writes that 'I should not be surprised to find that art was an expression of the same thing.... Certainly both have the power of transporting men to superhuman ecstasies; both are means to unearthly states of mind. Art and religion belong to the same world.... Rightly, therefore, do we regard art and religion as twin manifestations of the spirit; wrongly do some speak of art as a manifestation of religion.'[23] 'For the mystic as for the artist, the physical universe is a means to ecstasy', continues Bell. 'The mystic feels things as "ends" instead of as means. He seeks within all emotional exaltation.'[24] For the artist, 'the physical universe gives rise to ... that peculiar spiritual state that we call inspiration',[25] and the resulting work of art 'does affect the lives of men; it moves [them] to ecstasy'.[26] Bell concludes that 'if [art] be an expression of emotion ... it is an expression of that emotion which is the vital force in every religion ... [an emotion] felt for that which is the essence of all. We may say that both art and religion are manifestations of man's religious sense, if by "man's religious sense" we mean his sense of ultimate reality.'[27]

It was in New York that Milne first employed the motif of reflections, in his watercolours *Shimmering Water*, 1912 (p. 40), and *Dreamland Tower, Coney Island*, 1912 (p. 41), both of which show the influence of Whistler.[28] The series of paintings of reflections on Bishop's Pond at Boston Corners, such as *Bishop's Pond (Reflections)*, 1916 (p. 74), was inspired instead by Monet's *nymphéas*. Its pictorial construction—the flattening of the picture space, the asymmetrical shape of the pond, the cutting-off of the composition at the edge of the paper, and the contrast between areas of pattern and void—evokes the Japanese prints so admired by both Monet and Whistler. In this watercolour, Milne audaciously leaves the material elements, the trees and bank, blank and concentrates the detail on the immaterial, on the reflections. Much more than a stylistic device designed to catch the eye, this is a meditation on reality and illusion, one that Monet was employing in the *nymphéas*. By subsequently dragging a wet brush over dry pigment, he softens the focus on the surface of the pond, encouraging contemplation of this area. 'I work for unity', he said to his friend Stockton Kimball, 'by giving impression and then come to the center spot—emphasis. More emphasis on shape than color. Color is the servant. It's the Father-Son-Holy Ghost thing—you can't separate them.'[29]

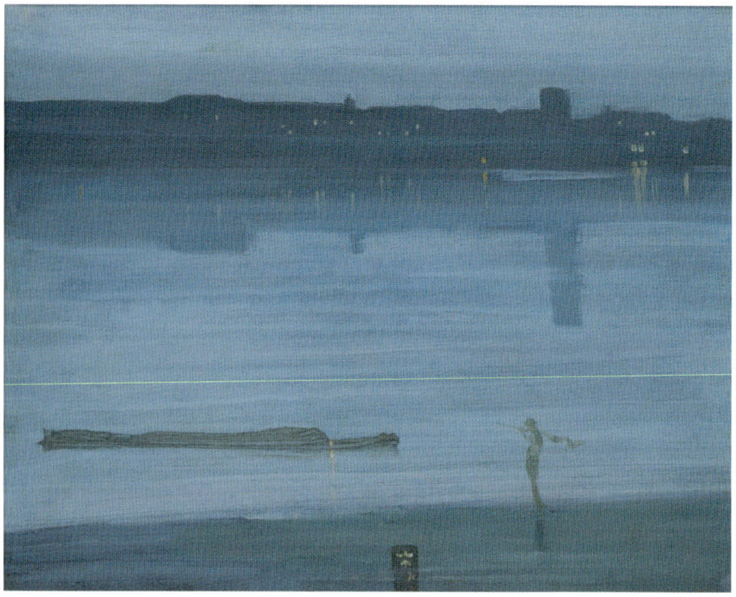

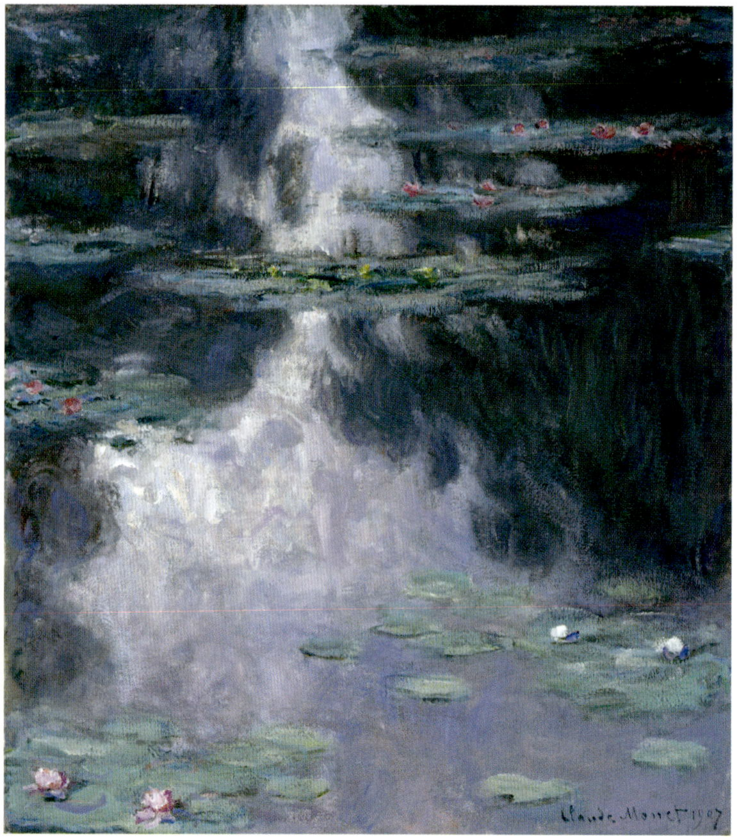

Top
James Abbott McNeill Whistler
Nocturne: Blue and Silver—Chelsea
1871, oil paint on wood

Above
Claude Monet
Water Lilies (Nymphéas)
1907, oil on canvas

After his service as a war artist, Milne returned to Boston Corners in late 1919 and began 'hammering the bayonet into a paint brush'.[30] He resumed his series of variations on the theme of the pond and reflections, mindful of Monet who, like Milne, 'would sit in front of the subject maybe for forty-five minutes or more sometimes, just looking at it before he made a mark'.[31] In *Bishop's Pond in Sunlight*, 1920 (p. 126), he once again leaves the material elements partially blank and concentrates the detail on the immaterial reflections, blurring them with a wet brush. However, in *Pink Reflections, Bishop's Pond*, 1920 (p. 127), he reverses the process and effect, with the material trees on the bank painted in textured detail, omitting the wet brush.

Milne told Stockton Kimball in 1935 that he 'found the mystery thing in quiet pools'.[32] He never stopped searching for 'the mystery' behind the surface of reality and trying to convey it in paint.[33] In his later years at Uxbridge and Baptiste Lake, Milne would produce myriad watercolours of saints and angels, even picturing the risen Christ (p. 76), but the devotional aspect of his work had always lain just beneath the surface. Recalling an afternoon spent with visiting clergymen at Six Mile Lake, Milne wrote:

> We went swimming and cooked our lunch on the outside stove and talked, mostly of art and religion with no fixed dividing line between the two. Most people find my pictures just blank but my visiting churchmen found little difficulty in grasping their essentials. They should. I would say that there could be no better introduction to the study of art than a reading of the four gospels where singleness of heart is taught and lived. Singleness of heart, sincerity beyond anything possible in daily life, is essential in painting.[34]

***Katharine Lochnan** is Senior Curator Emeritus, Art Gallery of Ontario, with special expertise in nineteenth- and early twentieth-century European and North American art. Among her many exhibitions and publications are* David Milne Watercolours: 'Painting toward the Light' *(2005), and* Mystical Landscapes: From Vincent van Gogh to Emily Carr *(2016).*

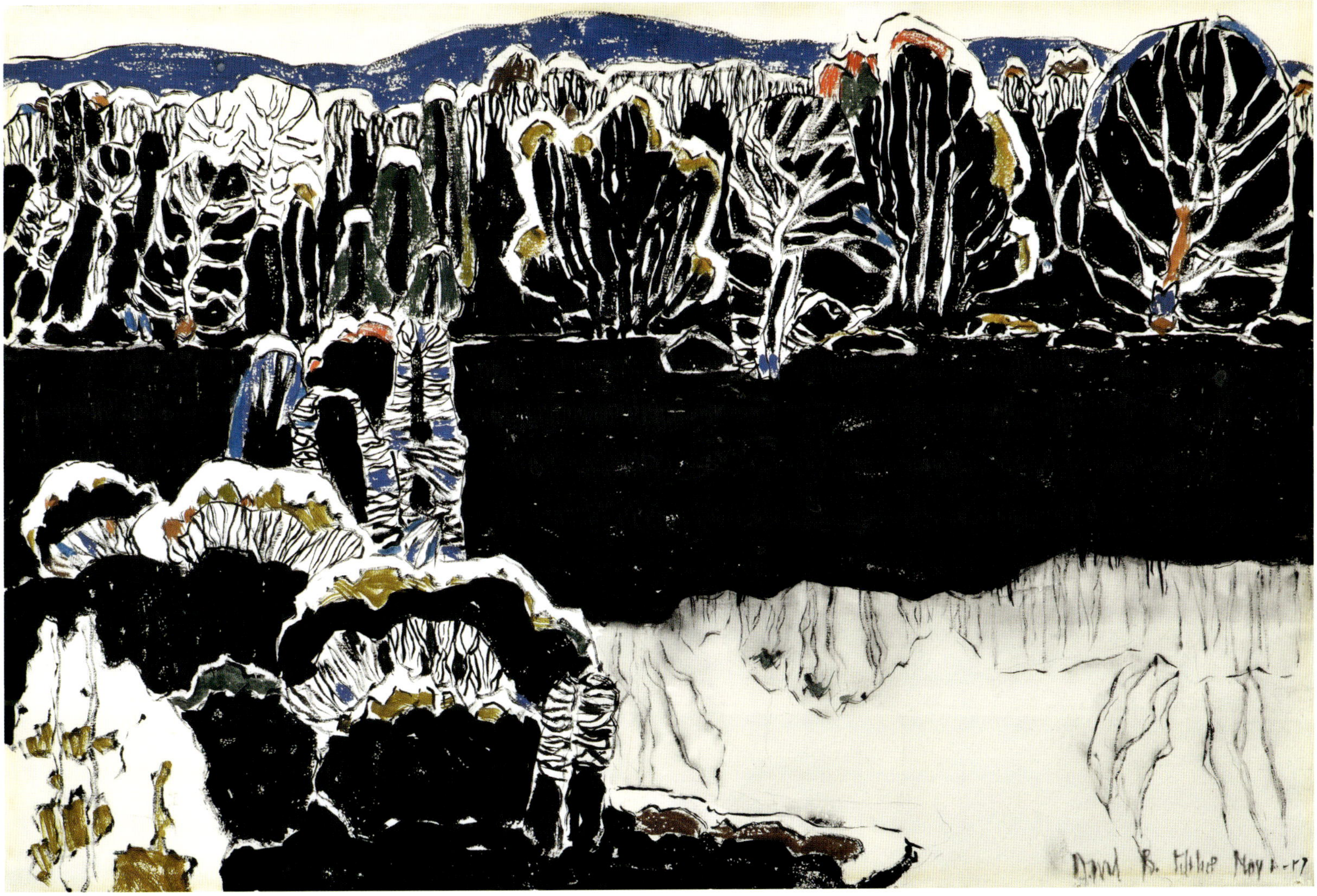

Reflected Forms
1917, watercolour and pencil on paper

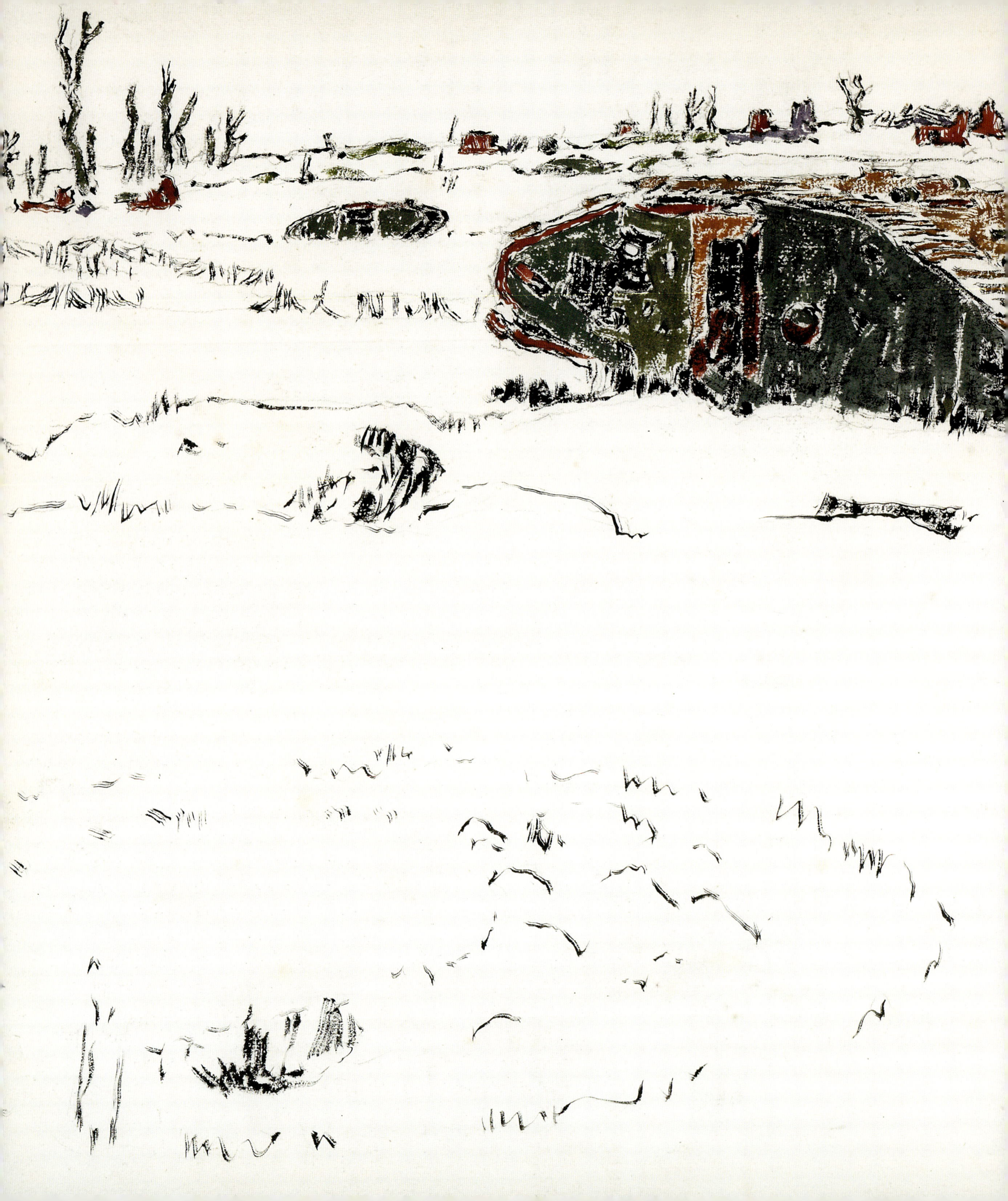

DOCUMENT OF WAR

Milne responded to the call of war, signing up in New York City in late 1917, but he was never to see active duty. Instead, he spent time in Quebec and in Kinmel Park Training Camp in Wales. On leave in London, however, he learned of the Canadian War Memorials Fund initiative and implored their representatives in London to commission him as a war artist. This they eventually did, first engaging him to record the Canadian training camps at Ripon, Kinmel Park, Bramshott and Seaford, then sending him to France and Belgium in 1919, where he documented the silent battlefields and trenches. Contrasting his experience with that of the thousands of Canadians who had fought there, Milne later wrote: 'I walked by day in safety, and sightseeing was part of my job. I was the first tourist, not the last soldier.'

Milne wrote of the experience with an odd detachment: 'I had no feeling of sadness about the battles of this place, no feeling at all except of interest, and amazement at the effort. The fighting perhaps was too hard to grasp; the effort, the labour was still evident at every step. The waste of a war that was over was to be seen underground as well as above: tunnels, trenches and dugouts, new and old, in perfect condition or in danger of falling in.' Periodically, Milne noted the return of birdsong or the abrupt detonation of ordnance. Occasionally, he witnessed makeshift burials, sometimes coming across charred or mutilated human remains in the torn-up battlefields. Dispassionately, and with fierce clarity, he documented it all.

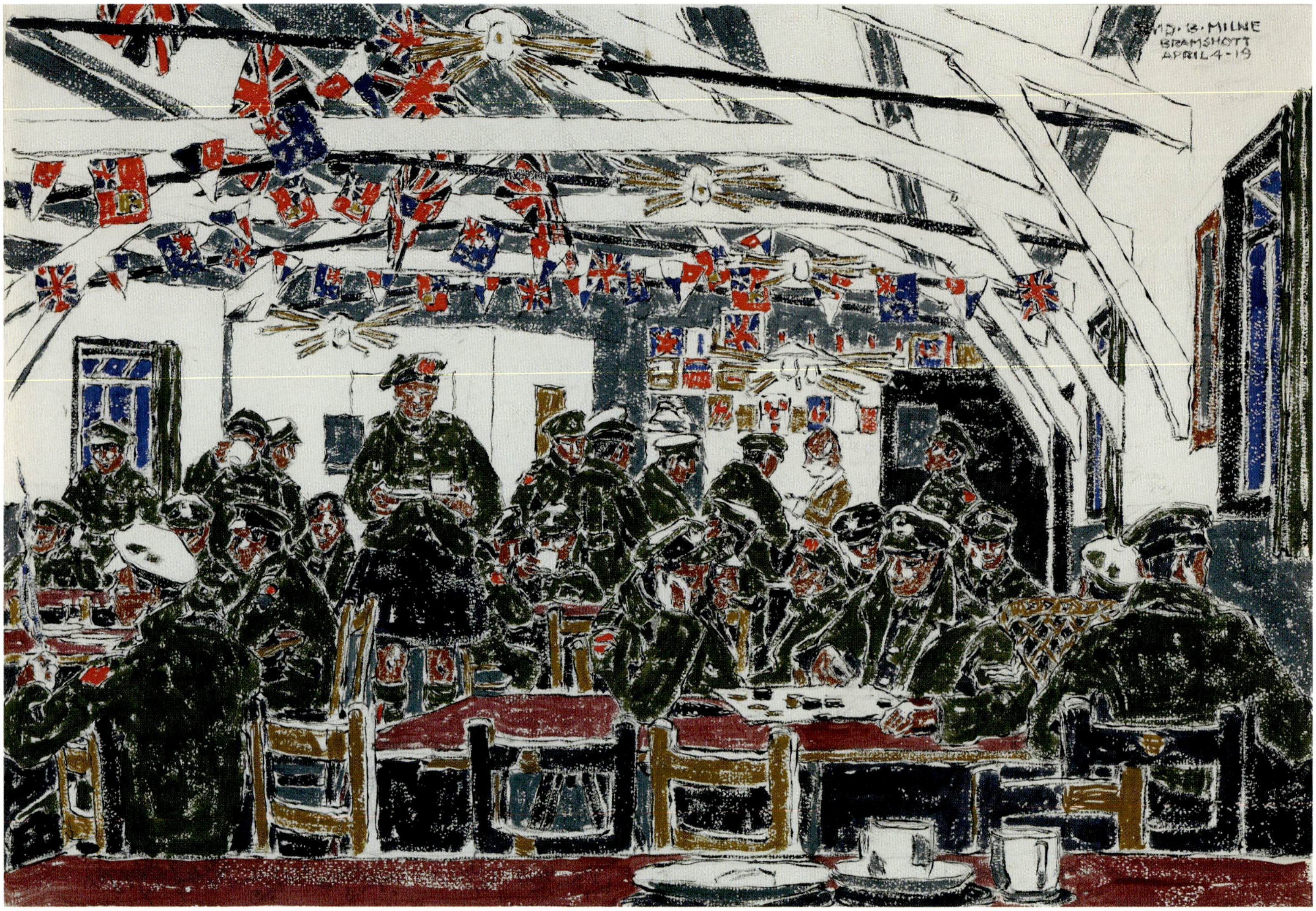

Bramshott: Interior of the Wesleyan Hut
1919, watercolour over graphite on wove paper

Opposite
Ripon: High Street
1919, opaque watercolour over graphite on paper

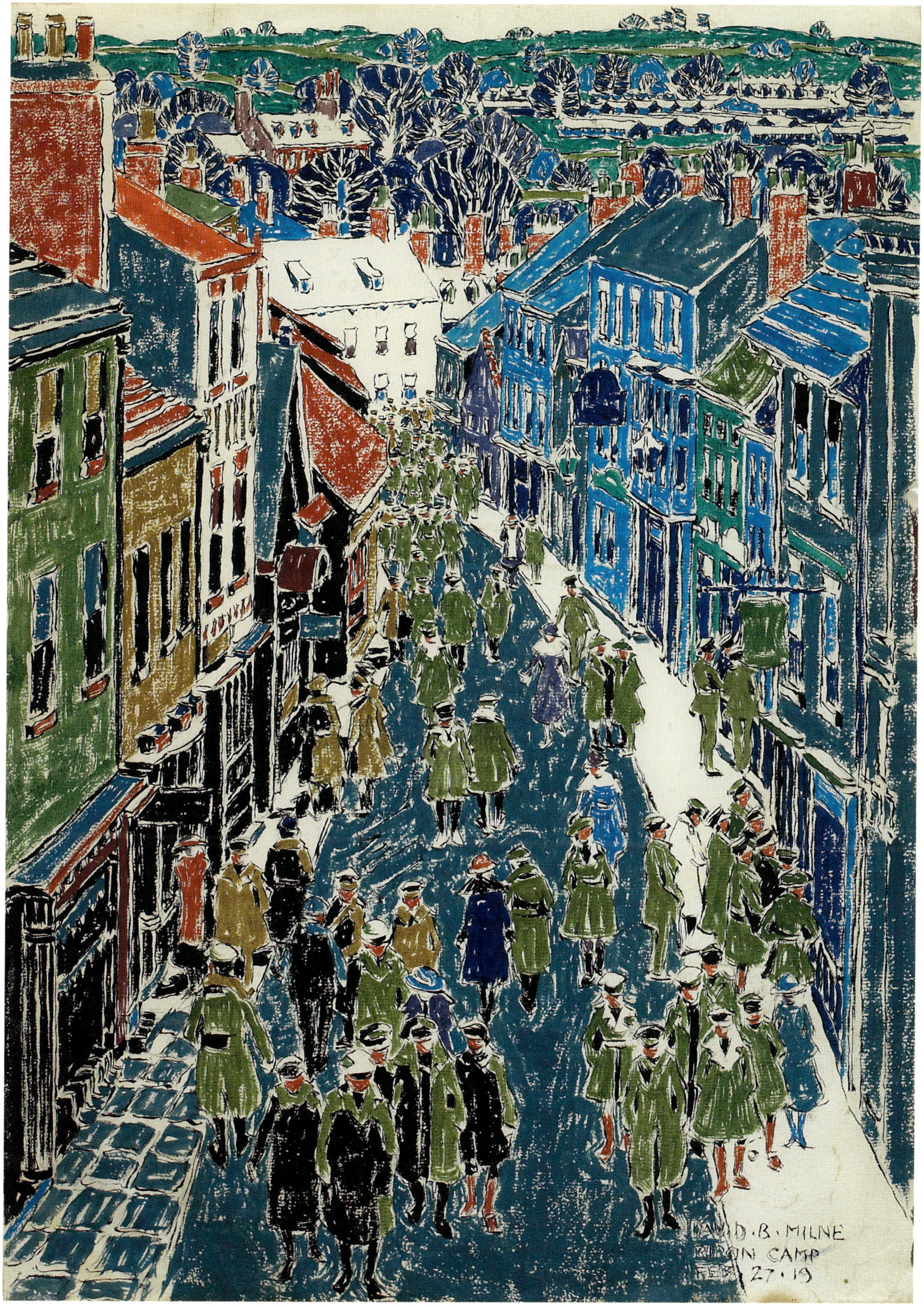
DAVID · B · MILNE
RIPON CAMP
FEB 27 · 19

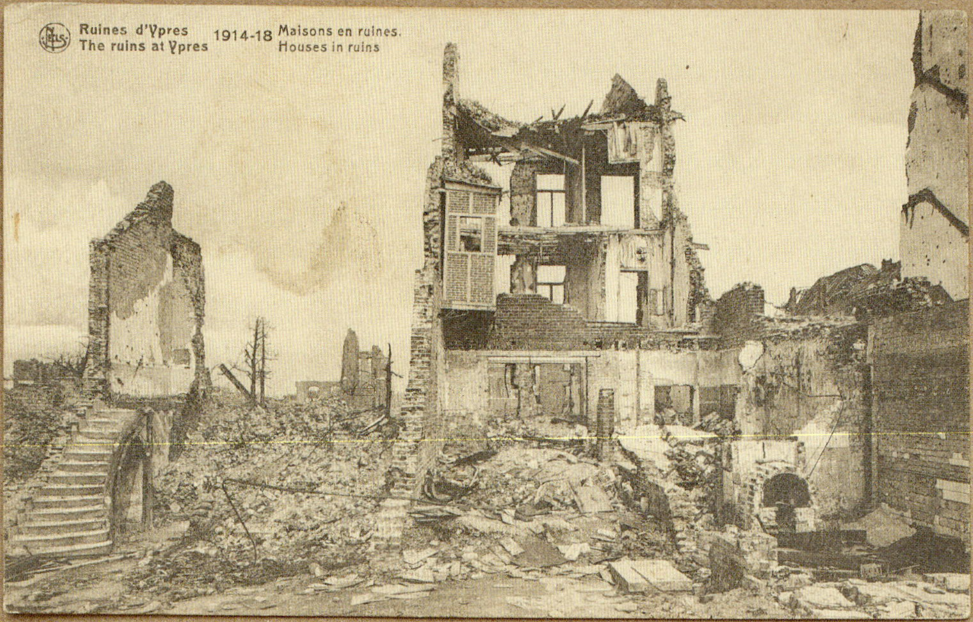
Ruines d'Ypres
The ruins at Ypres
1914-18
Maisons en ruines.
Houses in ruins

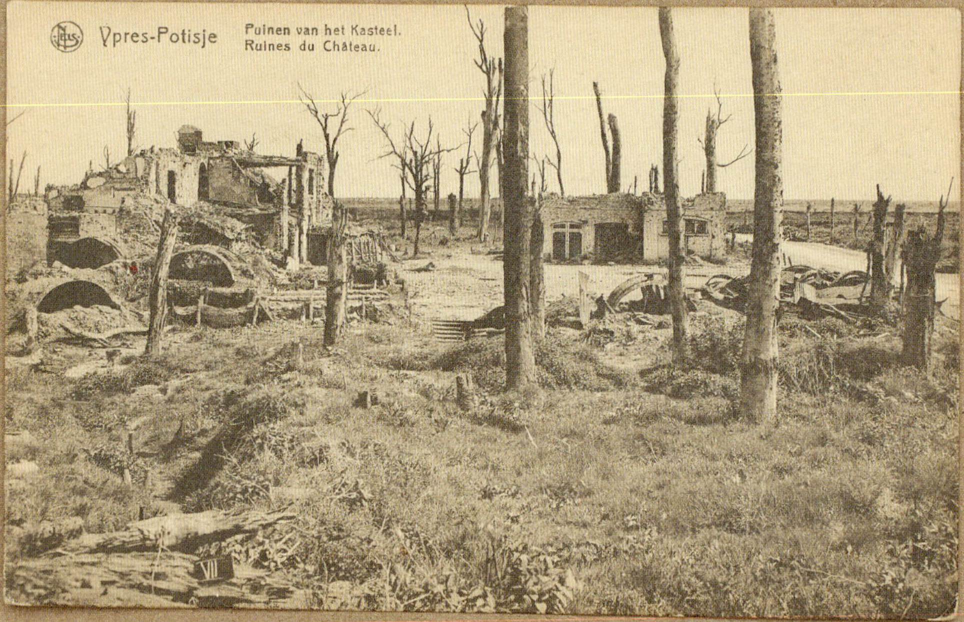
Ypres-Potisje
Puinen van het Kasteel.
Ruines du Château.

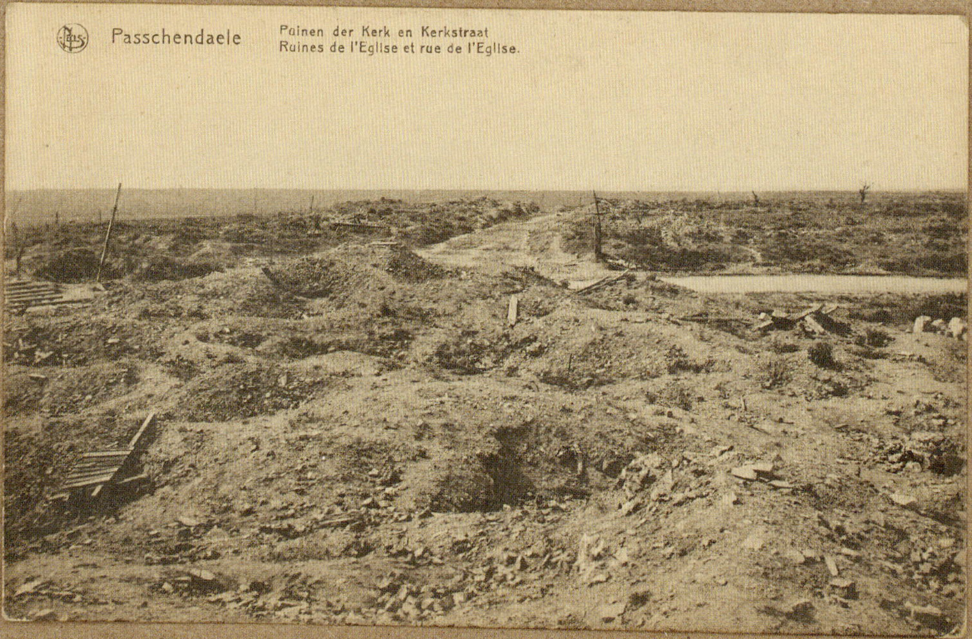
Passchendaele
Puinen der Kerk en Kerkstraat
Ruines de l'Eglise et rue de l'Eglise.

MODERN CATASTROPHE

Margaret MacMillan

If you travel today south through Belgium and into the north of France, you will see an unremarkable and placid landscape criss-crossed with rivers and canals and dotted with orchards, farms, villages and towns. The country is mostly flat, with only an occasional ridge, hill or church steeple to break the skyline. If you look closely, however, you will see odd dips and contours in the green land and fenced-off areas with warnings about explosives. A century ago this was part of the battlefields of the Western Front in the Great War of 1914–18. You can visit carefully preserved trenches, the cemeteries with their serried rows of crosses or the memorials such as the Menin Gate for British and Commonwealth dead at Ypres, the Newfoundland sites with their giant bronze caribou and of course Canada's Vimy Ridge.

When David Milne was there in 1919 to record the places where Canadians had fought, from Passchendaele in Flanders down to the Somme in France, the war had ended just six months before, and the scars it had left were open and raw. The soil had been churned up again and again over four years by tonnes of explosives. Thistles, poppies, wild roses, cornflowers, as Milne noted, were creeping back, and his watercolours have dashes of green where grasses and weeds had started to cover the wounded earth. The replacements for the blasted trees—some with shells still stuck in their trunks—would take much longer. *Zillebeke: Maple Copse and Observatory Ridge from Dormy House* (p. 102)—surely the name is intended as irony—shows the leafless splintered tree trunks near Ypres, where the First Canadian Division had fought its first major battle in 1915. In 48 hours of fighting, six thousand Canadians were killed or wounded.

A year before Milne arrived, the countryside had teemed with hundreds of thousands of men in a constantly expanding network of trenches, tunnels, supply routes, rear camps, airfields, ammunition dumps and makeshift hospitals. Now it was largely empty, save for the occasional civilian, the remaining prisoners of war and their bored guards, or observers such as Milne himself. As he noted, it was generally silent except for the songs of the birds, which were coming back, or the tinkling of tin rosettes on the graves in the French and Belgian cemeteries. From time to time, there were explosions of leftover ammunition, some spontaneous as the weather got hotter, others the work of teams trying to clear the land. The sound, as Milne described it, was 'a tearing, splitting noise that seemed to last longer than anyone's endurance'.[1] Every so often, he had to stop work and take shelter in a shell-hole.

Tangles of barbed wire, twisted iron posts, abandoned guns, wrecked vehicles, half-ruined pillboxes—the vast rubbish left by the war lay everywhere. Things that had once been essential for survival were suddenly useless in peacetime. In a letter to his close friend James Clarke, Milne tried to list 'the great mass of junk' he saw in a single crater: tinned food, shells, hand grenades, water bottles, bandoliers, gas masks, helmets, clothing. Some of the boots still had feet in them. And, as Milne noted, 'over all, the sweet sickish, but not offensive, smell of death'.[2]

The Great War, as it was known until a second dreadful world war came along, cost Europe and the world horribly. More than nine million people—many of them from the overseas European empires—died, and many more again were wounded. And then, just as the fighting was winding down, a deadly influenza epidemic flared, taking more than fifty million lives before it burnt itself out. Europeans who had once thought they were at the forefront of world civilisation had to face the awful truth that their great advances in science and technology, their huge industrial capacity and well-organised societies had produced endless death and the destruction of much of their wealth and heritage. In such works as *The Cathedral, Arras* (p. 109), *Passchendaele, Ruins of the Church at the End of the Road* (p. 105) or *The Belfry, Hôtel de Ville, Arras* (p. 108), Milne painted the pitiful remnants of beautiful buildings that had stood for centuries. Some have been rebuilt, but many ruins still stand as a reminder of the destructive machine that rolled over that part of Europe.

Milne arrived in France in mid-May 1919. Although he had his own car and driver for most of the time, the large-scale destruction meant that he frequently chose to walk. Often, he had to guess where a road once had gone. Sometimes, he reported, he could tell from a few small patches of brick that a farmhouse had previously stood there. On the outskirts of Lens, just a few kilometres north of Vimy Ridge, he painted the battered village of Liévin (p. 92), which had been used as a jumping-off point by Canadian forces in August 1917 in an attack on the German lines and which, in the spring of 1918, had been held, again by Canadians, in the face of the last great German offensive. He passed other villages so obliterated that he could only find them as coordinates on a map. South of Vimy, he visited the Canadian cemeteries at Neuville-Saint-Vaast and painted what was left of the village from across a field of poppies (p. 111). He clambered up and down its rubble. 'Here and there', he wrote to Clarke in June, 'a stovepipe sticking out of a pile of brick and stone, mostly pulverized, marks a cellar shelter. You are apt to tumble down the entrance if you are not careful.'[3] He painted piles of wrecked tanks at Monchy-le-Preux (p. 89), south of Vimy, where troops from Newfoundland, then a separate colony, had fought and died in 1917 and where Canadian forces had taken part in the great push against the Germans the previous August. There he also painted the gradually collapsing screens that had once hidden troops moving along a road from German artillery and snipers (p. 93). He travelled north too, to other battlefields where Canadians had fought, around Lens and then into Belgium, to the Ypres salient where the Germans had tried repeatedly to seize the Allied position, which jutted into their lines.

His letters to Clarke, as well as the tourist postcards of the battlefields and bombed villages of the Western Front that he collected there, help us to see what Milne was seeing. Reminders of the mass slaughter were everywhere, in hastily built graveyards and the makeshift crosses hammered together out of bits of wood. Milne ran across work groups searching for bodies and reburying the dead into new, more orderly cemeteries like the one he painted at Courcelette, which held Canadians who had died in the Battle of Somme in 1916 (p. 110). From time to time, he was roped into being part of the audience while priests blessed the new burial grounds and bored soldiers presented arms.

On one expedition, he found an abandoned letter, perhaps never posted because the writer had been killed. This unknown soldier complained about being fed up with 'this bloody country'. Milne sympathised: 'the lack of trees, the upheaval of the ground and the evidences of endless and monotonous labour oppress one, and of course it must have been infinitely worse then'.[4] Milne was fascinated by the countless German pillboxes that still punctuated the featureless land. Built of reinforced concrete to protect machine gunners or snipers, they often had several storeys. 'It was nice', he later wrote, 'to have something sticking above ground for a painting subject'.[5] Milne watched on occasion as army engineers tried to blow them up, but three of the watercolours (pp. 98, 99 and 106) show battered pillboxes still standing around Ypres in Flanders.

Moving back and forth across what had once been the battle lines between the Allies and the Germans, Milne spent considerable time on and around that crucial high point of Vimy, where thousands of men on both sides had fought and died. *Ablain-Saint-Nazaire Church from Lorette Ridge Looking toward Souchez and Vimy* (p. 101) shows the wasteland that was left. Milne had followed the Canadian capture of the ridge in 1917 with intense interest but face to face with the real place was surprised to find that it was no higher than the hills and ridges of his birthplace home in Bruce County in southern Ontario. 'It was only', he later wrote, 'when the crest was reached that the importance of Vimy ridge and the reason for all the heavy fighting was clear. It wasn't the highest ground, but, coming from the west it was the last high ground and from it I looked down over a plain stretching east into the haze.'[6]

Vimy was also about fighting underground, for it stood at the juncture where the heavy clay of Flanders and the northwest of France gives way to much harder chalk, ideal for tunnelling. During the war, the land around Vimy became a labyrinth of tunnels and bunkers carved deep underground as engineers on both sides tried to dig under each other's fortifications and blow them up. Tonnes of explosives were carefully and quietly put into place and detonated, leaving gigantic craters. Milne painted several, including those nicknamed the Twins (p. 97), as well as a nameless one near Vimy railway station (p. 96). He also started work on what was called the New York crater but fragments from explosions set off by the work parties fell uncomfortably close, so he moved along to the Montreal crater, created in November 1916 when 24 tonnes of explosives sent German lines sky high and created one of the largest craters on the Western Front. 'After all', Milne commented, 'one crater was very much like another'.[7] The consequence, however, is one of his most famous works, *Montreal Crater, Vimy Ridge* (pp. 94–5). Tiny human figures just on the skyline show the crater's sheer size—Milne described it as 'deep enough to hold a house or even a church'[8]—and highlight its emptiness. It looks as though an asteroid had landed.

When Beaverbrook set up his War Memorials Fund, he did not think that there were any Canadian artists worth commissioning. Milne's work—and that of his fellow Canadian artists such as A.Y. Jackson and Frederick Varley—show how wrong that assumption was. Milne's war paintings are among his greatest works and provide a fitting memorial to one of the deadliest conflicts in modern history.

Margaret MacMillan *is a professor of history at the University of Toronto and specialises in the international history of the nineteenth and twentieth centuries. Her latest book is* The War That Ended Peace: How Europe Abandoned Peace for the First World War *(in North America titled* The Road to 1914*).*

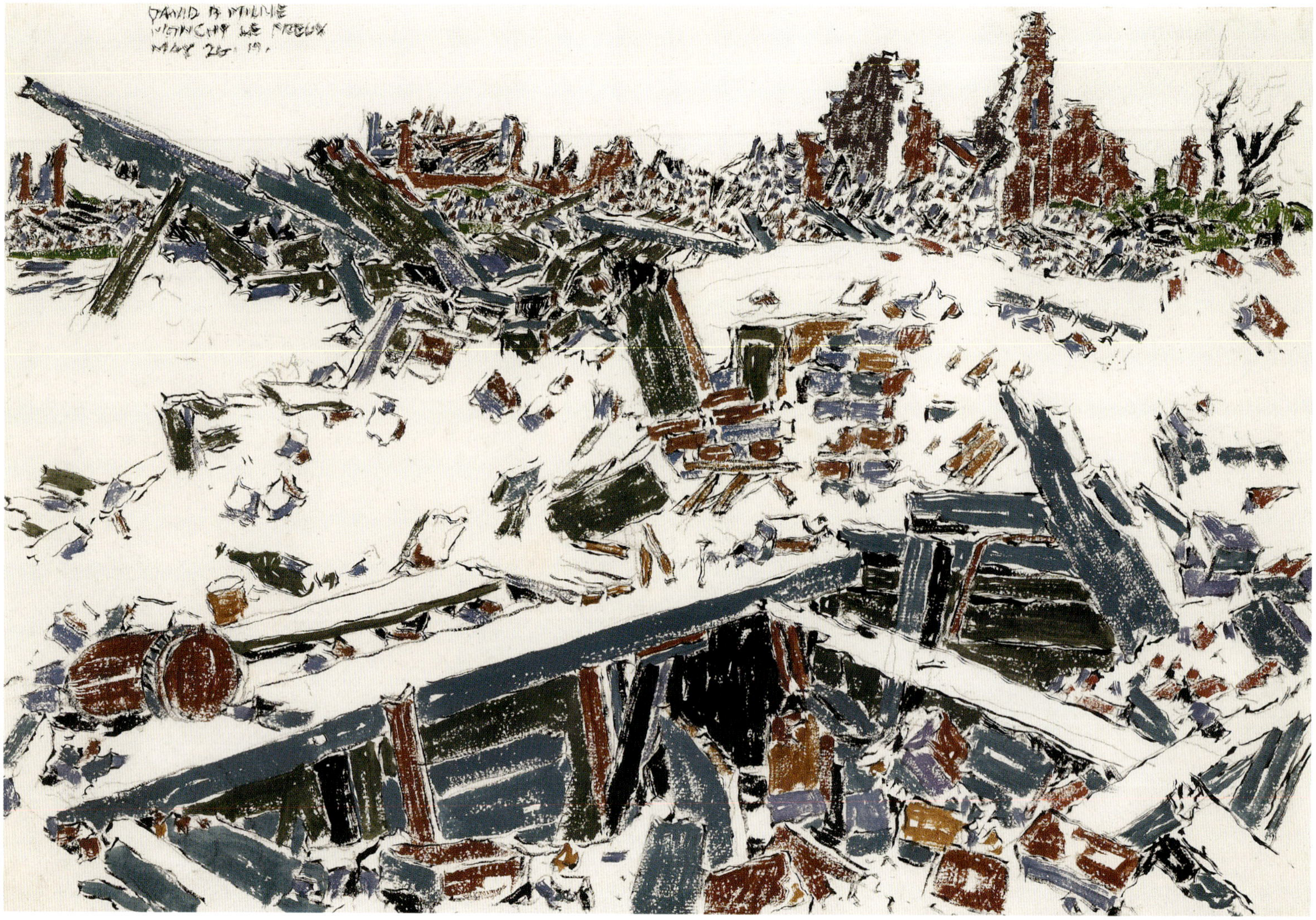

Entrance to Cellar Shelter in Monchy-le-Preux
1919, watercolour over graphite on wove paper

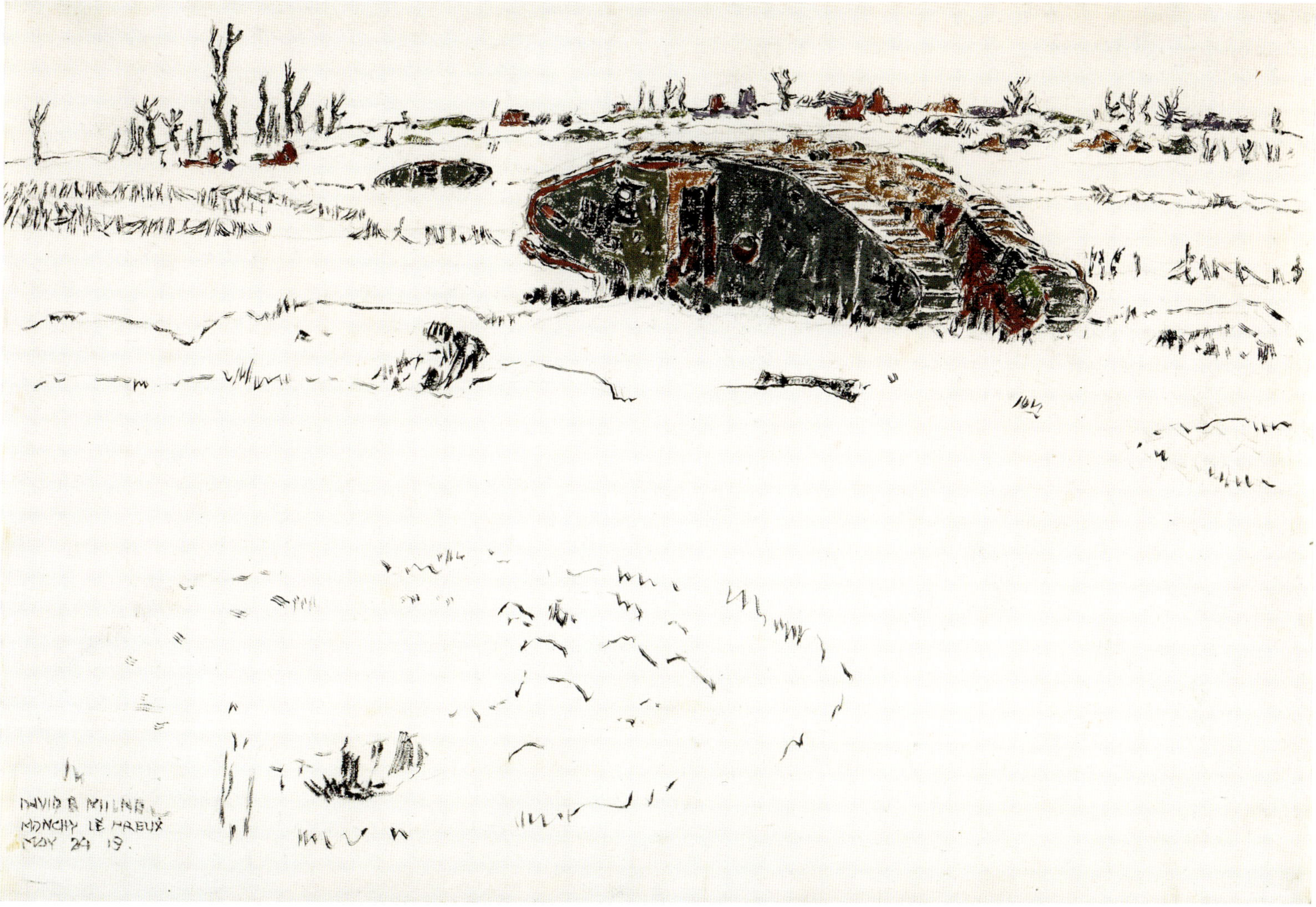

Wrecked Tanks outside Monchy-le-Preux
1919, watercolour over graphite on wove paper

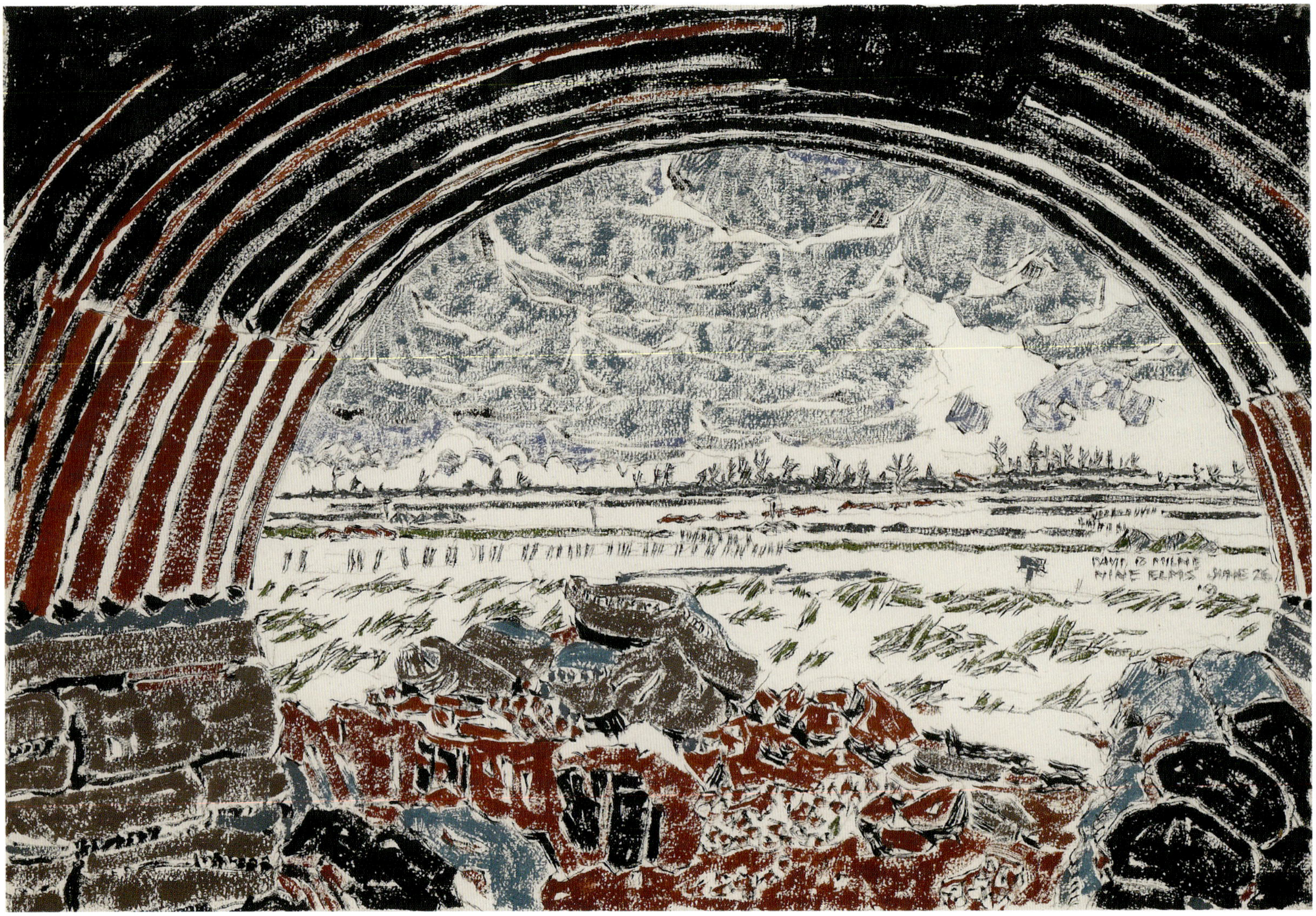

Looking towards Thélus and Thélus Wood from a Nissen Hut under the Nine Elms
1919, watercolour over graphite on wove paper

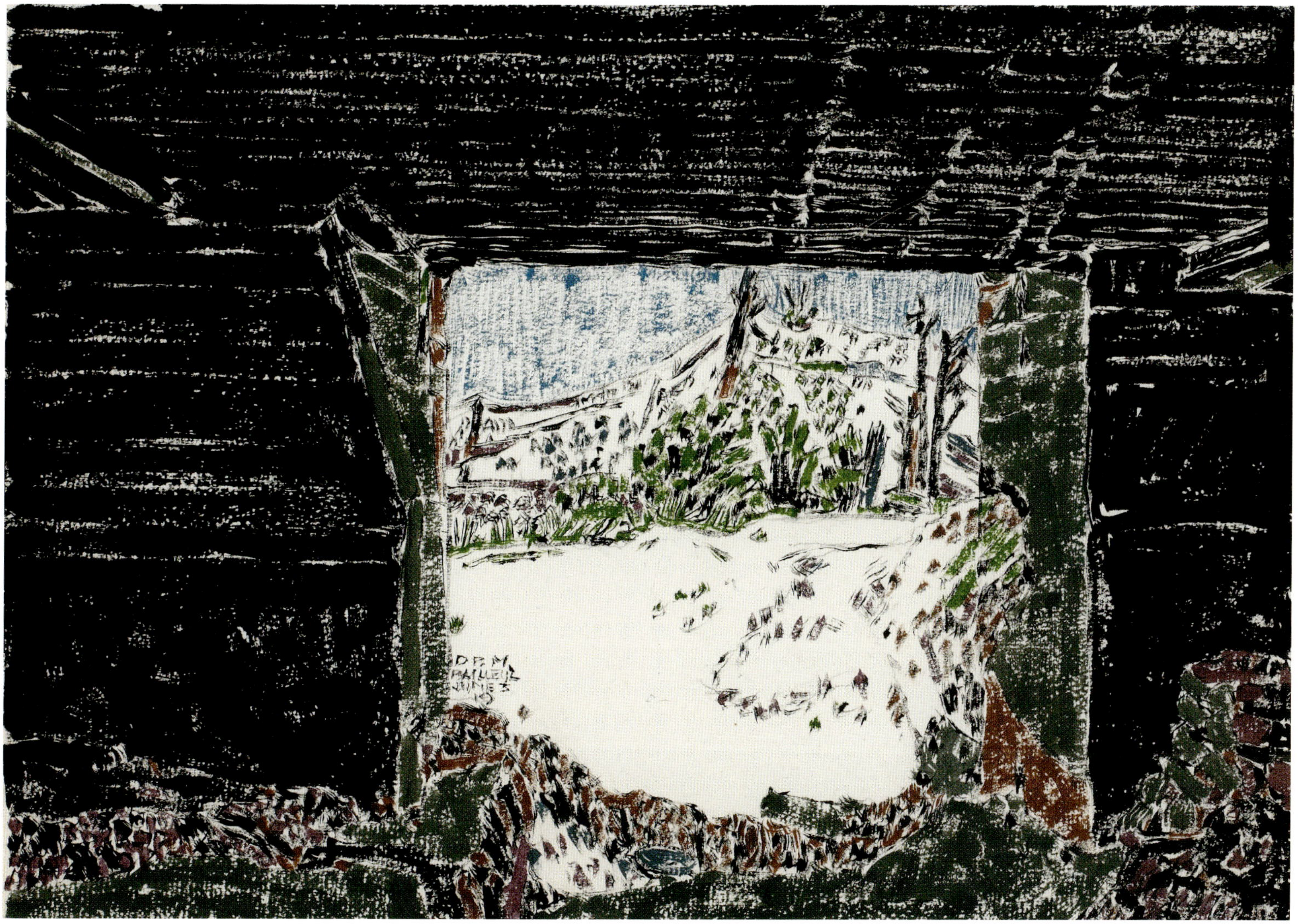

From a German Gun-pit at Bailleul, East of Vimy
1919, watercolour over graphite on wove paper

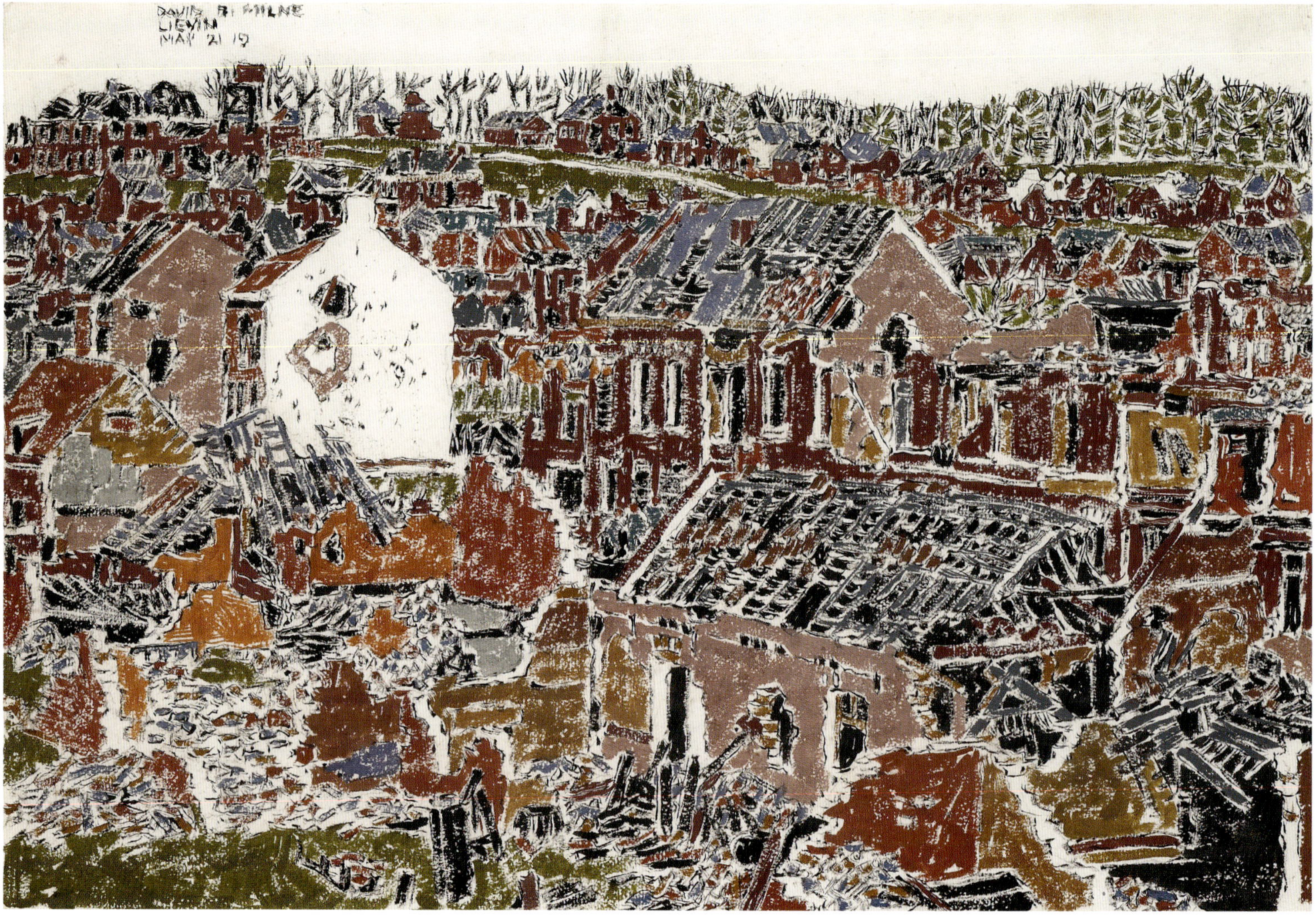

Liévin
1919, watercolour over graphite on wove paper

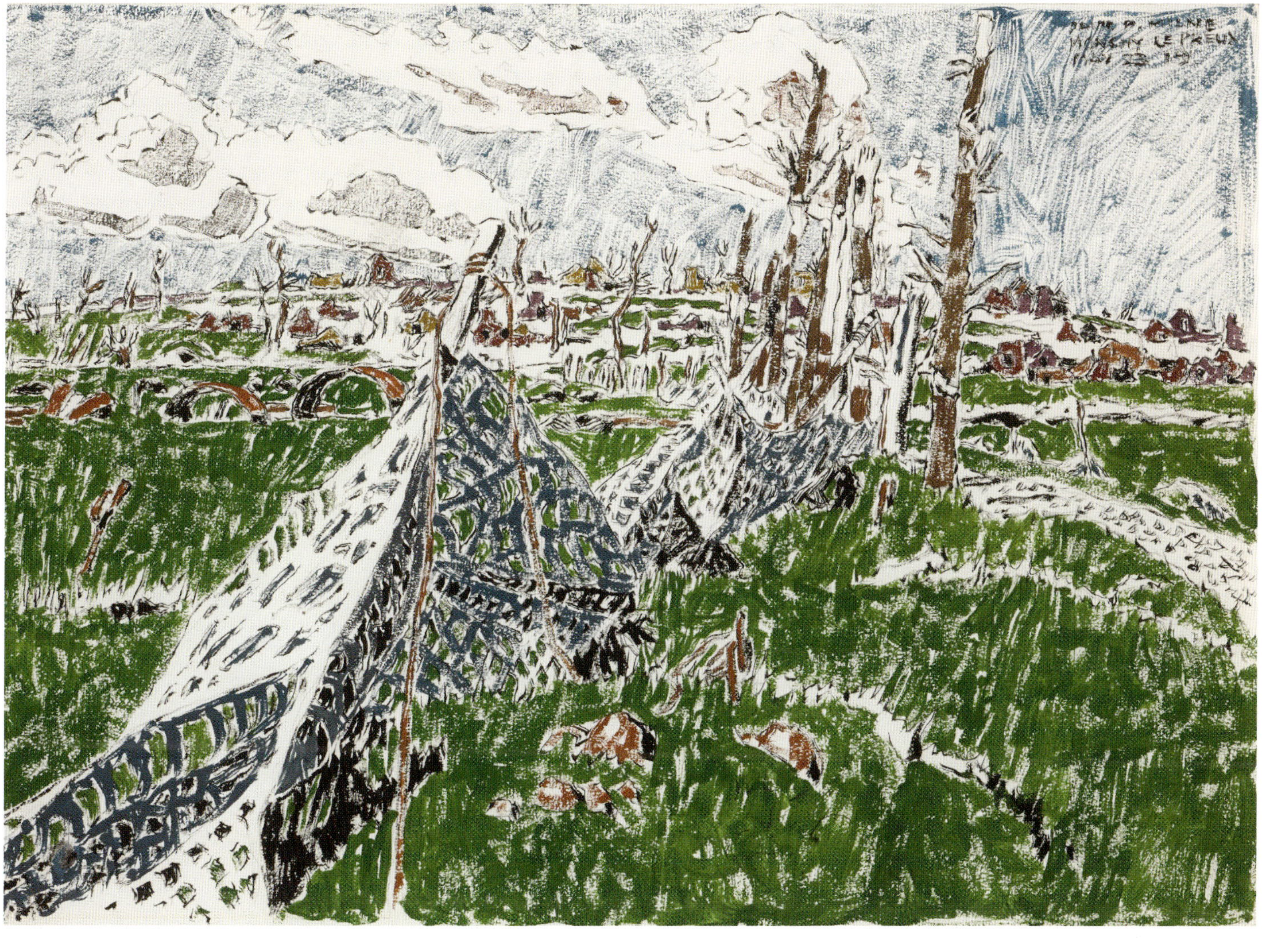

Screened Road into Monchy-le-Preux
1919, watercolour over graphite on
wove paper

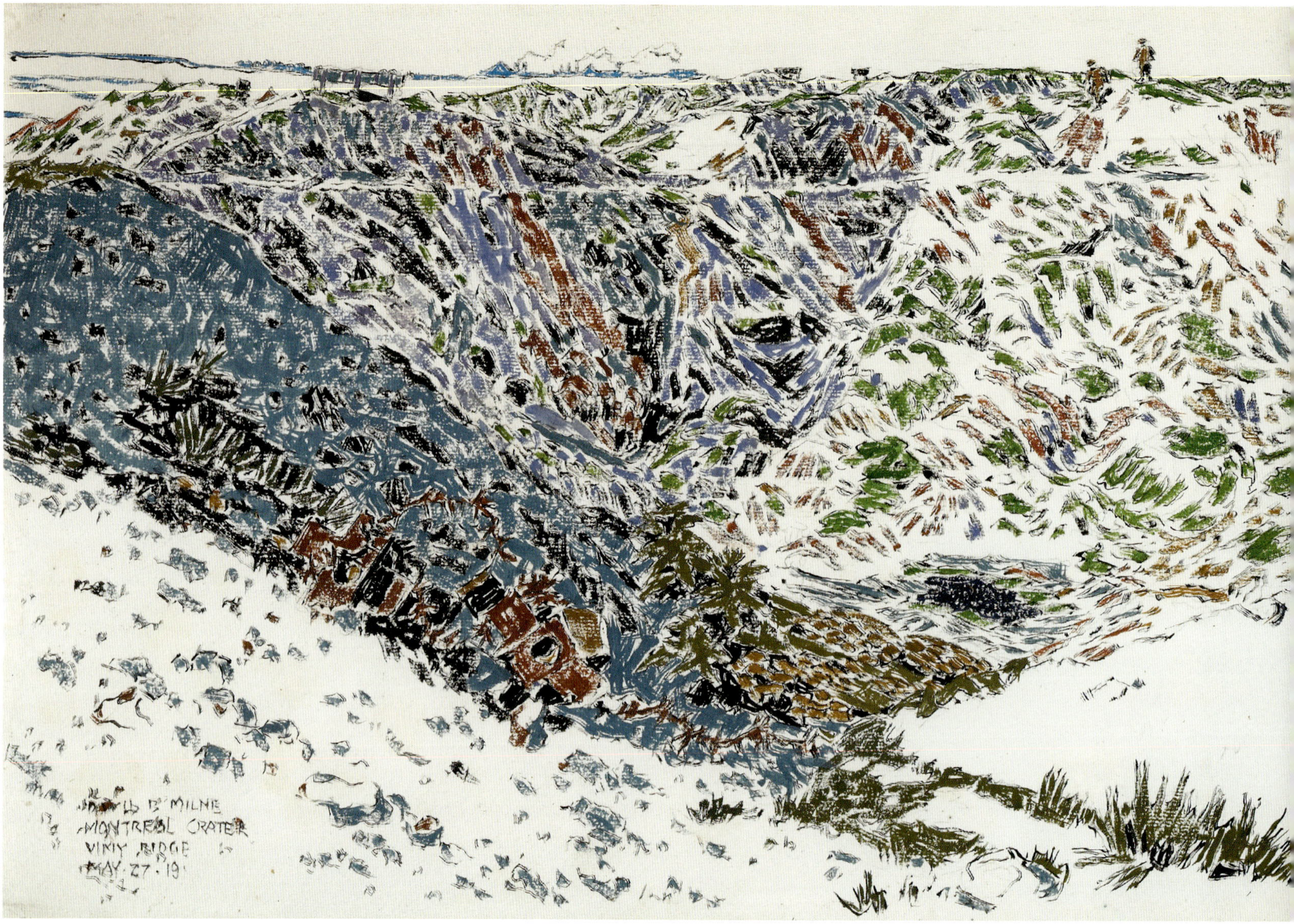
B. MILNE
MONTREAL CRATER
VIMY RIDGE
MAY 27 19

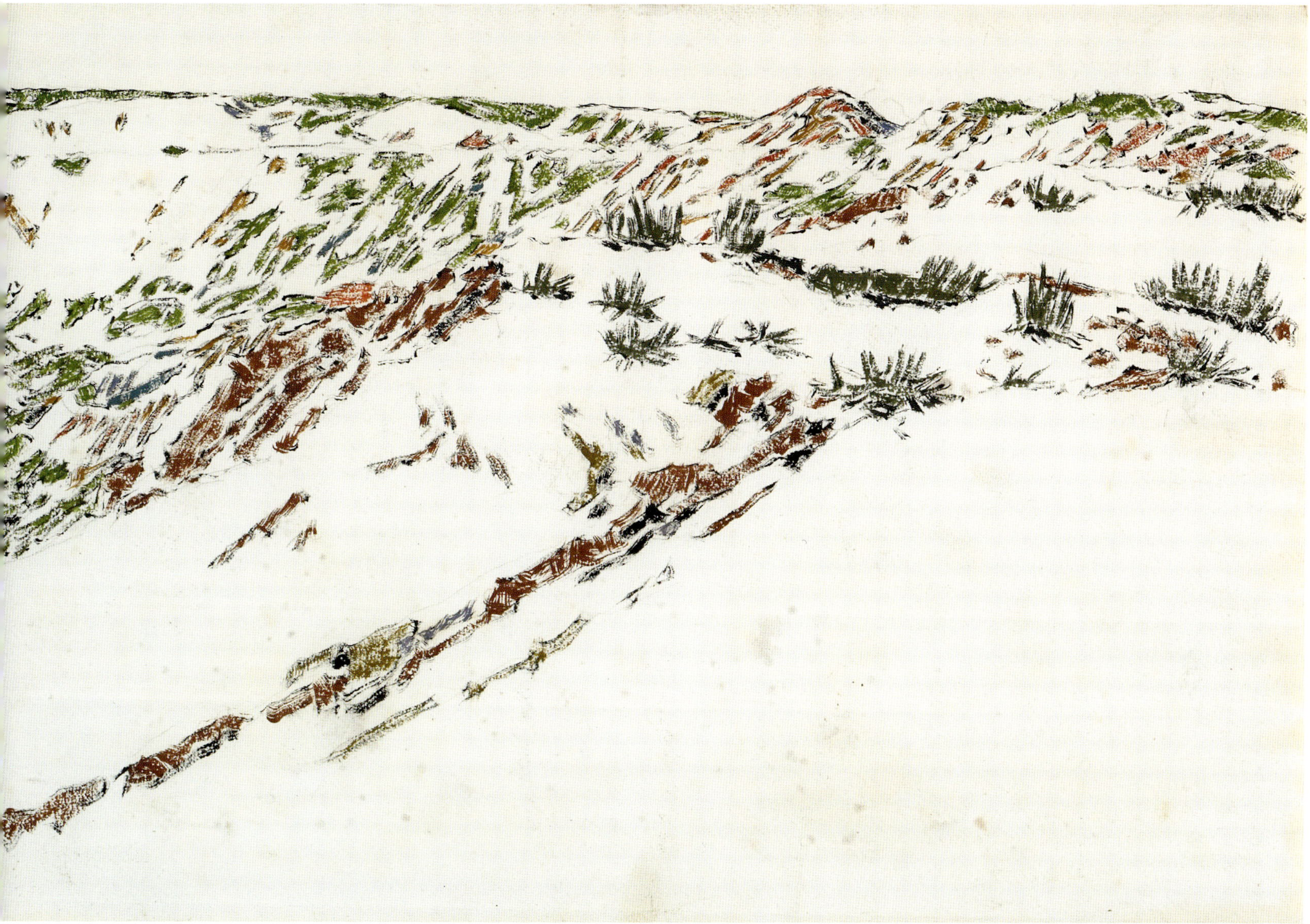

Montreal Crater, Vimy Ridge
1919, watercolour over graphite on
wove paper

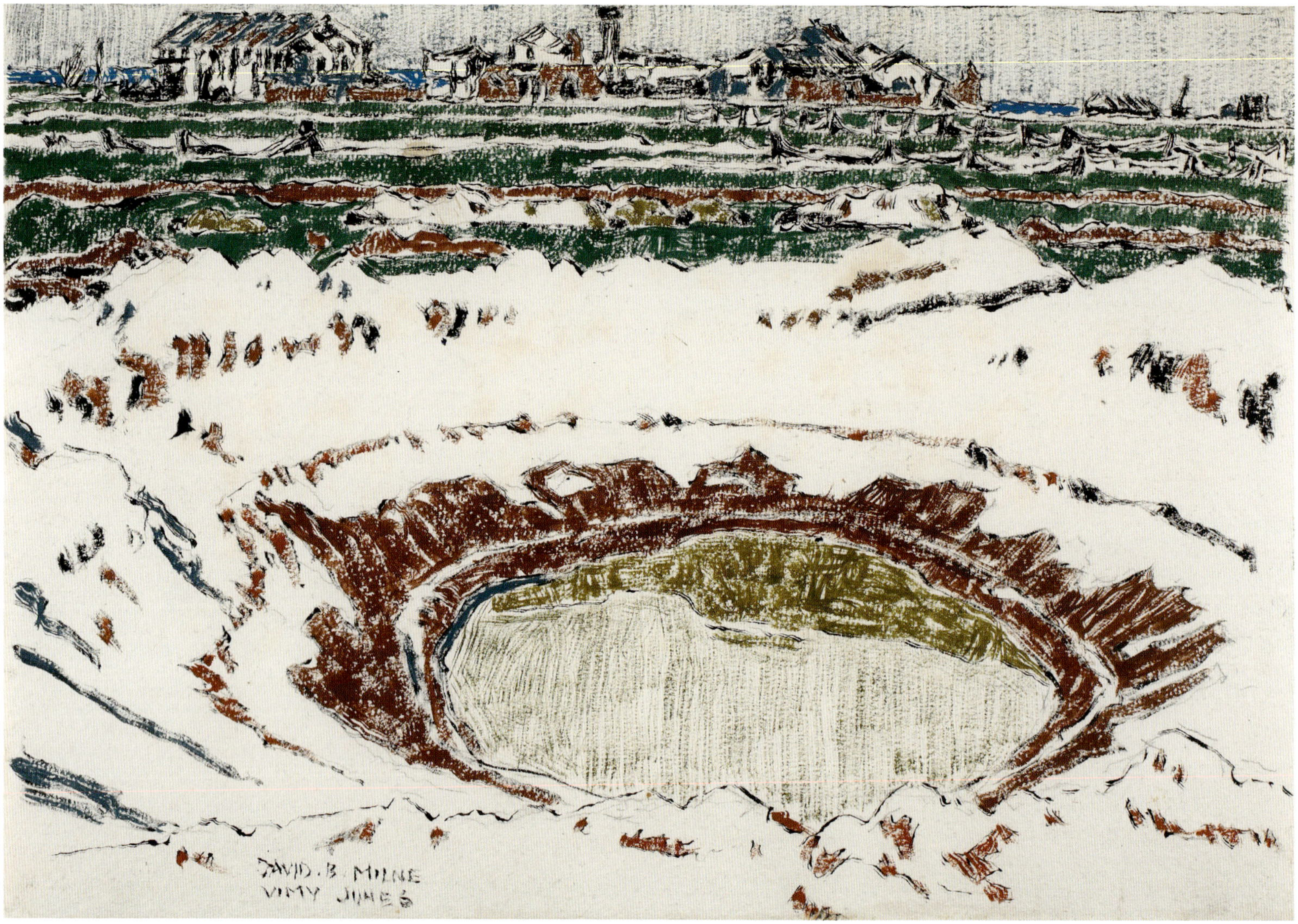

Bomb Crater behind Vimy Station
1919, watercolour over graphite on wove paper

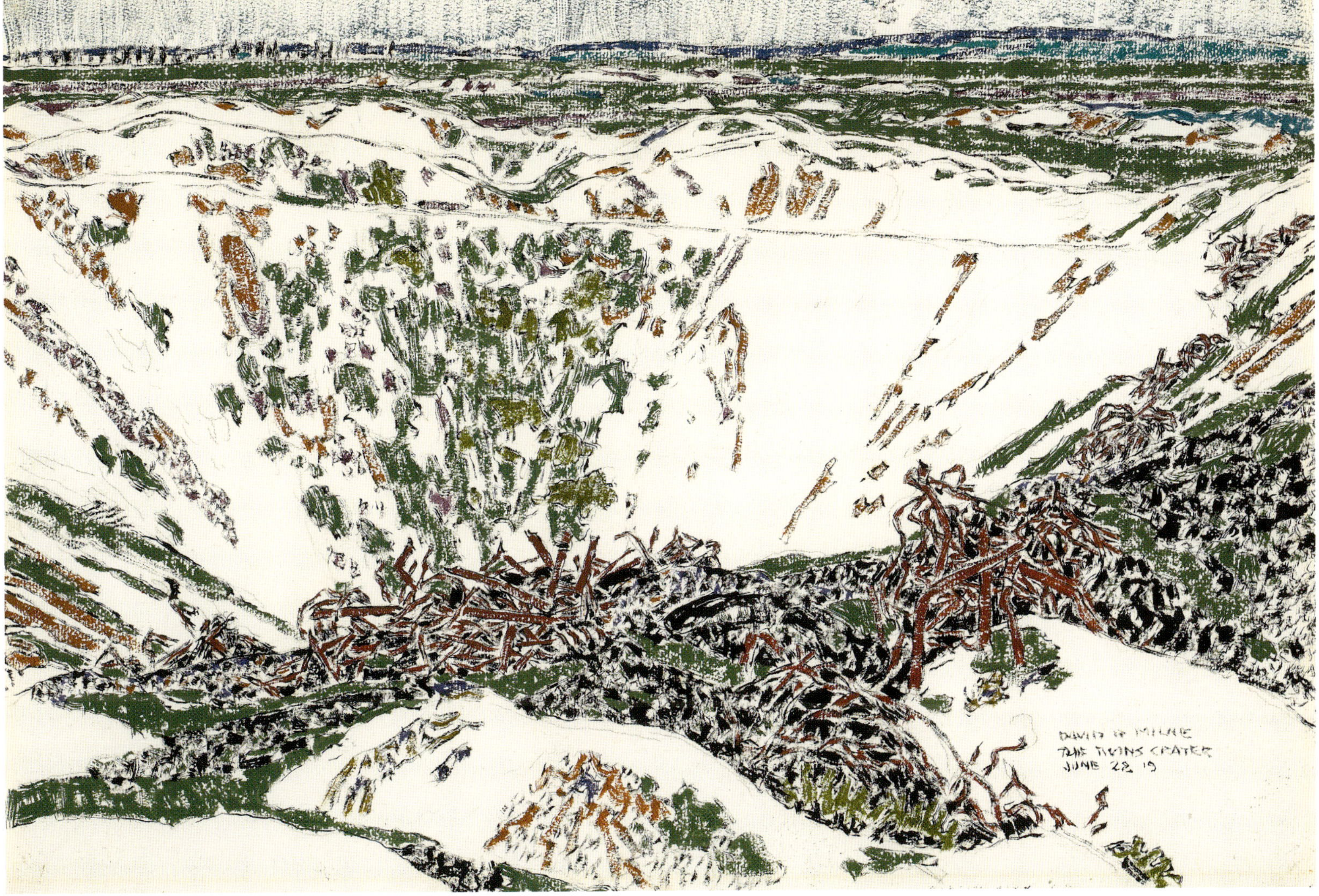

'The Twins' Crater, Vimy Ridge
1919, watercolour over graphite on
wove paper

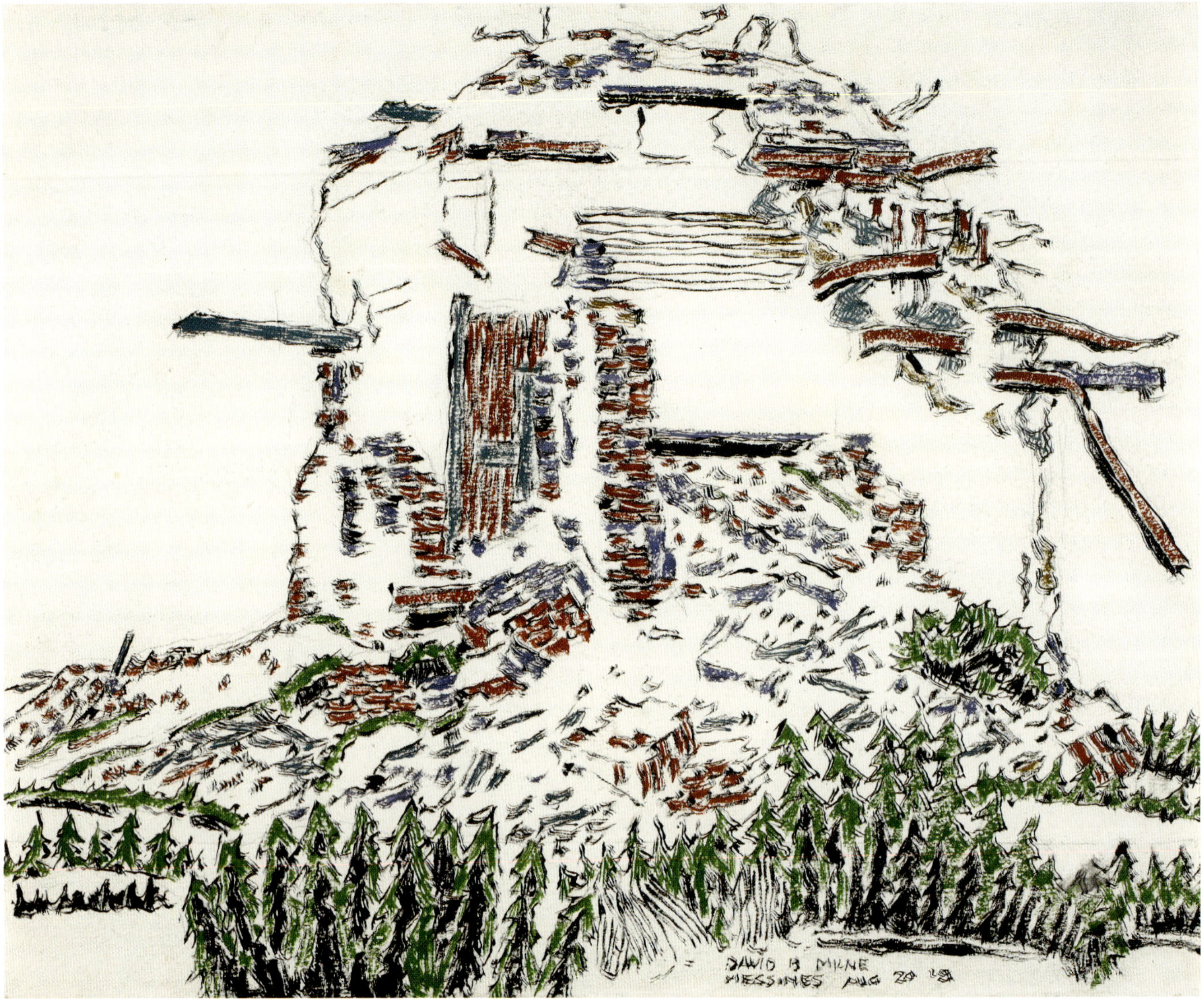

German Pillbox at Messines
1919, watercolour over graphite on
wove paper

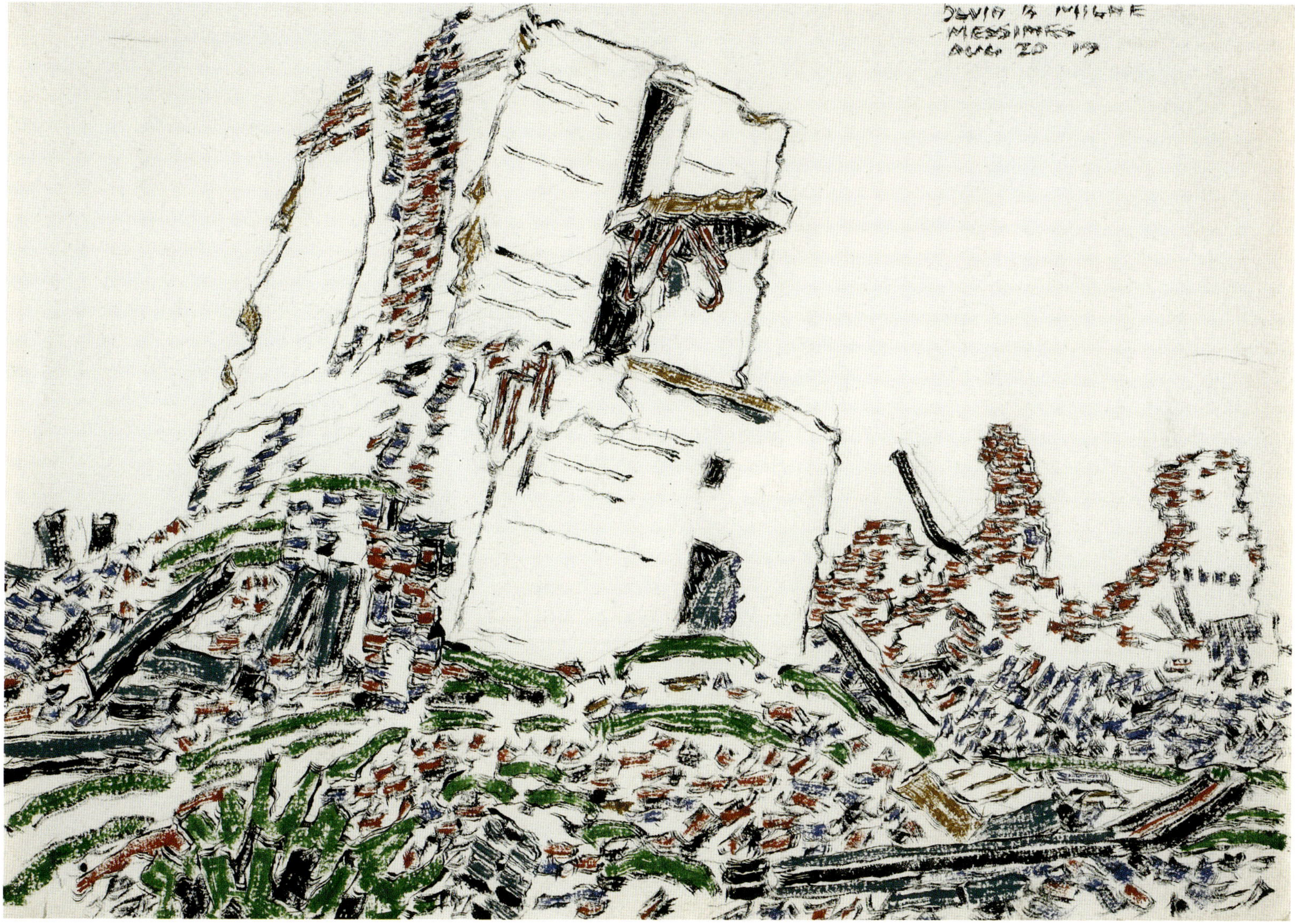

Skyscraper Pillbox at Messines
1919, watercolour over graphite on
wove paper

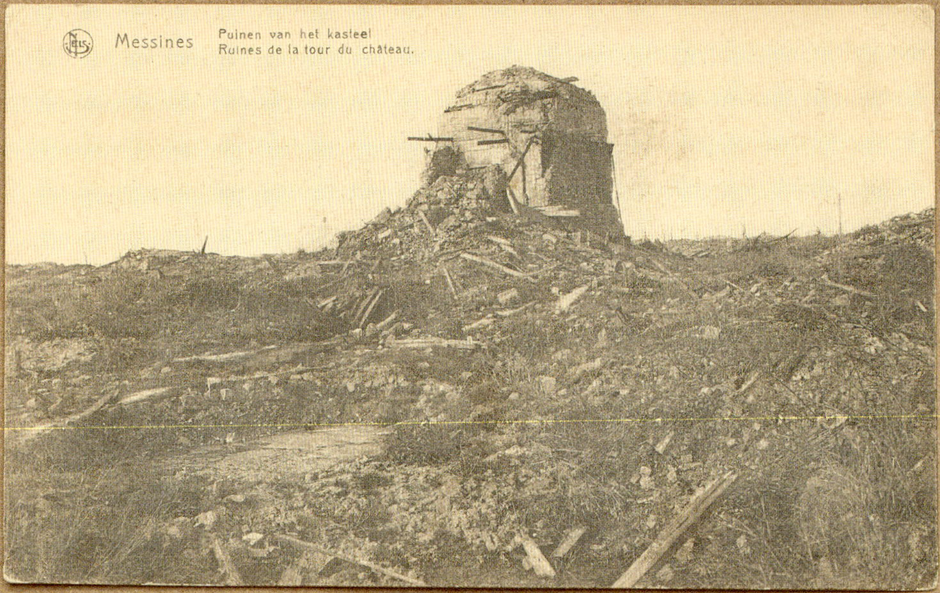
Messines
Puinen van het kasteel
Ruines de la tour du château.

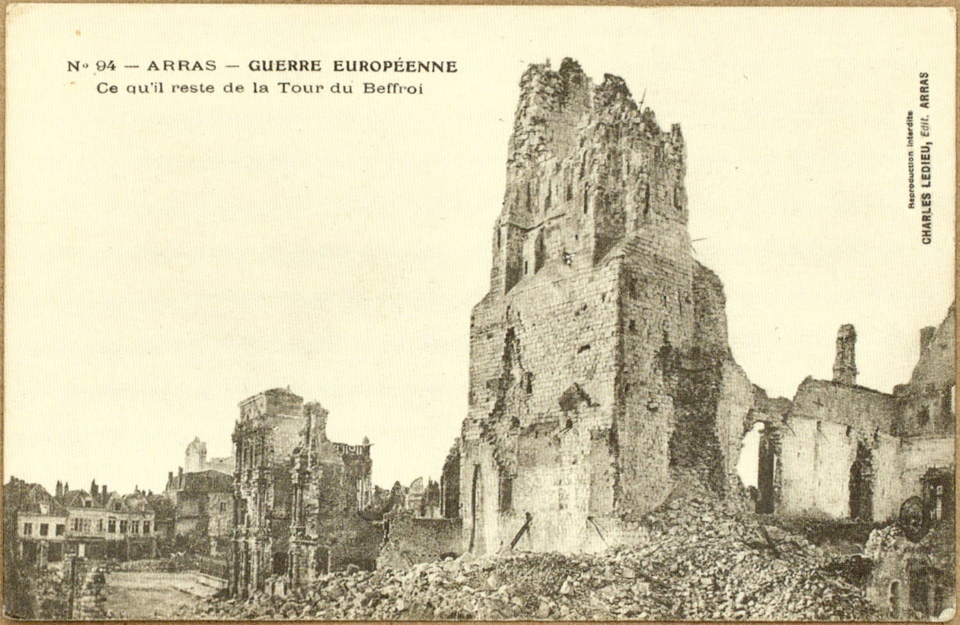
N° 94 — ARRAS — GUERRE EUROPÉENNE
Ce qu'il reste de la Tour du Beffroi
Reproduction interdite
CHARLES LEDIEU, Edit. ARRAS

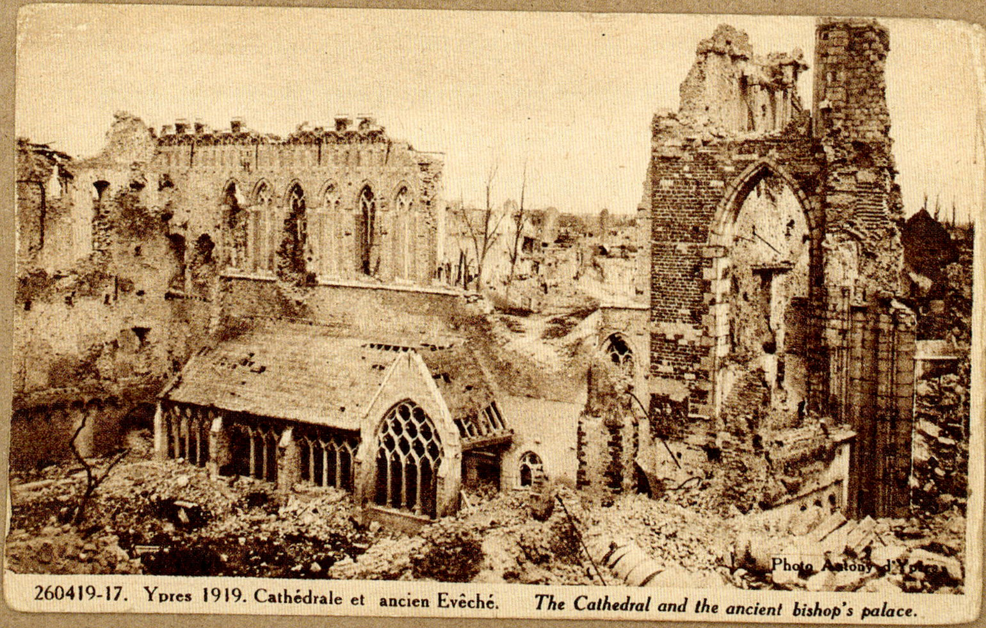
Photo Antony d'Y
260419-17. Ypres 1919. Cathédrale et ancien Evêché. *The Cathedral and the ancient bishop's palace.*

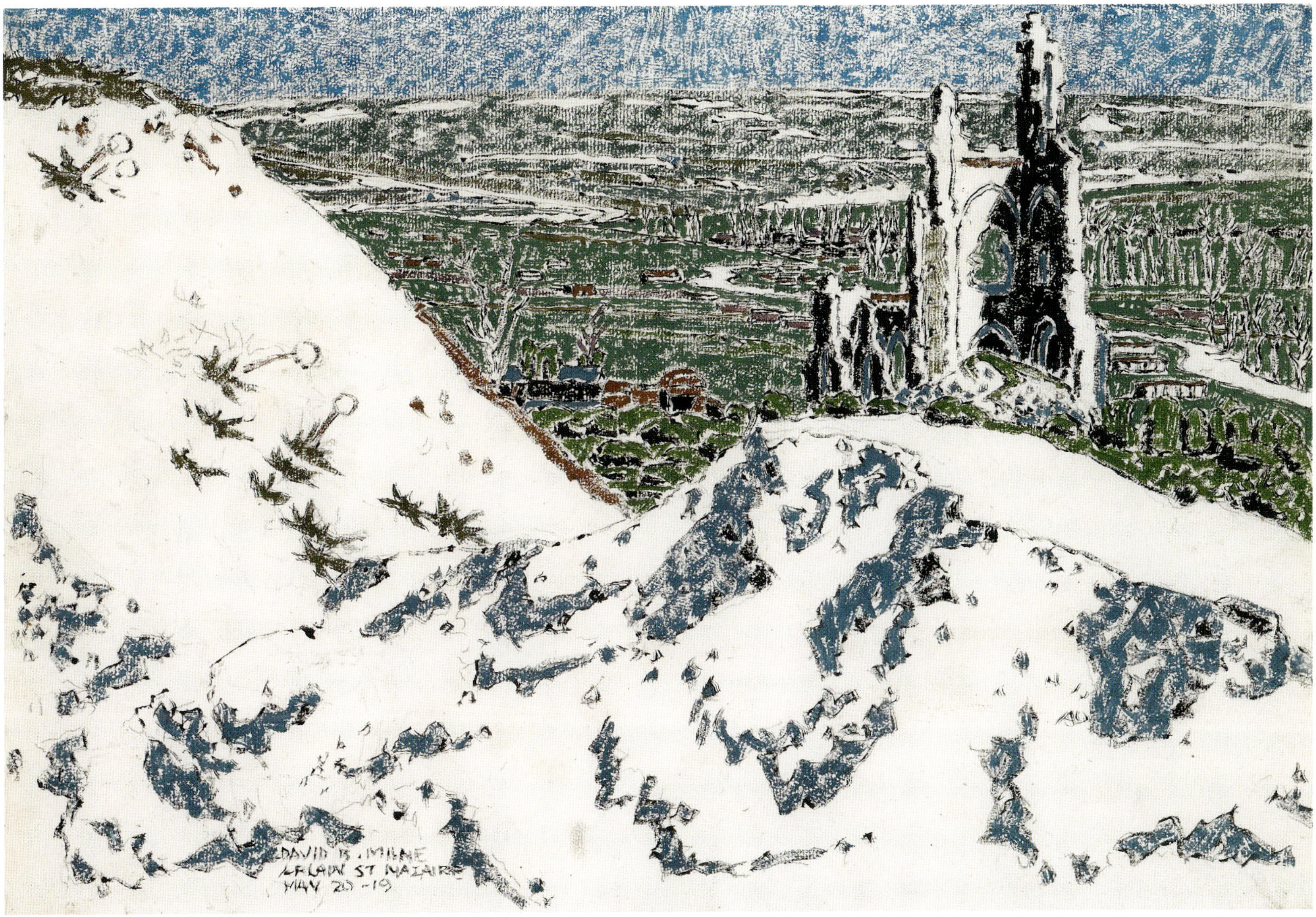

Opposite
Postcards
Acquired by David Milne in France or Belgium in 1919

Ablain-Saint-Nazaire Church from Lorette Ridge Looking toward Souchez and Vimy
1919, watercolour over graphite on wove paper

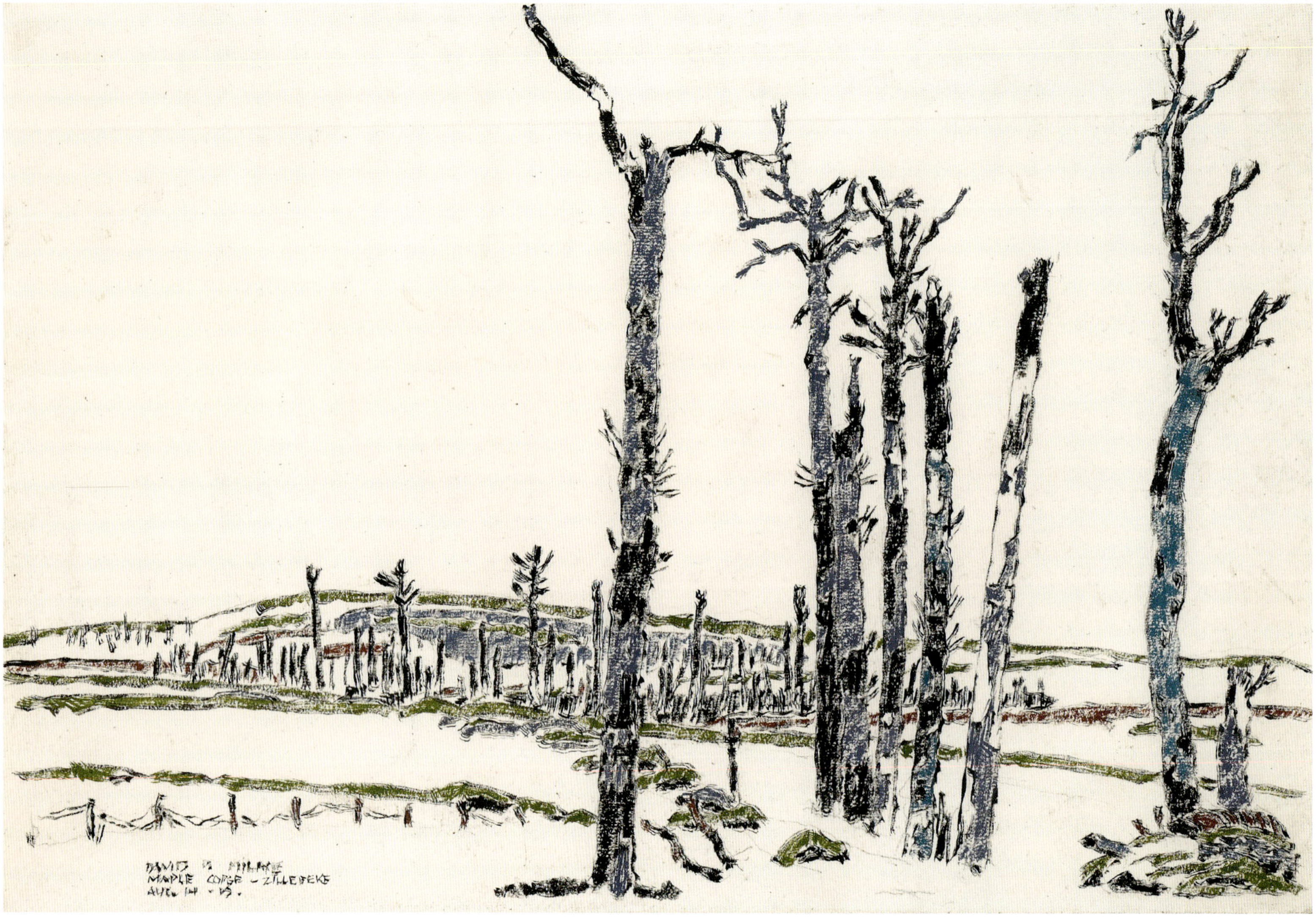

Zillebeke: Maple Copse and Observatory Ridge from Dormy House
1919, watercolour over graphite on wove paper

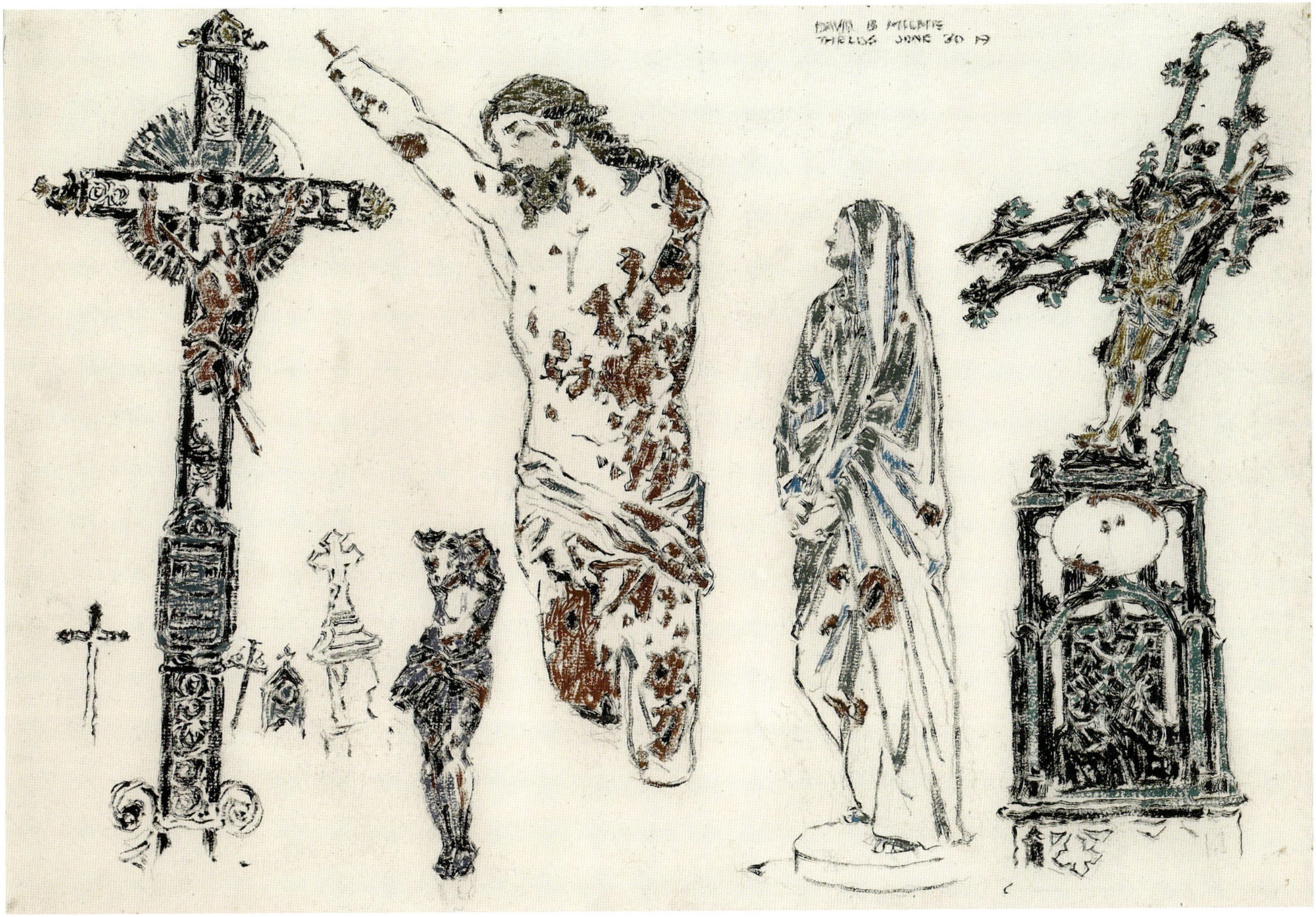

Shattered Images in Thélus Cemetery
1919, watercolour over graphite on
wove paper

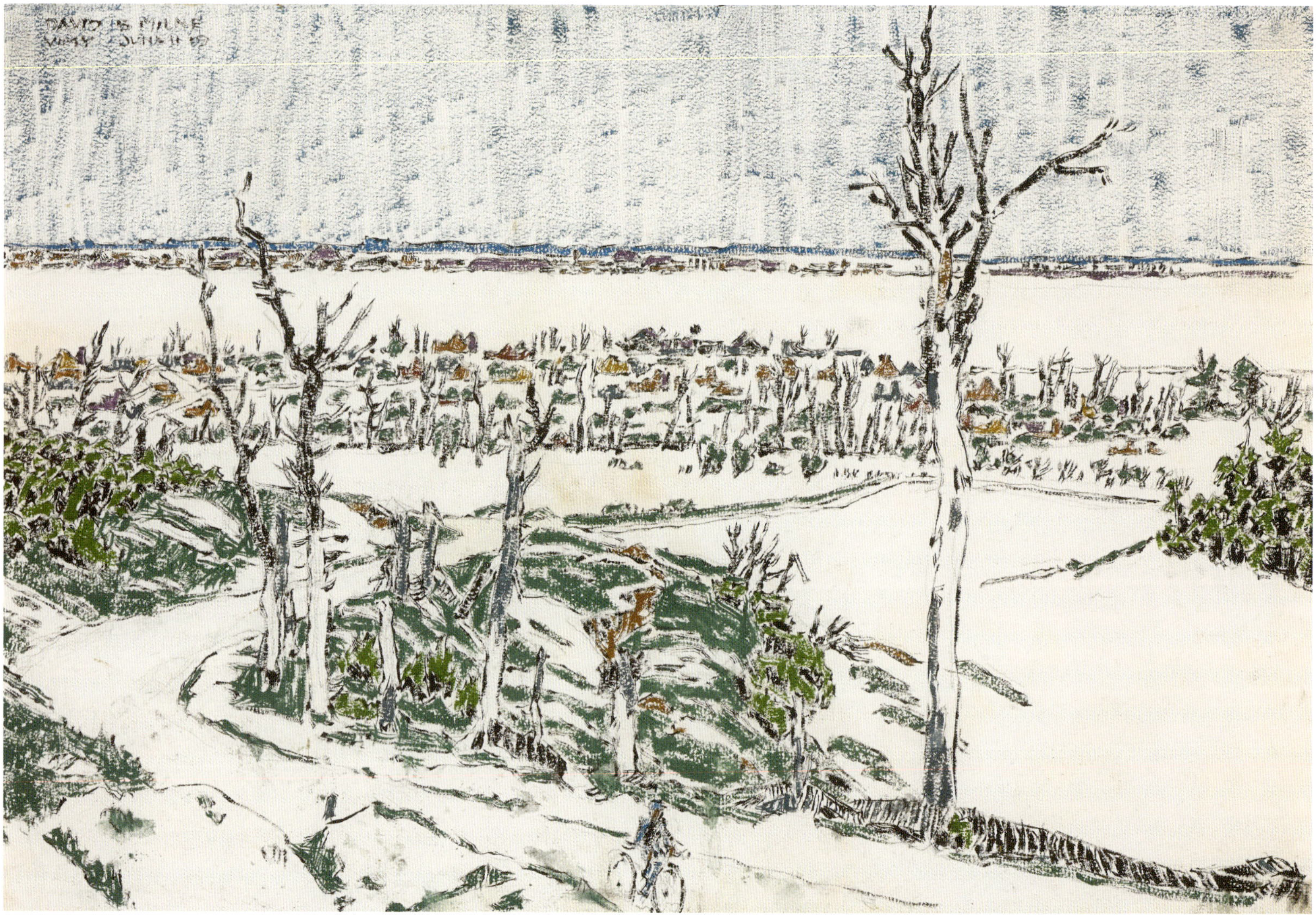

The Bend in the Arras–Lens Road above Vimy Village
1919, watercolour over graphite on wove paper

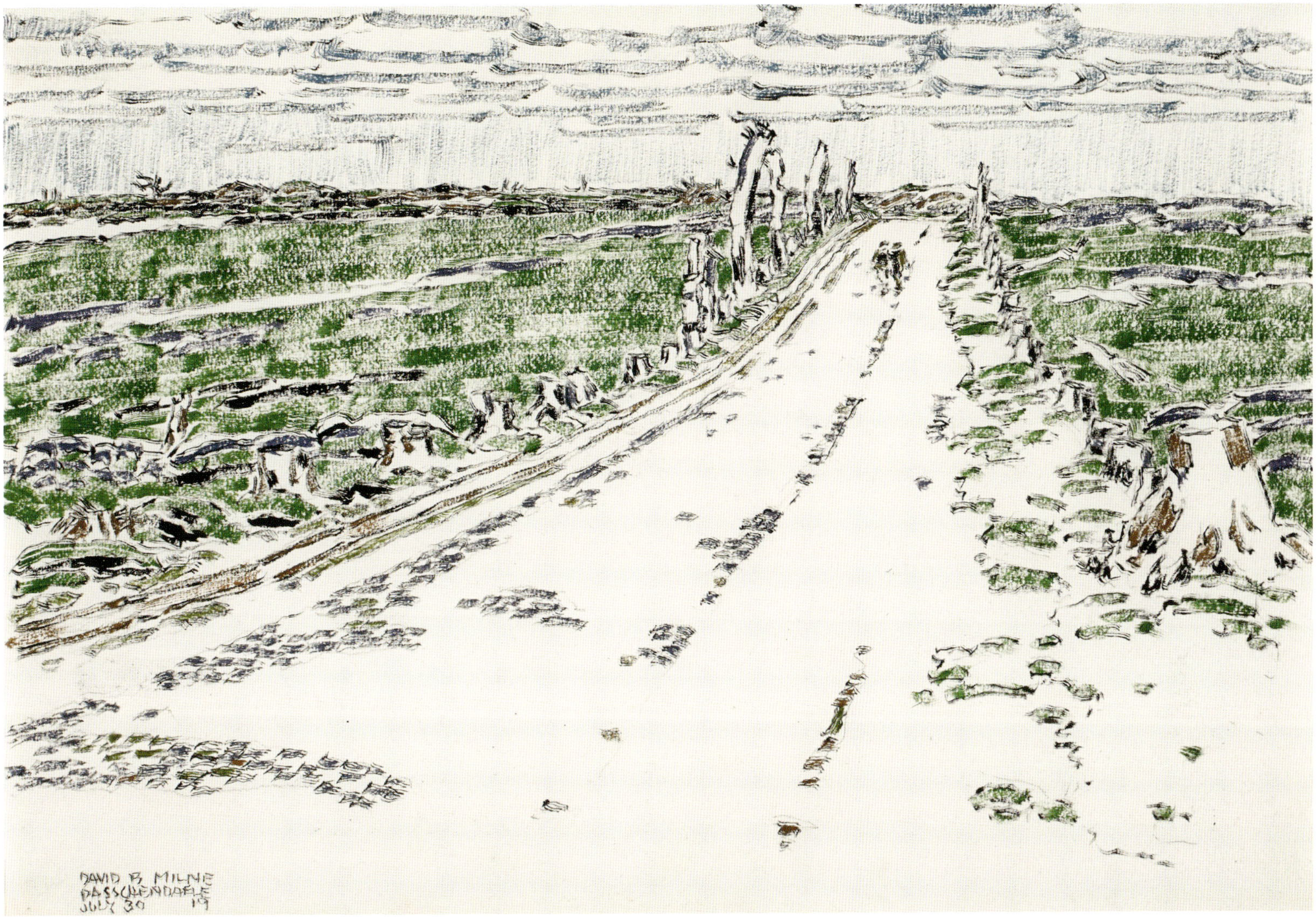

Passchendaele, Ruins of the Church at the End of the Road
1919, watercolour over graphite on wove paper

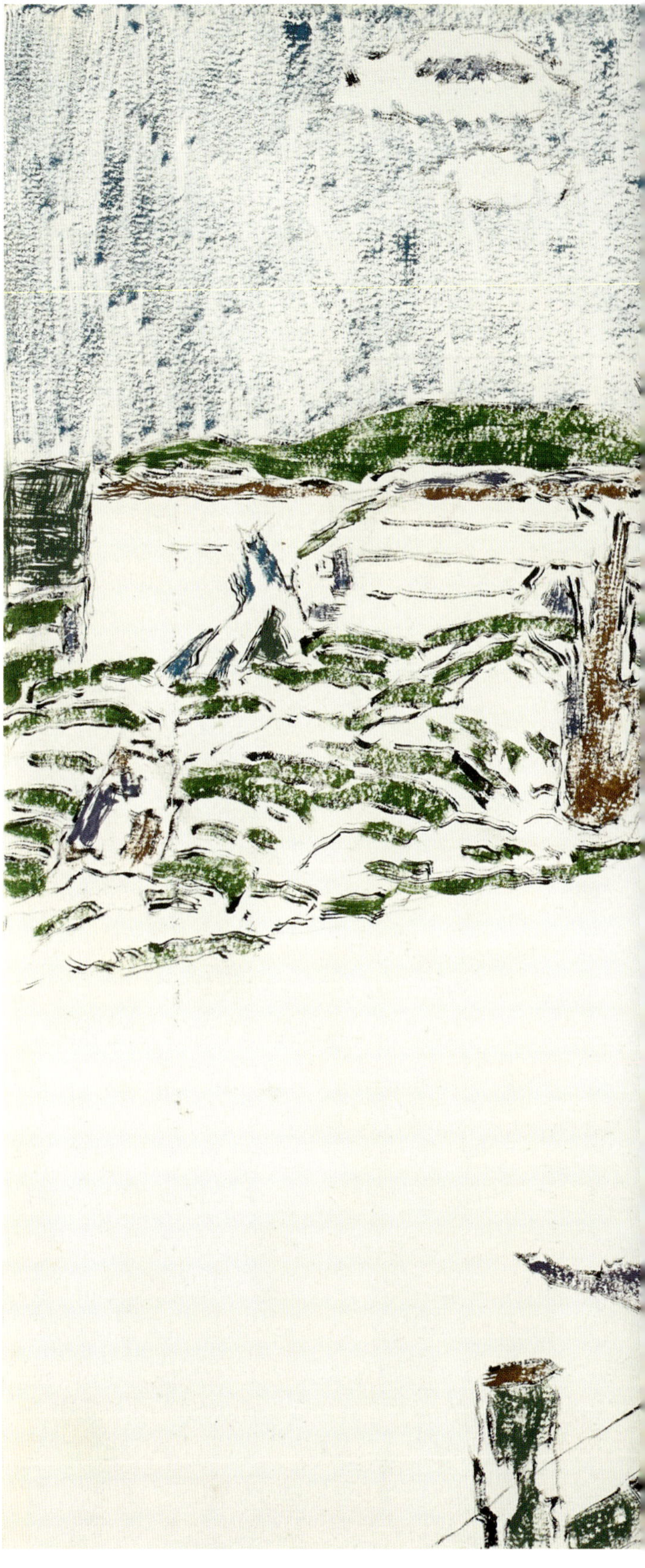

The Road to Passchendaele, German Pillboxes on Each Side
1919, watercolour over graphite on wove paper

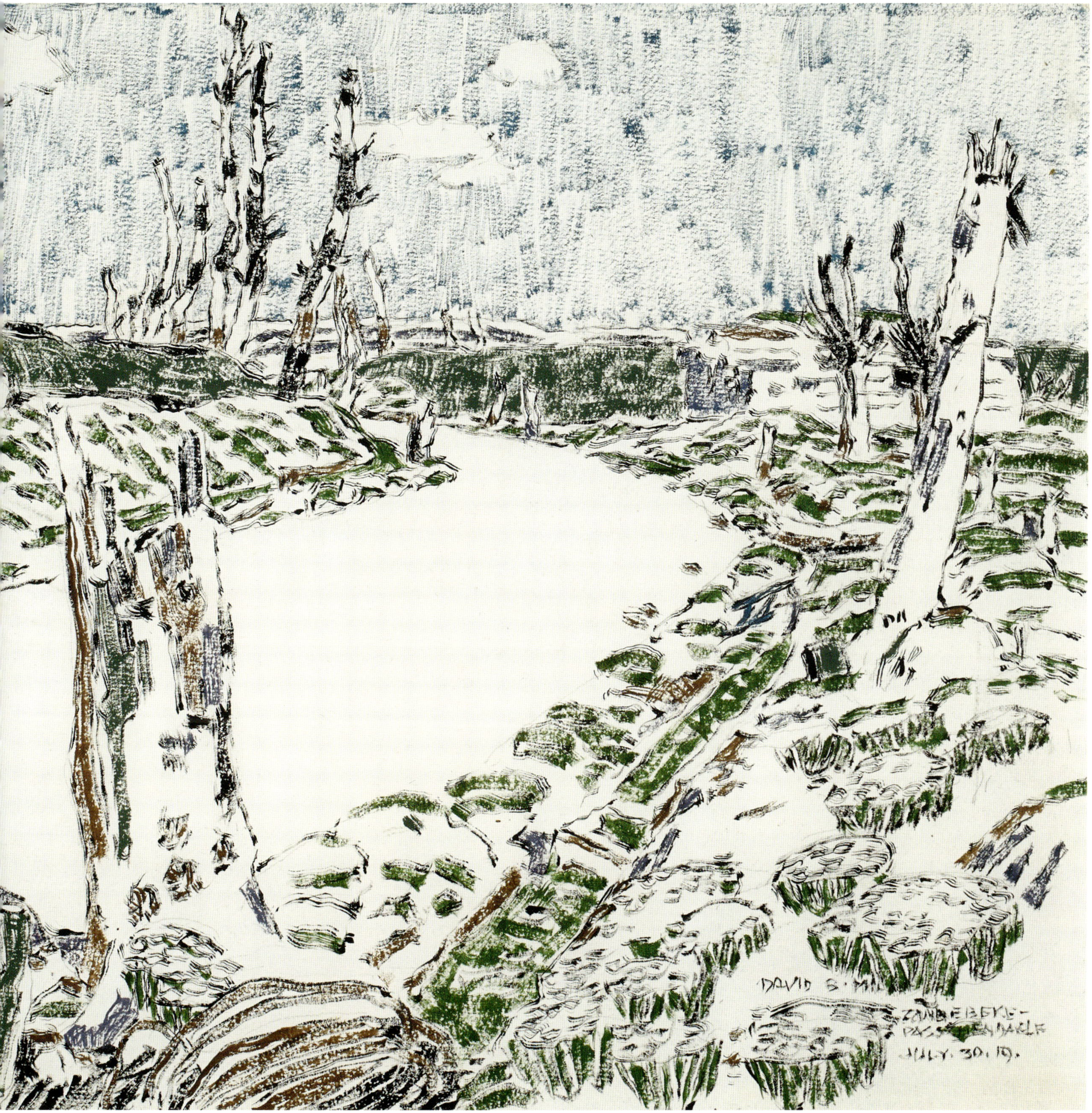
DAVID B.
JULY. 30. 19.

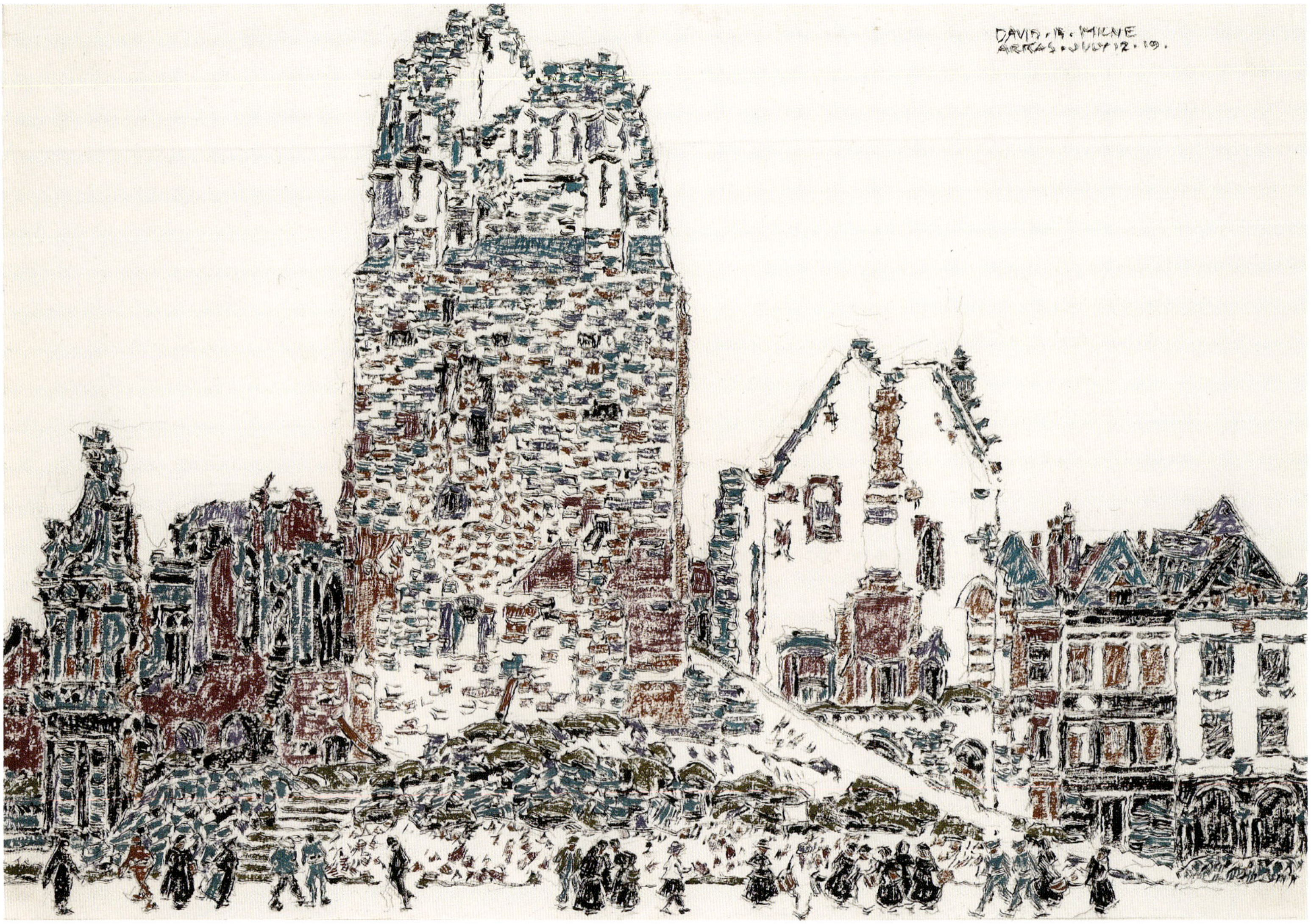

The Belfry, Hôtel de Ville, Arras
1919, watercolour over graphite on
wove paper

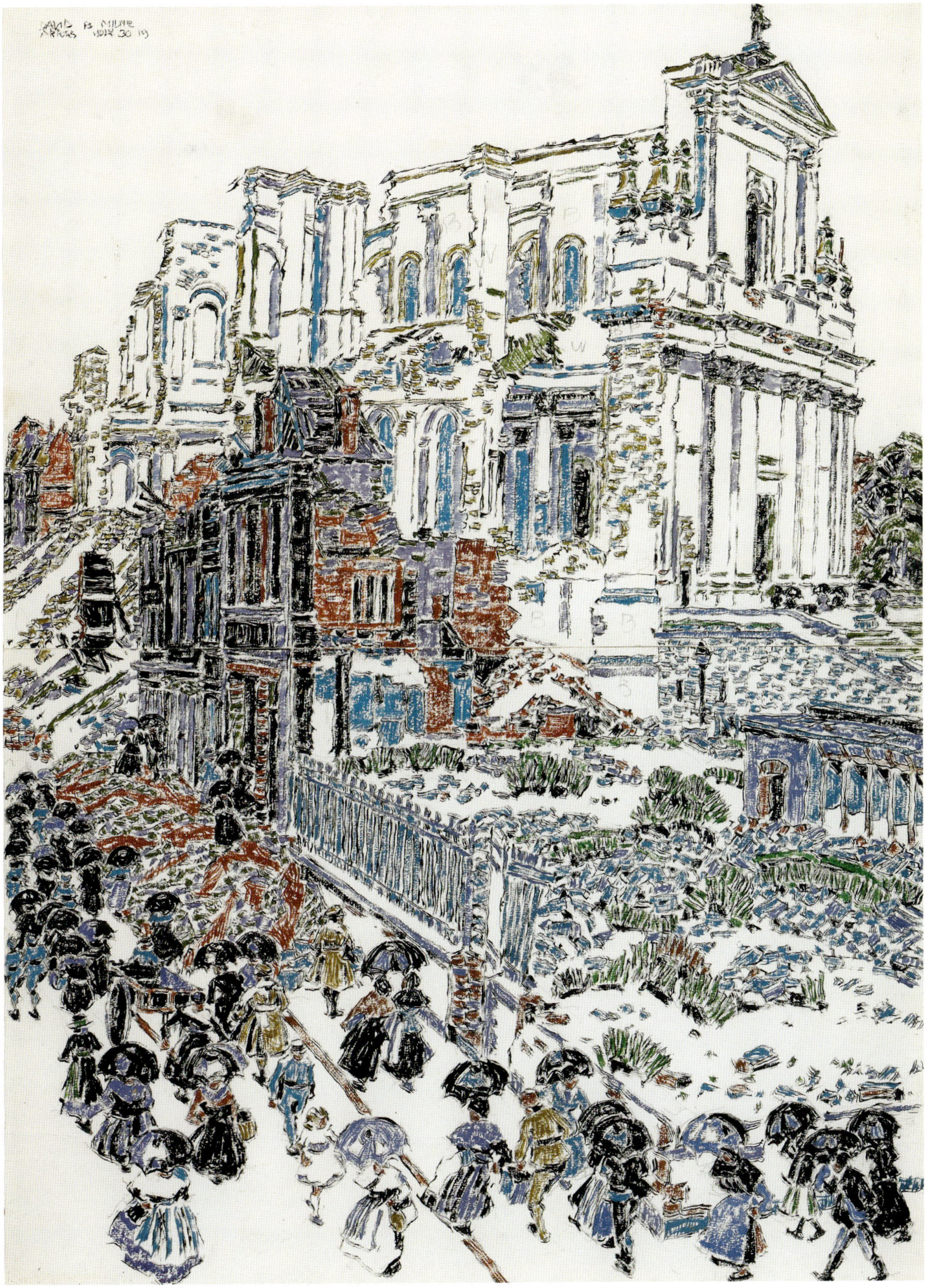

The Cathedral, Arras
1919, watercolour over graphite on
wove paper

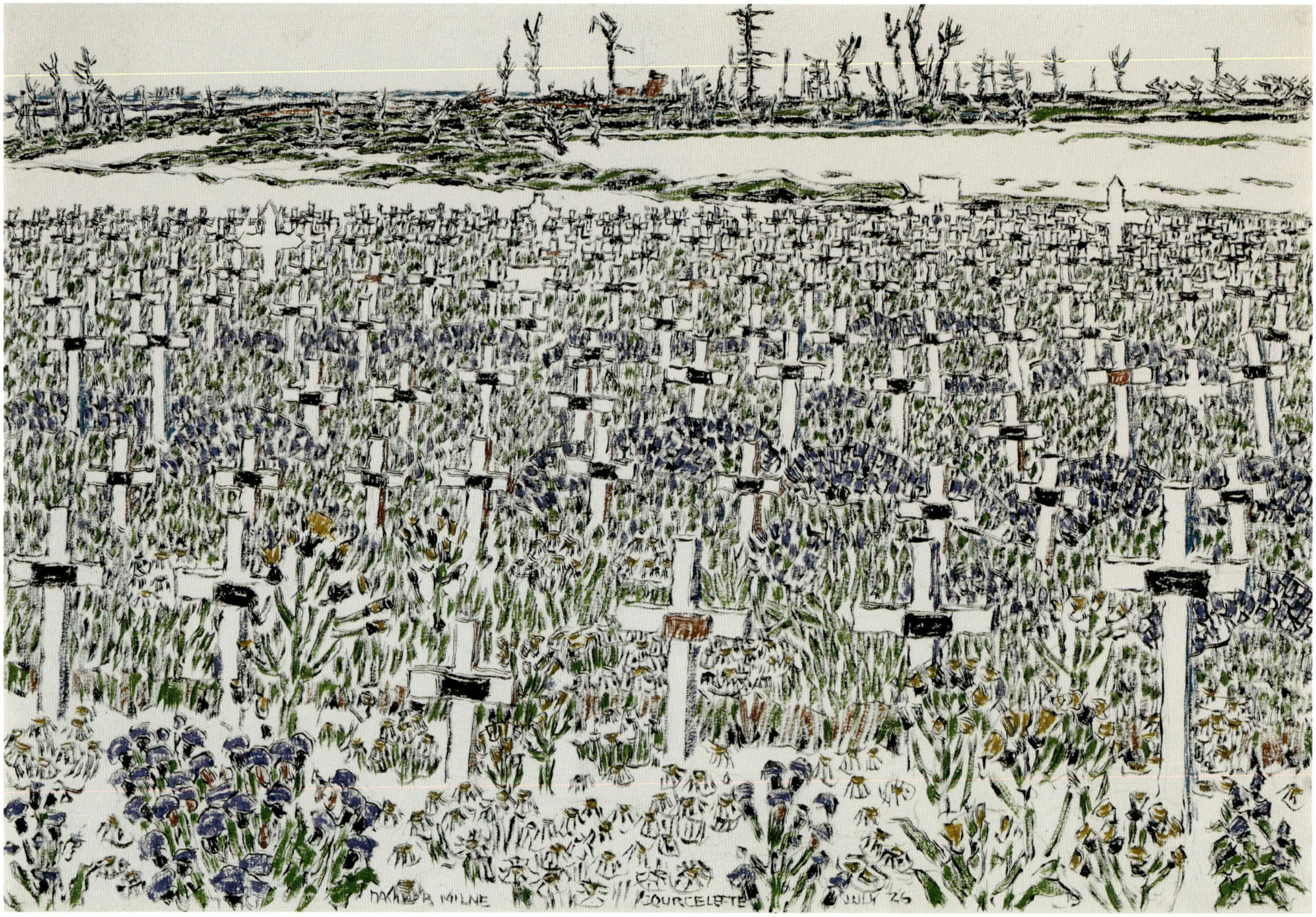

Courcelette from the Cemetery
1919, watercolour over graphite on
wove paper

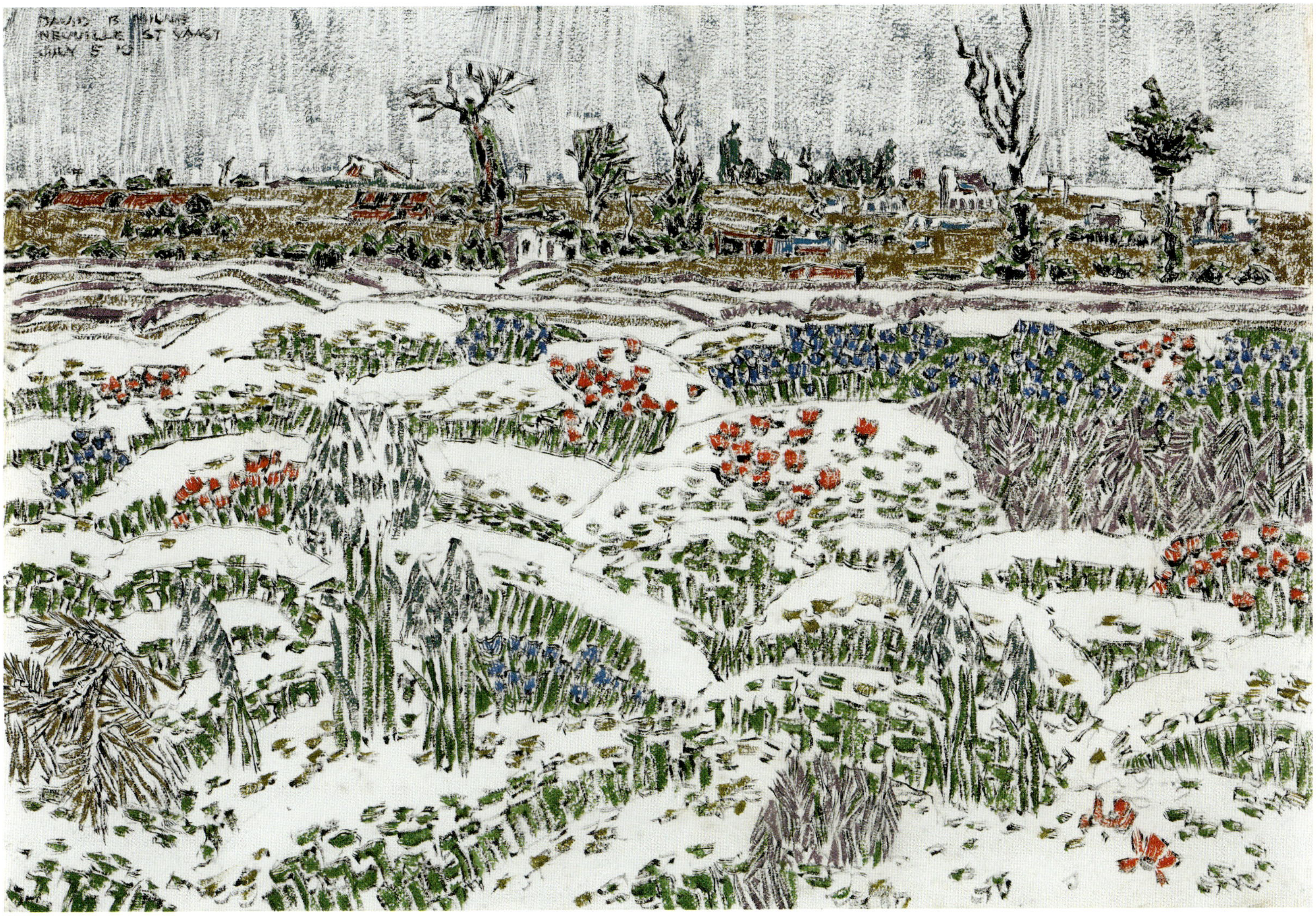

Neuville-Saint-Vaast from the Poppy Fields
1919, watercolour over graphite on wove paper

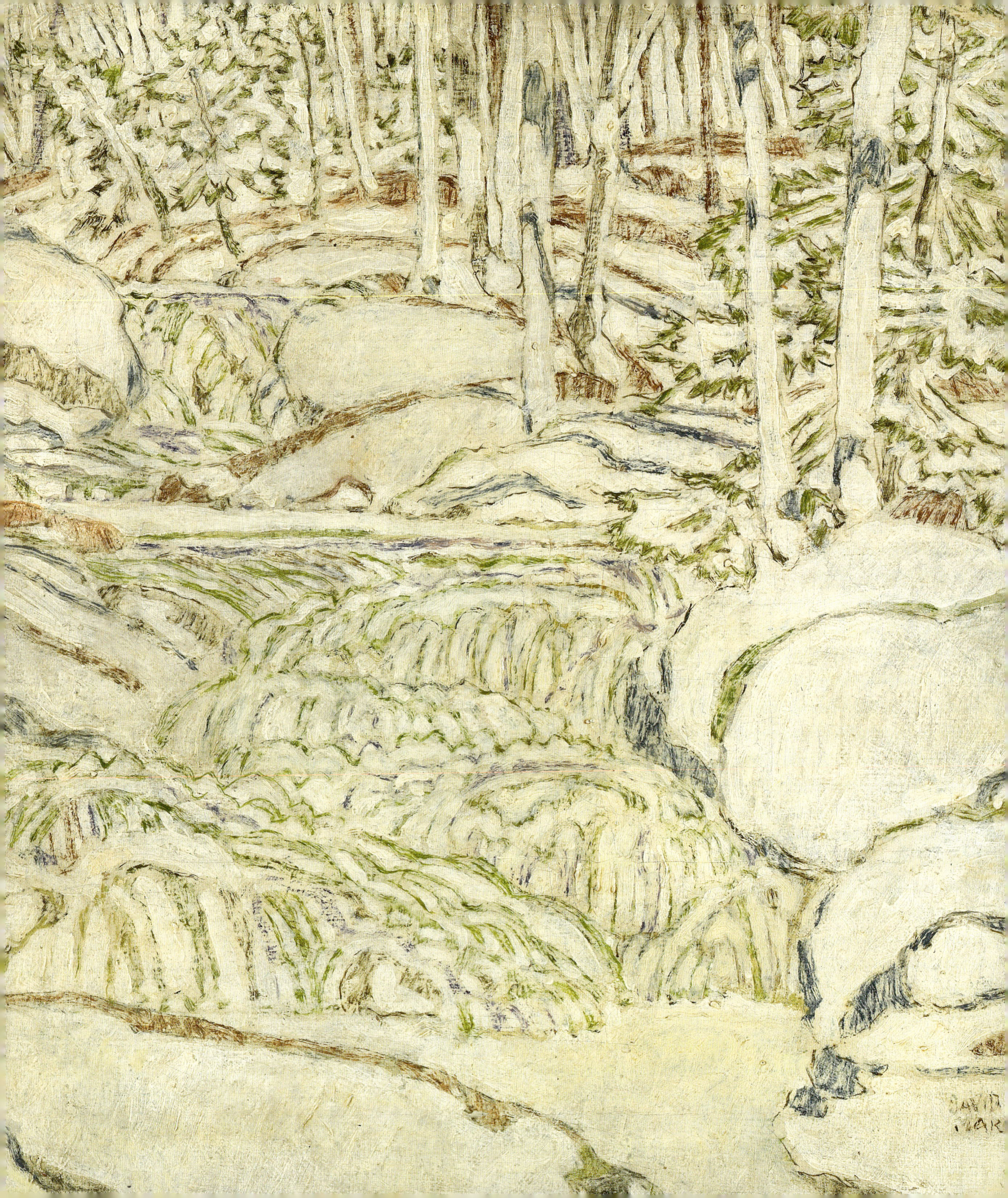

AFTERMATH

Still absorbing his experiences of the landscape of war, Milne returned to Boston Corners and to married life, though his reacquaintance with the writings of Thoreau soon prompted an experiment in living alone. Milne retreated for the winter of 1920–1 to Alander mountain, behind Boston Corners, where he built himself an 11-by-13-foot hut, capped with a curved roof in the style of the military Nissen huts he had seen in Europe. As snowstorms built around him in the depths of that winter, he managed to affix a front door and windows, to scrounge a cast-iron stove and to secure for himself a shelter from the elements. Milne's journals from this interlude reveal the intensity of his internal life and his drive to strip away distraction from his days. A series of remarkable paintings engage with the stump outside his front door; one senses its role as companion. Others describe the natural calligraphy of tree bark and branches against the snow. *White, the Waterfall*, one of Milne's favourites among his own works, is an exercise in subtraction and economy. All that is inessential has been bleached away from the act of painting.

The decade that followed Alander would be one of roving, resettlement and endless frustration, as Milne sought to find a way to support himself, undertaking various odd jobs, hospitality work (he and Patsy ran two tea houses) and construction work in the Catskills and the Adirondacks. His fascination with the effects of light continued—whether it was light mirrored on a lake's surface or captured in the curve of a glass bowl. There is a stillness and gravity about Milne's painting in the 1920s that is haunting, at times suggesting tranquillity, at others a quiet desolation.

Gentle Snowfall
1919, oil on canvas

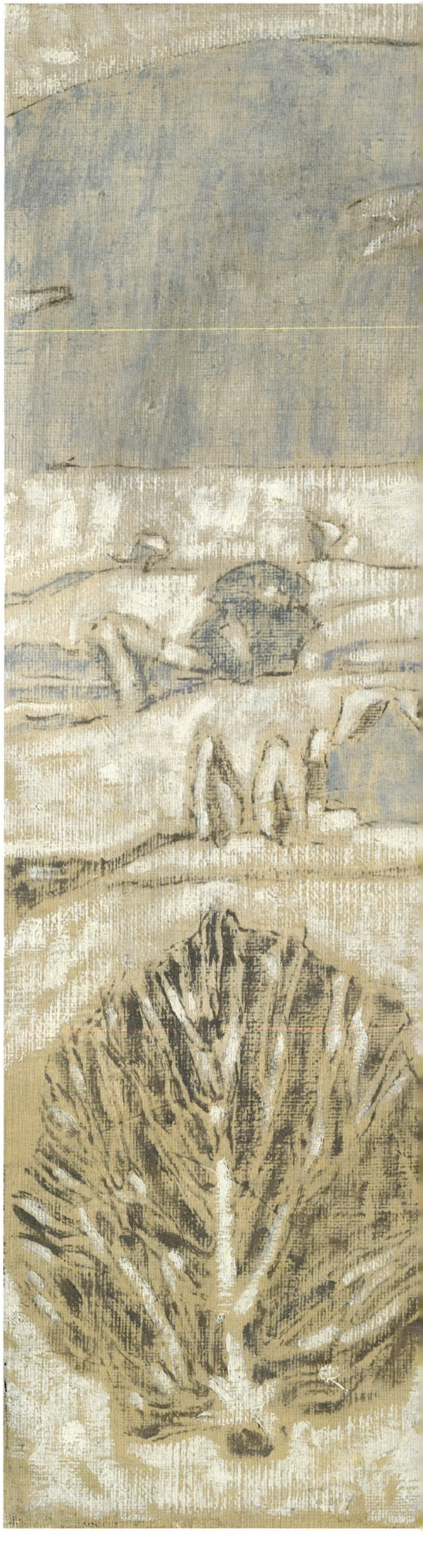

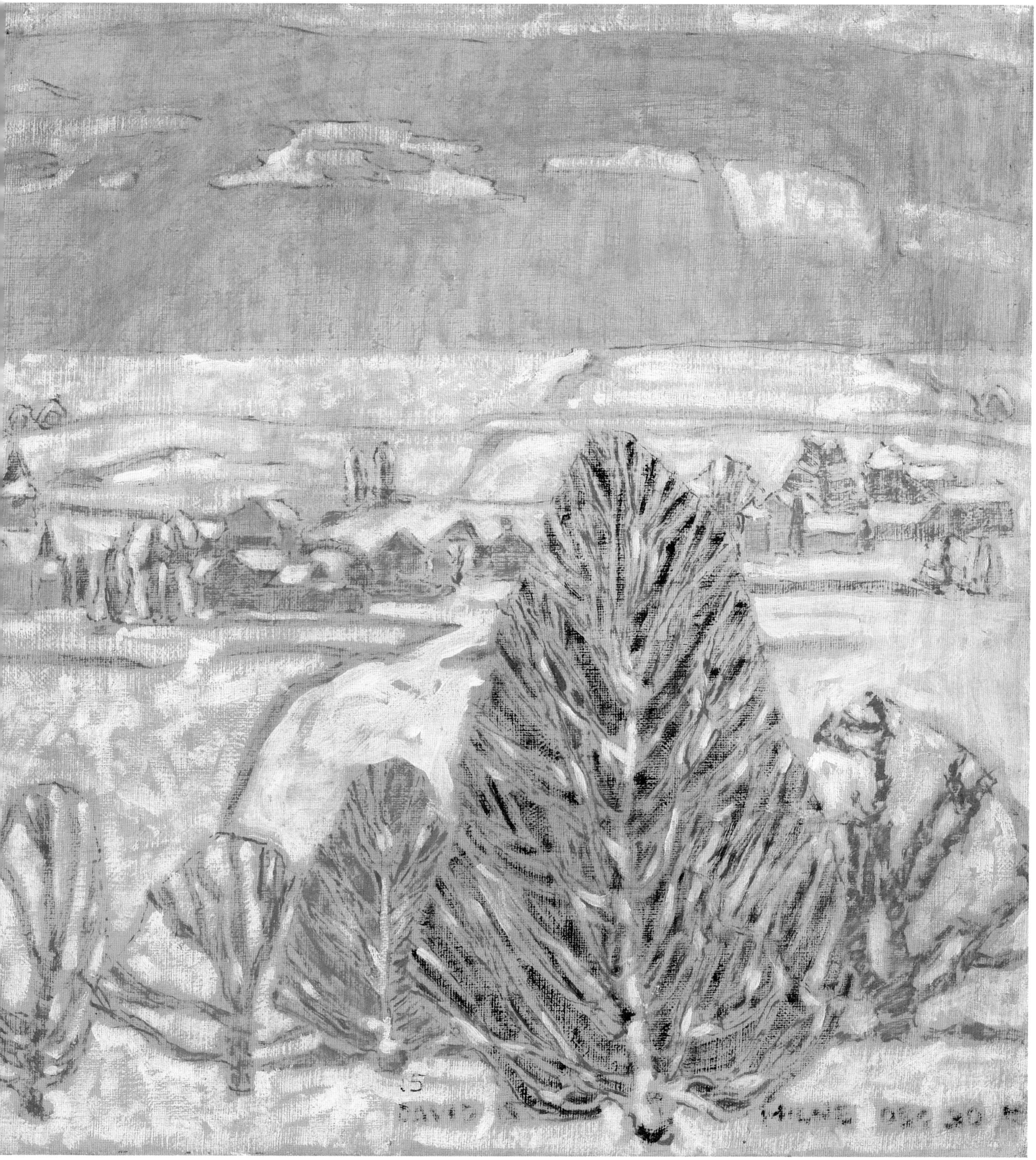

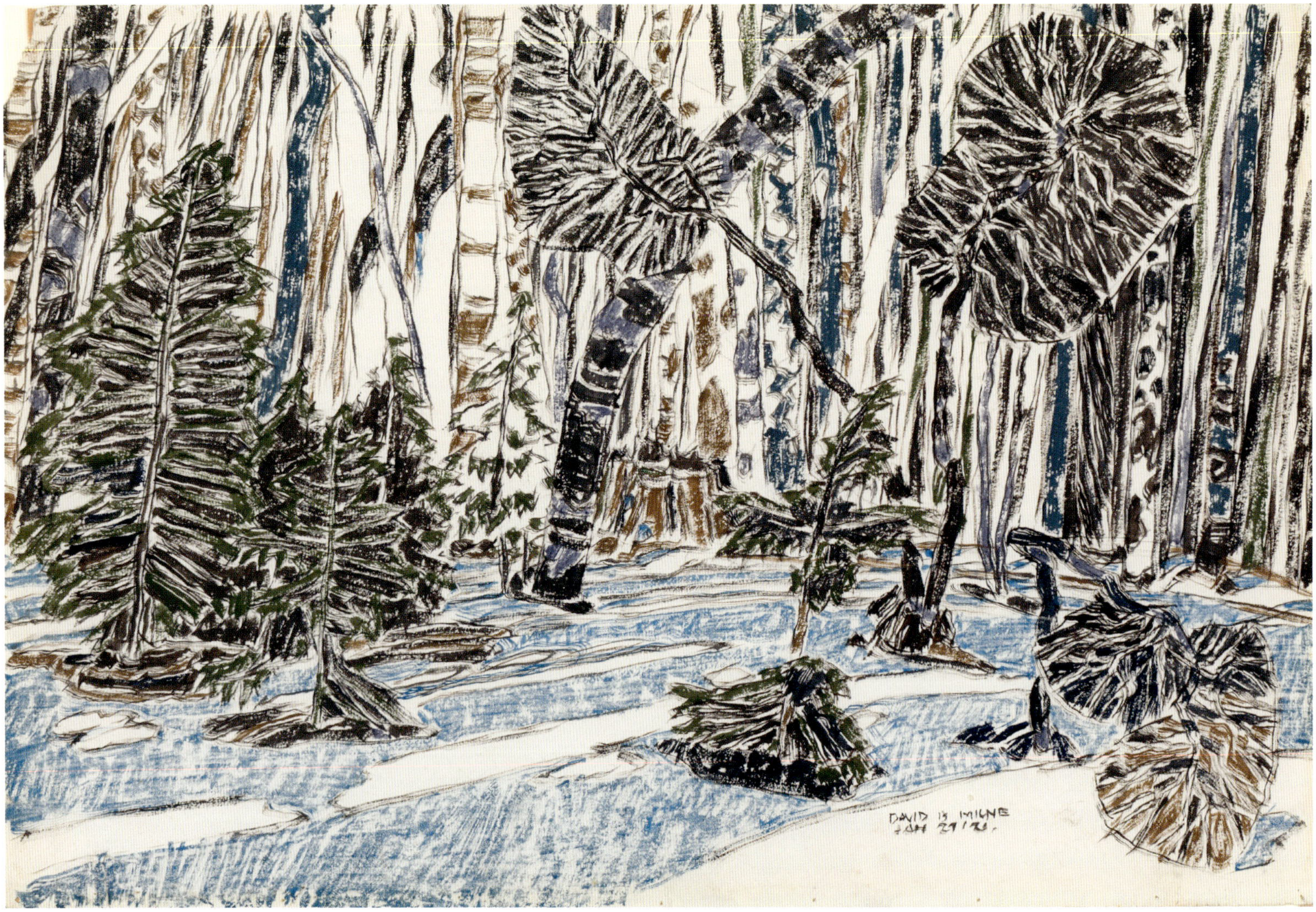

Shadows in the Woods
1921, watercolour on paper

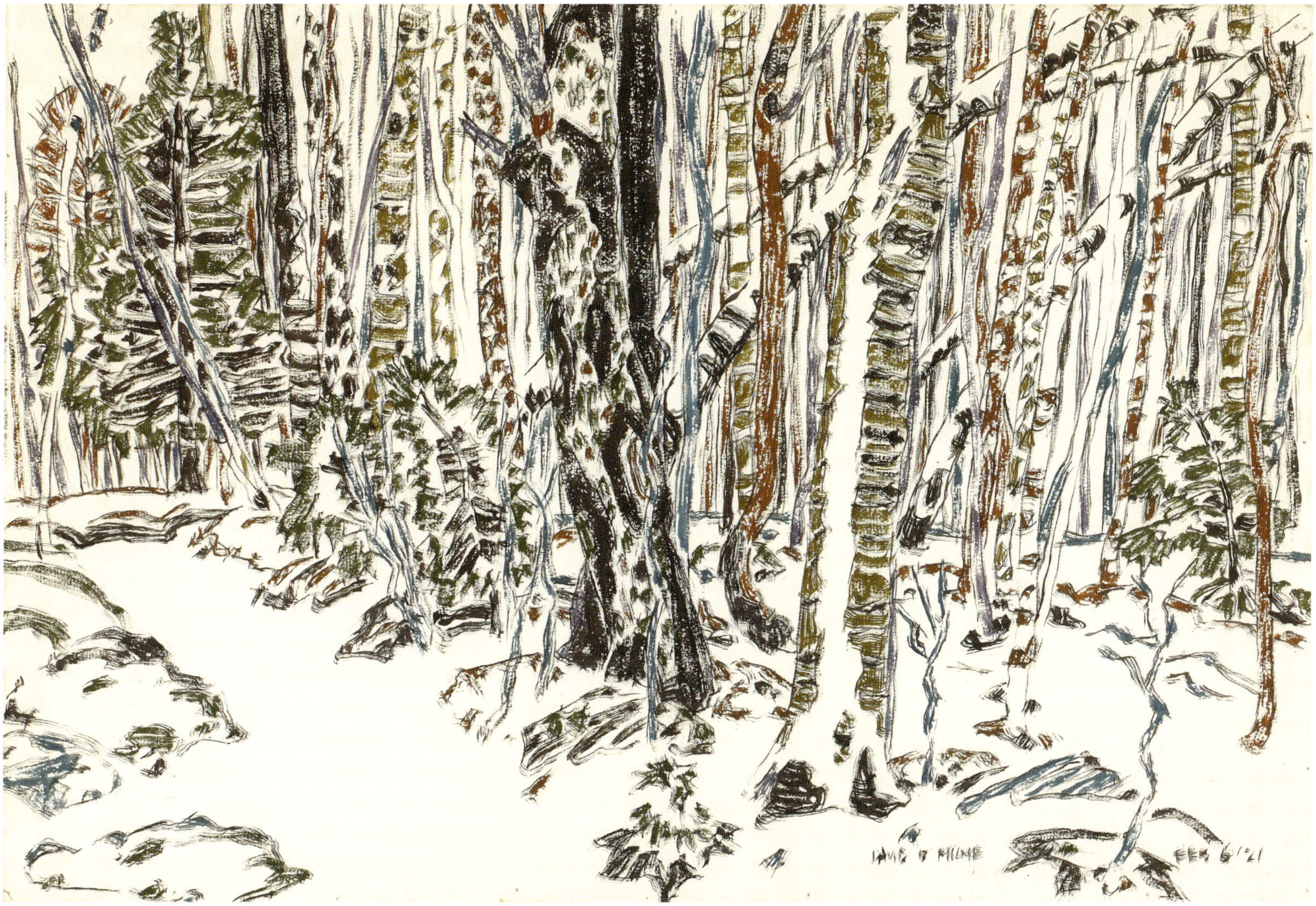

Path in the Woods
1921, watercolour on paper

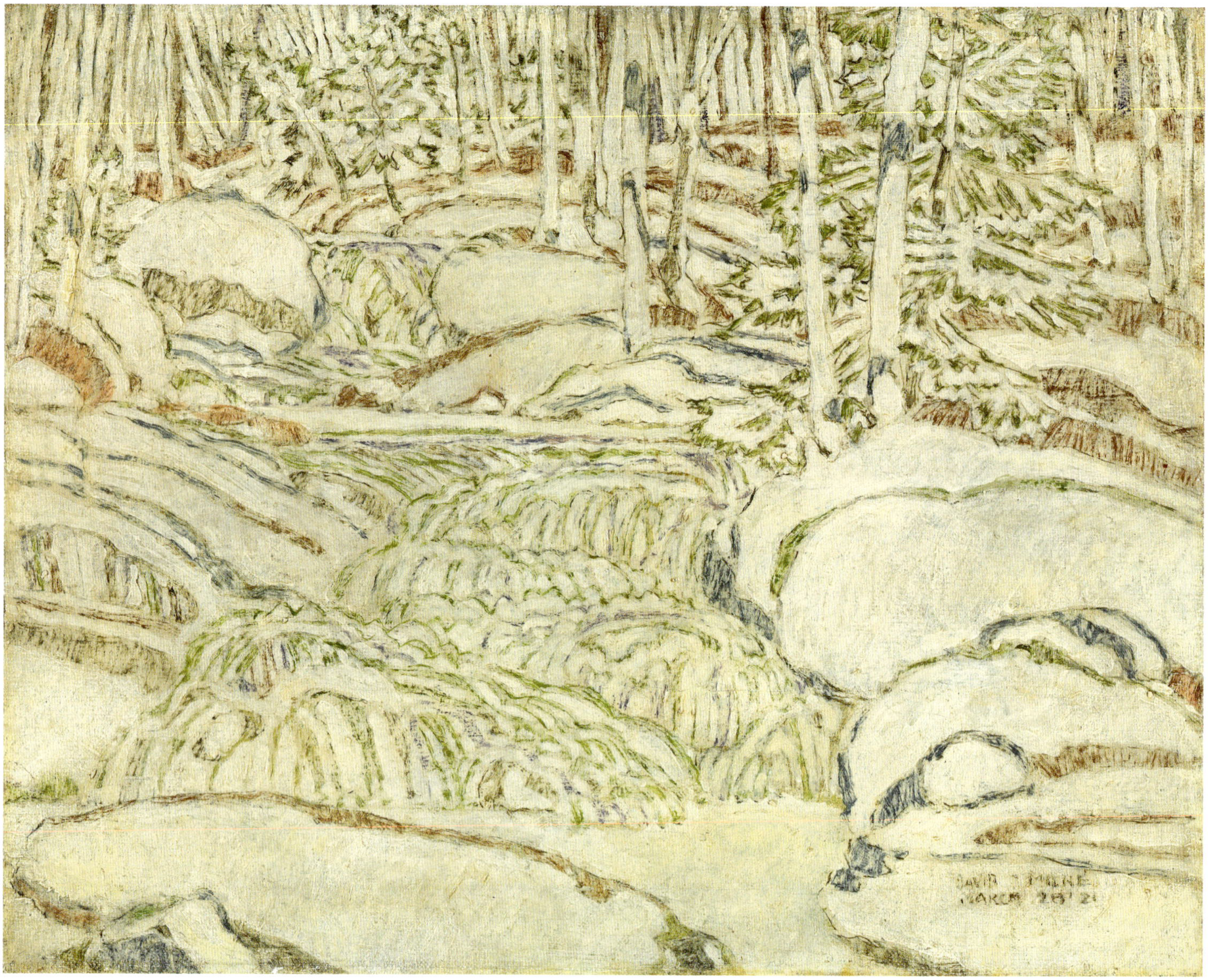

White, the Waterfall
1921, oil on canvas

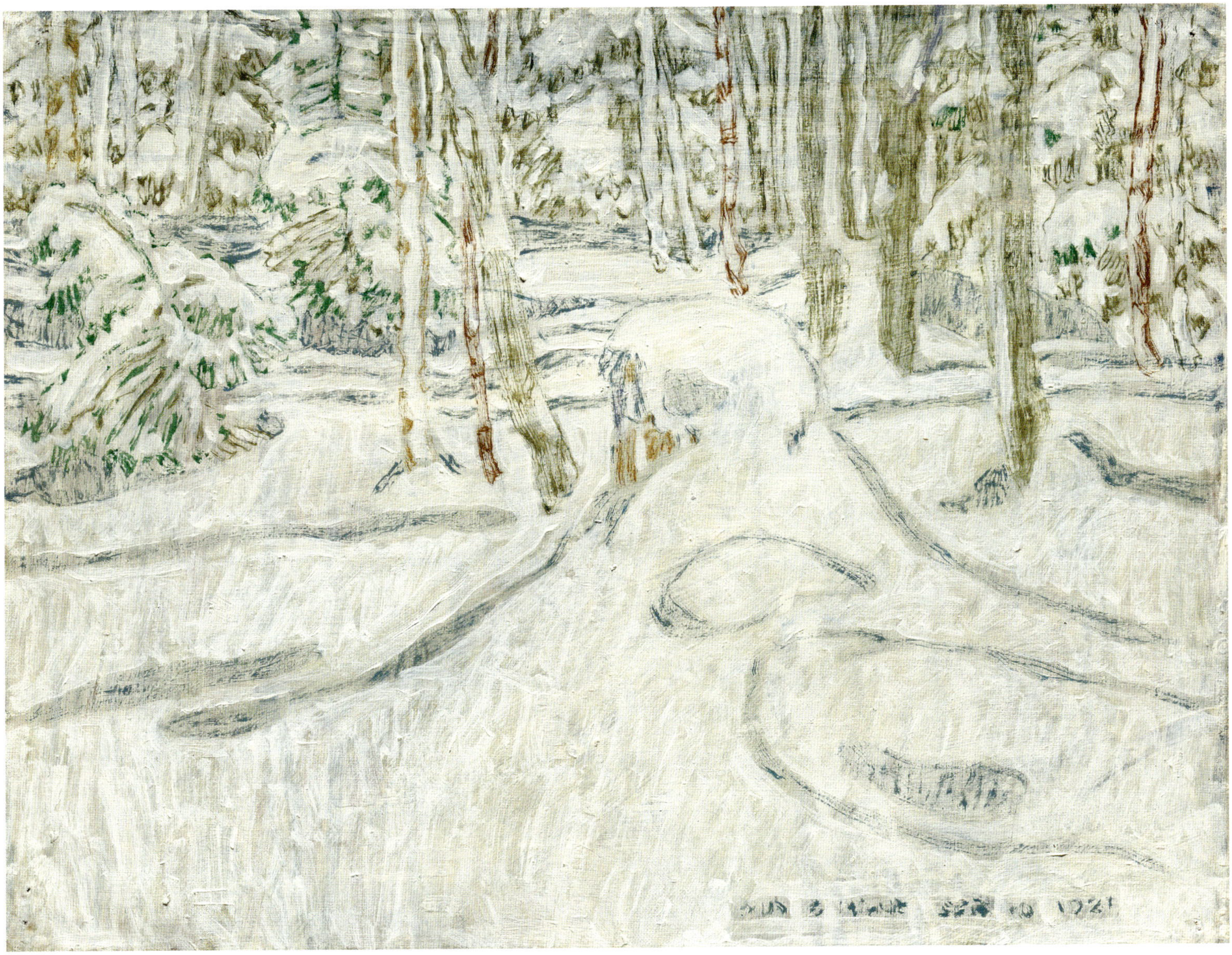

Drift on the Stump
1921, oil on canvas

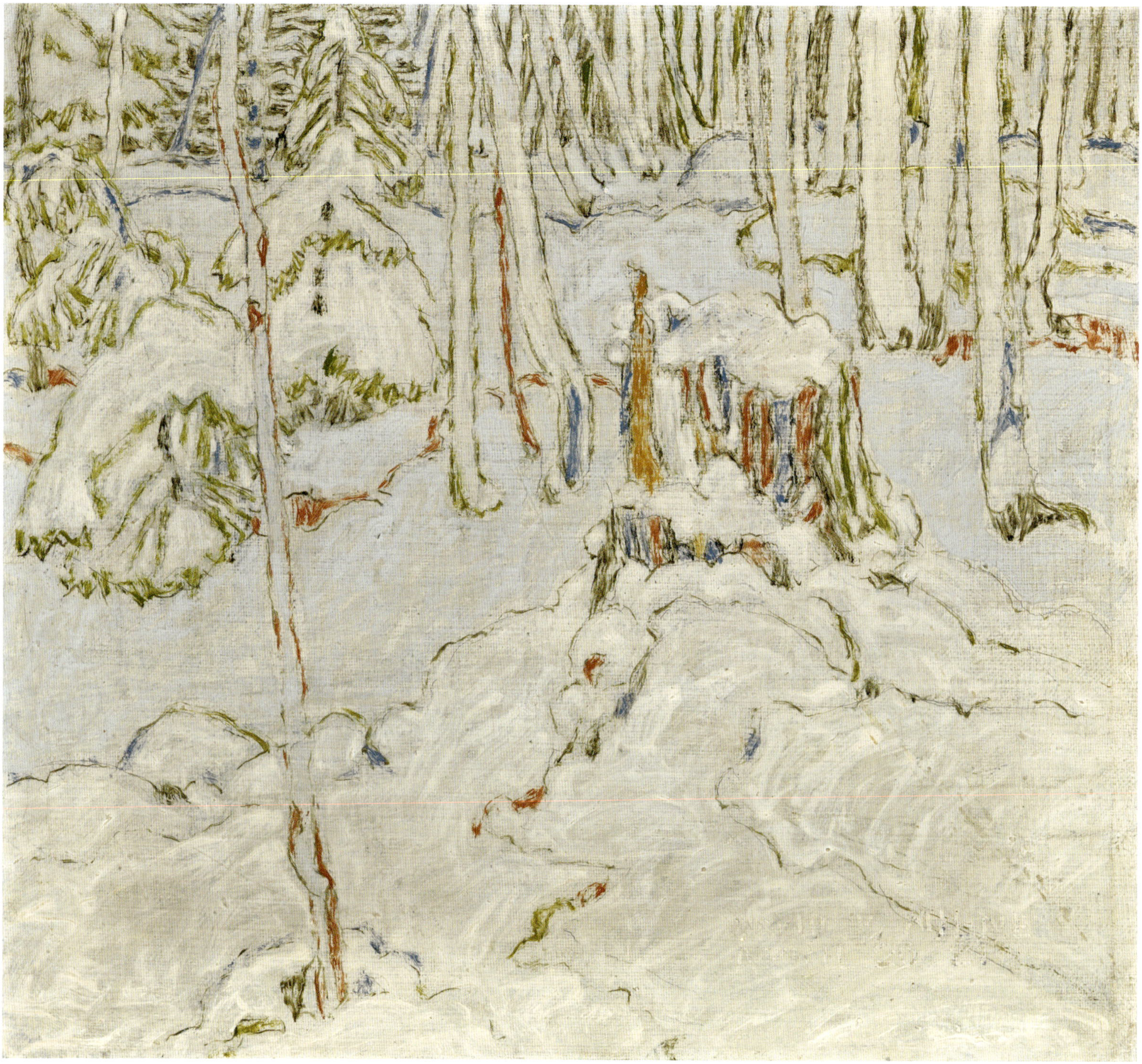

Snowy Hemlocks
1921, oil on canvas

FIVE STUMPS

Anne-Marie Ninacs

Is it a stump you see? David Milne would almost certainly have said no.[1] In *Drift on the Stump* (p. 119), *Thaw in the Woods* (p. 125) and *Snowy Hemlocks*, there are no stumps, only lines, shapes, colours and a considerable effort to achieve aesthetic unity. Painting these three pictures at the beginning of 1921, Milne was indeed taken by the main question of material and formal simplification, premising his approach on his 'Scotch motive' or 'getting the result with the slightest possible means'[2]—a concept he developed during the Great War and carried further after reading Clive Bell's *Art*. To translate into oil the blank paper and dry pigment effects of his war watercolours, he reduced his palette to three colours plus white, for the first time using the latter, instead of black, 'as a sharpening tool'.[3] He was also very interested in a contrast of textures, a pictorial problem he explored by playing with the oil paint's ability to appear sometimes dry, sometimes greasy; he scrubbed and scratched the paint in different directions until it looked like crayon. The viewer will first see the painting subject as a stump, but Milne resisted that easy understanding. Subject matter was his pretext to work out specific formal problems—for example, the contrast of textures between the pillowy-soft blankness of the snow and the roughness of the branches, with the whole arrangement 'hammered into simplicity and order'.[4]

These three stumps are depicted from the same vantage point, and together they generate a serial effect akin to Claude Monet's modern approach to painting. The stump is somehow Milne's haystack, a stable subject anchoring aesthetic permutations. The Impressionist master is actually the only direct artistic affiliation Milne ever claimed. 'The great effect Monet had on me would be hard to trace. No one has ever noticed it,' he wrote while explaining what he learned from his elder: 'I was thrilled by just one thing, his singleness of heart, the unity of his pictures. There was no straying into bypaths. He clearly aimed at one thing and one thing only.'[5]

It is crucial to understand that aiming at a single thing was neither a romantic figure of speech nor a theoretical posture for Milne. It was a *method*, which he referred to as 'singleness of purpose,' and it consisted of a conscious and repeated decision to concentrate all his energy, time, assets, thoughts and most subtle attention on a specific creative

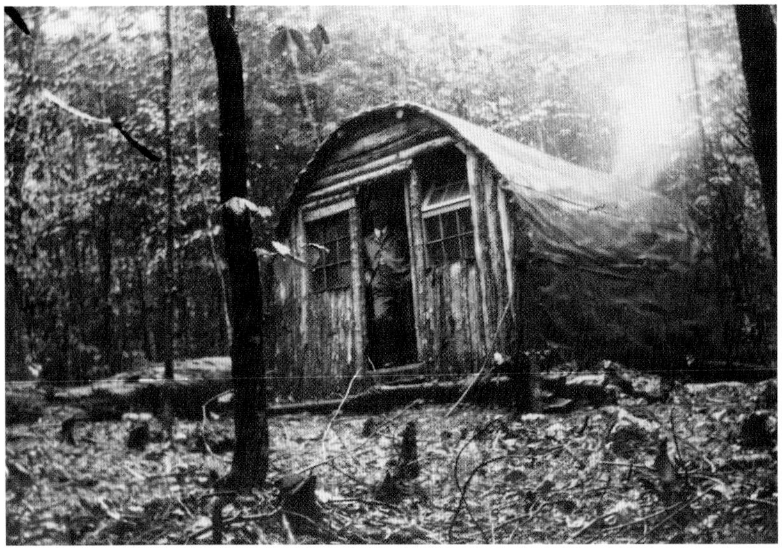

David Milne at his Alander cabin, 1921

goal. Faced with any two demands in the making of a work of art, he would advise, you must submit to one and focus all you have in a single direction, for that is the only way to achieve aesthetic unity. Milne also applied this single-purpose method to his approach to life, a principle affirmed by the lessons in ethics and economics that he drew from Henry David Thoreau's *Walden*. Rereading the book produced 'an explosion in my mind',[6] the painter confided in September 1920, and just two months later he was himself launching his first attempt at a Thoreauvian life. Alone in the New England woods near Alander mountain during the winter of 1920–1, he tried to become 'one of the worthies of the world' while keeping '[his] accounts on [his] thumb nail'.[7]

Milne could see the stump from the door of his handmade cabin; it is what he used daily for the woodcutting necessary for his survival in the winter cold and was therefore at the centre of his new-found artistic realm. Milne's animist comment on *Drift on the Stump* leaves no doubt indeed about his deference to this humble but central presence: 'Incidentally, I nabbed the old stump and chopping log. He looks like a white-crowned-and-robed king with two big beautiful grease spots on his train.'[8] Milne similarly saw the reduction of his material needs to a woodsman's way of life as a direct benefit for creative continuity and attention—conferring a wealth that made him feel fully alive and no less than 'one of the kings of earth'.[9]

Milne's relationship to the Alander stump would remain merely anecdotal were it not for the recurrence of the stump as a subject in his art. After he left his Alander cabin in the spring of 1921 until winter 1950 on Baptiste Lake, Milne painted or engraved more than 30 different images of stumps.[10] He tackled the subject regularly enough for the observer to take notice and wonder why one would paint again and again something so utterly plain. Wouldn't most artists omit such a commonplace object when framing a landscape? What exactly was so compelling in that specific subject that a formalist painter would want to return to it so often?

Painted in 1932, *Stump among the Saplings* (p. 168) serves as a perfect example of Milne's ongoing interest in the subject. He wrote that it represents 'one of the early workings of a theme not yet fully developed, the use of pure blue to dominate values and the other hues',[11] and the picture indeed announces what would become a few years later his forceful 'bright blue theme'. What Milne left untold was why he chose to depict the stump not simply as an object in nature but almost as a portrait, so closely framed that it appears decontextualized, magnified, alive with tentacles and dark insides, placed here against a piercing blue backdrop, with a jewel-like colour scheme that makes 'him' look as royal as the earlier manifestation in *Drift on the Stump*.

Not all stumps are granted such stature in Milne's art, and the secretive painter never once explored openly the symbolic or emotional meaning of his iconography, making it a very delicate enigma to unravel. Nevertheless, the recurring stumps betray his subliminal attraction to the subject. They reveal the imaginative function of the mind, which in a glimpse catches in the world what concerns the painter and entices him enough to pursue the painting process all the way into 'singleness of heart'—an ephemeral yet extraordinarily dynamic sensation of unified action which constituted for Milne the actual meaning of the verb 'to paint'.[12] The painter seldom described any special artistic experiences from his childhood, but he did remember very vividly seeing 'brush and stumps being burned',[13] as well as the feeling that had overtaken him when he stood on a certain stump high up on a hill:

> Anyway I was the small boy and the farm was on the stage road between Port Elgin and

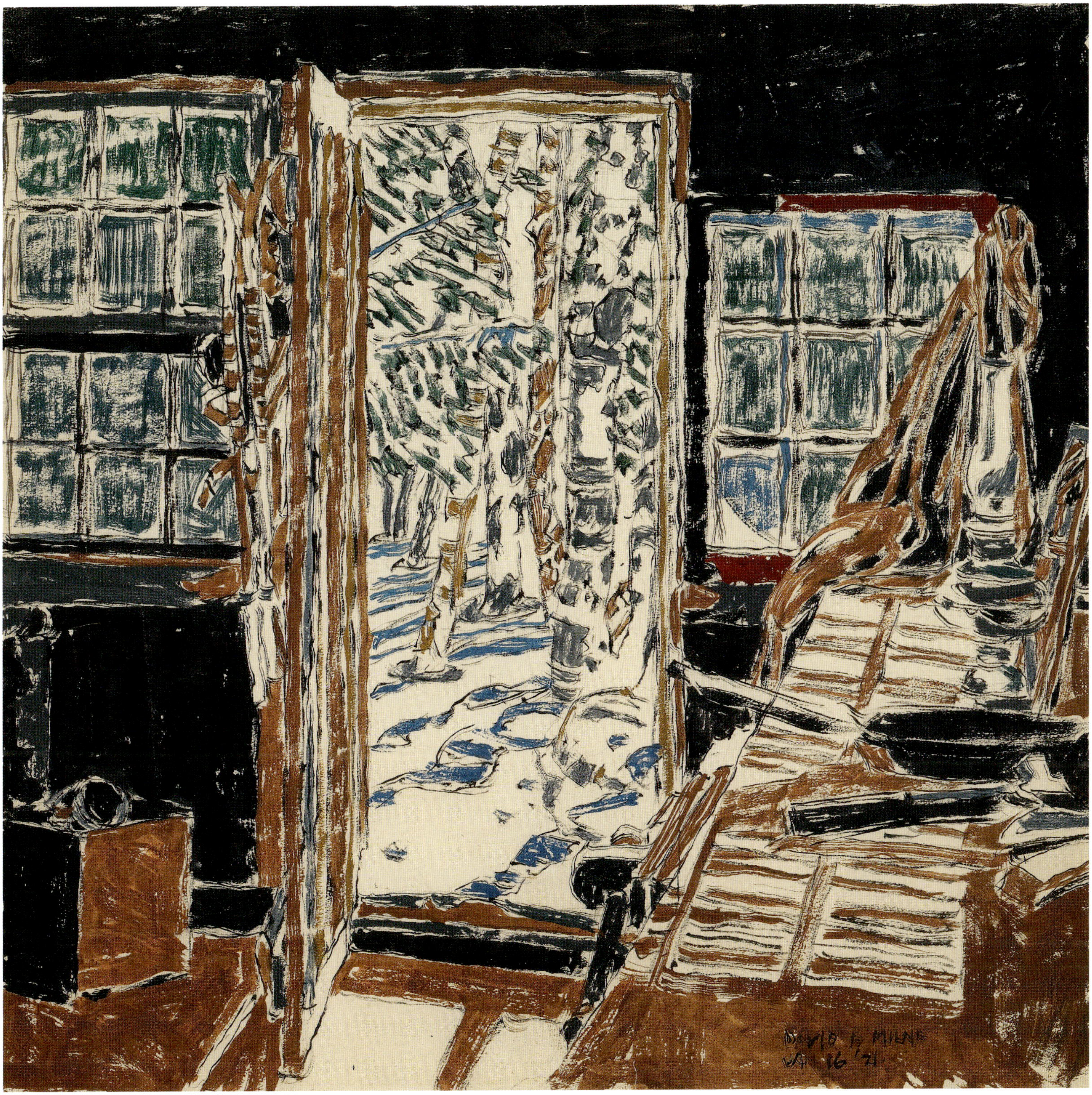

Doorway of the Painting House
1921, watercolour over graphite on
buff wove paper

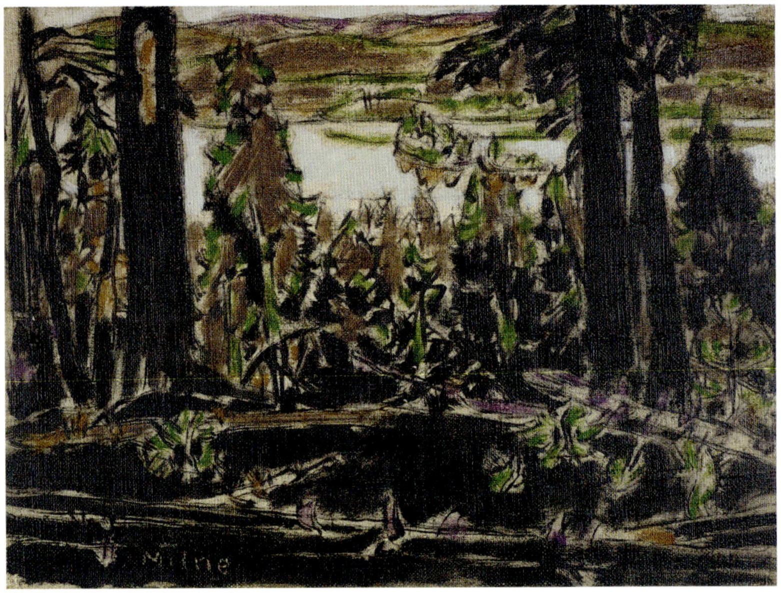

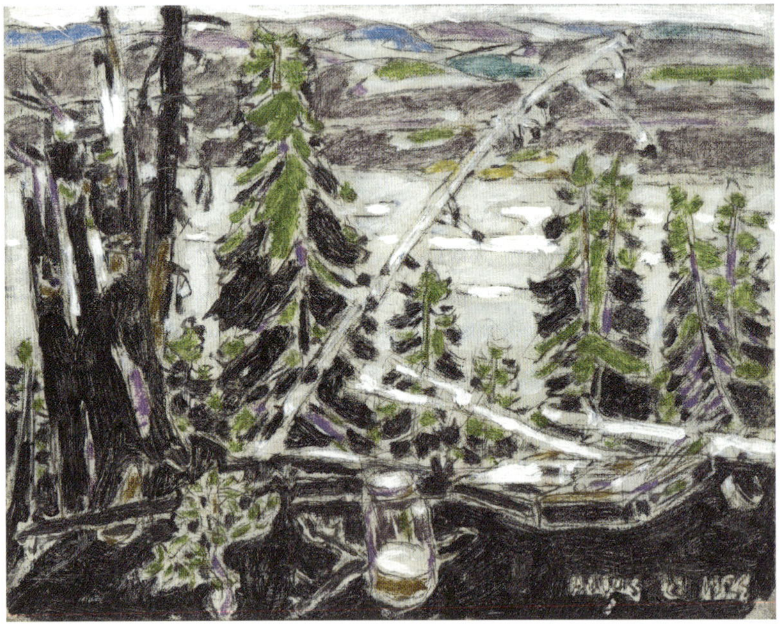

Top
David Milne
Painting Place: Brown and Black
c. 1926, oil on canvas

Above
David Milne
Painting Place I
1926, oil on canvas

Owen Sound.... On the back of it, along the edge of Black's bush there was a hill and from the top of a stump on that hill we could see mostly everything, our own fields and barn and part of the house, Finnie's pasture and berry patch, another farm and then the valley through which the Saugeen River flowed, Brown's farm very small and faint, and beyond it sand hills. Beyond the sand hills a long straight streak of blue, sometimes with a white moving speck on it, Lake Huron. From that stump for the first time I was brought face to face with Infinity where anything might be and anything might happen.[14]

That childhood memory seems to have played an important underlying role in the evolution of *Painting Place III,* 1930 (p. 157), Milne's most famous representation of a lake and rolling hills captured from a mountaintop vantage point. His progressive treatments of the subject clearly show that there was no stump when he first noticed 'the frame of the mirror that grips your heart' in August 1926.[15] In a letter written on the spot to his friend James Clarke, neither his description of the scene nor the accompanying sketch, which resembles *Painting Place: Brown and Black, c.* 1926, includes any stump.[16] One comes to suspect, though, that the view was so intimately connected to Milne's remembered feeling of possibility back in Bruce County that this memory manifested itself in the form of a stump, which makes its appearance the next day in *Painting Place I*, 1926,[17] likely painted from a slightly different vantage point.

For four years following these initial efforts with the scene, Milne would create further variations in prints and paintings, asserting the stump, from one version to the next, as an ever more important and defining element of the design. In the final 1930 *Painting Place III,* he even used white outlining to visually uproot the stump from the soil and set it apart from the landscape, alongside the paintbox, brushes, water jar and flowers on the dark foreground where he, the artist, is standing. Milne thus positioned the stump as an essential component of his painting kit—a symbolic touchstone for that feeling he aimed for while painting. Today, we can see that the humble stump also stands in for the practice of painting itself, rooted in the earthly existence that Milne jumped on daily to come face to face with Infinity.

***Anne-Marie Ninacs** is an art historian and curator with a special interest in the relation between subjectivity, ethics and the artistic process. She is a professor at the School of Visual and Media Arts of the Université du Québec, Montréal. She has recently completed the first doctoral thesis on the life and work of David Milne.*

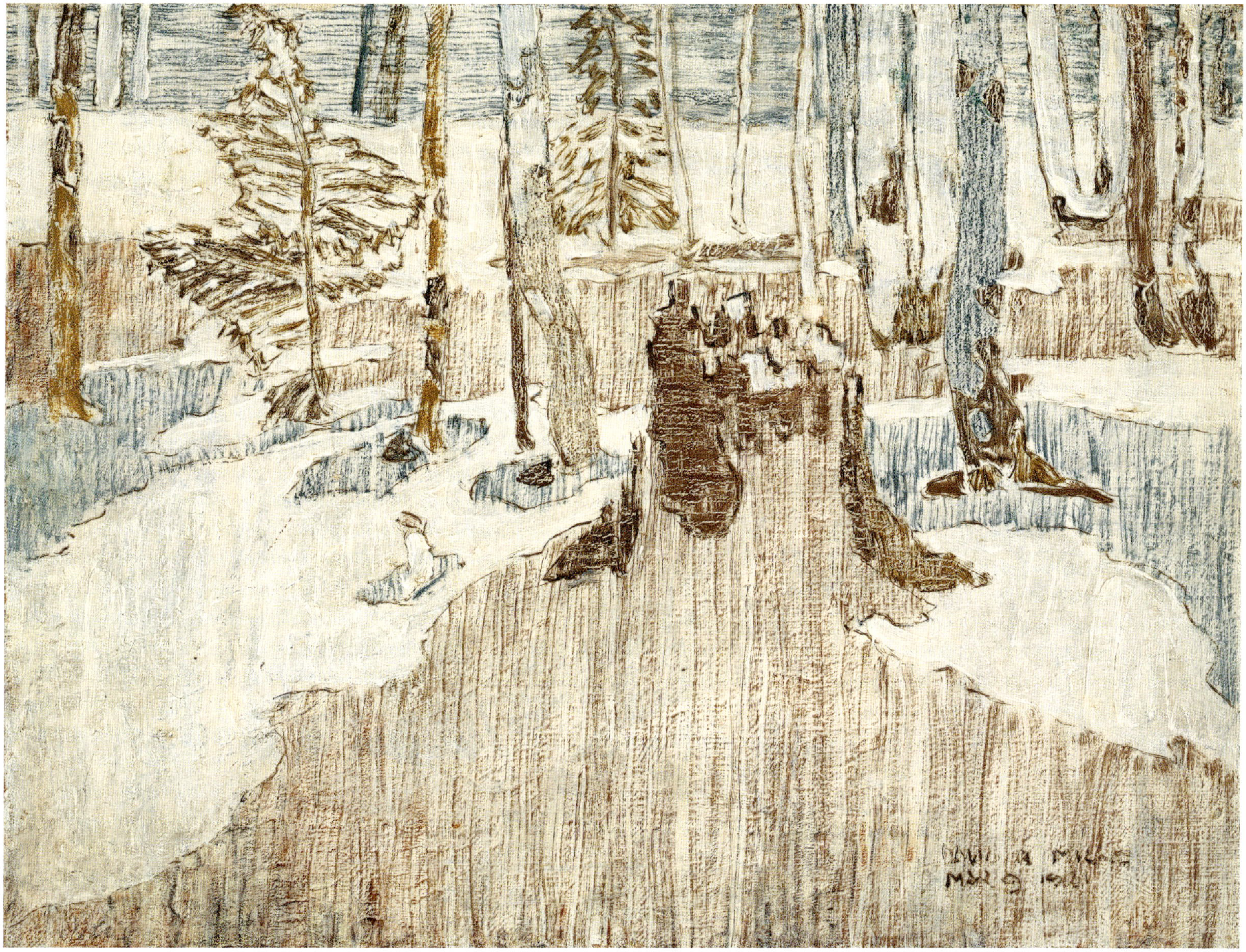

Thaw in the Woods
1921, oil on canvas

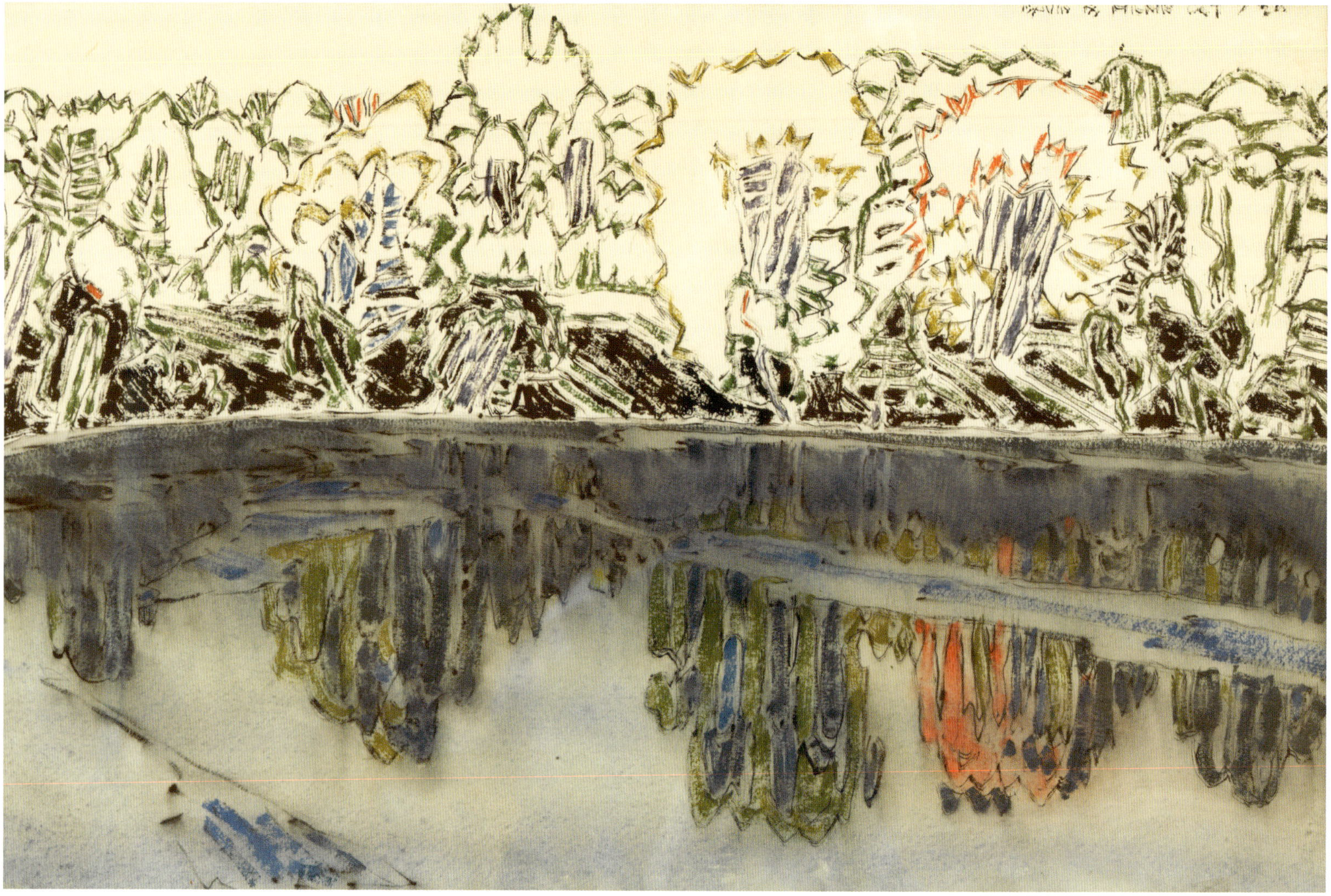

Bishop's Pond in Sunlight
1920, watercolour on paper

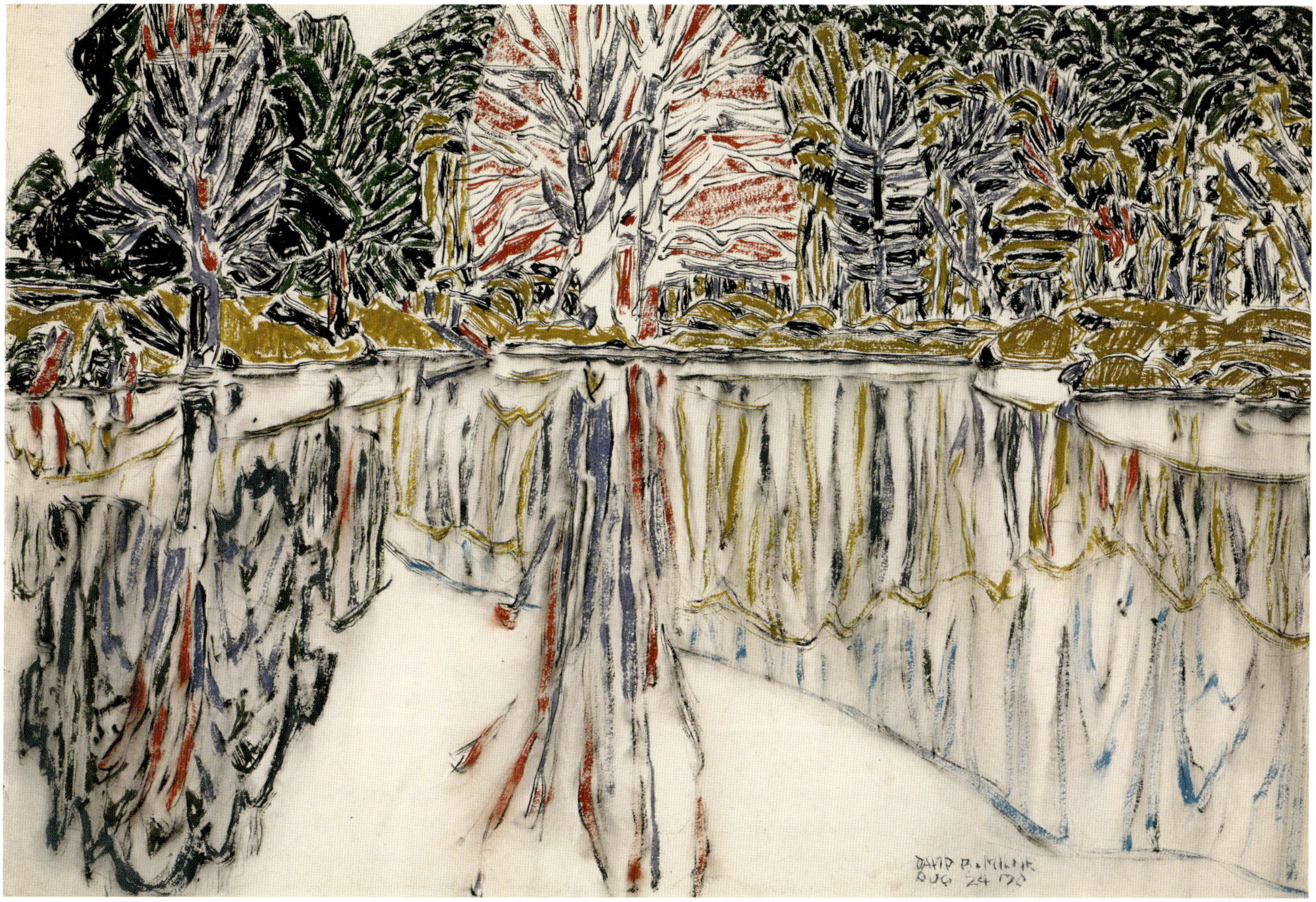

Pink Reflections, Bishop's Pond
1920, watercolour over graphite on wove paper

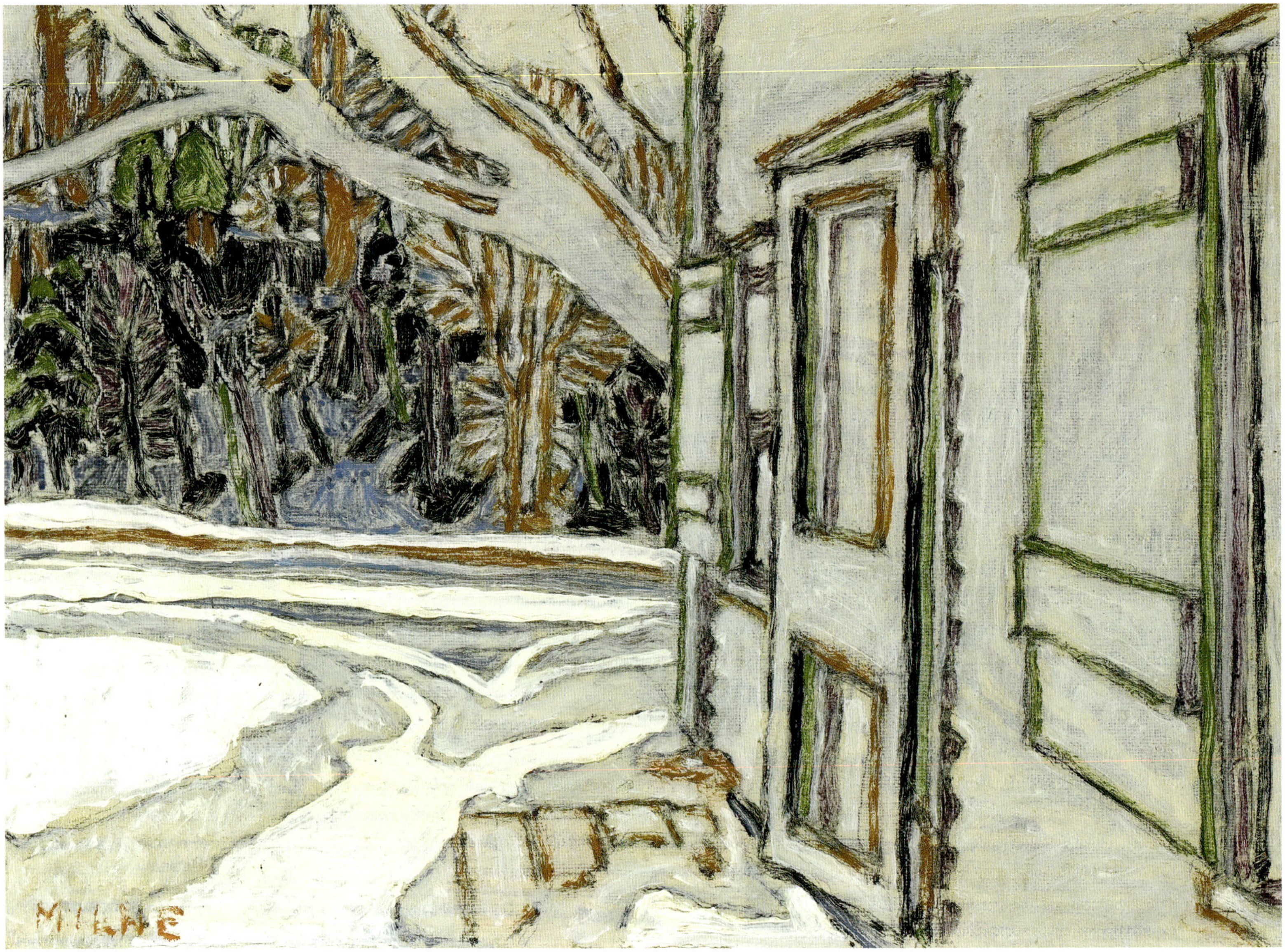

Side Door, Clarke's House
c. 1923, oil on canvas

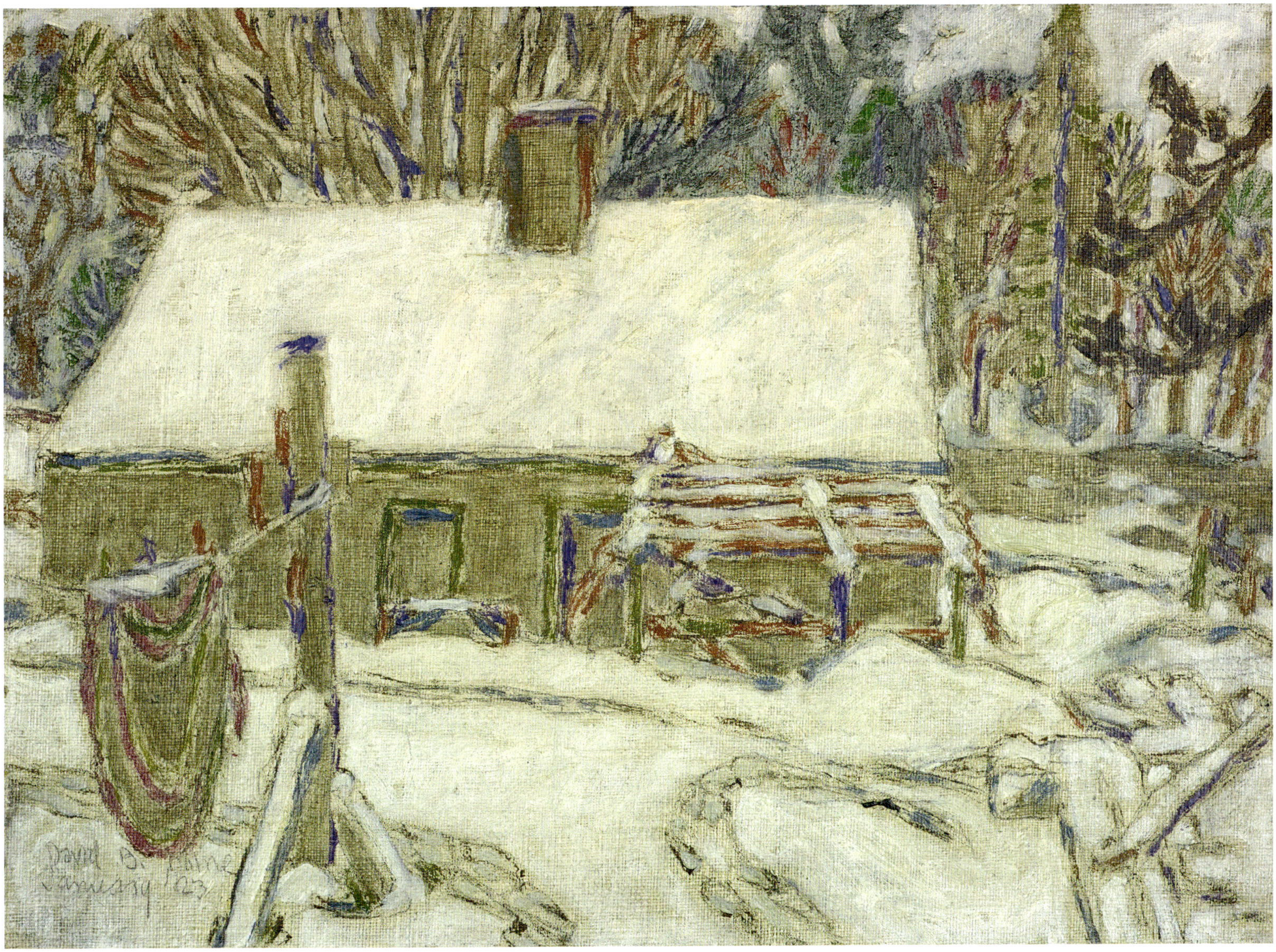

Back of Clarke's House
1923, oil on canvas

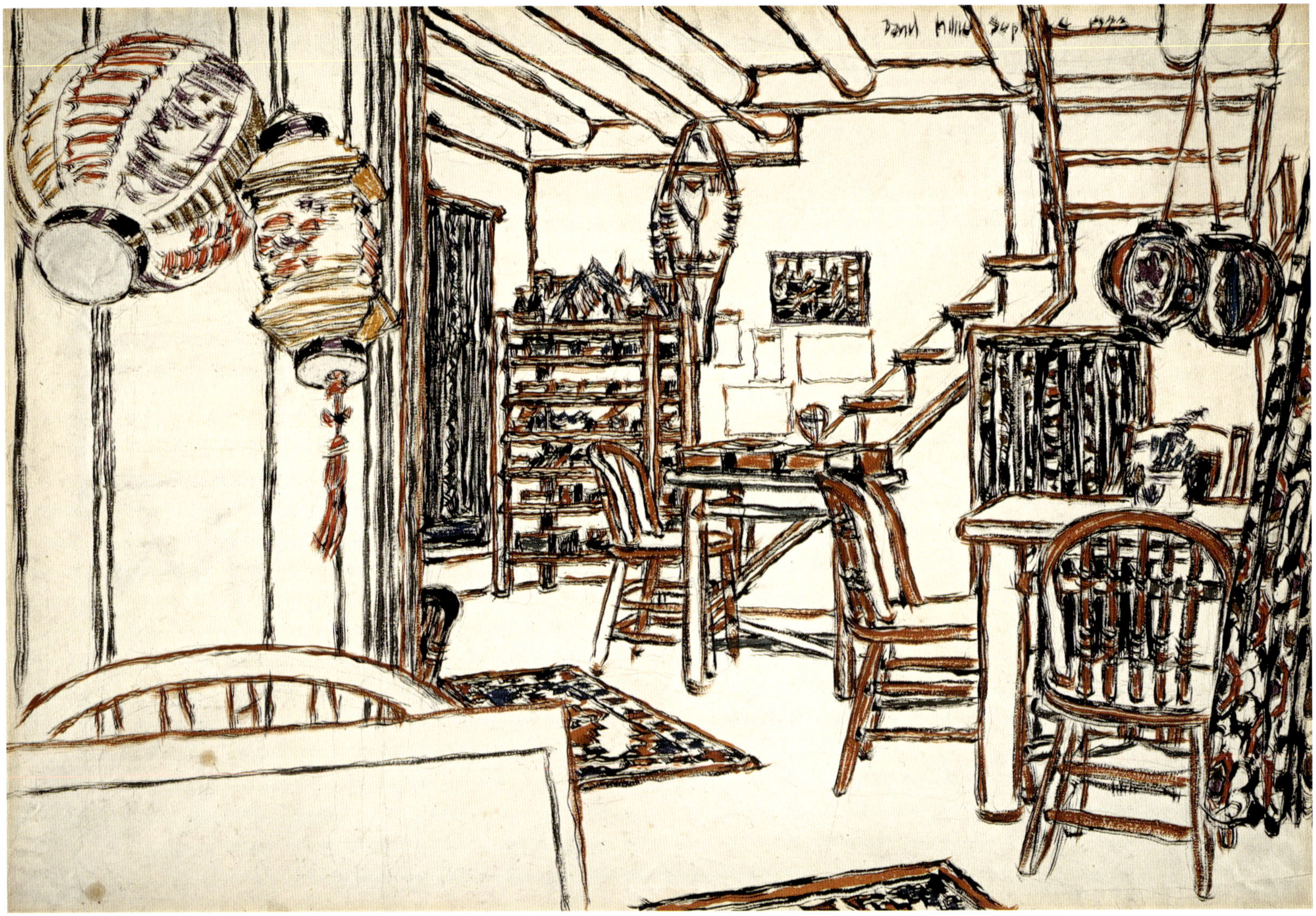

Lanterns and Snowshoes (Interior of Tea-House)
1923, watercolour on paper

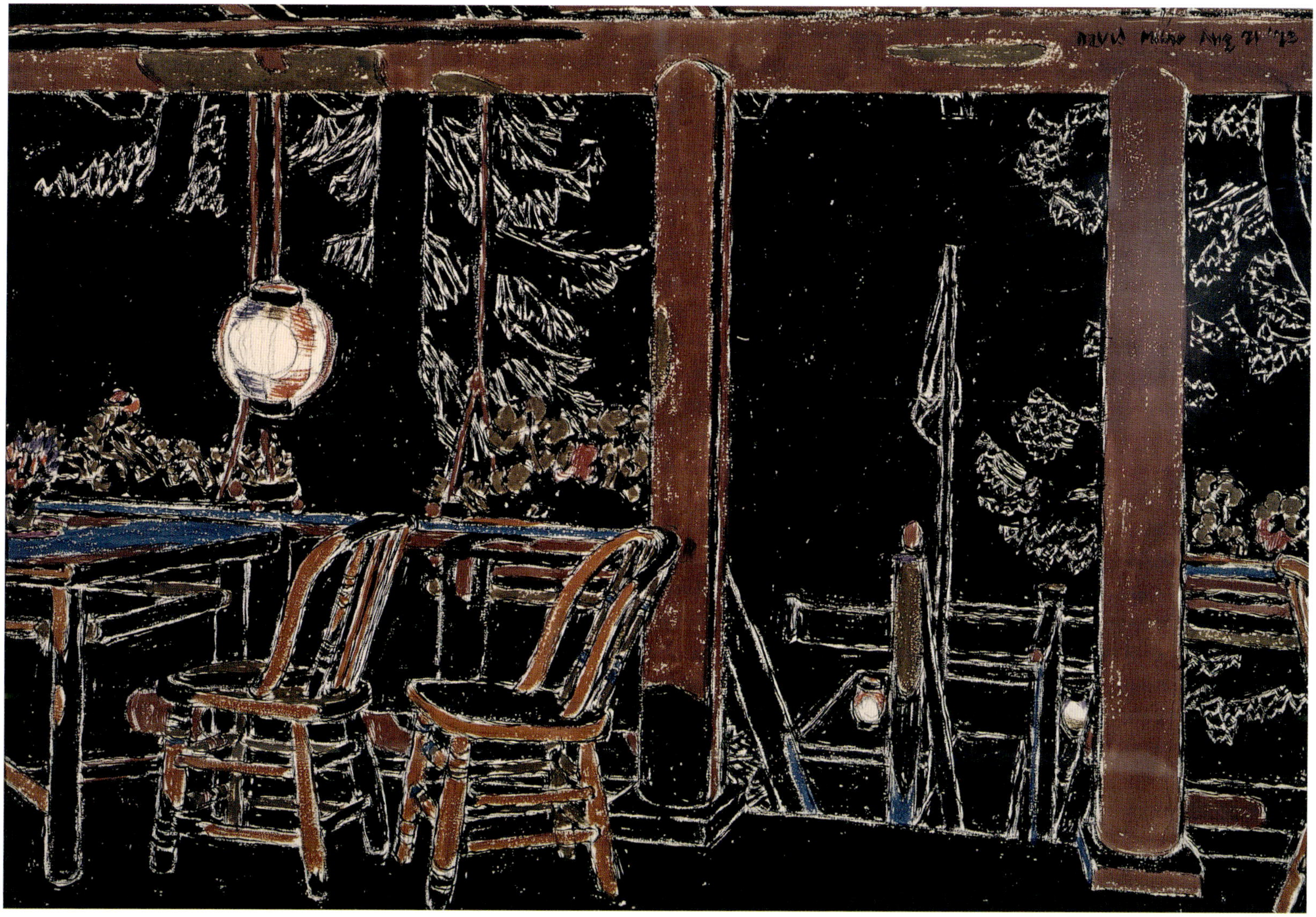

Verandah at Night II
1923, oil on canvas

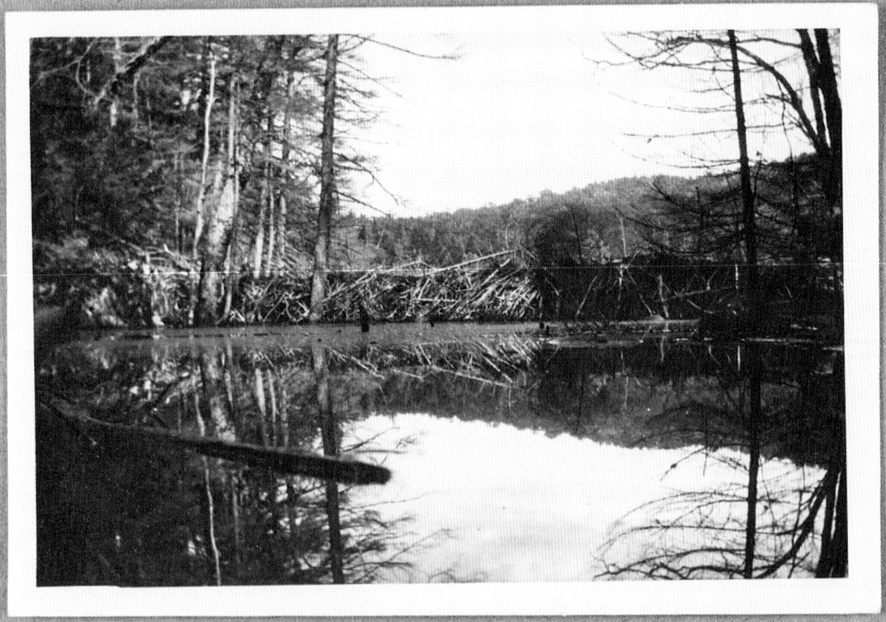

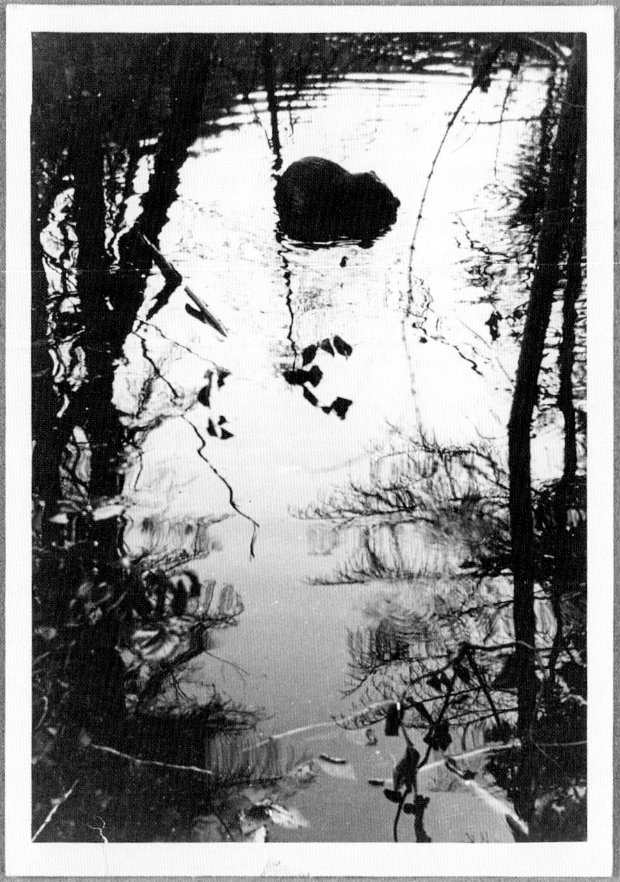

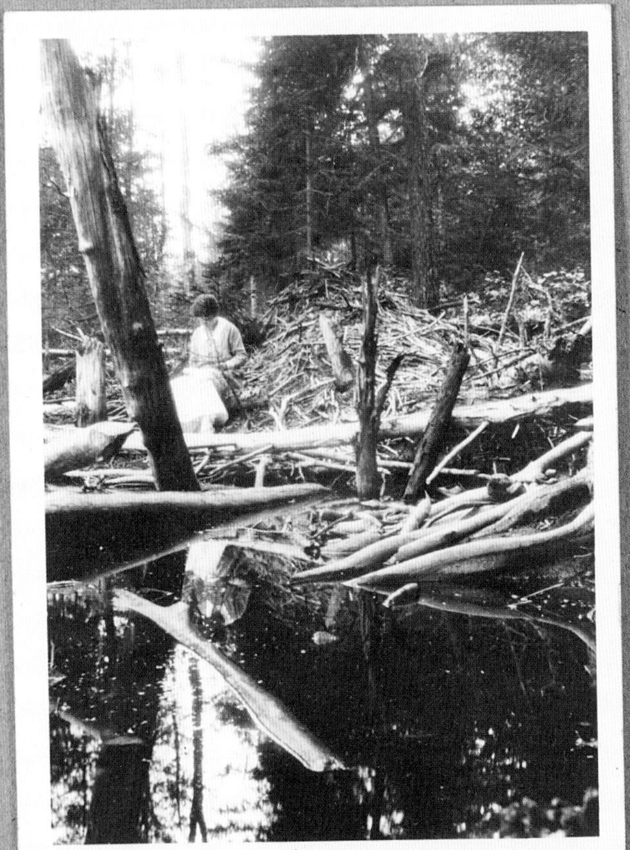

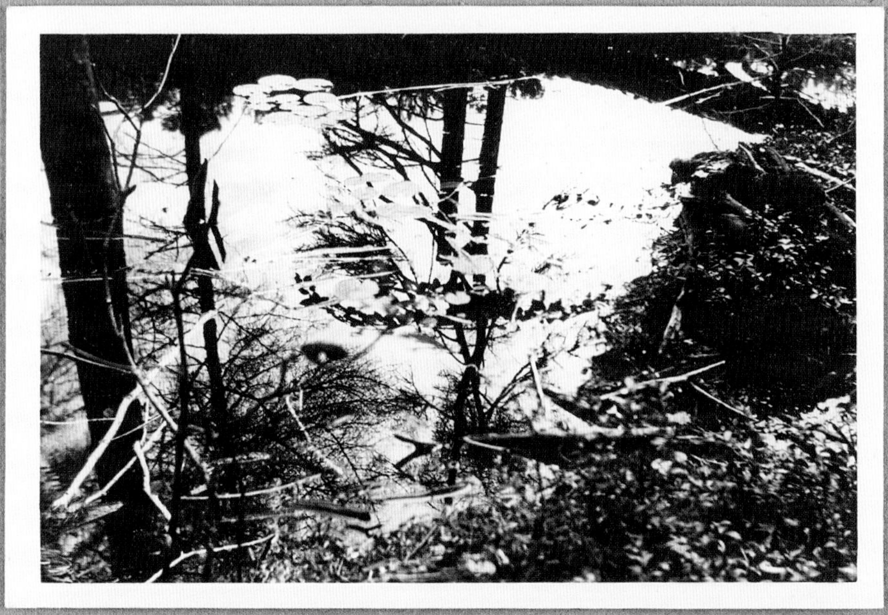

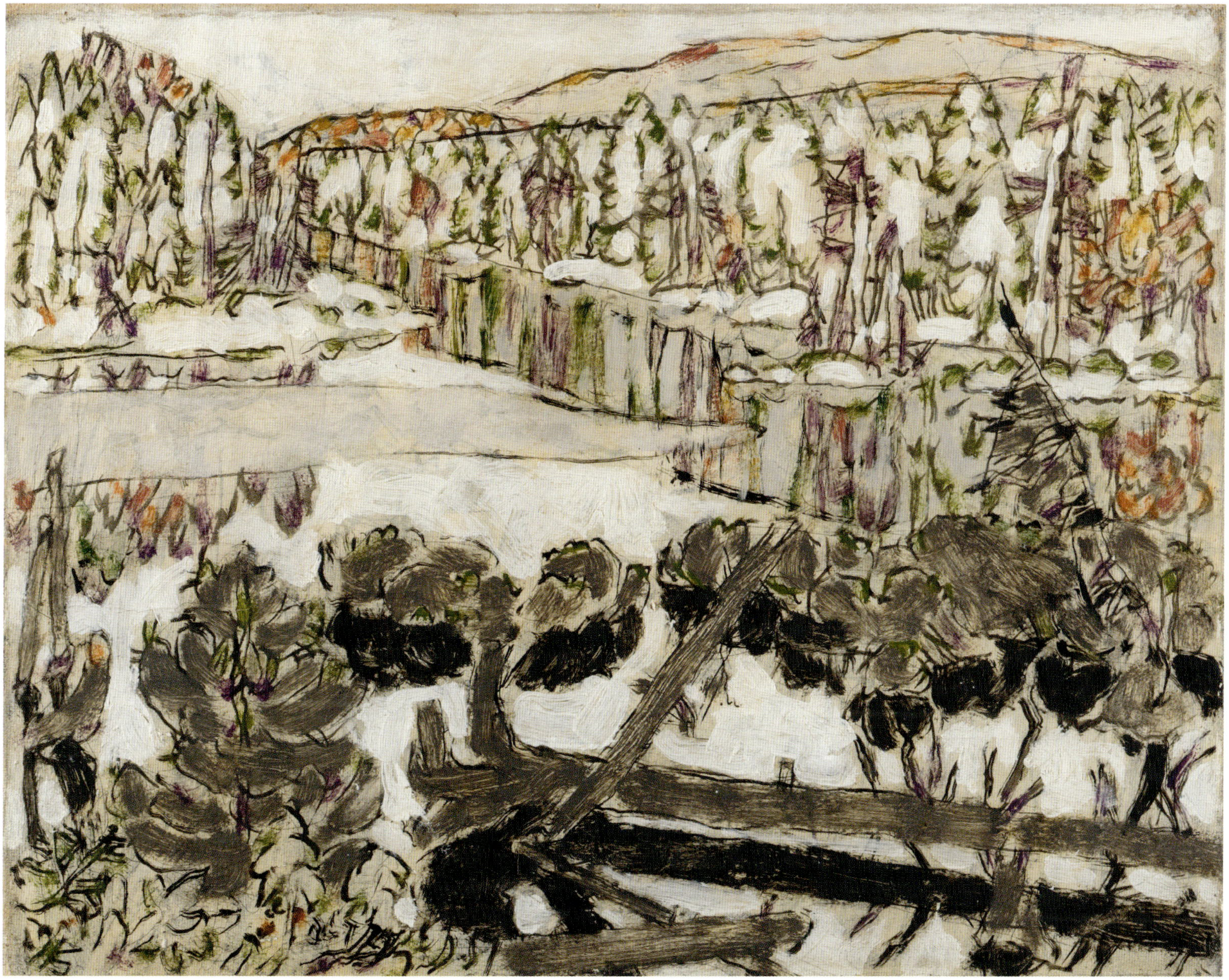

Opposite
David Milne
Dart's Lake
1921
Top right, beaver and reflections;
Bottom left, Patsy Milne seated

Pond at Big Moose
(Outlet of the Pond I)
1926, oil on canvas

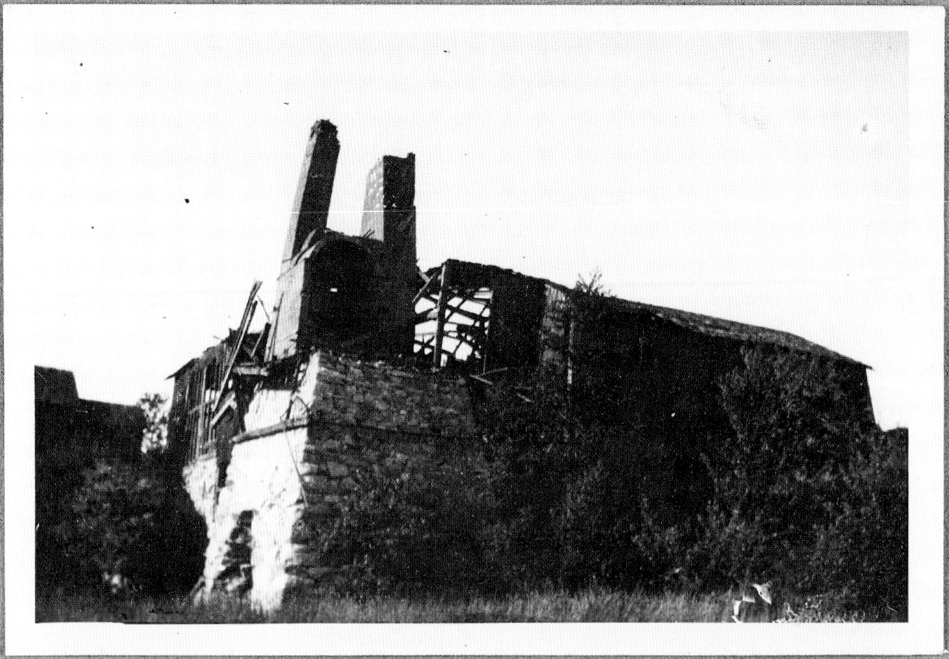

BC 10

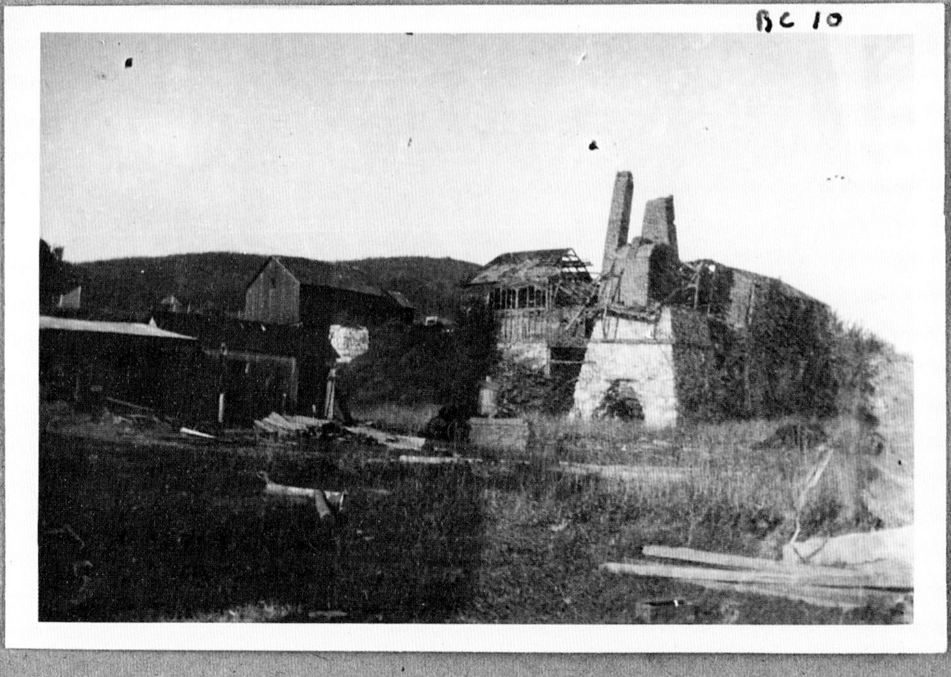

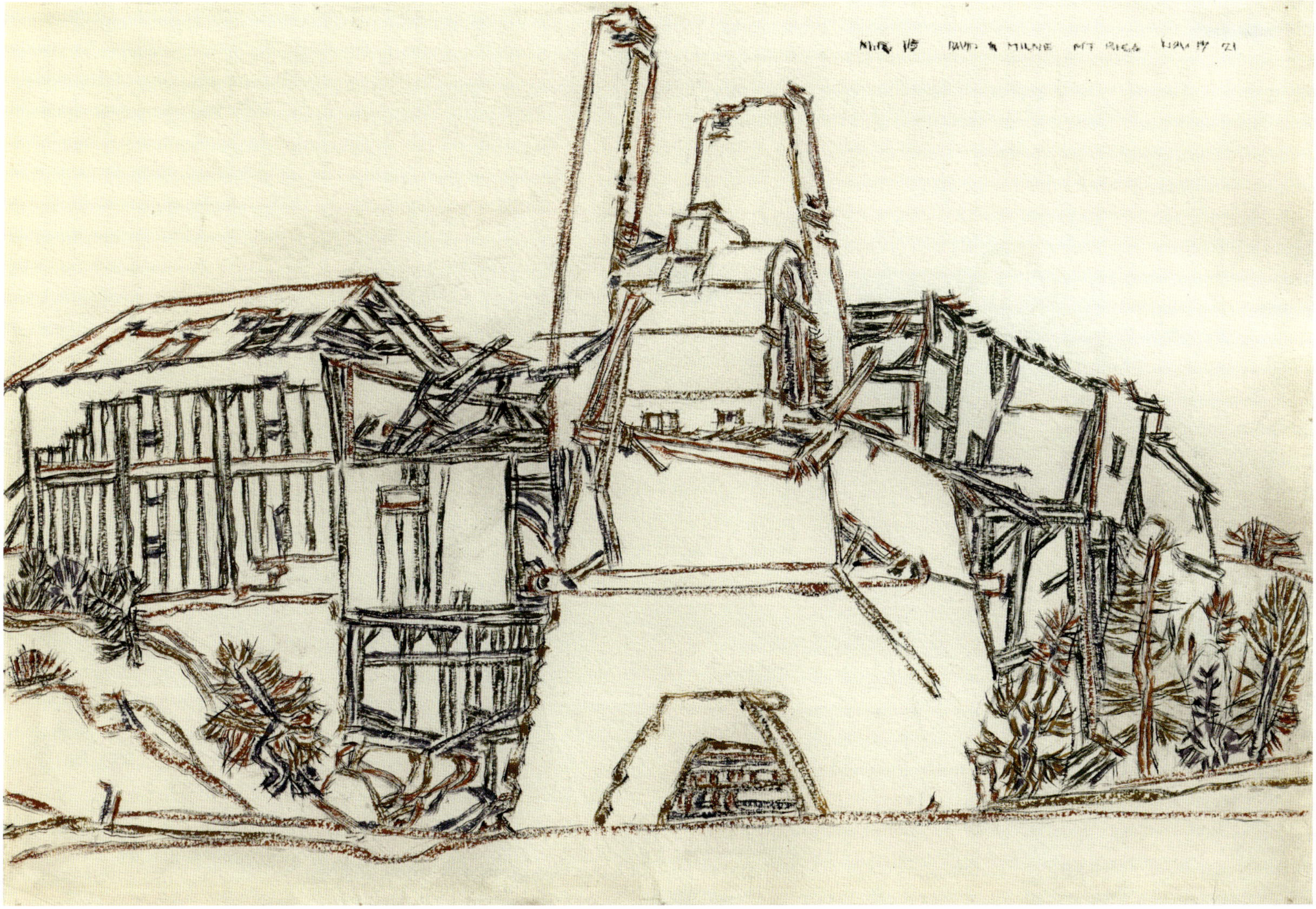

Opposite
David Milne
Charcoal furnace near Riga Lake
1921

Ruined Furnace
1921, watercolour on paper

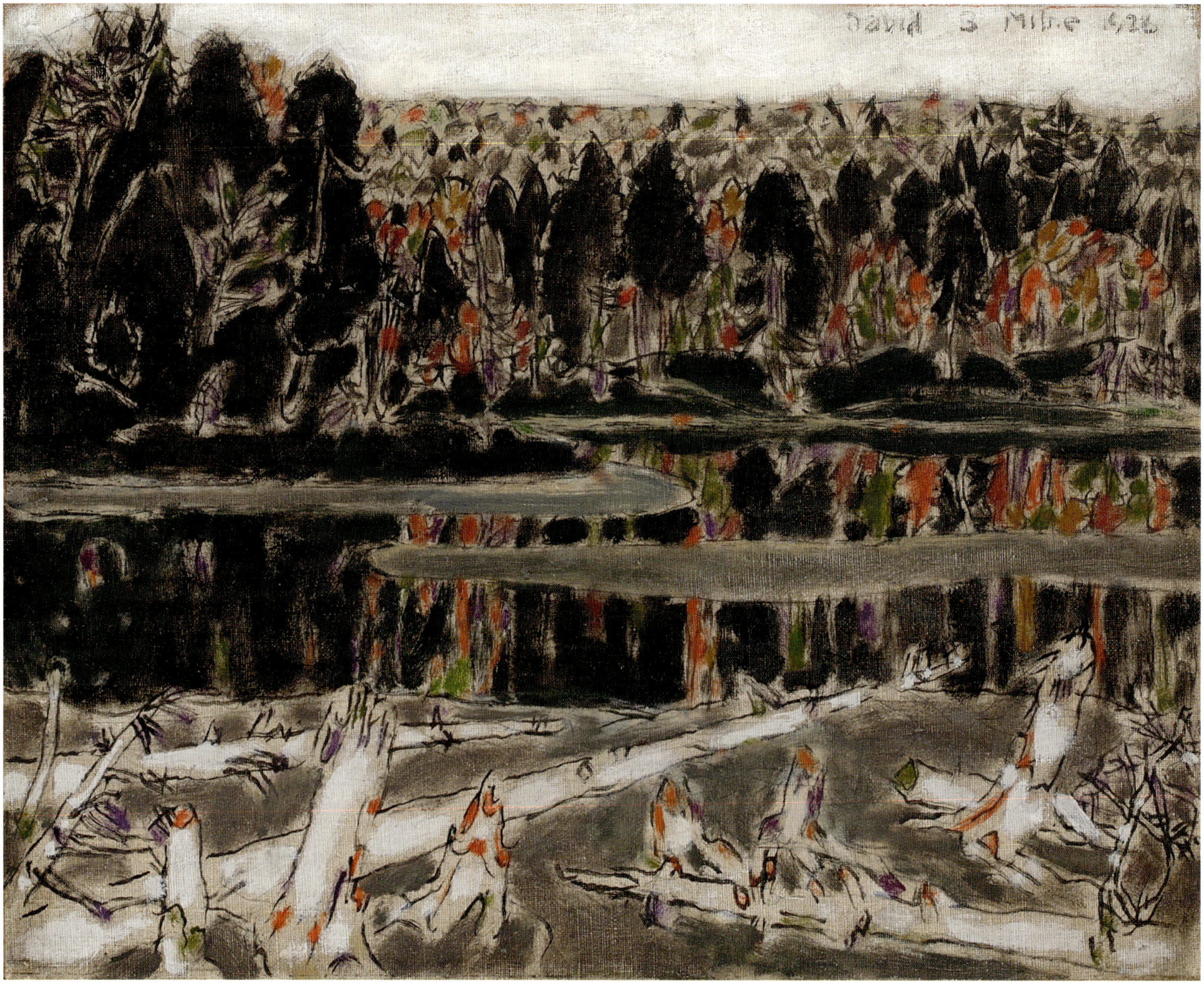

Outlet of the Pond, Late Afternoon
1926, oil on canvas

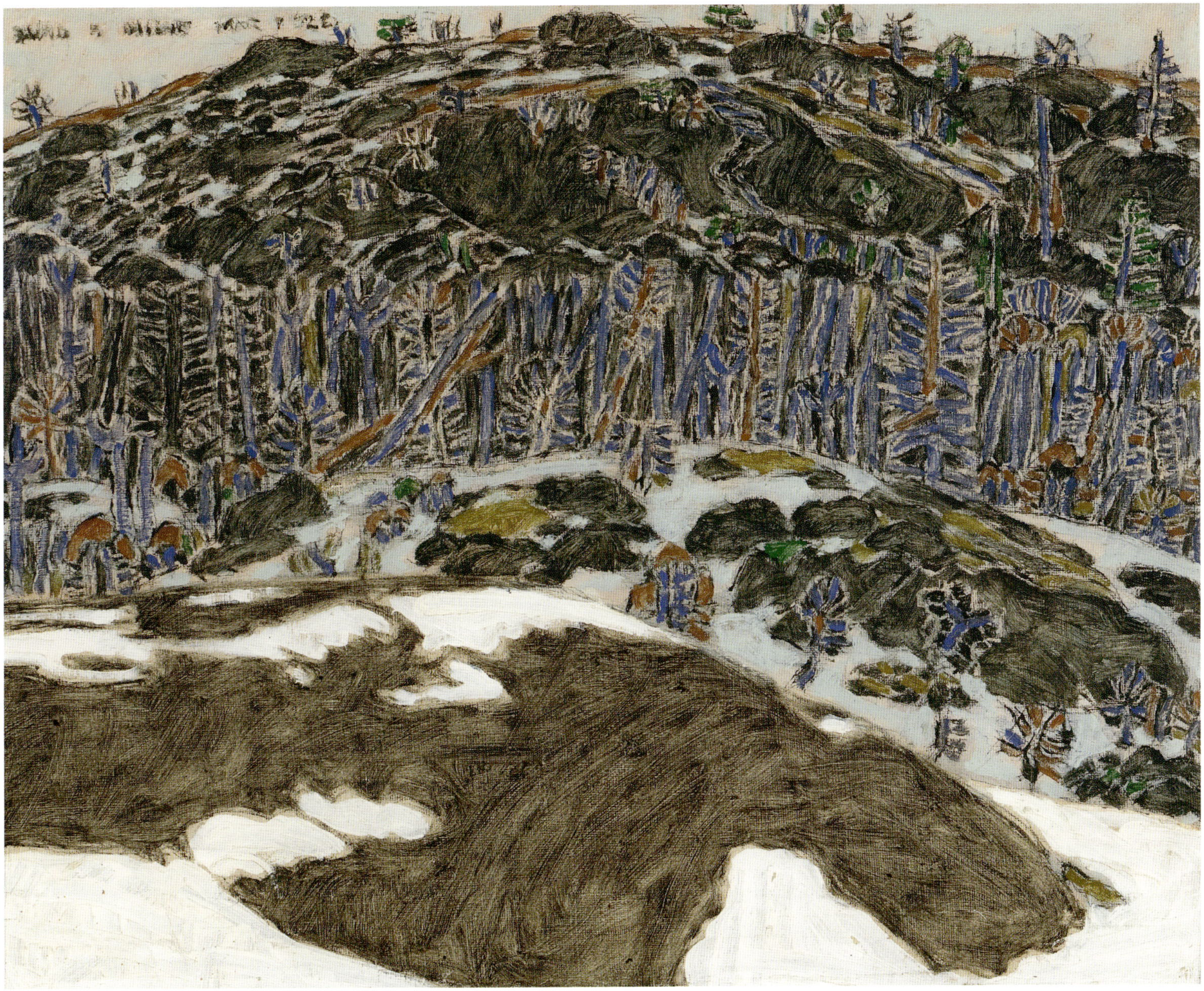

Rocks in Spring
1922, oil on canvas

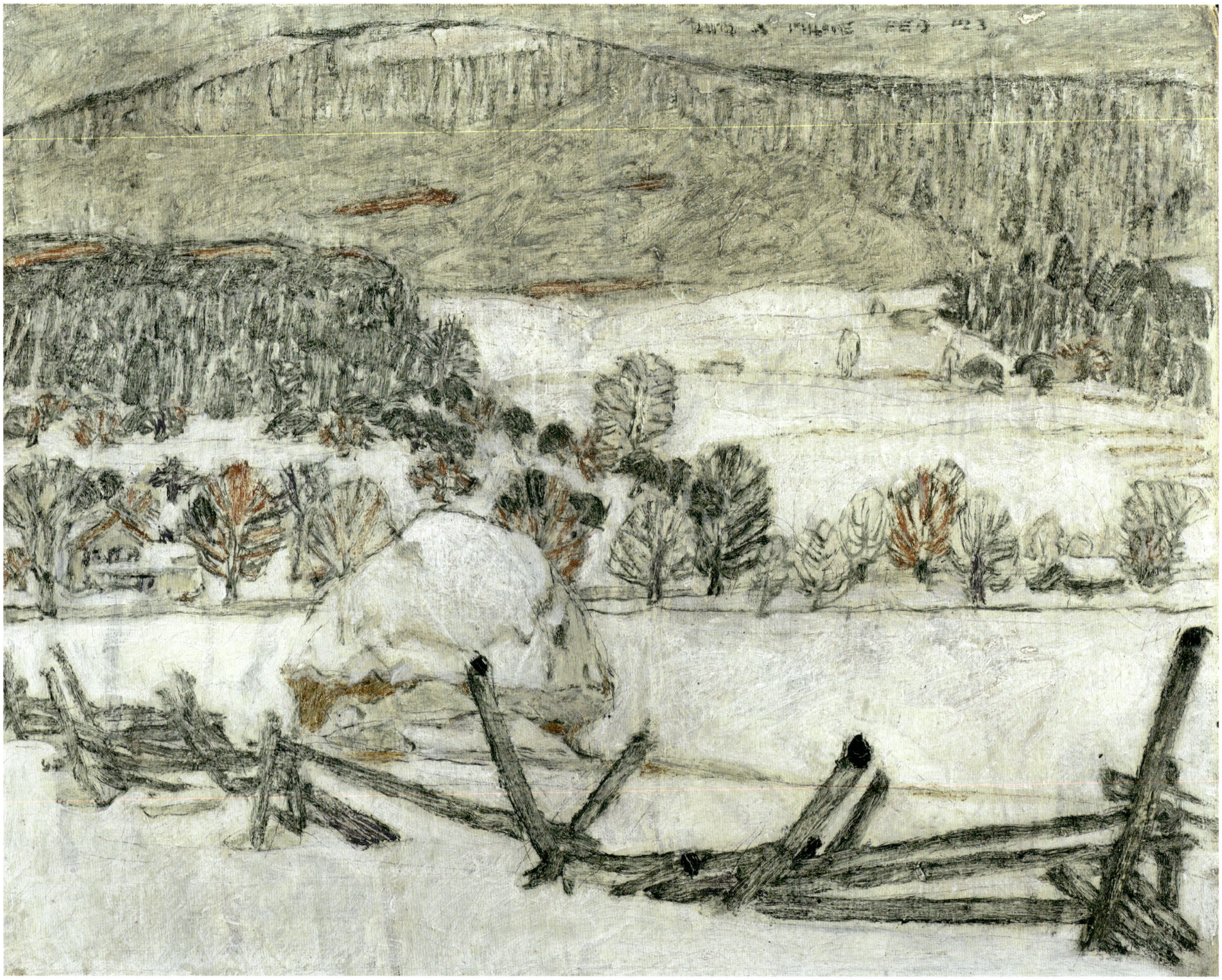

Haystack
1923, oil on canvas

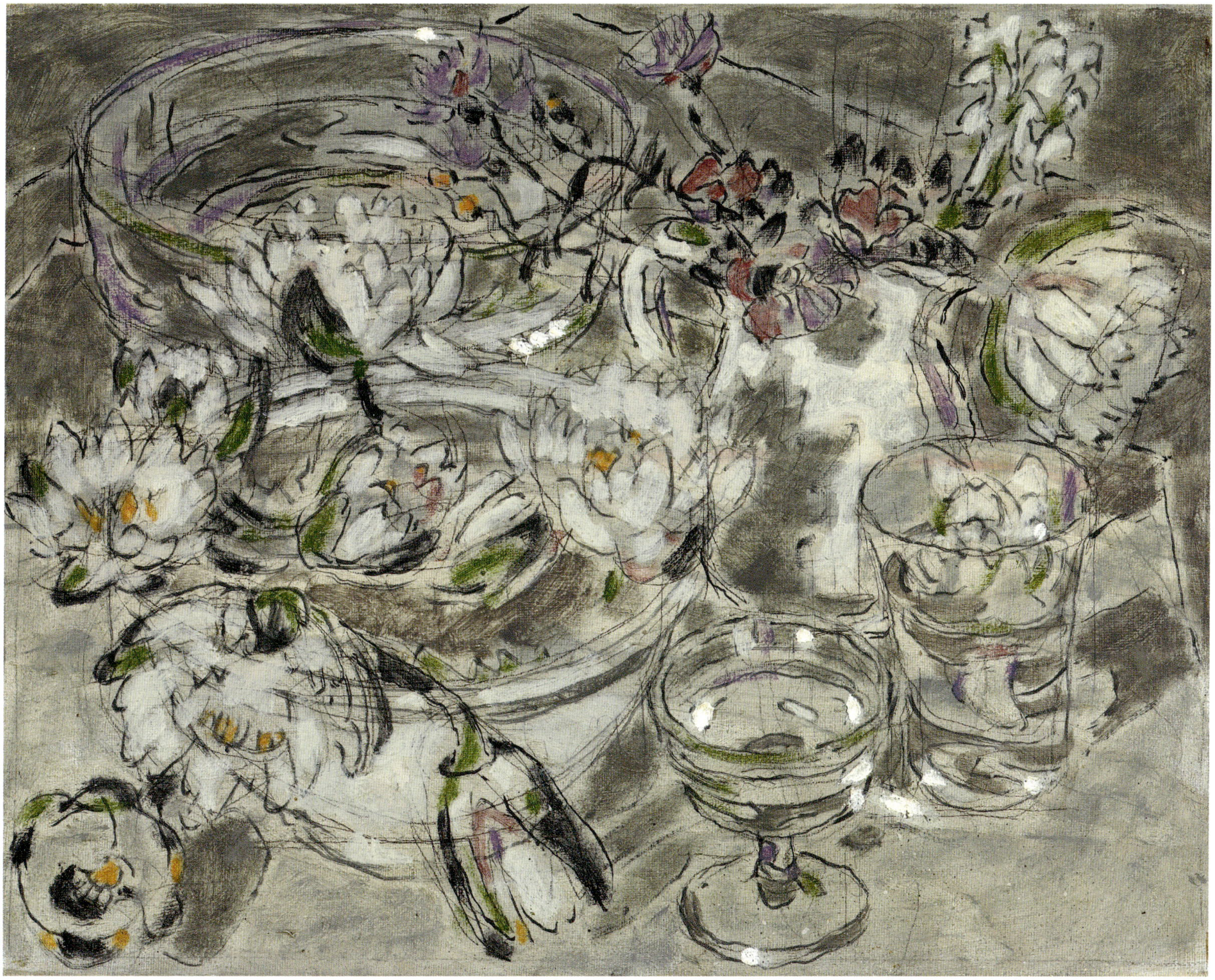

Sparkle of Glass
1926 or 1927, oil on canvas

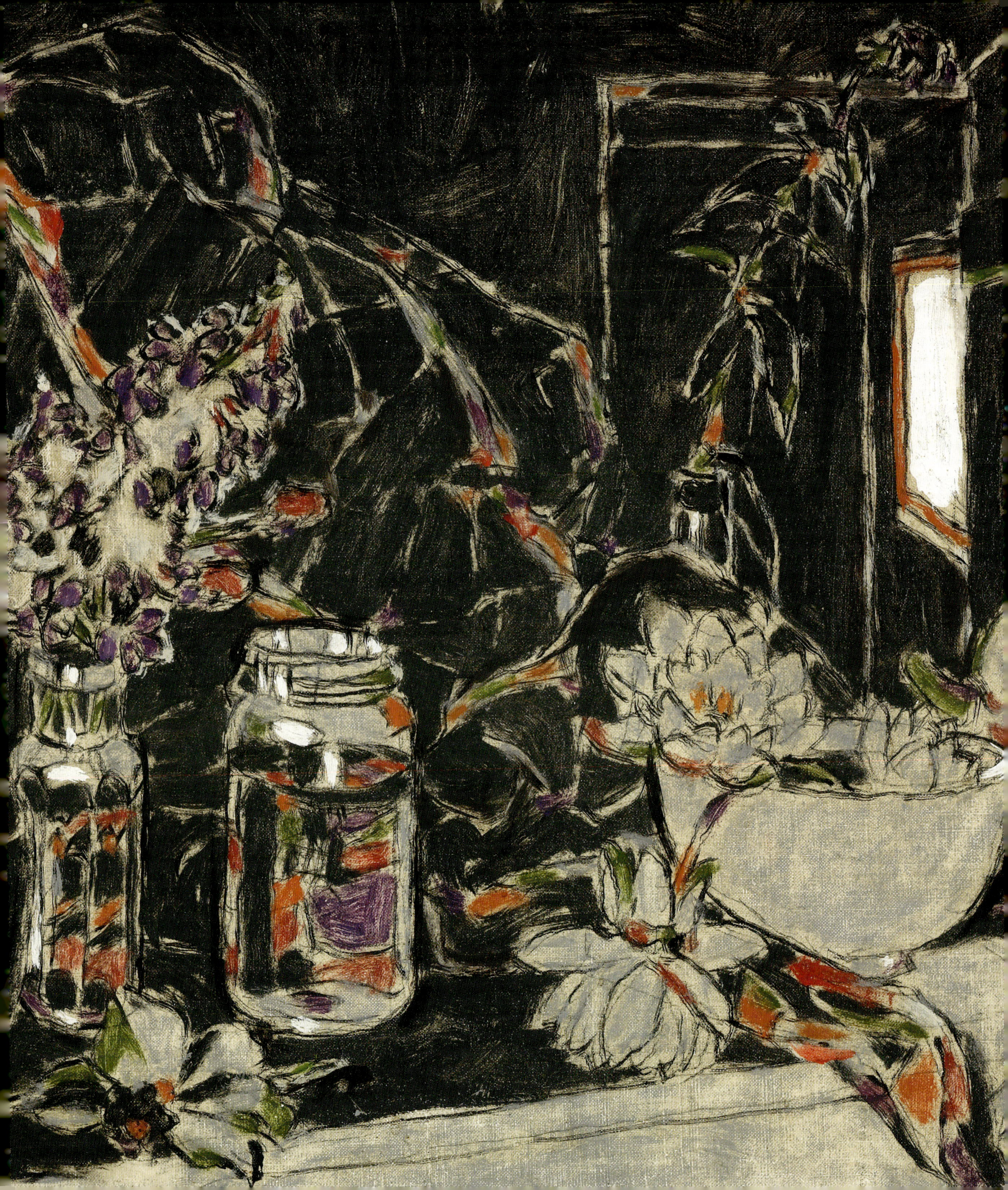

RETURN TO CANADA

Milne had returned to Canada briefly in 1923–4, but for the most part felt discouraged in his efforts to connect with his artistic peers in his country of origin. In 1929, however, he came home for good, settling for a time in Temagami, a remote mining and logging town on the threshold of northern Ontario. Here he lived in a tent, with occasional visits to an abandoned prospector's cabin, creating a series of remarkable works that explore the extremes of subject matter.

On the one hand, Milne painted a series of still lifes at Temagami, many of which carry representations of his own paintings within them—a kind of self-referentiality that suggests both his modernist sophistication and his fundamental aloneness. The water lily appears repeatedly in these works, bespeaking Milne's long memory of Monet's art, and the water lilies Monet painted in the shadow of World War I, not far from where Milne had walked the trenches. Nothing could be further from the French master's heavenly paradise on earth, however, than Milne's hardscrabble life in the bush.

On the other hand, Milne was also drawn to paint the flooded prospect shafts at Temagami, which he discovered in the nearby woods. 'To the miner it may be a disappointment', he wrote of one such abandoned shaft, its waters suffused with leaching minerals, 'but to the painter in search of colour it is a find'. These are among his grittiest works, some of them smouldering with a kind of infernal intensity. For the most part horizonless, they plunge us facedown into the blast holes, formally recalling the artist's earlier encounters with the craters of the Western Front. Milne bears witness to the earliest scars of industry on the landscape here, but as in his war art, he documents more than he proselytises. These are modern landscapes of a new order, reflecting a changing world.

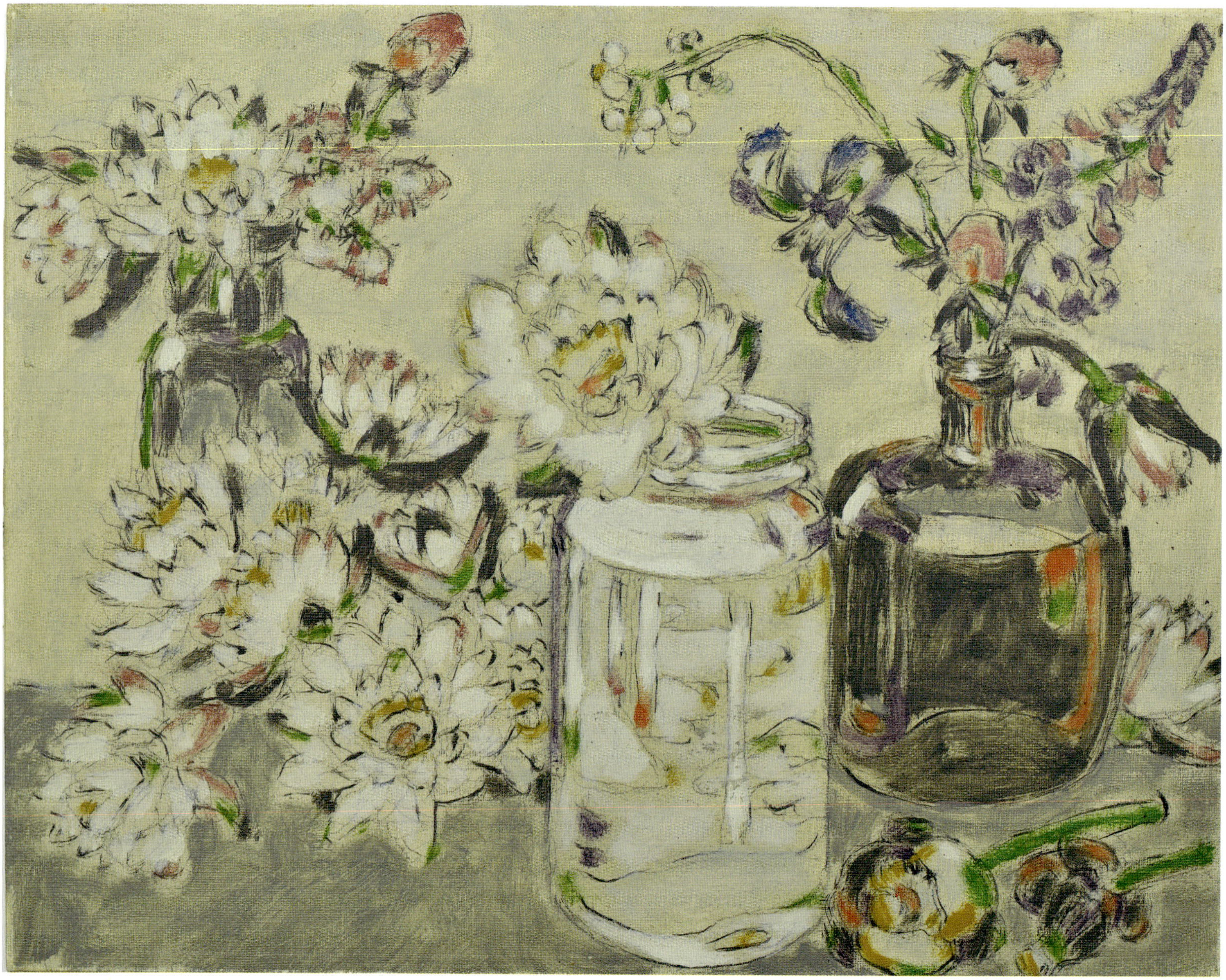

Water Lilies
1928, oil on canvas

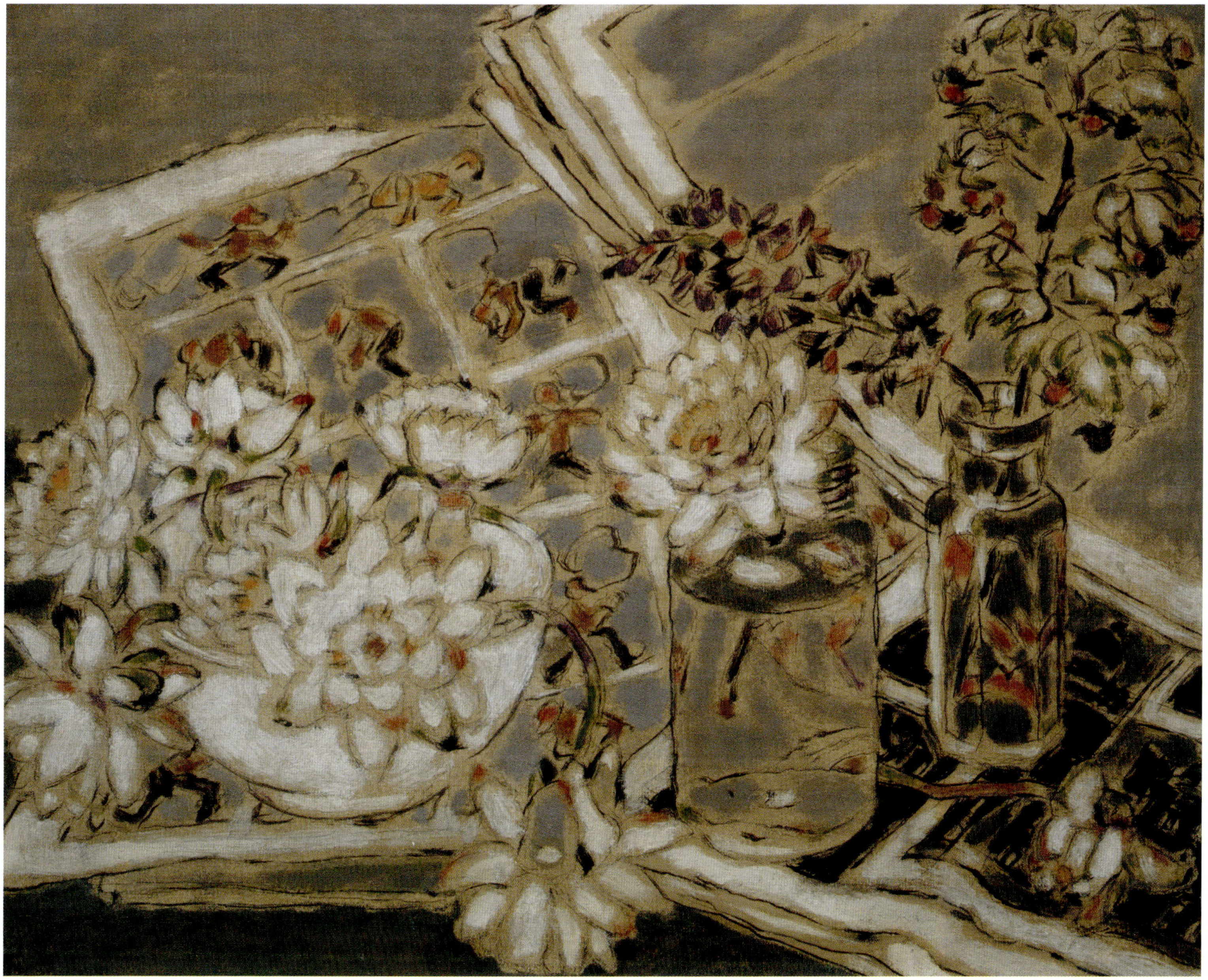

Waterlilies and the Sunday Paper
(Water Lilies, Temagami)
1929, oil on canvas

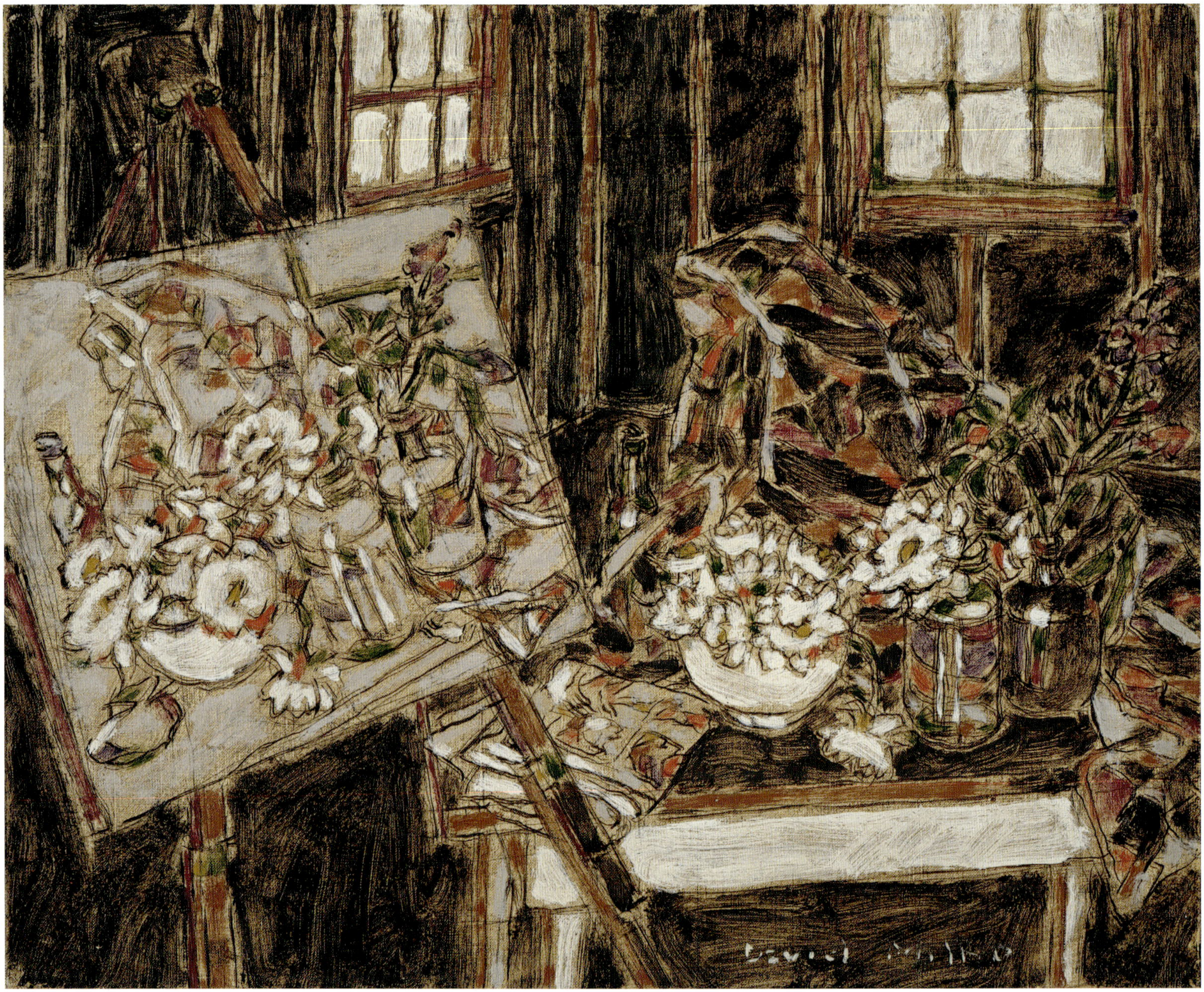

Flowers and Easel
1929, oil on canvas

MILNE'S GREAT INDOORS

Jane Urquhart

David Milne was 47 years old when he returned to Canada for good. Like a fugitive on the run, he abandoned Ottawa after a few days and travelled through the seemingly endless landscape of water, rock and pine trees that lies to the north. Finally, he arrived at the Ontario town of Temagami, almost 500 kilometres to the northwest, carrying with him his art supplies and everything he had learned about life and aesthetics—both in and out of his native land—in the intervening years. There, close to town, he set up house in a tent with a wooden floor and a stovepipe and, by his own admission, never moved farther than five kilometres away from his campsite. As he would discover to his delight, almost every subject he needed was right at the end of his outstretched arm—or his paddle—as he toured in his canoe along the shores of the serene lake. And if nature's arrangements did not suit, he could seek out the plants and flowers that had obsessed him since his childhood botanical studies, arranging his specimens in the few vessels that were among his current possessions.

The cabins, shacks, tents—even the simple lean-tos—of bush architecture had always appealed to Milne, but here he seemed to seek a thinner and thinner membrane between himself and the woods outside. Inside these provisional shelters, the plants he had harvested appeared to push through and around their containers, as if every surface and object were germinating with signs of that outdoor life. In *Waterlilies and the Sunday Paper*, 1929 (p. 143), for example, the daily news has been overtaken by nature, and the cartoons and photographs on the newsprint can be read as only slightly more geometric blossoms, with the same colour and texture as the plucked flowers close by.

The fact that Milne had access to a Sunday paper at all speaks to the existence of the haphazard mining settlements in the area—such as the silver town of Cobalt 50 kilometres away, or the village of Temagami itself. Milne would have been aware that mining operations smaller than these would sometimes bloom in the bush overnight, then almost as quickly disappear, leaving behind a skeletal headframe or the flooded shafts that so interested him as painter. The Sunday paper, too, is ephemeral, with its description of fleeting events. The composition thus speaks to this sense of human transience on the one hand, and the persistence of nature on the other. But the water in the jars animates everything, mixing the stems of the plants and the illustrations refracted from the newspaper beneath them in a wild, joyful dance.

Milne claimed that one-third of his efforts in Temagami went towards painting the wild water lilies found in the dark lakes and ponds of the forest. No artist in 1929 could choose the subject of water lilies without the shadow of the by-then very famous French artist Claude Monet darkening his or her mental doorstep, but Milne's bush flowers were a far cry from the pastel panoramas of Monet's painted garden. Monet's water lilies were fully cultivated, both in the ponds of his garden and, to a certain extent, in his paintings, while Milne's water lilies were wild and uncultivated. And while the French artist painted his subjects *en plein air*, the Canadian brought his blooms inside.

Once they were under his roof, however, Milne took no pains to formally arrange his bouquets. Instead, he thrust casual handfuls of water lilies into water-filled bowls and glass jars and watched as the combination of moisture and glass reflected and quickened the shapes and colours of the flowers. Added to this visual carnival were the shapes and colours that migrated onto the glass and into the water from every corner of the room, and from the windows giving access to the natural world outside. As Milne confessed to a friend in a letter, the water lilies themselves were not really what moved him; they were 'just an excuse for having bottles of water around to diffuse and refract light'.[1]

In *Flowers and Easel*, 1929 (p. 144), he begins to pay attention to both the refraction and the source of the light itself, when he paints two rectangular cabin windows, then echoes their shapes with a 'painting inside the painting' as bright, and as seemingly transparent, as the windows' panes of glass. The interior is darkening down in this picture, with the light picking out the parallel line of the table (complete with Sunday paper), the painting and the floral subject, leaving the surroundings in shadow.

Those shadows deepen in Milne's most mysterious—and most Canadian—version of this motif: *White Waterlilies in a Prospector's Cabin*, 1929 (p. 156). Even the title of this painting seems like a tip of the hat in Monet's direction. But there is much more going on here than a gesture from a new world to an old, or a statement from the bush concerning nature versus culture. The light in this chamber, the source of which is a small rectangle high on the picture plane, is echoed *only* in the reflections carried by the bottles of water, the thick dark jug and in the almost phosphorescent glow of the bowl and the flowers. Everything else is clothed in darkness—the darkness of a mineshaft (with its opening rectangle on the upper right) or, indeed, the darkness of the tomb. It was as if Milne, with his eagerness to be less and less protected from the environment, had found a way to imaginatively enter the earth itself—to be fully embraced by nature.

No still life of Milne's could ever be confused with a European *nature morte*; they are too full of vitality for that. This is particularly true of the still lifes that he painted in the precarious shelters of the Temagami region, situated in a wilderness that continued—practically untouched—for more than 1,000 kilometres to the north. In this frontier, any settler endeavour had to be seen as ephemeral. 'The property went back to bush' was a familiar mining colloquialism in the area, one I often heard growing up in the mining town of Little Longlac, another several hundred kilometres to the north-west. Nature was ready to move in where humankind left off, given the slightest chance. Yet, as Milne knew, the light of the natural world shines persistently on, and these paintings, with their transparencies and spatial confusions, the insistent glitter of moisture and the shine of reflections on glass, are enhanced and quickened by light. And they carry this light—this life—into even the darkest of places.

***Jane Urquhart** is an award-winning Canadian novelist whose works have been published internationally, including* The Whirlpool *(1986),* Away *(1993),* The Underpainter *(1997),* The Stone Carvers *(2001) and* Sanctuary Line *(2010). She currently holds the 2017–18 Craig Dobbin Chair in Canadian Studies at University College Dublin.*

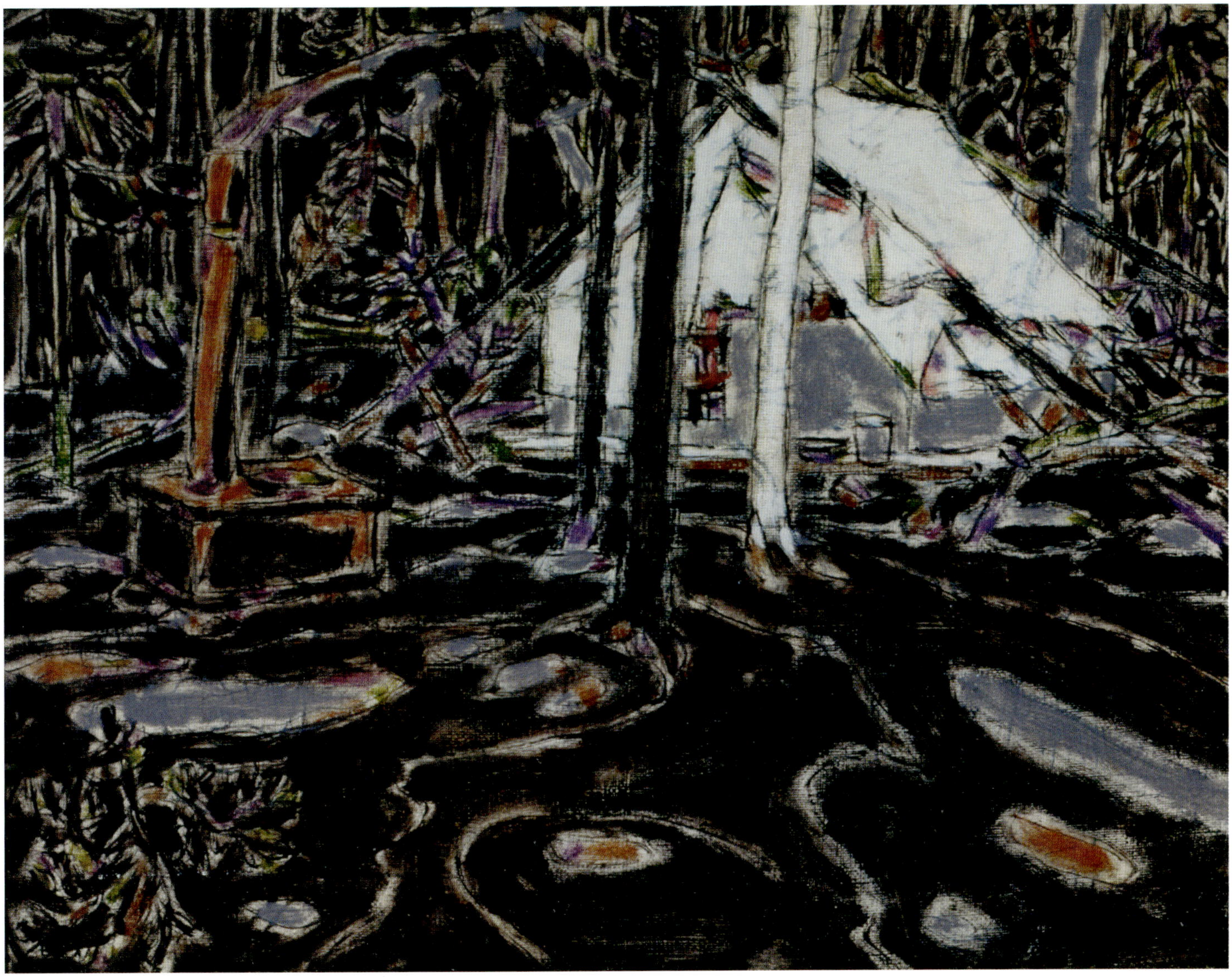

Tent in Temagami
1929, oil on canvas

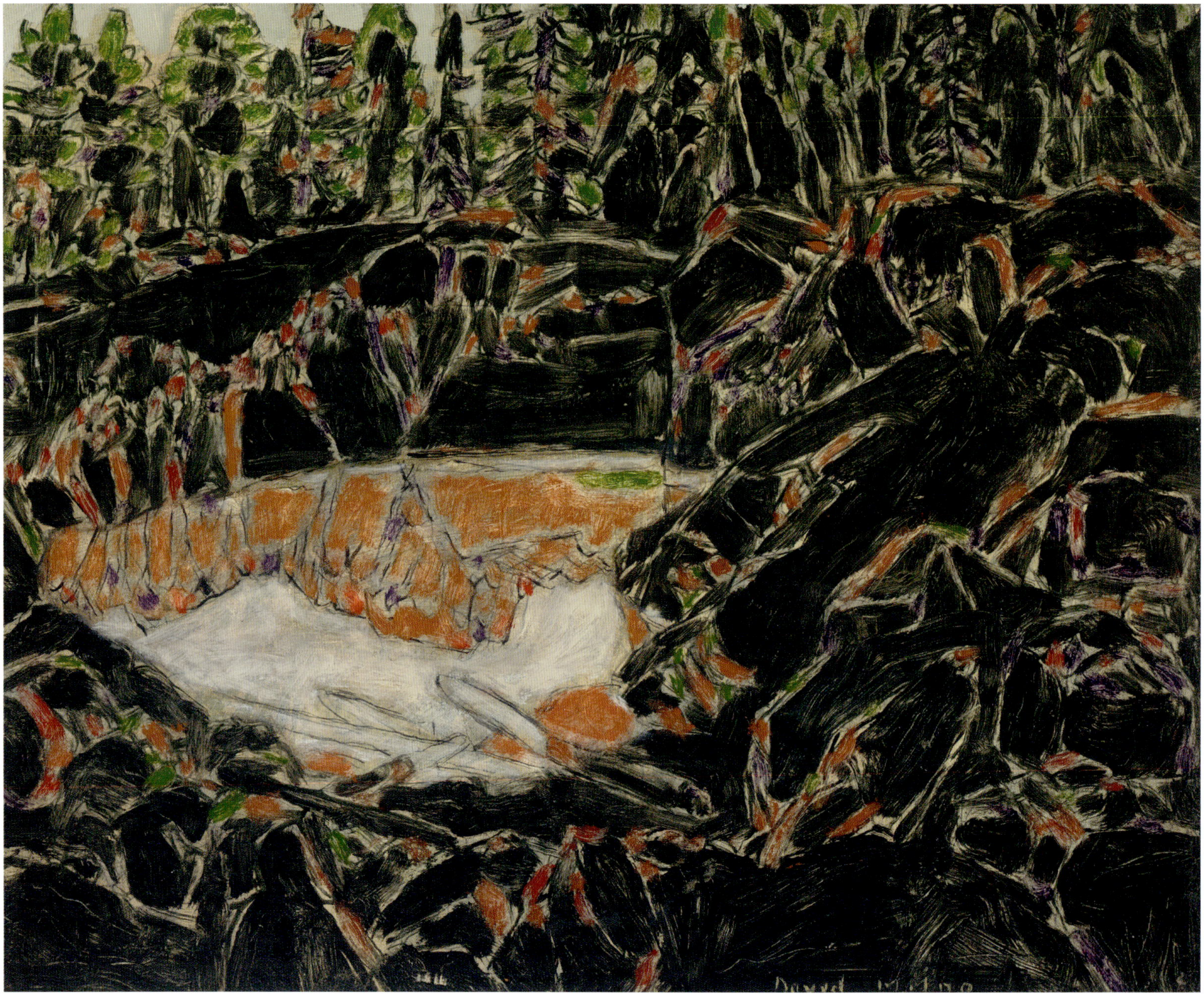

Red Pool, Temagami
1929, oil on canvas

MILNE'S MINESHAFTS: A CONVERSATION

Edward Burtynsky and Sarah Milroy

SM Mining has been such a consistent interest of yours as a photographer. How did your own relationship to that industry begin?
EB Just before I started out as an art student here in Toronto, I needed to get some money together to buy equipment and so on. A friend of mine worked up at the mine at Red Lake, which is literally the end of the road in Ontario, north of Dryden, on the border of Manitoba—about a twenty-hour drive northwest from Toronto. The first week up there, I found a job in the Red Lake Gold Mine, which for a long time was Canada's richest gold mine. My friend worked at the Griffith Mine in Ear Falls in a big open-pit iron-ore mine, so I went to see him too. I was, I think, 19 when I saw that first big open-pit mine.

I was there at the end of the day, when they were doing a blast. Rocks were flying up in the air, and then they just rained down. The earth shakes because these are massive explosions taking off a whole bank at a time. The team might spend two weeks loading up a wall of rock with dynamite. It was an incredible thing to see, but I just filed it away and never really thought about it. I made quite a bit of money that summer, and I came back and started my photography course. It never occurred to me that it would become subject matter.

Later, in 1981, I was working on my last year's portfolio. I had been doing a lot of horizonless work, looking at the landscape more as a raw material that I could use the way a painter would. In a picture like *Grasses, Bruce Peninsula, Ontario*, 1981 (p. 150) I was interested in the compression of space, looking at it from a painterly aesthetic, trying to fill my frame. There's a sense of Pollock, I think, of something gestural, an all-overness. But I realised that I was just not that engaged with the subject matter itself. It was largely a formal exercise, and it seemed to suggest a yearning to be of another time.

About then I came across mined areas in Pennsylvania. That was the first time I shot a mine as a subject. It seemed more in keeping with my own moment in history. I had an intuition that if I kept working with these kinds of images I could come to understand our relationship to nature, how we use it, how we usurp it. To me that was more interesting. In 1982 also [the German photo-conceptual artists] Bernd and Hilla Becher came to North America, and they were shooting makeshift headframes [structural frames above mineshafts] in the mining country in Virginia. These are the only other photographers that I knew who were dealing with this kind of subject matter back then.

Edward Burtynsky
Grasses, Bruce Peninsula, Ontario
1981, chromogenic print

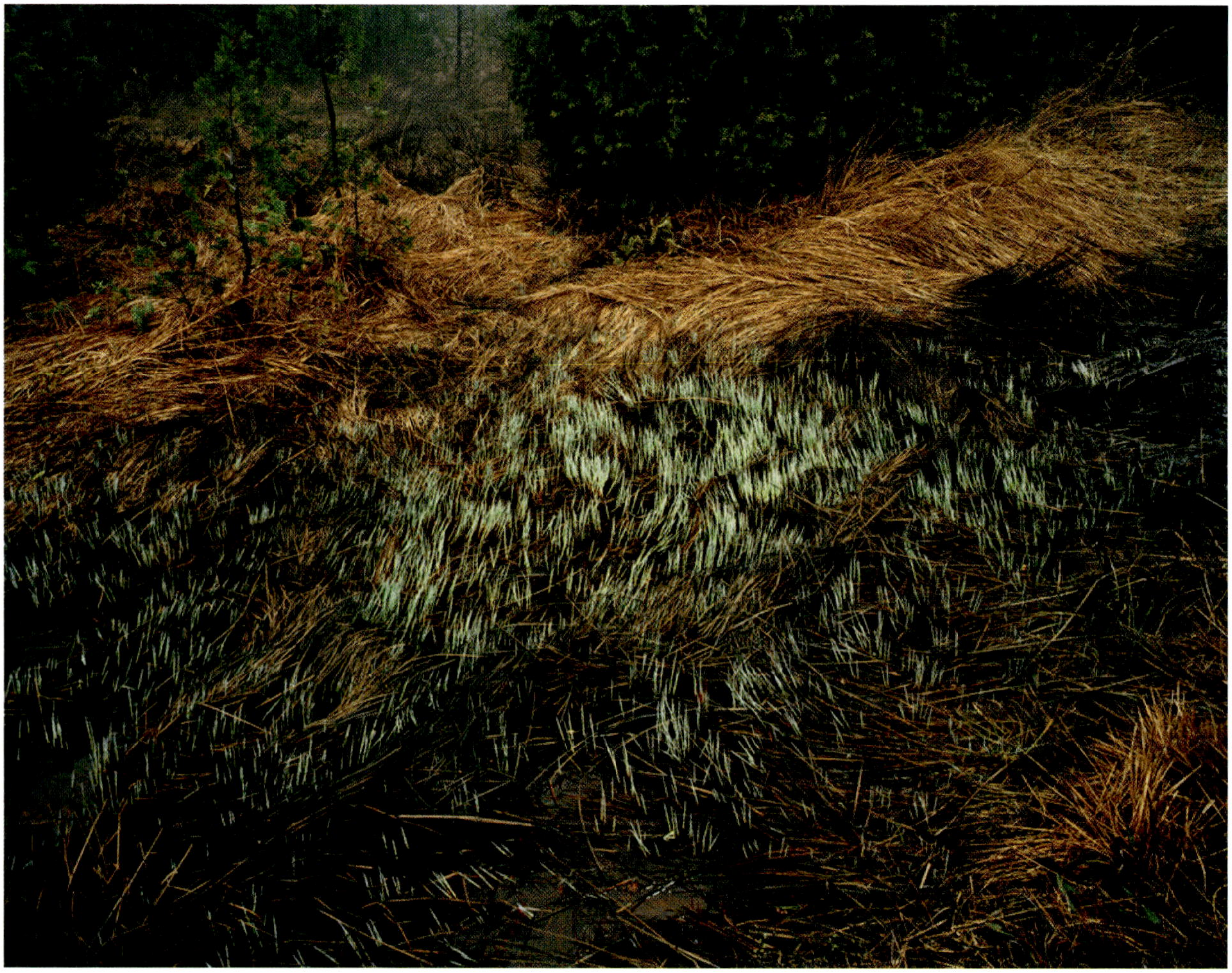

SM So many of the mines that you have documented have been on an almost epic scale. Milne's paintings look back to an earlier, smaller scale of operation.
EB These are artisanal human-scale mines that Milne was looking at. I have been to Temagami, and I've also seen prospect holes in the woods. They were known in the industry at the time as 'glory holes'—a guy takes all of his possessions, cashes out everything and goes out into the wilderness with dynamite, a pick axe and a shovel and on a hunch stakes out a place and says, 'There's gold here.' There are hundreds and hundreds of these 'lost lives', I call them, where the hope was of hitting the jackpot. The sites are all grown over now, but I find myself thinking about that person's life and what he had to give up to do this. How alone was it, out there digging away by himself? Did he leave a family back home? Each one of these holes has a human story attached to it. In a way, mining is a fascinating metaphor for life: you're not sure the gold is there but you just keep toiling away.

SM Well, that's very much the stage of life that Milne was at when he made these pictures at Temagami, in northern Ontario. He had just returned to Canada after 26 years in the USA, he was living in a tent, not certain anyone would ever care about the work that he was doing. He had no prospects.
EB There's that, but if I had to project what he might have been thinking about here, it's also an encounter with the human mark within a largely repetitious environment. You go over every hillock of the Canadian Shield and one place looks very much like the next. It's fairly monotonous. But here was a human incursion. It adds that element to the landscape, an event.

SM These paintings are very raw and gritty. When you look at them, do you see any evidence that he saw this mining activity in a negative light?
EB At the time, Canada was just endless resource, forest from sea to sea, and we were still a very small population, just ten million people across the whole country. The notion that we were tipping the scales against nature was not on anybody's mind. The fact that we could annihilate each other was certainly on a lot of people's minds, after World War I, but that we were a species that would have a planetary impact? No. [The Canadian photographer] Michael Torosian once referred to the idea of 'residual landscapes', showing the traces that we leave behind. There's something of that residual landscape in these paintings by Milne, but in its infancy.

SM Milne wrote to H.O. McCurry, the director of the National Gallery, about painting a prospect shaft, saying that it 'looks like the collision between Winsor & Newton's and a coal mine, good for painting'. These were evidently iron mines, but Milne described them as 'iron, copper, silver, gold, arsenic, sulphur, molasses'.[1] What about the colours here?
EB When I work with these kinds of landscapes, it's often about the colours. Where minerals are found, there are usually a lot of traces of them in the water. Most ore bodies are the result of some ancient catastrophic event, where a meteorite hit the planet. The whole Sudbury basin was the site of a meteorite impact, so all the mines are around the edges where the magma gushed out. Hudson Bay was created by a meteorite impact. What happens when you have that high level of mineralisation and you start removing rock—that rock that has been sitting underground, benign—is that now you have broken it up, exposed it to oxygen and other gases and water, so these sulphurs and coppers, which might give you a green colour, and iron ore and all these other chemicals are being released into the environment. That's how you get the weird-coloured pools, like the ones that Milne painted. You don't normally find these colours in nature. In our current time, you find them only when you get that intersection with us.

SM Tell me about your photograph *Abandoned Mine Shaft Crean Hill Mine, Sudbury, Ontario*, 1984 (p. 152). You said it was one of your most important earlier works.
EB I almost didn't get that shot. I was walking by it and saw it, but it was in deep shadow. But then I went back and had the idea of using a very long exposure to get that colour. They had been mining there for nickel and copper—all the mines in Sudbury are fifty-fifty nickel and copper. It's all here in this image: the compression of space, the flattening of the image. I felt a recognition that visual interest can be cultivated from multifaceted rock when the rock face is exposed.

SM It strikes me how much this image is structured like Milne's *Flooded Prospect Shaft II*, 1929 (p.153), which we are showing in the exhibition.
EB In both pictures, there is a bifurcation of the foreground and the background. In both cases, we are looking at an altered rock face. There is a dynamic that begins to unfold. To me it's important to the image that you can see the reflection in the visual field below. Then there are those fantastic greens. This is the painting of Milne's that really grabs me.

SM What about the composition of these two pictures?
EB Well, it's kind of like short-wave radio, attending to a very, very faint frequency, and that delicate moment when you find it. It's elusive. My camera could have been 8 inches to the right, or 8 inches to the left and the picture would have fallen apart. That ability to dial in is the key. I often tend not to include sky in my compositions, because I want the eye to wander over the whole plane. Maybe for me, initially, this has something to do with the particularities of this place, of this landscape in Ontario. Everything visual is happening down on the ground.

SM Do you see these as very Canadian pictures?
EB We have a reputation in Canada of being closer to nature because we have so much of it, and many of us have had the experience of being out there in the presence of what nature intended. Our experience of nature is therefore different

from that of people who grew up in Holland, where every plant and every tree has been placed. We still have untouched nature but, for a smallish country population-wise, we have done a very aggressive job of removing the forests. We are prodigious takers. Fort McMurray is the largest surface-mining project on the planet. We are the leading mining and drilling country in the world, owning and operating more than half of all mining operations internationally, from South America to Africa to Asia.

As a subject for art, though—this is not normally something that an artist would pursue. I mean, [the American landscape photographer] Carleton Watkins did some early works, but he was often hired by the mining companies back at the end of the nineteenth century. At around the same time, [the Scottish-Canadian photographer] William Notman and his studios were hired to shoot the building of the railway as well, and then there was [the American] Darius Kinsey with his logging pictures—these are all early examples of industrial photography; there is this history. But in this case, Milne's interest was strictly voluntary, documenting the mineshafts as a kind of relief from the monotony of the landscape.

SM Just one visual prospector, maybe, meeting up with another, looking for some gold.

EB You could say that, for sure.

Edward Burtynsky*'s photographs of industrial landscapes are in the collections of more than 60 major museums, including the National Gallery of Canada, the Museum of Modern Art, the Guggenheim Museum in New York, the Reina Sofia Museum in Madrid, Tate Modern and the Los Angeles County Museum of Art. Among his distinctions are the TED Prize and Governor General's Awards in Visual and Media Arts.*

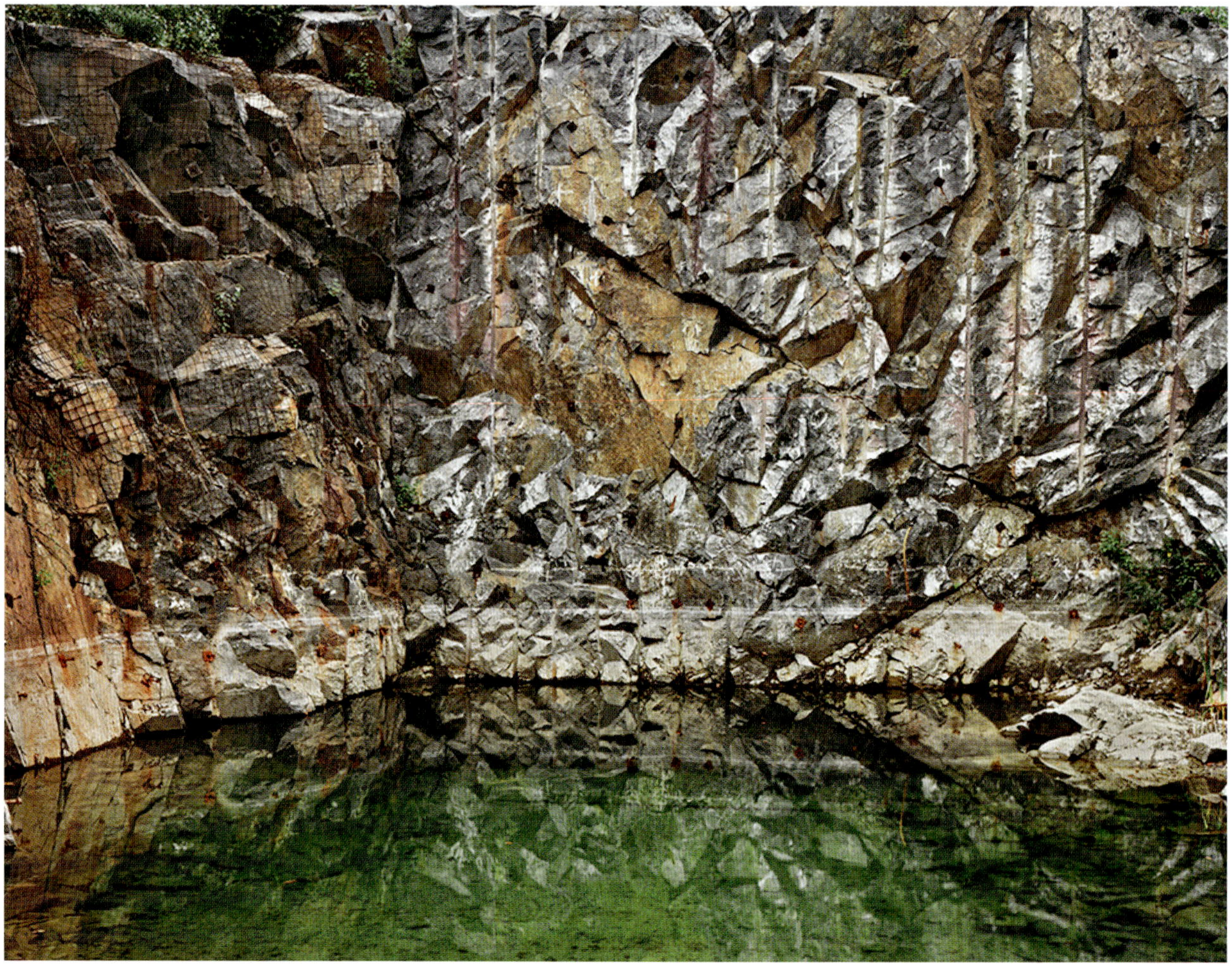

Edward Burtynsky
Mines #13, Inco—Abandoned Mine Shaft, Crean Hill Mine, Sudbury, Ontario
1984, chromogenic print

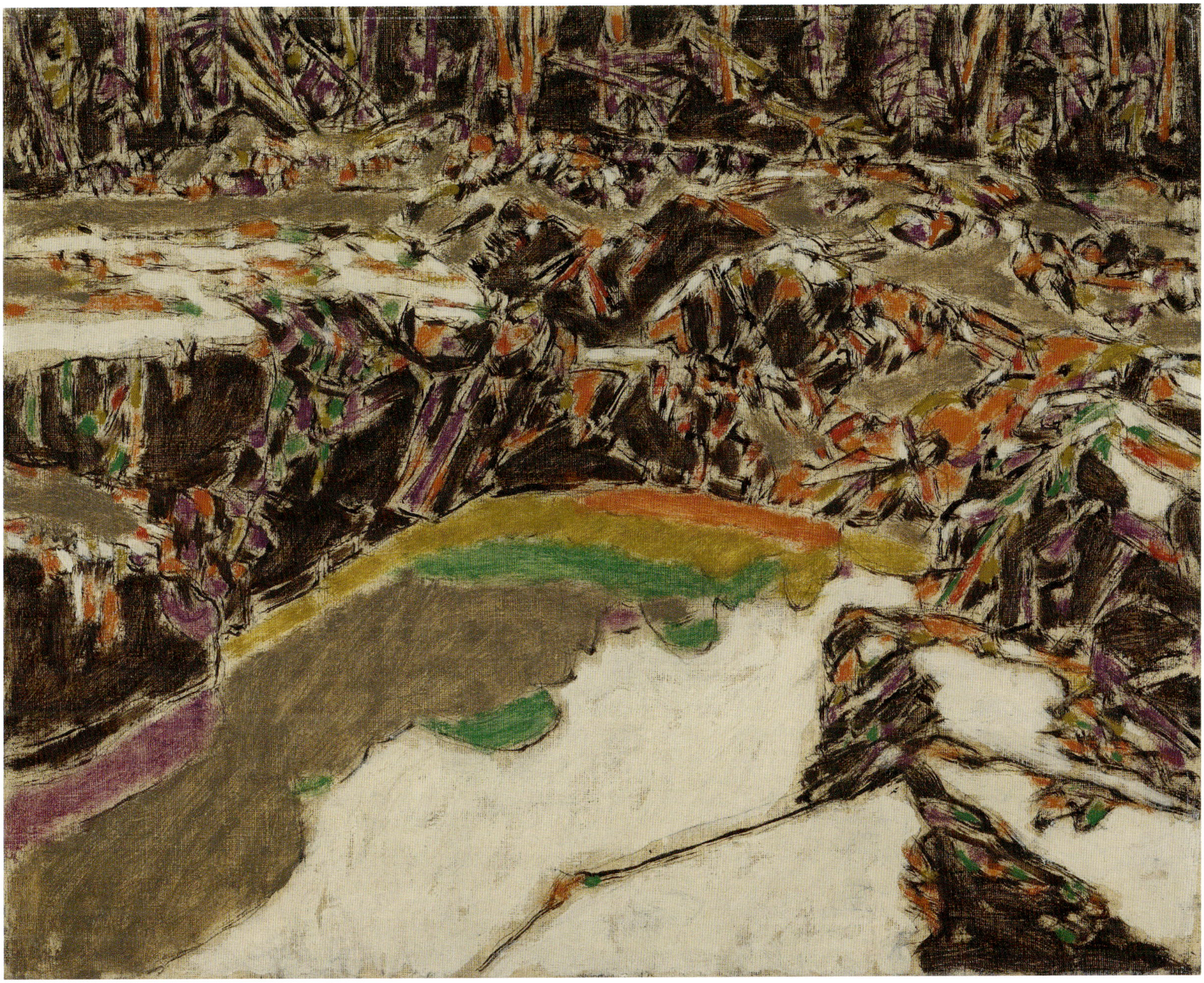

Flooded Prospect Shaft II
1929, oil on canvas

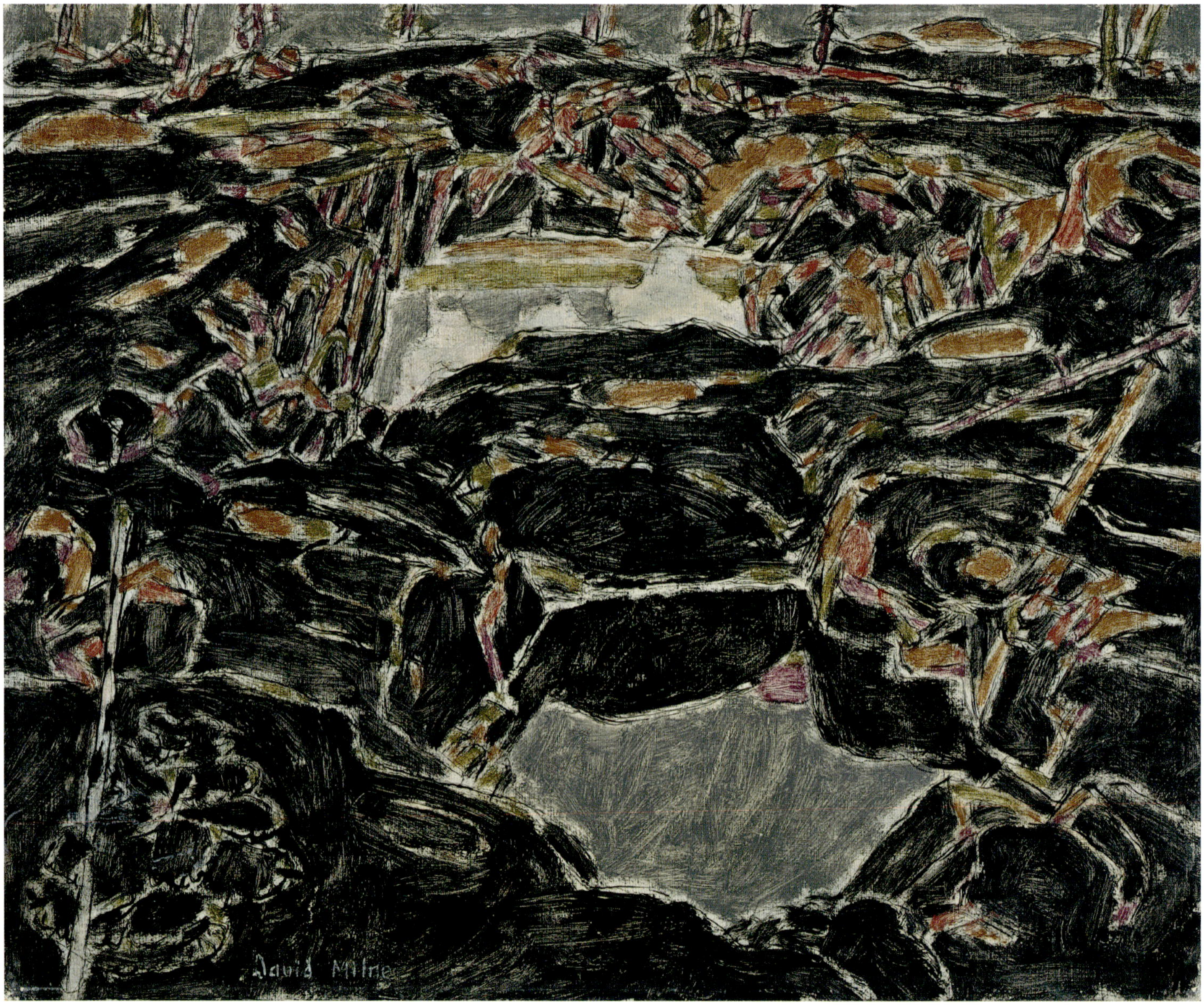

Gray Pool
1929, oil on canvas

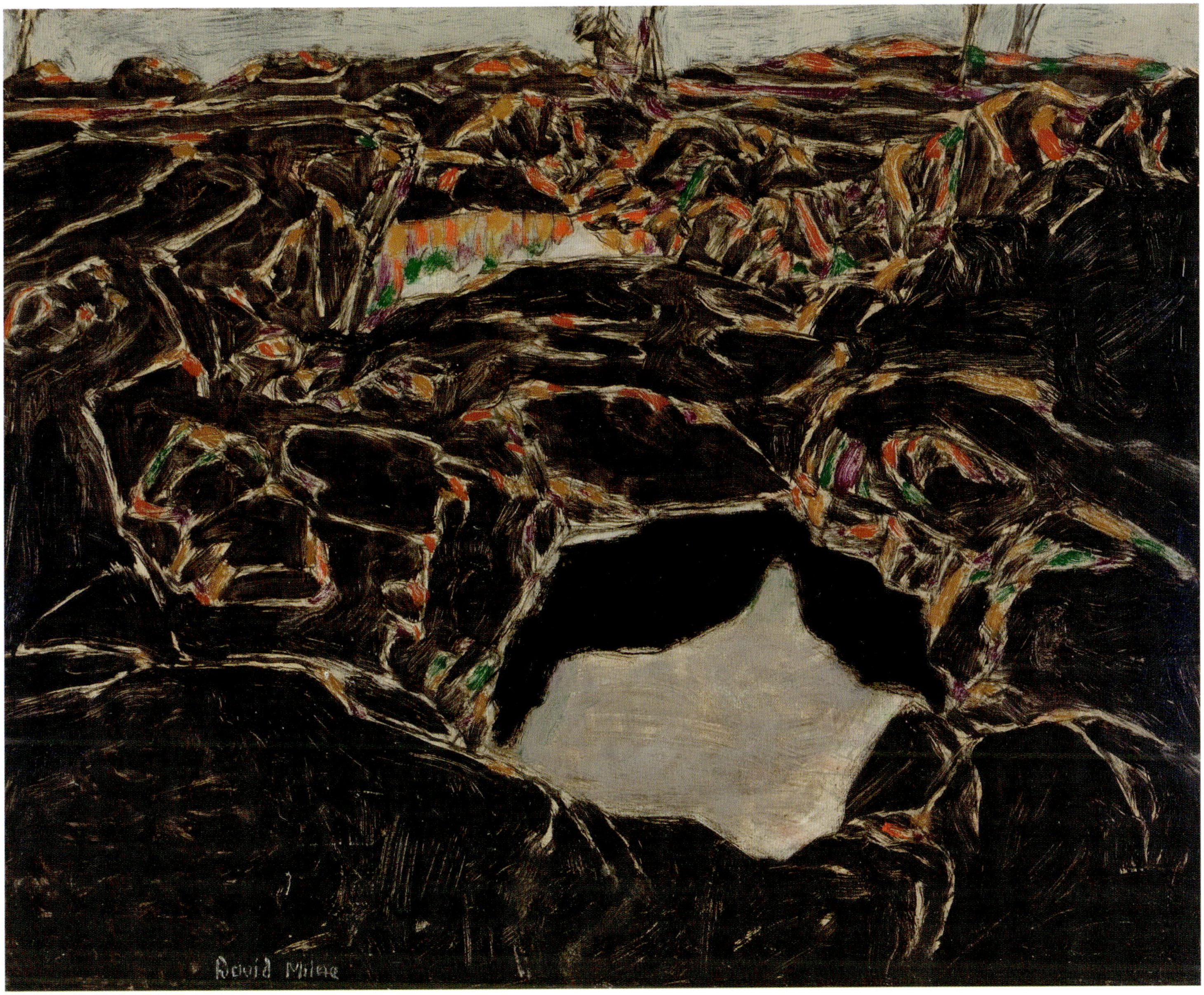

Prospect Hole
1929, oil on canvas

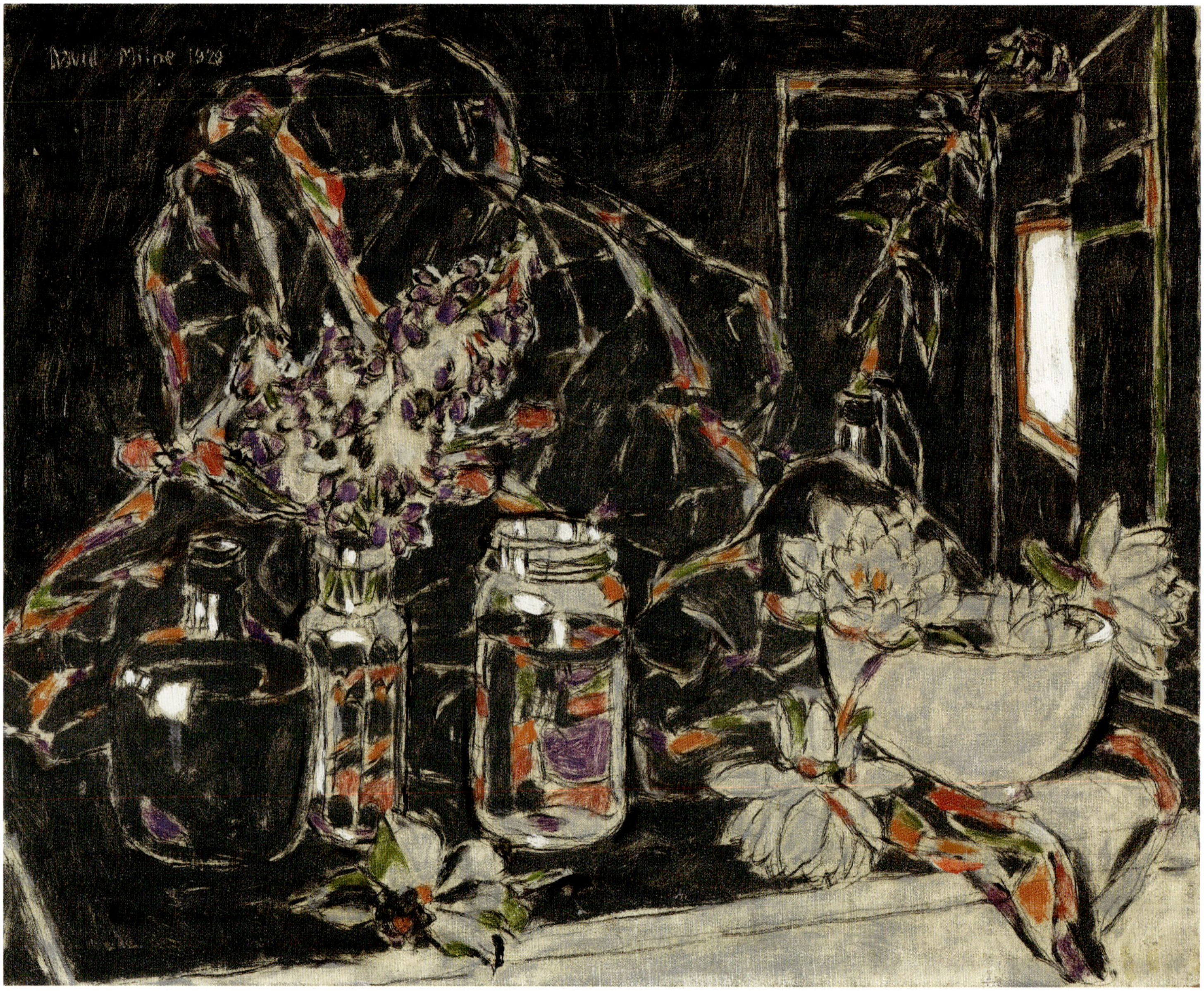

White Waterlilies in a Prospector's Cabin
1929, oil on canvas

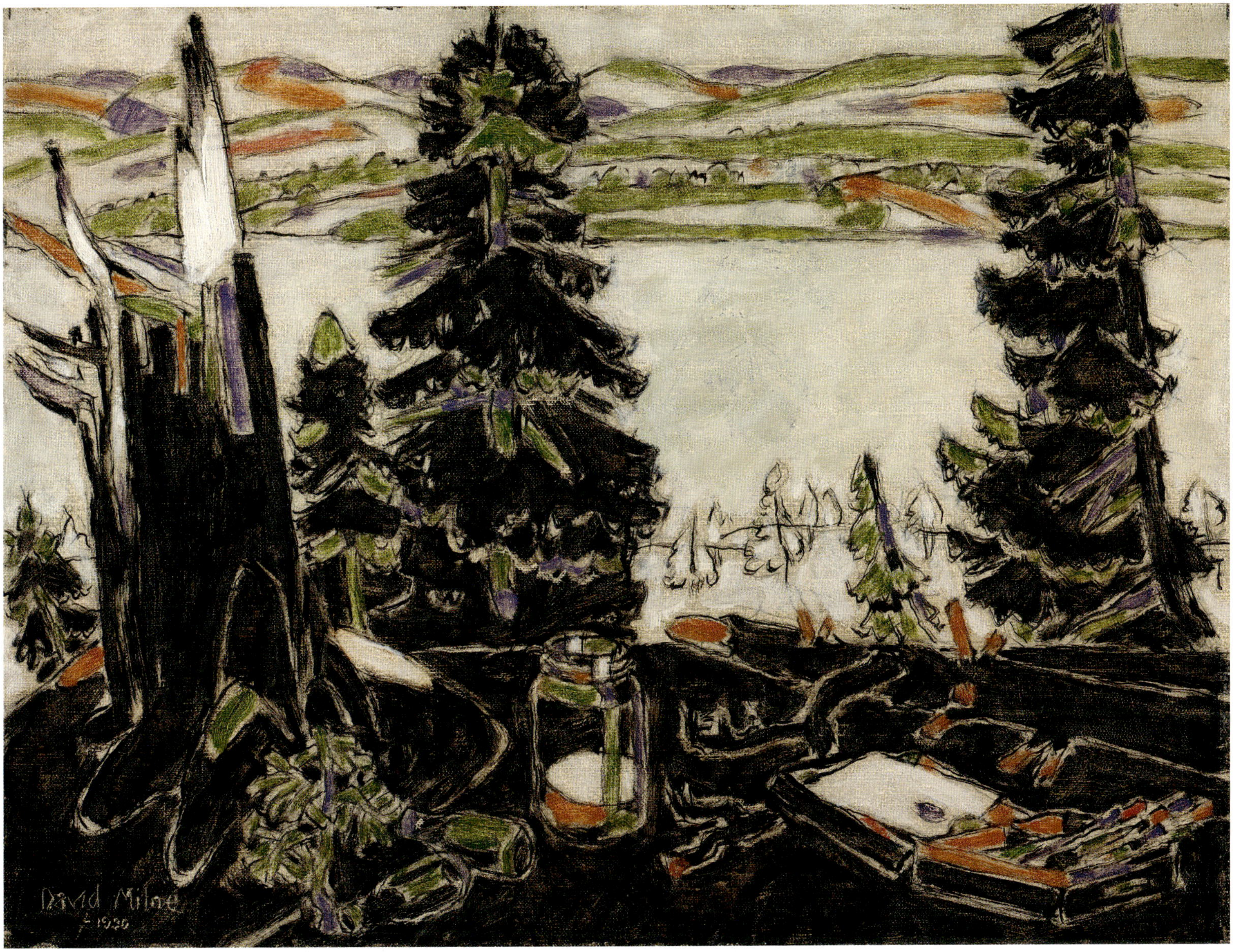

Painting Place III
1930, oil on canvas

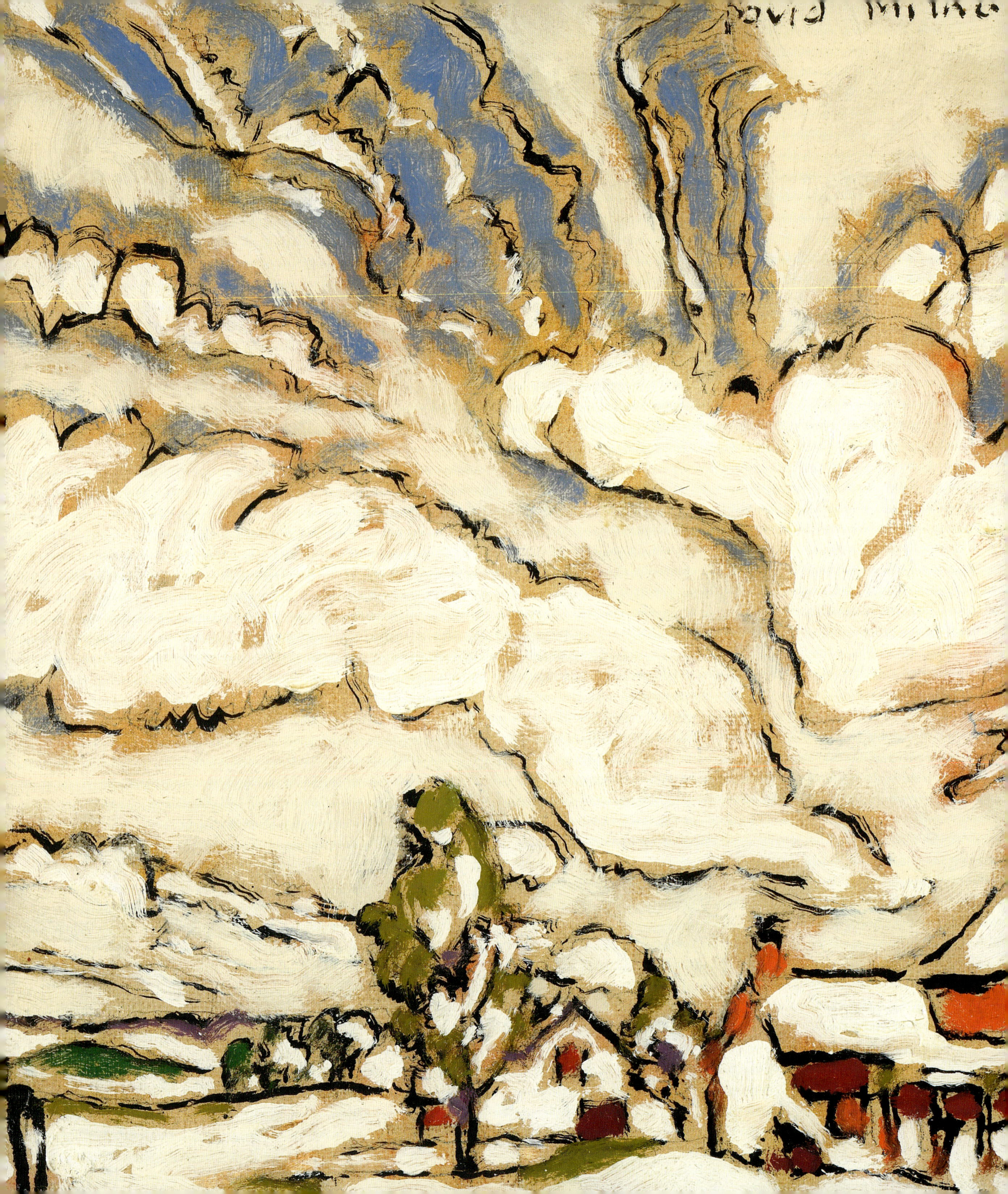

A SUDDEN OPENING

By 1930, Milne had left Temagami for the town of Weston and then Palgrave, closer to Toronto. For the first time, Milne was beginning to have sustained contact with artists and critics in Toronto and he finally began showing his work commercially in the city in 1934. The year before, he had parted ways with Patsy, making a move to remote Six Mile Lake, farther north. Here his creativity was unleashed anew in still-life studies and in sky paintings that express a euphoric connection to the natural world. Once again, Milne lived alone in a cabin he built for himself, and his letters and recollections of this period brim with vivid accounts of neighbouring birds, plants and the odd porcupine in search of a free dinner. Milne delighted in it all, and in the occasional company of visiting art world figures from Toronto or the National Gallery of Canada in Ottawa. In 1934, he made a deal to sell a parcel of some three hundred works to the leading Toronto art collectors Alice and Vincent Massey, who would soon move to London, where Massey served as Canadian high commissioner. The deal did little to keep the financial wolf from the door—the Masseys drove a hard bargain—but Milne managed to scrape by, and sales slowly built through word of mouth and via his association with the pioneering Canadian art dealer Douglas Duncan. At last, Milne had found a wider community of influential and likeminded artists, writers, museum professionals and collectors with whom he could share his ideas.

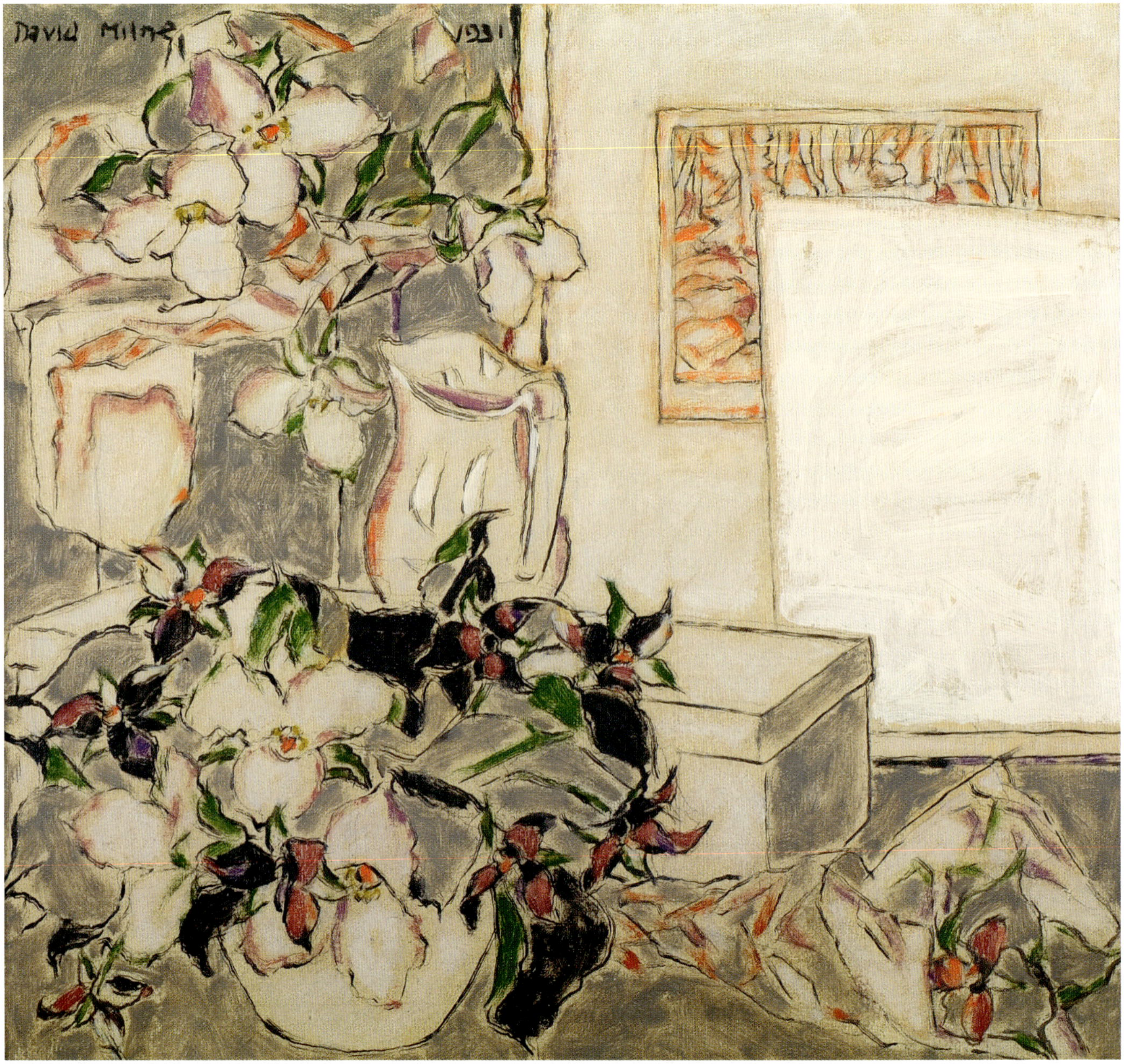

Framed Etching (Lilies from the Bush)
1931, oil on canvas

MOTIVE FOR METAPHOR

John O'Brian

Framed Etching (Lilies from the Bush), painted in 1931, is one of David Milne's most complex compositions. Viewers cannot readily synthesise what they are looking at, and vision is stymied.[1] On a barely discernible table, indicated by loose patches of grey paint, red and white trilliums are arranged in vases on either side of an oblong cardboard box. A porcelain jug sits on the box—at first glance it seems to be floating, unsupported in space—and to its right a framed colour drypoint etching leans against a wall. The visual syntax of the painting reveals itself only bit by bit. The complications include an optical disturbance triggered by a rectangular white reflection bouncing off the glass of the framed etching. This 'dazzle spot', as Milne called it, is calculated. 'It is a blow, a push, violence', the artist wrote, 'but with a purpose'.[2] As an area of strong contrast, the dazzle spot is designed to heighten the impact of the painting. It strikes the eye before anything else—and jolts it. Although the eye moves on quickly to other parts of the composition—there is nothing in the reflection to sustain interest—the force of the contrast destabilises it.

The contents of the painting are also slow to reveal themselves. Located in the bottom right corner, lying on the surface of the table beside the cardboard box, is a posy of trilliums. The conically packaged bouquet requires some consideration. Why has the artist juxtaposed store-bought trilliums with trilliums found in the wild that, by his own report, were gathered in the woods not far from his house in Palgrave, Ontario?[3] (The trilliums are of two kinds, white *grandiflorum* and red *erectum*, both in the lily family.)[4] Is the collocation of cultivated and natural trilliums, the juxtaposition of what is domesticated with what is not, significant to how the painting should be interpreted? And where, one might wonder, did Milne acquire the boxed nosegay? During the Depression years of the early 1930s, the town of Palgrave had no flower shop and Milne had no money, especially not for the luxury of commercially grown trilliums when wild trilliums could be had at his back door.[5] *Framed Etching* functions more like a stage set, it seems to me, than most of Milne's still-life paintings. There is a 'motive for metaphor' in the tightly structured composition, to draw on the title of a poem by Wallace Stevens, in addition to the artist's persistent concern for dramatic formal effect.[6]

Framed Etching was acquired for the collection of the Canadian diplomatic mission in Paris in 1935 on the advice of Donald W. Buchanan. As the biographer of James Wilson Morrice, who painted with Henri Matisse in Tangier during the winters of 1911–12 and 1912–13, Buchanan must have observed that some of Matisse's aesthetic concerns were reflected in Milne's work. Colouristically and spatially, *Framed Etching* relates closely to Matisse's studio paintings of the 1910s, a connection acknowledged by Milne himself. Some years before he painted *Framed Etching*, Milne wrote about Matisse's *The Red Studio*, 1911 (p. 21), and the effect that resulted from reducing the palette to a single dominant colour.[7] The rust red that spreads through *The Red Studio* makes the depicted objects scattered across its picture plane spatially unstable, just as the grey that spreads through a large part of *Framed Etching* produces similar if less radical results.

Buchanan may have selected *Framed Etching* for Paris because he thought it held its own against French modernist painting. I would concur with the assessment, if that is the case, but the diplomatic mission failed to catch the message. When David Milne Jr was undertaking research with David P. Silcox for their catalogue raisonné of the artist's paintings, he went to check on *Framed Etching* and discovered that it had disappeared. It was not hanging in any of the legation's offices, and no one knew where it was. Eventually, it was located in a broom closet with the janitor's mops and pails.[8] A likely explanation for the painting's banishment is that the diplomatic mission wanted to hang something more declaratively Canadian on its walls, a winter landscape by A.Y. Jackson or Lawren

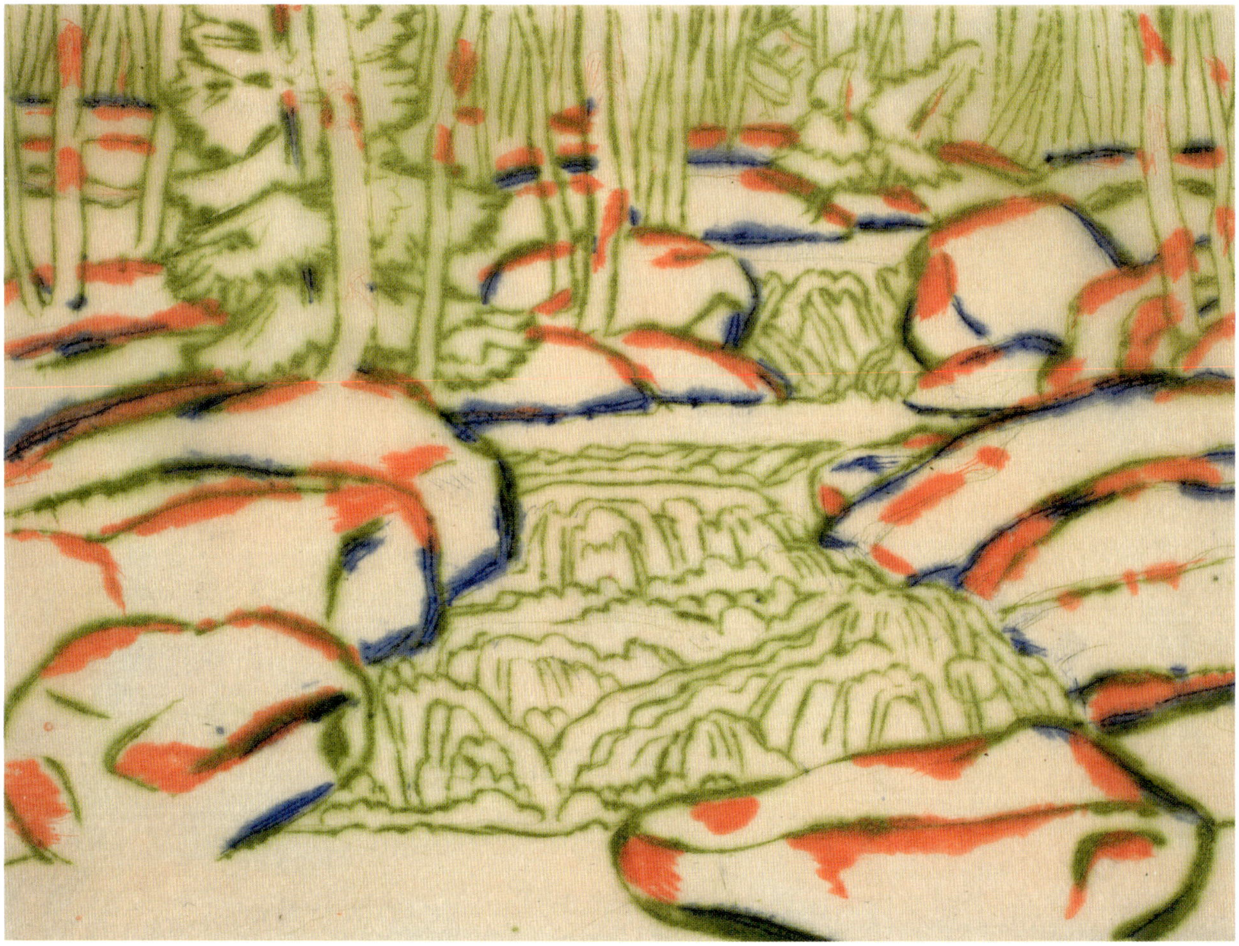

David Milne
Waterfall
1930, colour drypoint
on Japan paper

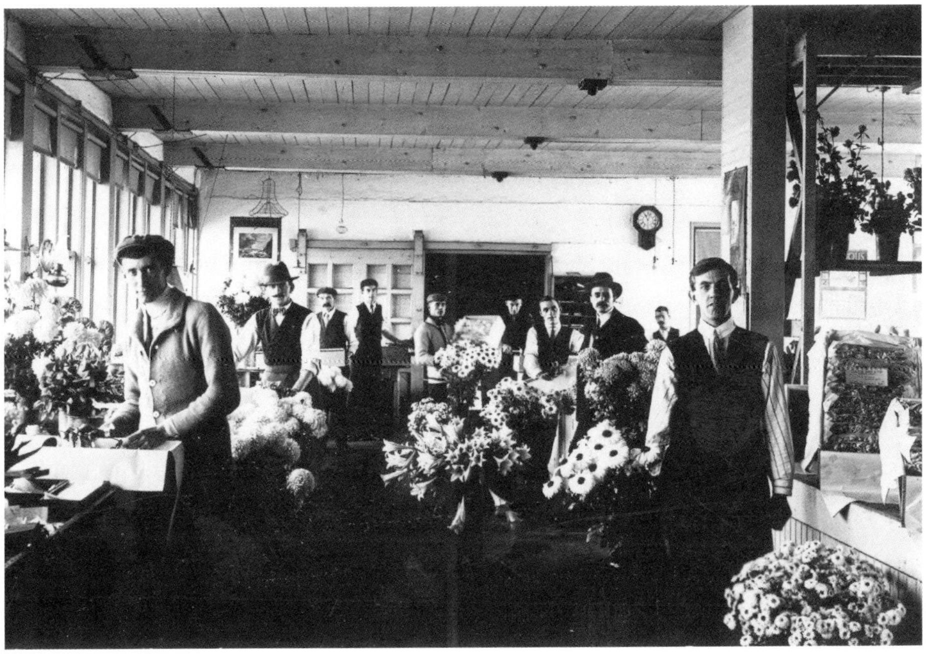

Dale Estate shipping room, Brampton *c.* 1910, gelatin silver print

Harris. But it is also possible that the painting's formal complexities perplexed the mission staff. Early critics of Matisse wrote of their 'stupefaction' in front of his work, of being unable to make sense of his mark making and use of colour.[9] Milne's painting may have elicited a similar response.

Milne's signature as well as the date of *Framed Etching* are written in black across the top edge of the painting on the left side. There is a gap between the two parts of the inscription that contributes to a visual pun. The width of the inscription seems to transform the trilliums painted below into a representation of a painting within the painting—until, that is, the viewer realises that flower petals and the handle of the jug obscure the frame of the etching and do not constitute a picture within a picture as first thought. *Waterfall*, which is the title of the etching, and not the abstracted trilliums to its left, is the real picture within the picture.[10] Milne often placed pictures within his paintings for the same reason Matisse did: to help transfigure pictorial space into a decorative field. *Interior with Paintings* (p. 55) and *Alcove* (pp. 21, 54), both from 1914, and *Flowers and Easel*, 1929 (p. 144), are strong examples of this practice.

The metaphorical element in the painting derives from the juxtaposition of cultivated and wild trilliums. Although Palgrave had no flower shop, it did have a general store that sometimes sold flowers. Two large wholesalers, Dale Estate and Walter Calvert Limited, located 35 kilometres to the south in Brampton, shipped flowers across southern Ontario as well as globally.[11] Dale Estate was one of the largest greenhouse growers in the world. It would have taken less than a minute for Milne to scavenge the oblong cardboard box and some wrapping paper from the back of the general store, which was located no more than 100 metres from his house. The box and the paper provided him with additional shapes and textures for his painting, but they also gave him a reason to contrast what was domesticated with what was wild, which is to say, they provided him with a motivation for metaphor.

In 'The Motive for Metaphor', Stevens opposes an objective world that is set against us—he diversely describes it as 'the weight of primary noon, the ABC of being, [the] dominant X'—with subjective inventions of the mind.[12] Poetry and painting are products of the latter. In 1931, the objective world set against Milne was the Depression and a failing marriage. Milne could not afford to buy a posy of hothouse trilliums, but he could make his own bouquet and arrange it on a studio table with vases of wild trilliums, a scavenged box and other items in the studio. He could construct a stage set. Although line and colour may be the primary concerns in *Framed Etching*, they are motivated by metaphor. Line, colour and metaphor are sutured together.

***John O'Brian** is an emeritus professor of art history at the University of British Columbia. His books include* David Milne and the Modern Tradition of Painting *(1983),* Ruthless Hedonism: The American Reception of Matisse *(1999) and* Clement Greenberg: The Collected Essays and Criticism *(1988). His current research is on the engagement of photography with the nuclear era.*

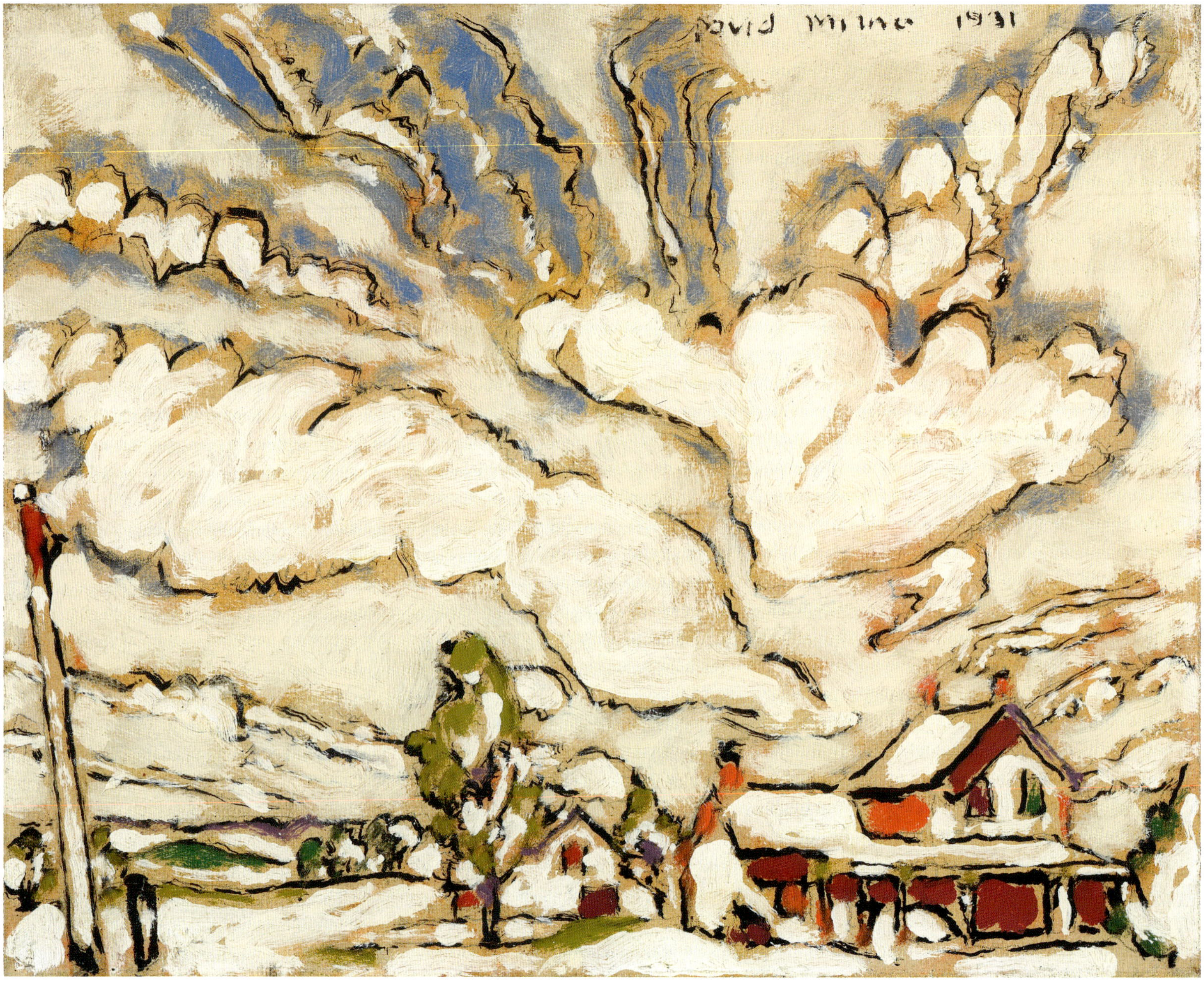

Ollie Matson's House Is Just a Square
Red Cloud
1931, oil on canvas

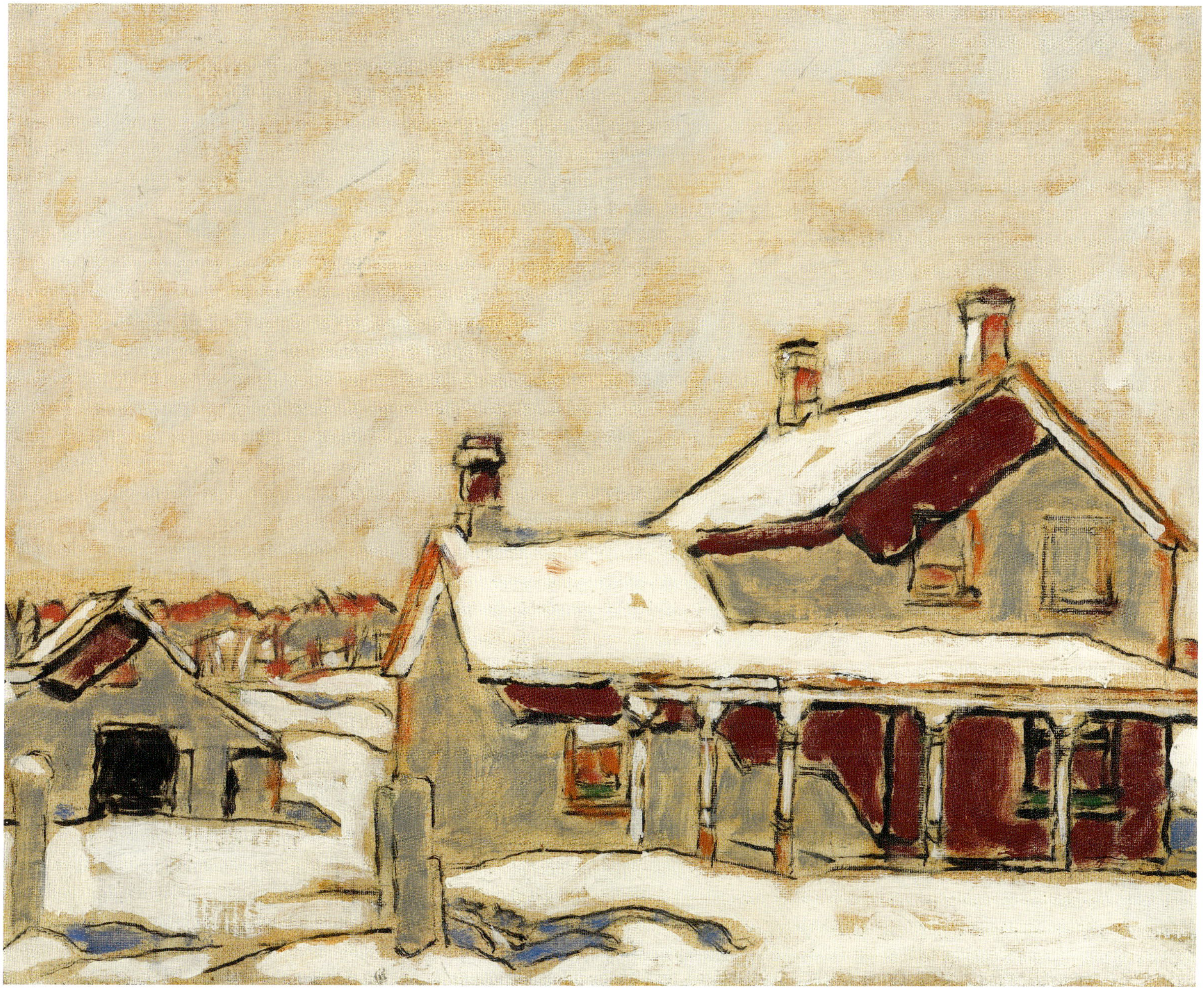

Ollie Matson's House in Snow
1932, oil on canvas

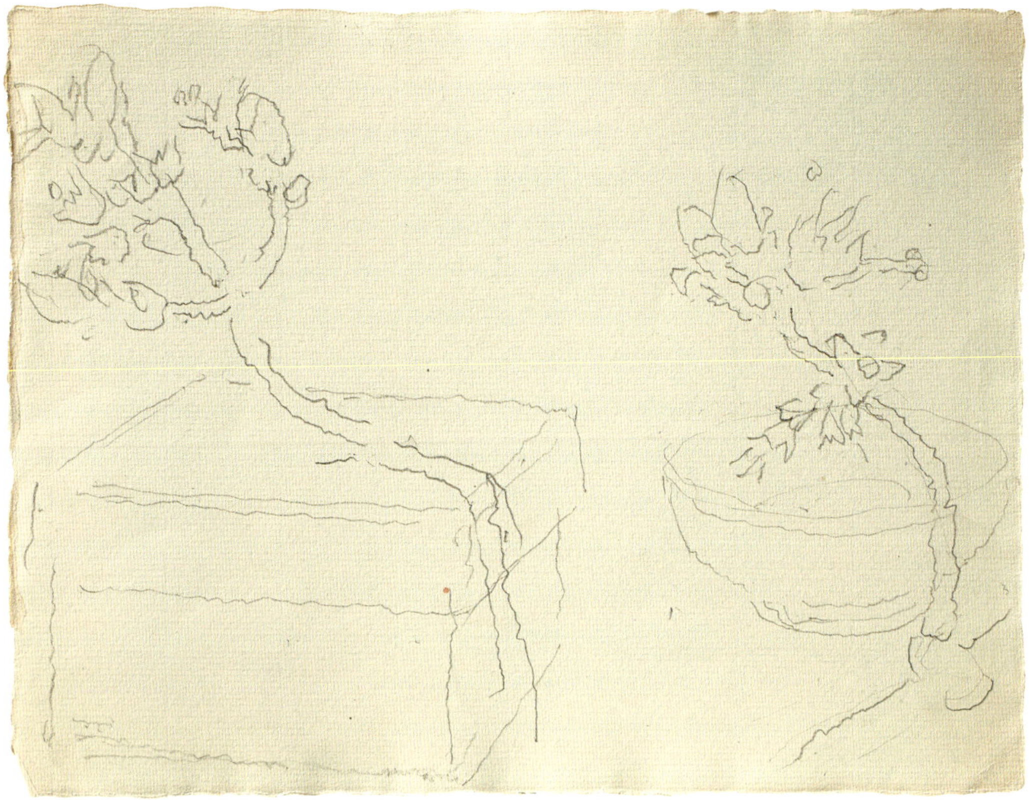

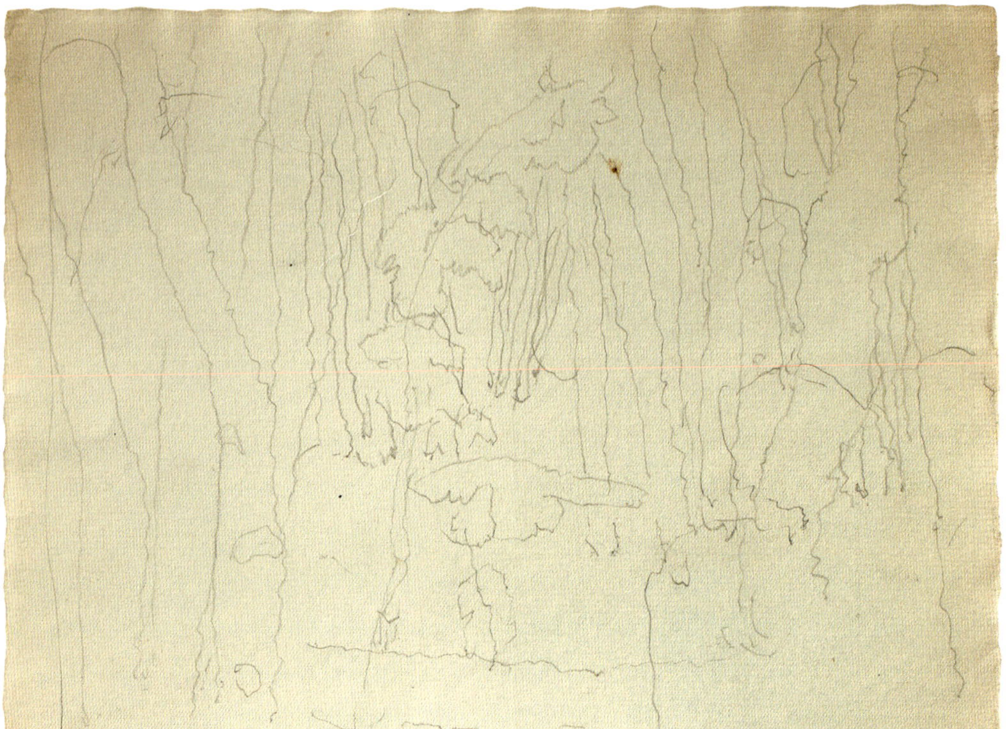

Untitled drawings
c. 1936, graphite on paper

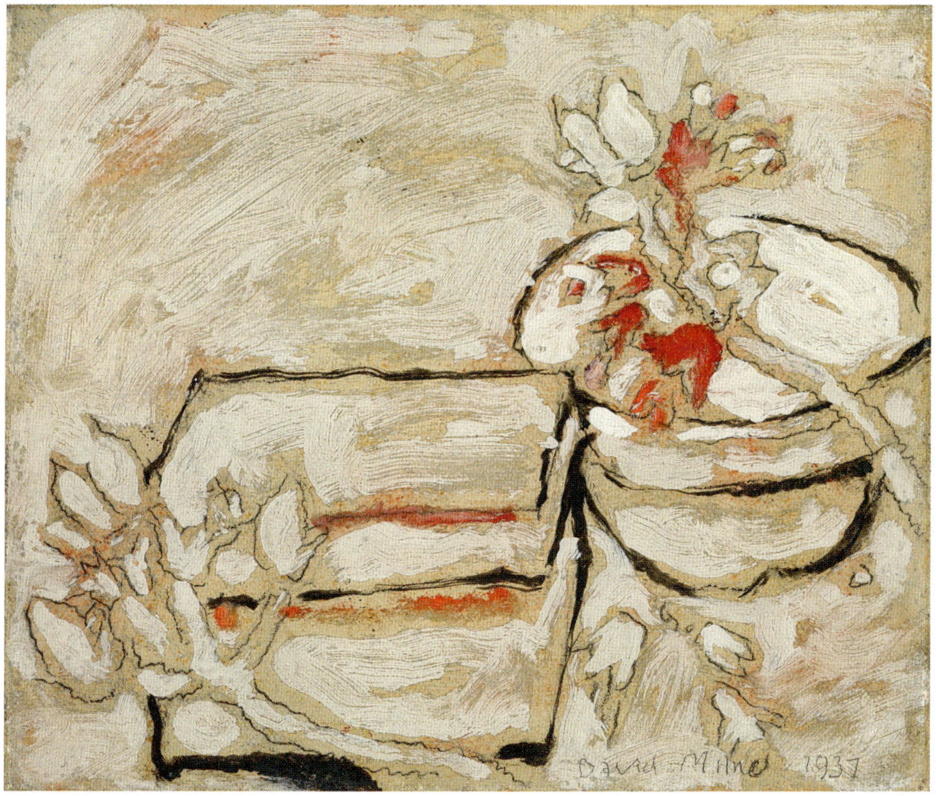

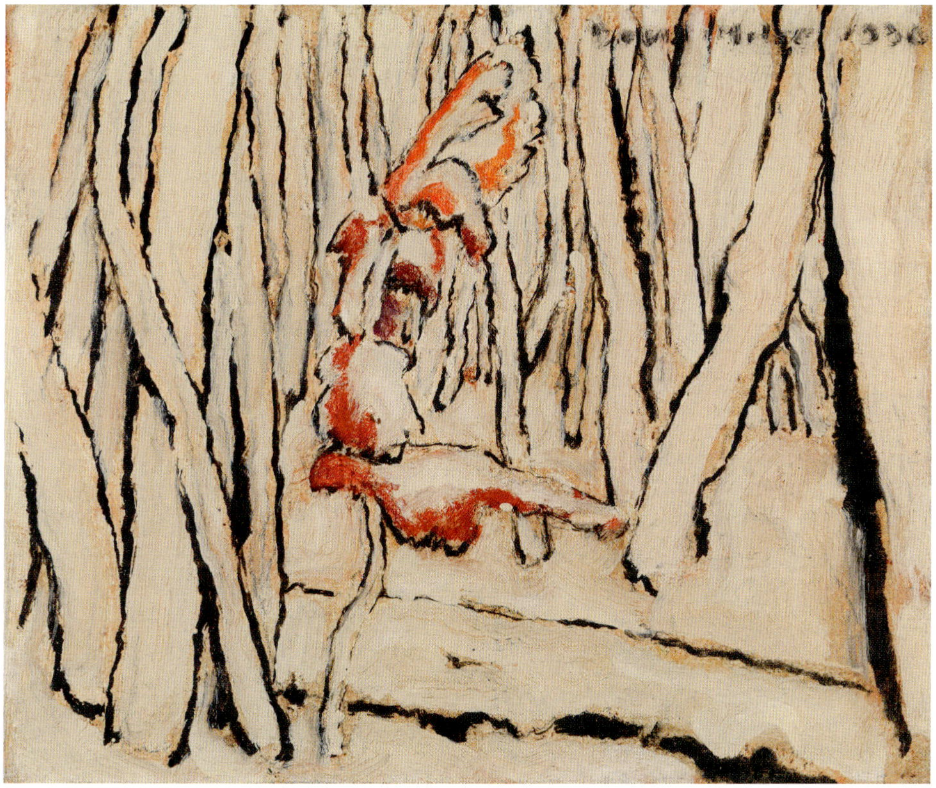

Top
Flowers of the Maple
1937, oil on canvas

Above
One Small Maple
1936, oil on canvas

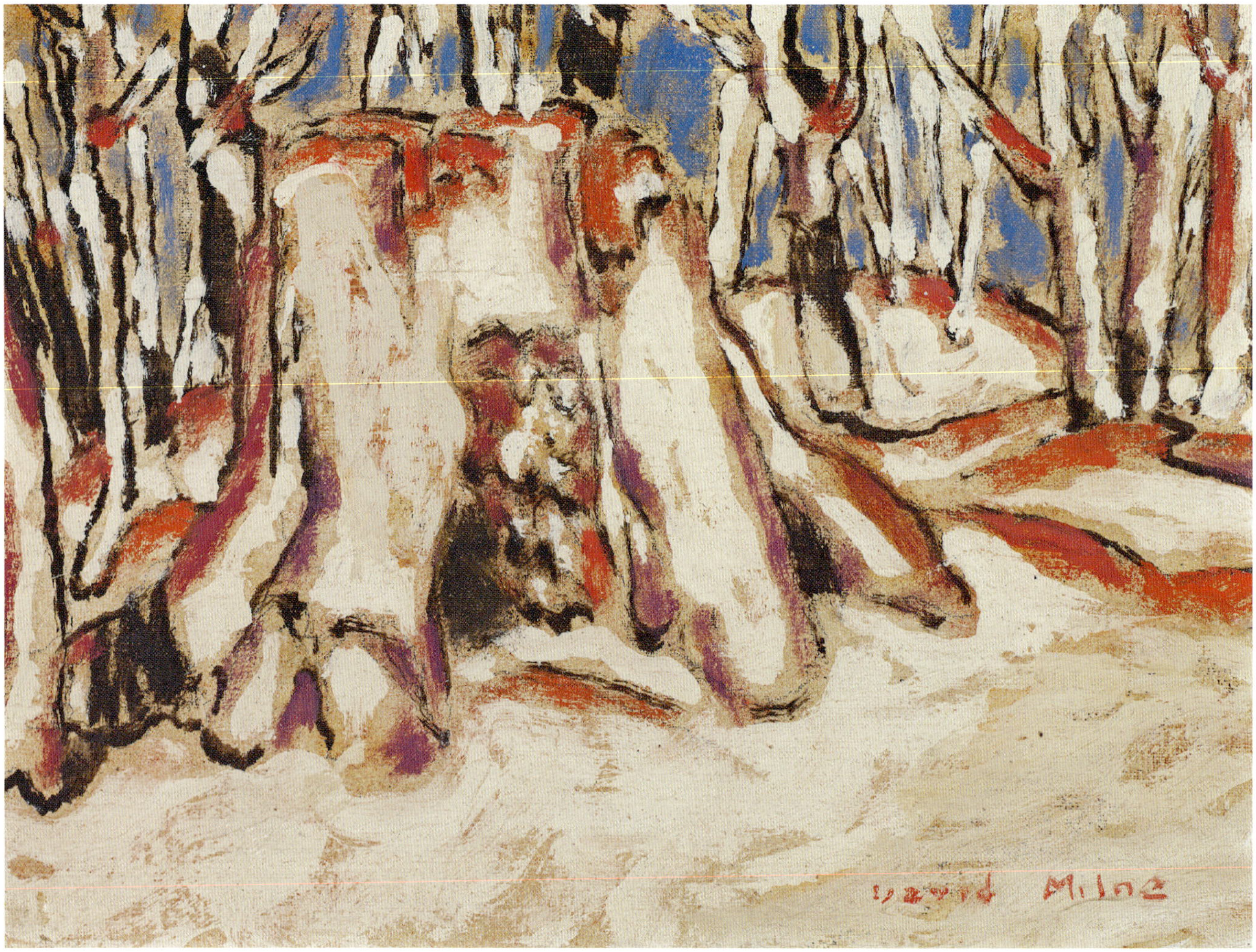

Stump among the Saplings
1932, oil on canvas

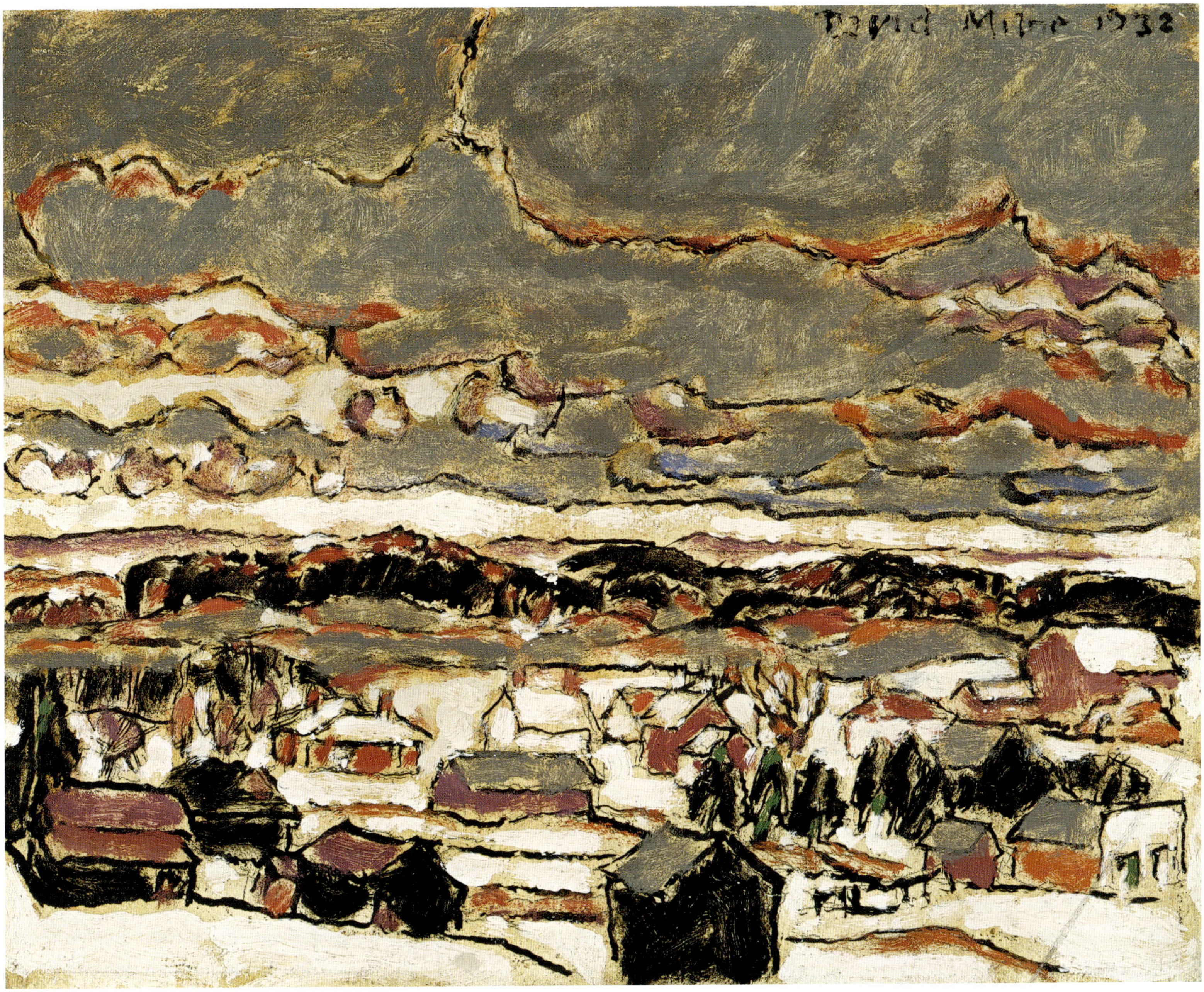

Clouds over the Village
1932, oil on canvas

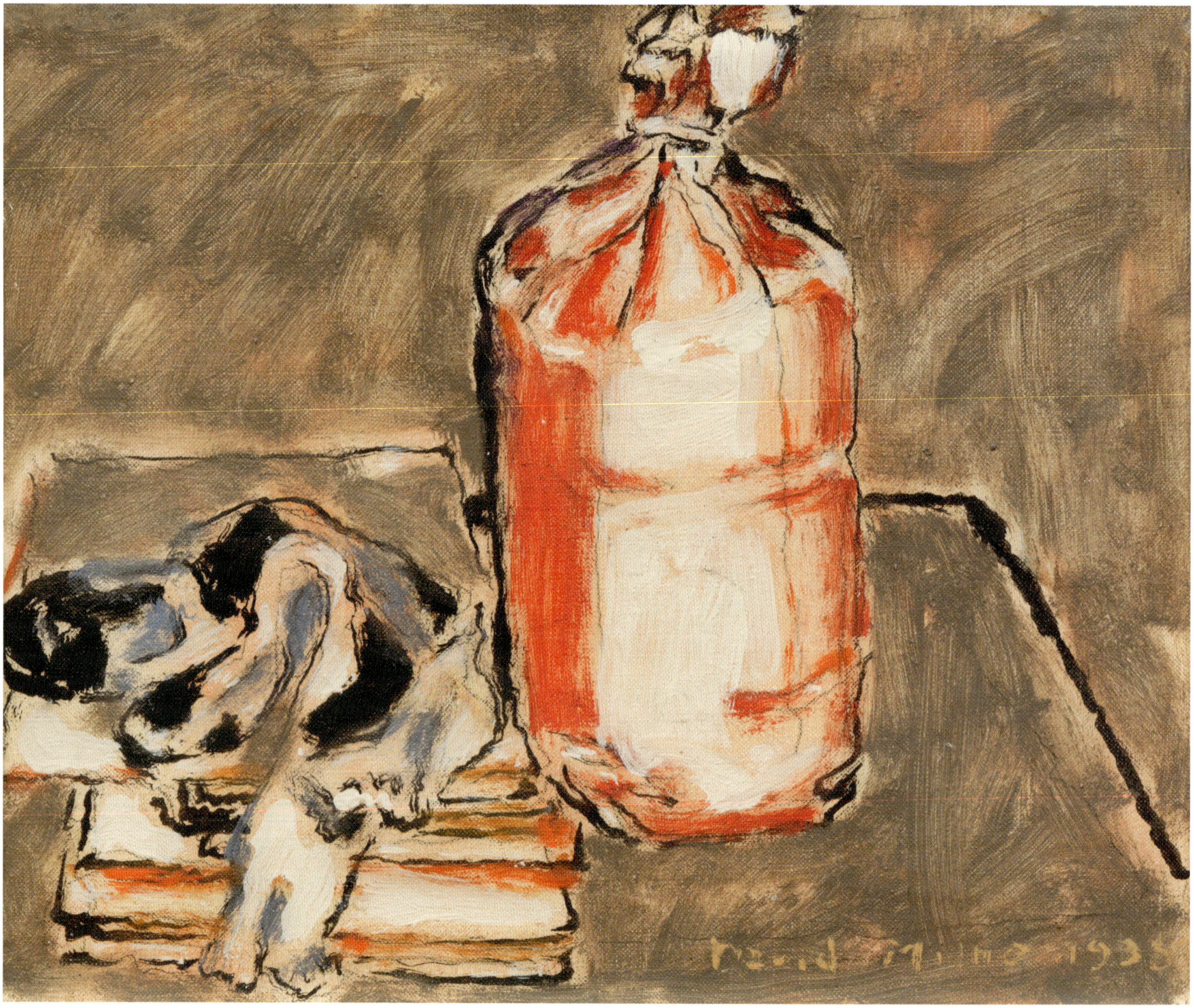

Flour Bag
1935, oil on canvas

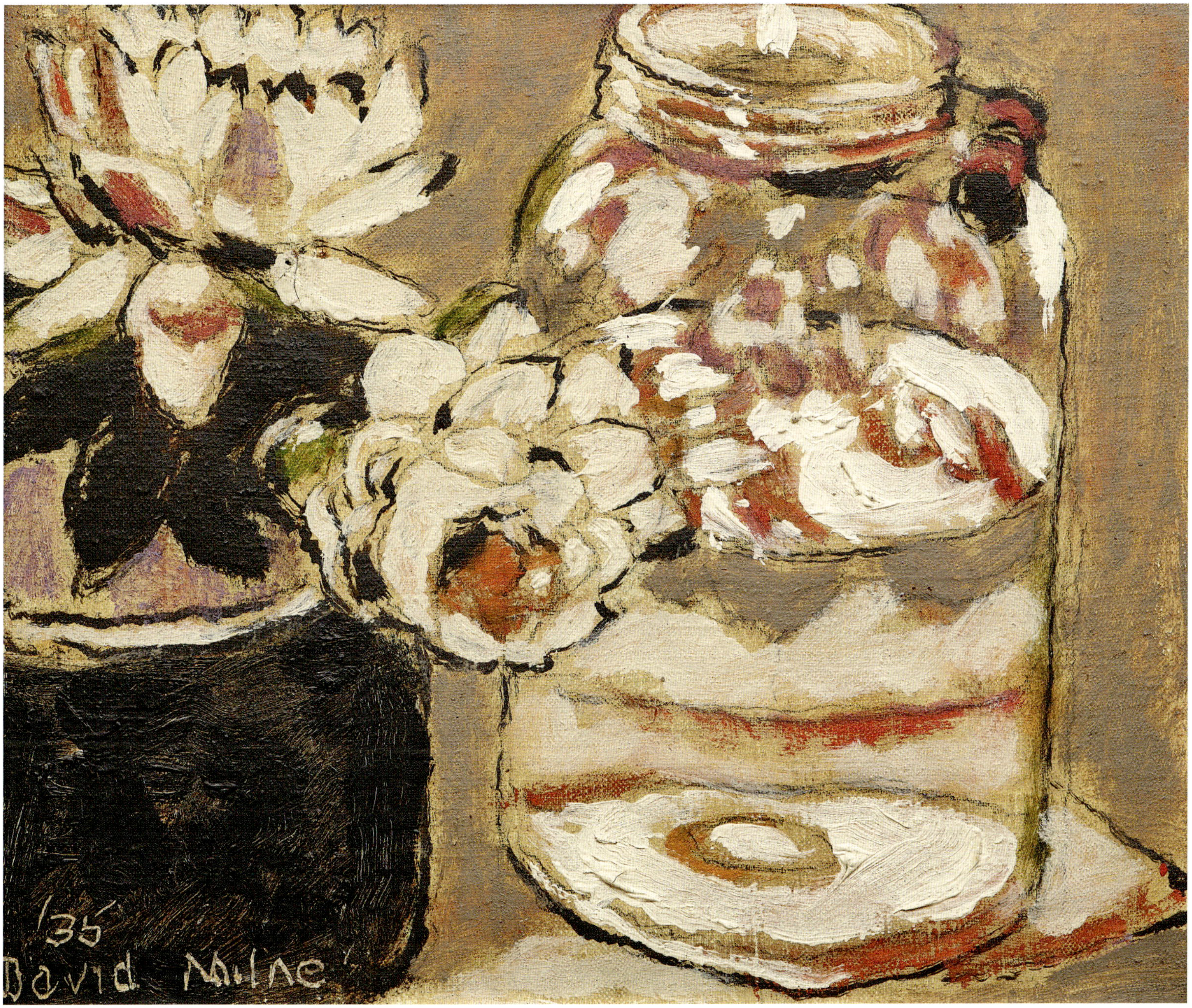

Water in a Jar
1935, oil on canvas

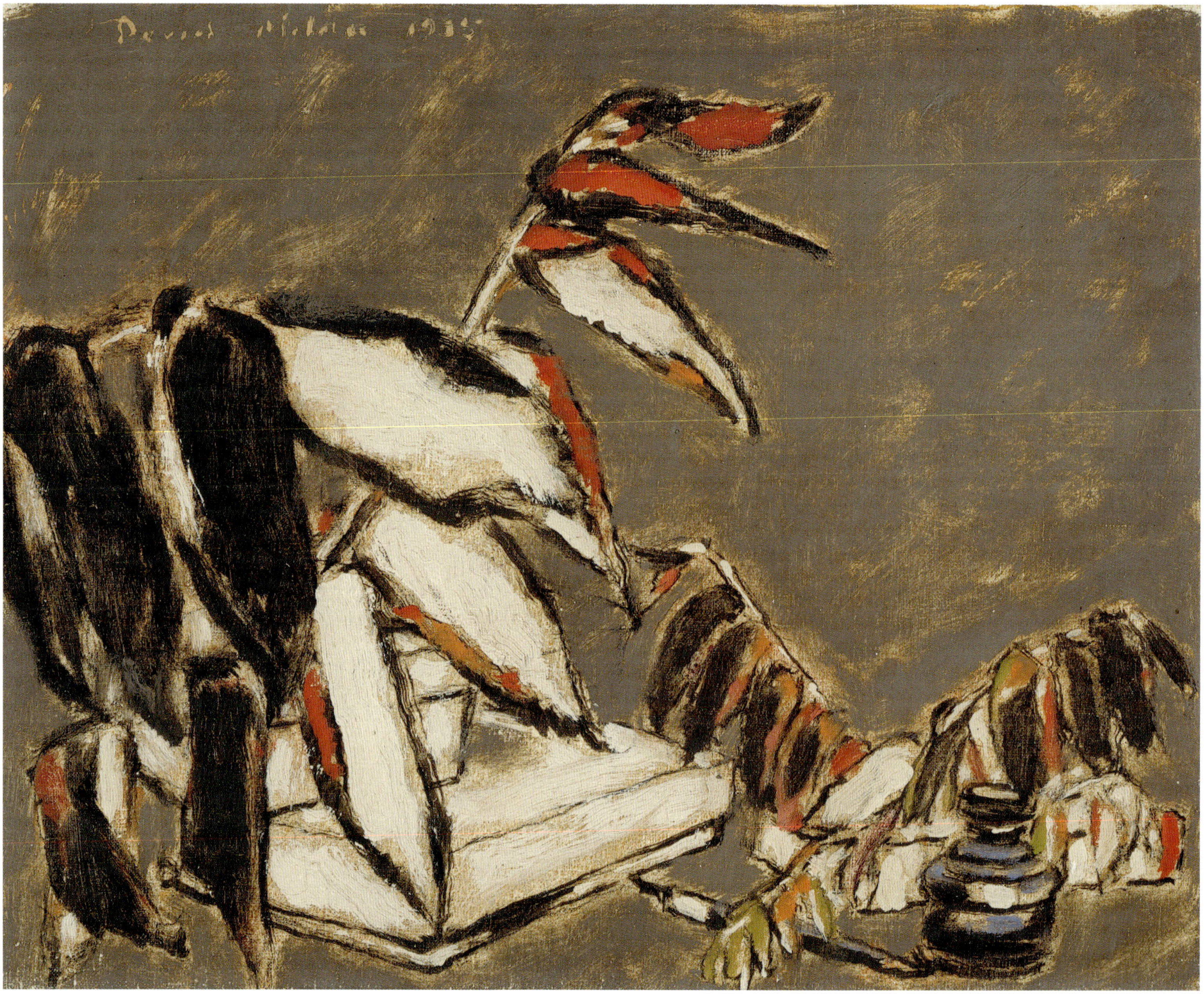

Sumach
1935, oil on canvas

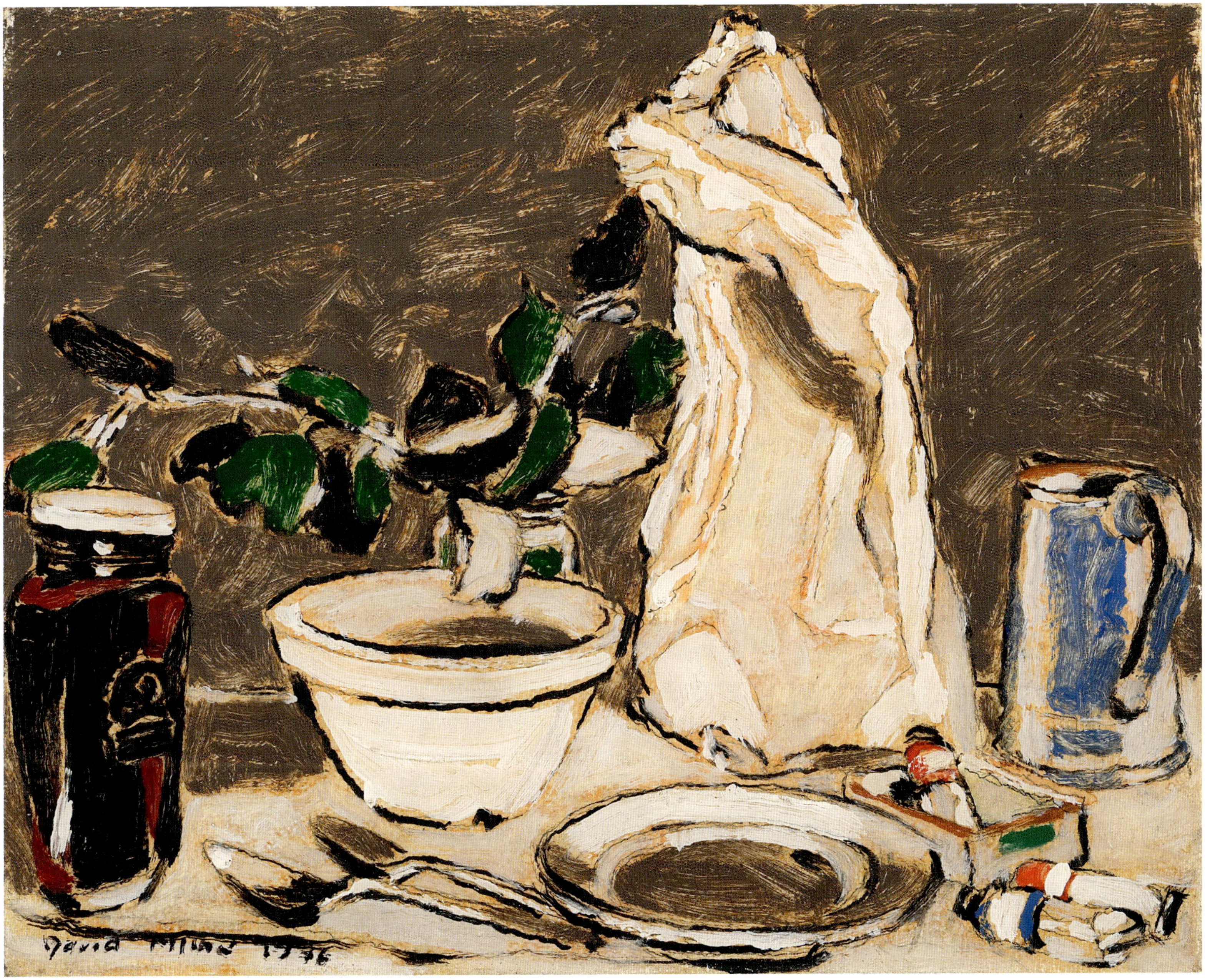

Raspberry Jam
1936, oil on canvas

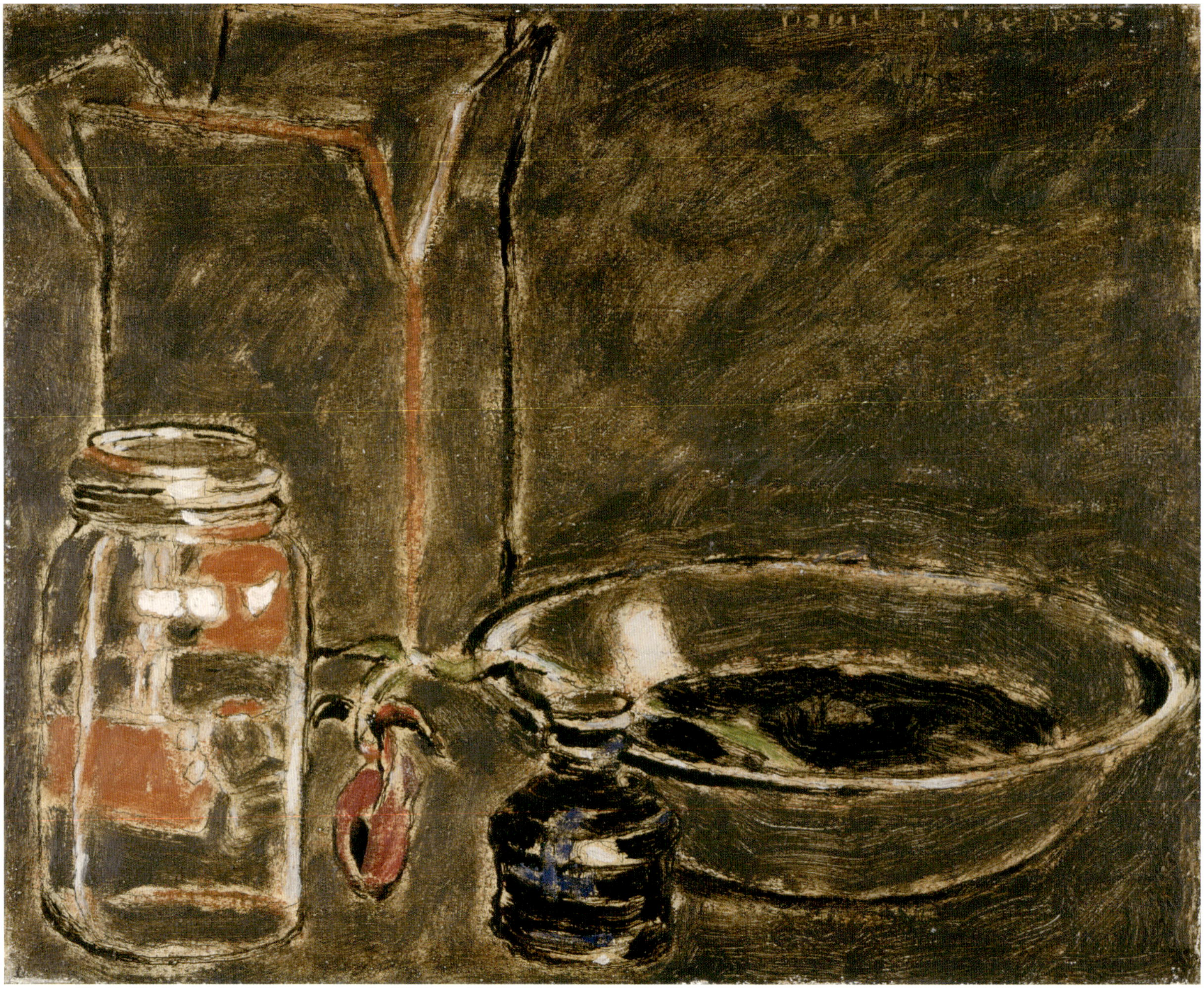

Moccassin Flower
1935, oil on canvas

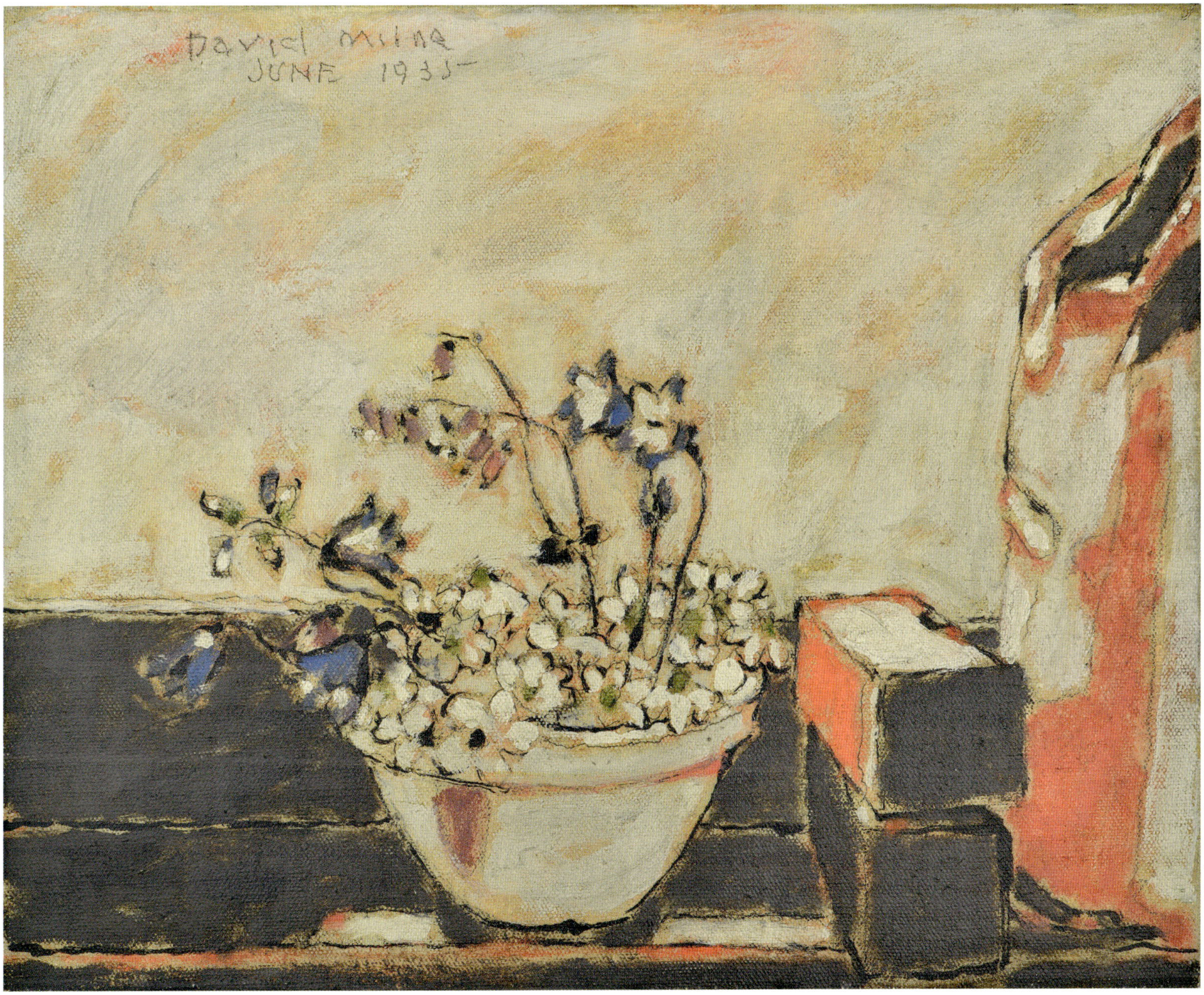

Rock Flowers
1935, oil on canvas

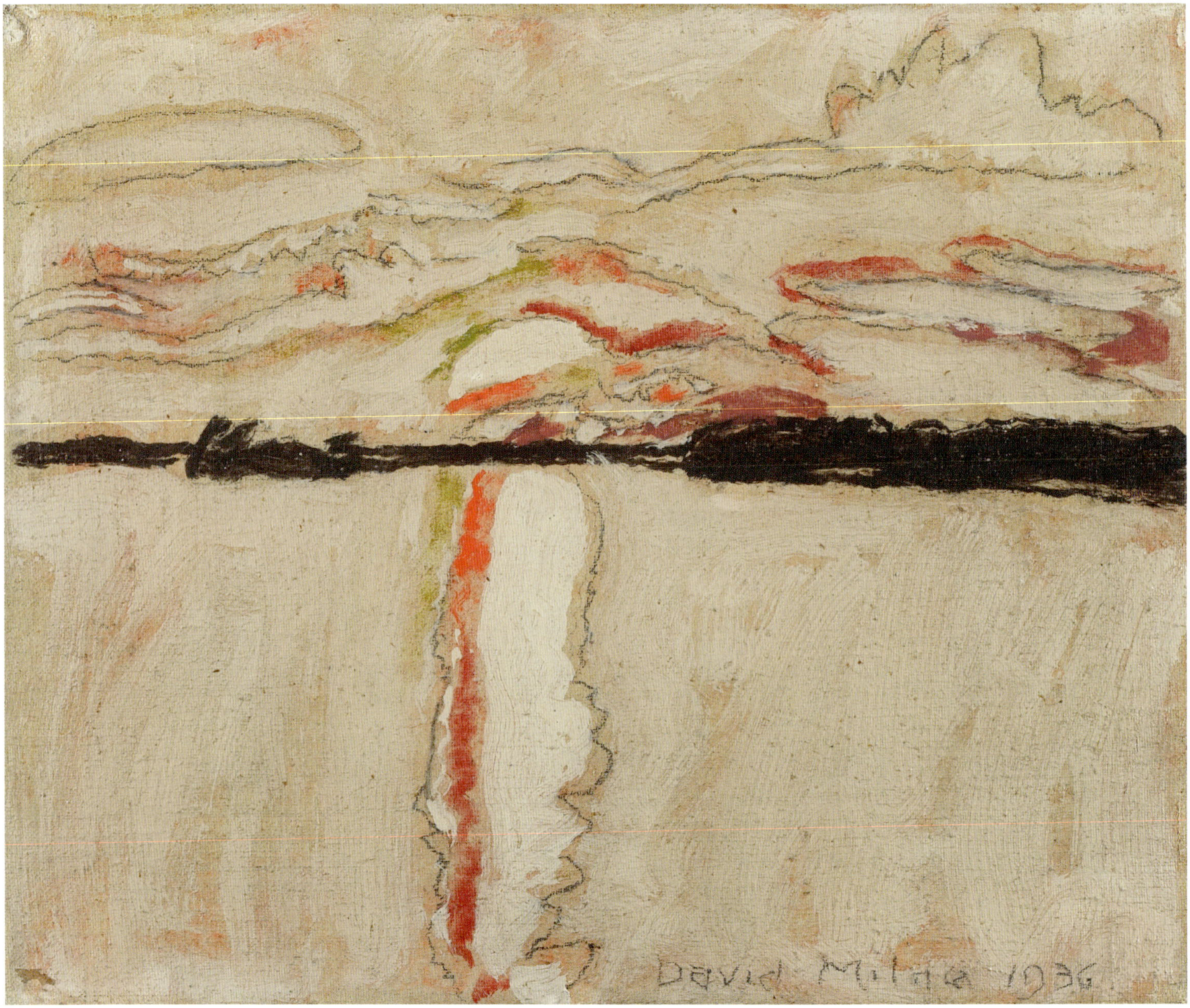

Across the Still Lake
1936, oil on canvas

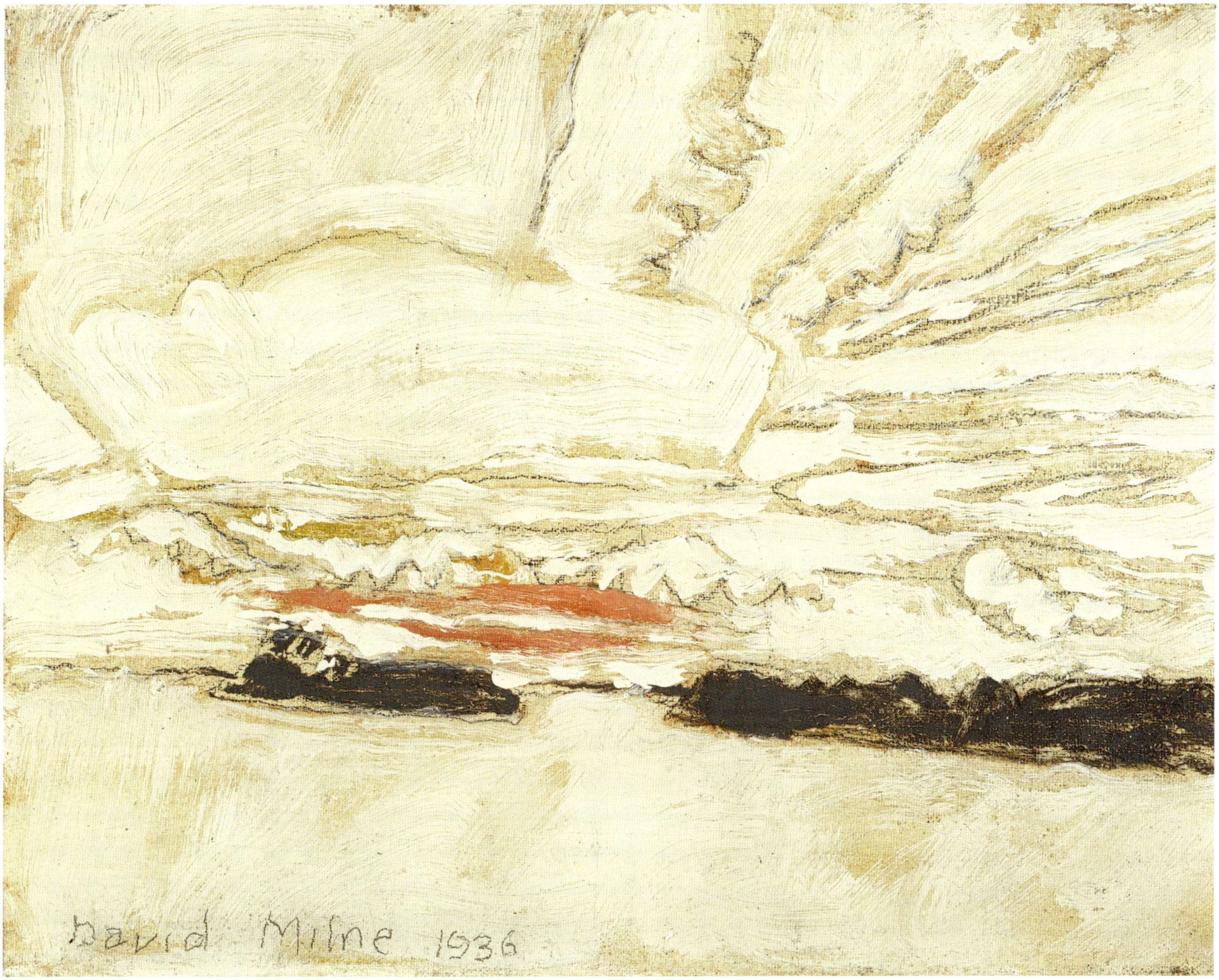

Sunset beyond the Islands
1936, oil on canvas

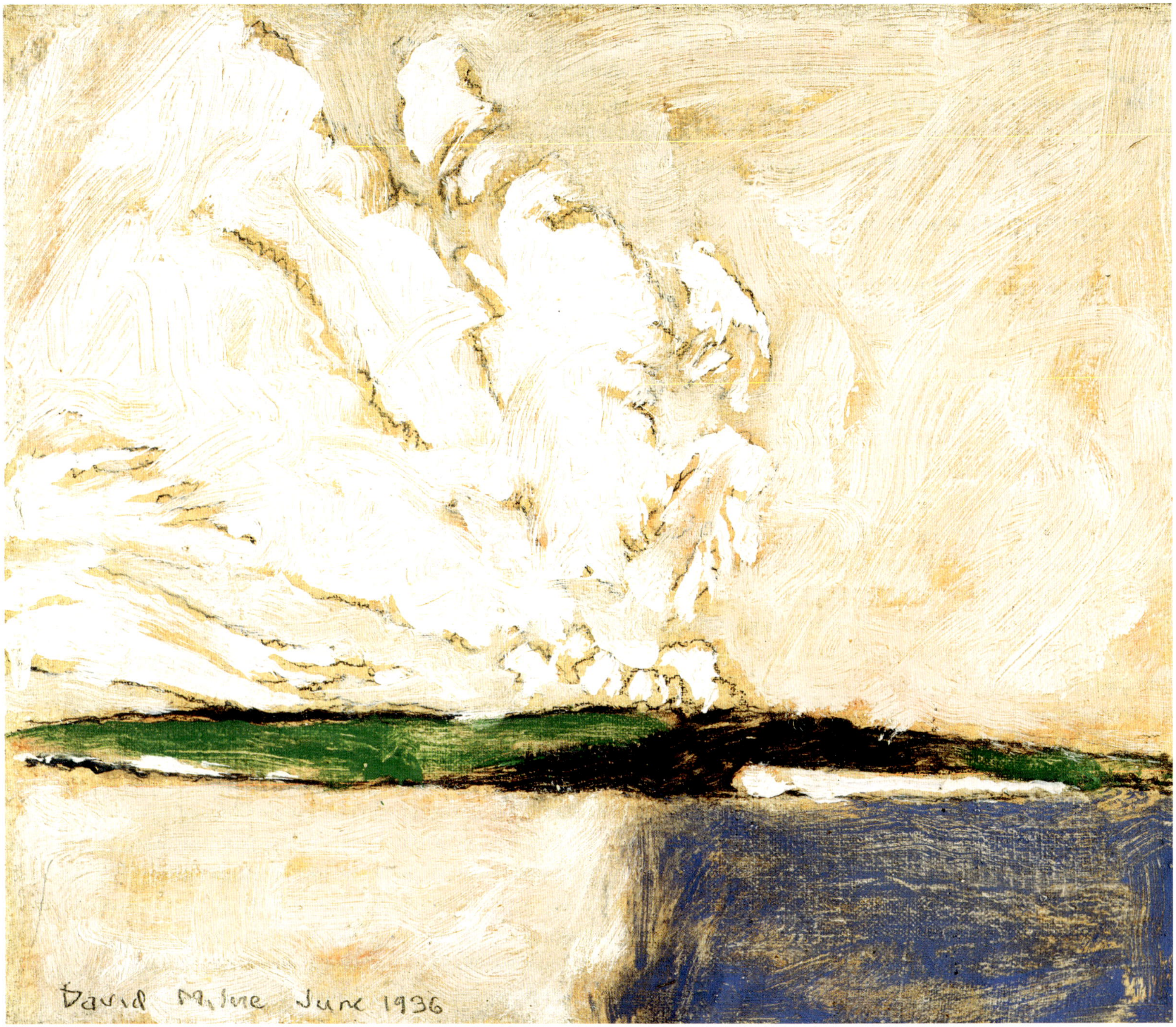

Summer Colours
1936, oil on canvas

A RADICAL SHIFT AT SIX MILE LAKE

David P. Silcox

After he and his wife separated in April 1933 at Palgrave, Milne bought a canoe and made his way northwest on Lake Couchiching, along the Severn River system, until he finally came upon Six Mile Lake in southern Muskoka, close to Georgian Bay, with its subtly coloured granite rock formations and weatherworn pines. There he rigged up a temporary camp on the eastern shore to enjoy vivid sunsets and face prevailing west winds. He began assembling driftwood to build a permanent place to live and work and, with some purchased lumber and tar-paper insulation, had a 12-by-14-foot cabin finished by Christmas. As he paddled around the lake's perimeter, he was pleased to discover that he was its only inhabitant and delighted that he would not be interrupted in his work.

Milne would live at Six Mile Lake for six years, the longest he ever spent in one place, and it was here that he painted his small but powerful masterwork *Summer Colours*, 1936, one of dozens of powerful skyscapes that signalled a surge of energy and renewal. At the lake, his life and art took an abrupt and profound turn in relation to the outside world. He found patrons in Alice and Vincent Massey, who in 1934 purchased, for $1,500, some three hundred of the fifteen hundred paintings Milne offered to sell to them for $5 each. The sale enabled him to buy art supplies, to pursue painting ideas, to buy clothes—he had but one pair of trousers, one shirt and one coat—and to have necessary dental work done.

In the serenity of his rustic location, Milne's art flourished—he even began painting watercolours again in 1937 after a 12-year hiatus. Furthermore, the connection with the Masseys was proving strategically important—through them, his work was shown and sold commercially in Toronto, Ottawa and Montreal, though largely to the financial benefit of the Masseys and their picture dealers than to Milne's. Through his new contacts he met Douglas Duncan, who became his agent/dealer from 1938 onwards, and Alan Jarvis, a second-year University of Toronto student, future director of the National Gallery of Canada and one of the first to write, in 1934, about Milne as a great artist. Critics and curators such as Graham McInnes and Donald W. Buchanan also sought Milne out and wrote about his work. Picture sales and periodic payments received

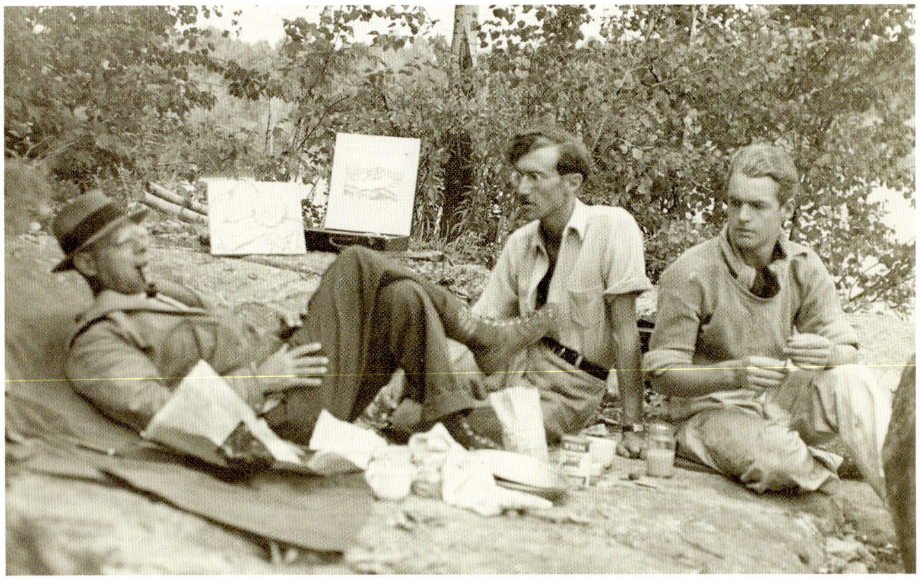

David Milne, Douglas Duncan and Alan Jarvis at Six Mile Lake *c.* 1936

on the mortgage Milne held on the cottage he had built and sold at Big Moose Lake in the Adirondacks led to his at last attaining a modicum of stability.

The paintings Milne made at Six Mile Lake, especially in the first three years, represent his final surge of energetic modernist work—after 1937 he abandoned his loyalty to modernist principles in pursuit of a more narrative and fanciful approach—but *Summer Colours* captures Milne's essential thought processes as a modern painter as well as, or perhaps more succinctly than, most of the other pictures. In the hands of a lesser artist, the painting's modest size—just 31 by 36.5 centimetres (12 by 14 inches)—might have diminished its luminosity and enduring impact, but as Milne wrote in an undated painting note, 'The thing that makes a picture is the thing that makes dynamite—compression.'[1] Dynamite can come in small quantities and still be effective.

Milne's inclination in both art and life was towards economy. The trailblazing Toronto artist Harold Town, an admirer, later provided an apt description: 'Milne was a master of absence. He could leave more out of a picture than any painter I know of, yet still retain its essence.'[2] In *Summer Colours*, Milne did just that—left out almost everything and still managed to summon the essentials. 'They are mostly extremely simple', he wrote to Clarke, describing the series of small works, offering answers 'to the old conundrum, how little does it take to make a picture'.[3]

Dividing his small rectangle into four unequal segments, he sets the two large creamy areas above a thin but strong low horizon line/shoreline in black and green, and two smaller segments below it—the right-hand one a blue lake surface, the left a differently textured creamy white also representing a stretch of water, with the clouds above reflected on its surface. In all, Milne uses six colours on the canvas, but he supplies further variety through the range of his paint handling: each of the three cream-coloured areas has been given a unique texture by his adding highlights of a pure white, with the most extensive use of white in the upper left, where he depicts an assortment of clouds that look as if they have been whipped into a soufflé. Milne's placement of the various shapes demonstrates his inventiveness, his ability to create a means to catch the eye, define the subject clearly and provide a dramatic counterweight to the composition.

The strongest element in the picture is the green-and-black horizon, which binds the four segments of the painting together and, paradoxically, keeps them apart. Despite their different sizes, the visual balance among the segments is remarkably exact. Milne takes into account the hues and tones of each of the five elements of the composition; the weight of each component is contingent on its size, its colour, the way it is brushed or drawn onto the canvas and the manner in which it relates to each of the others. One segment may be darker, but another is brighter; one is flatter, another more textured. Each has its own visual strength but is held in perfect tension with the others.

The upper-left segment has the additional power of being the largest in the painting; it has the airy buoyancy provided by the white highlights, which can be read as one massive, dissonant cloud or as a dozen rebellious ones. This unit reveals Milne's fascination with skies (he had long been an admirer of Turner, Constable and Van Gogh) as well as his incisive observation of his immediate environment. His sensitivity registers and conveys the pressure and temperature of the air, detects the scent of possible rain and notes the effervescence in clouds as they execute a divine choreography overhead—changing every minute, yet persisting in their shifting forms and changing colours,

Paterson Ewen
Lightning Storm
1971, acrylic and metal on carved linoleum on board

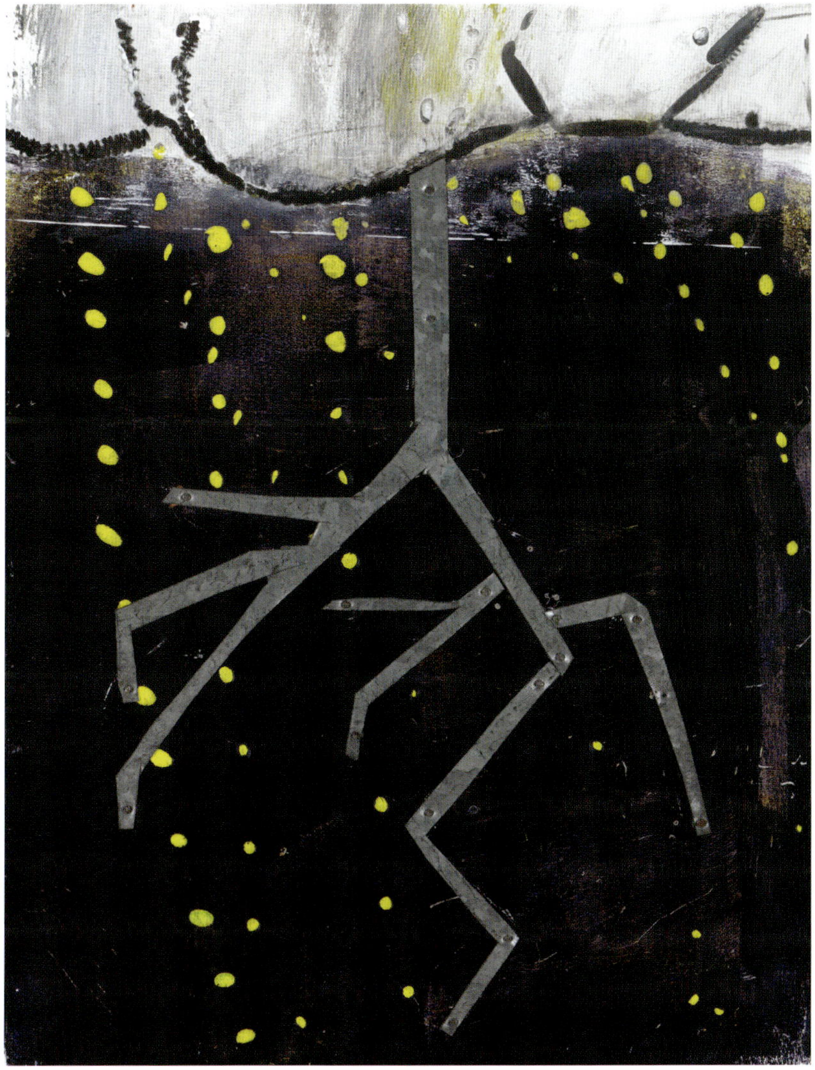

intimating things to come. The texture of the brushwork is varied and seems casually done but is distinct in each segment.

Unlike other painters of the Canadian landscape, Milne was attuned to the subtler qualities of temperature, humidity, wind and light. His only near competitor in this regard was Tom Thomson, in Thomson's last two years' work especially. Milne seems to have taken his measure of landscape by the feeling of it on his skin, by the height, formation, colour and character of the clouds, and by the effect of sunlight on the whole vista. 'I have done a dozen or twenty very small pictures—12 x 14 or 12 x 16 mostly—from memory', he wrote to Clarke. 'The method is pretty much the same in all—a very quick observation, usually when doing something else, a slight pencil sketch at the time, or sometimes later, then the actual painting done next day or later, in some, months later.'[4] *Summer Colours*, along with *Northern Lights*, 1935 (p. 189), *Lightning*, 1936 (p. 183), *The Big Dipper*, 1936 (p. 187), and *Across the Still Lake*, 1936 (p. 176), are all depictions of striking natural phenomena. These and other paintings from the period at Six Mile Lake seem to prefigure Canadian art to come, suggesting a rough and ready relationship to the natural world, and to making art, that recurs on an epic scale in the routered plywood paintings of Paterson Ewen half a century later.

Milne's lifetime achievement as an artist has been admired and revered by artists, curators and collectors over several generations. If he had been a musician instead of a painter, he would be described as having perfect pitch, or, visually, as having the sense and skill to put the right colour in the right place, in the right composition, sensing the right point of view for the right subject.

The American art critic Clement Greenberg once told me that he rated David Milne as the equal of Winslow Homer and John Marin, considering the trio to be the best artists of their time in North America. Milne might have been surprised to know this, but in his heart he would have been pleased to be recognised for realising what he set out to be, and indeed what he became, and is still.

***David P. Silcox** is the author of* Painting Place: The Life and Work of David B. Milne *(1996) and the co-author (with David Milne Jr) of* David B. Milne: Catalogue Raisonné of the Paintings *(1998). His other publications include* Tom Thomson: The Silence and the Storm *(with Harold Town, 1977 and 2017), and* The Group of Seven and Tom Thomson *(2011).*

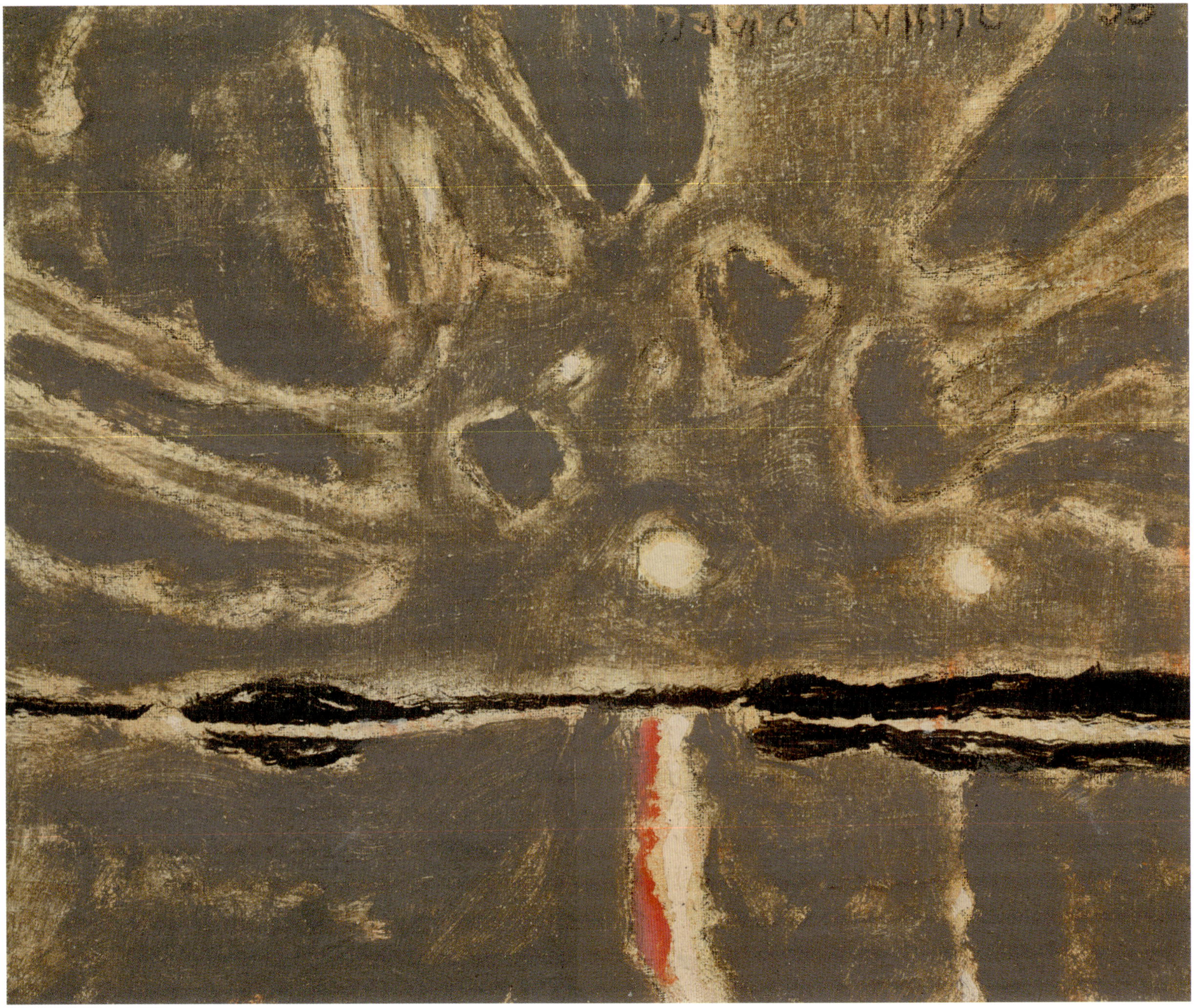

Setting Stars
1935, oil on canvas

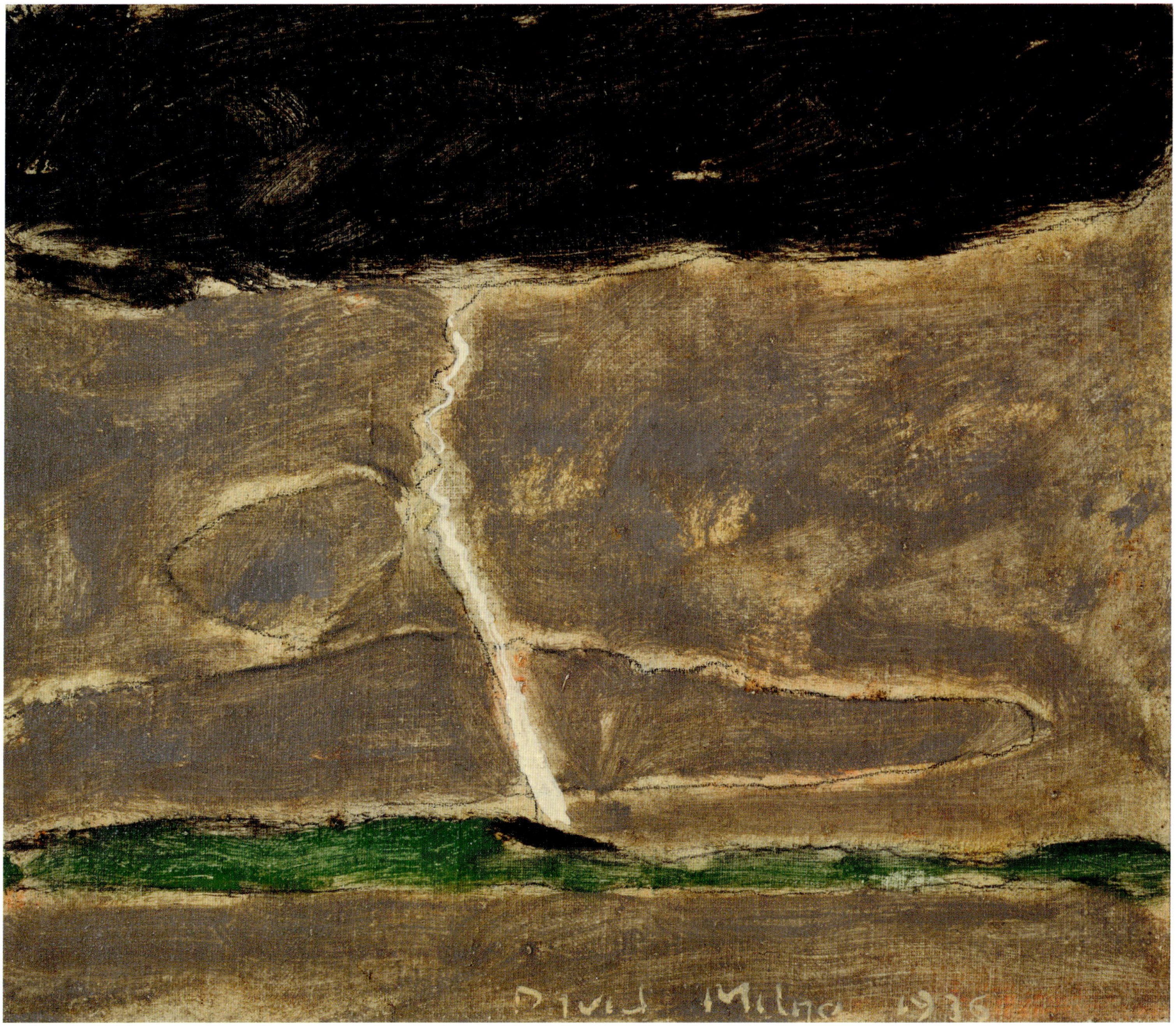

Lightning
1936, oil on canvas

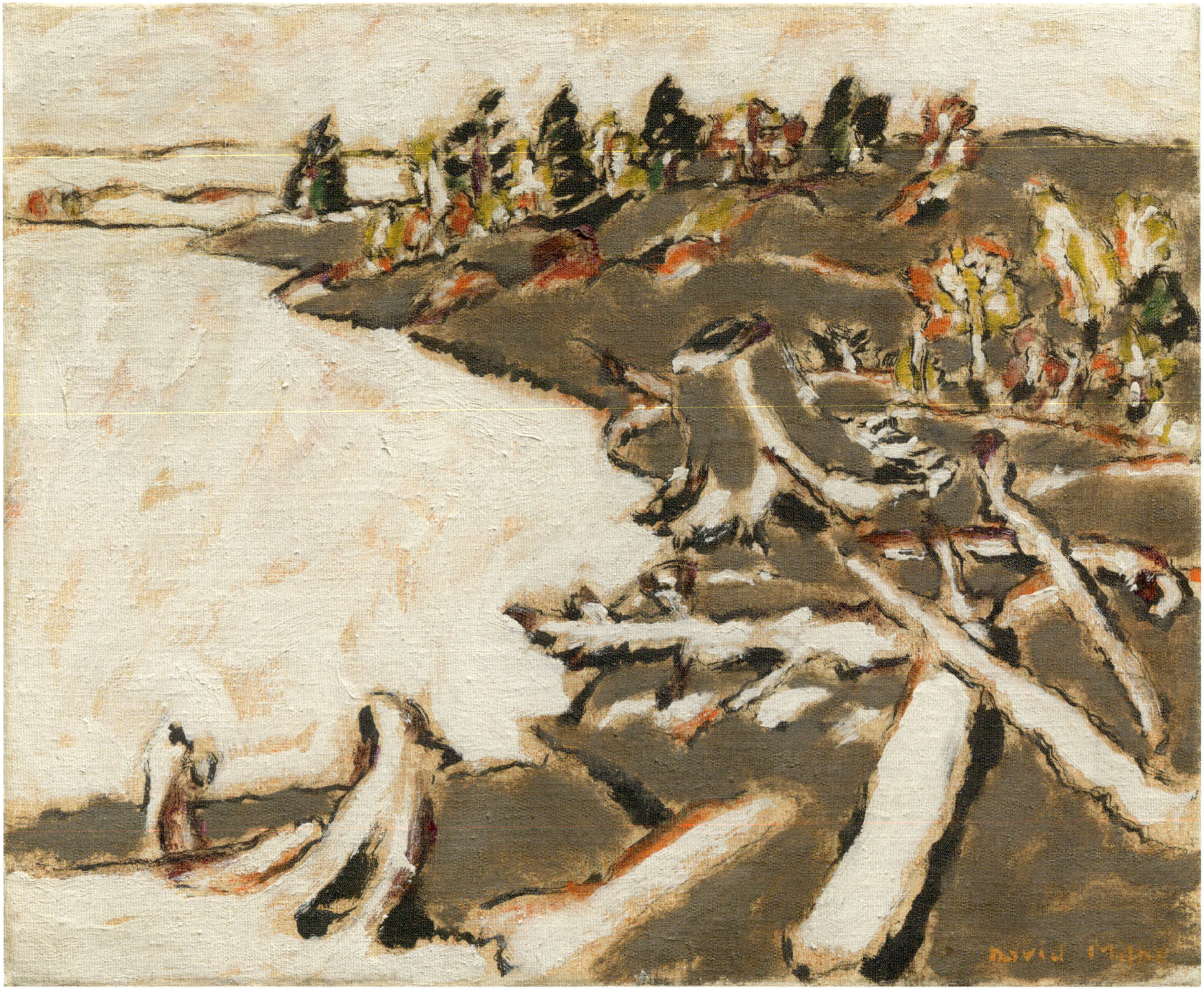

Shore Line, Six Mile Lake
1936, oil on canvas

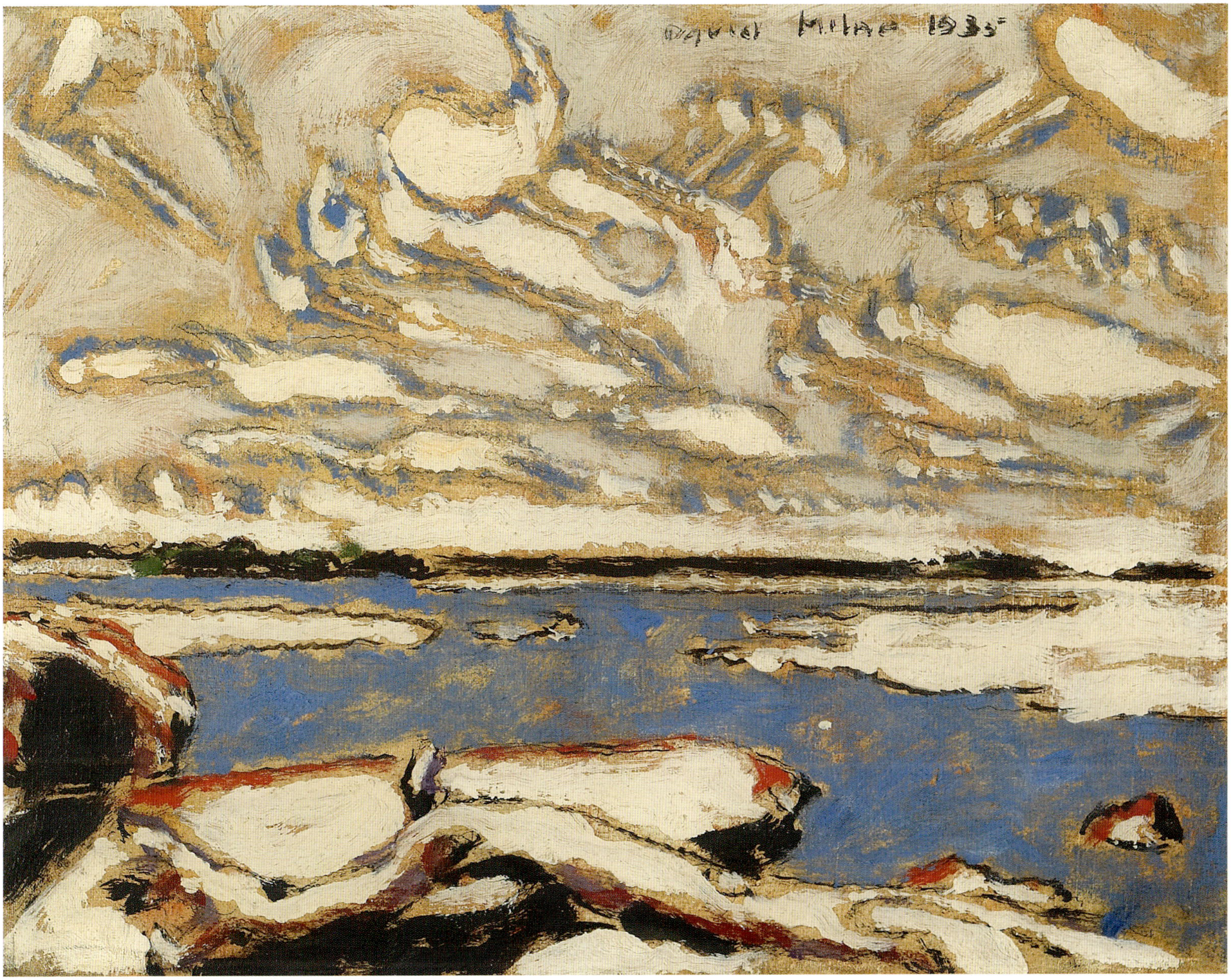

Blue Lake
1935, oil on canvas

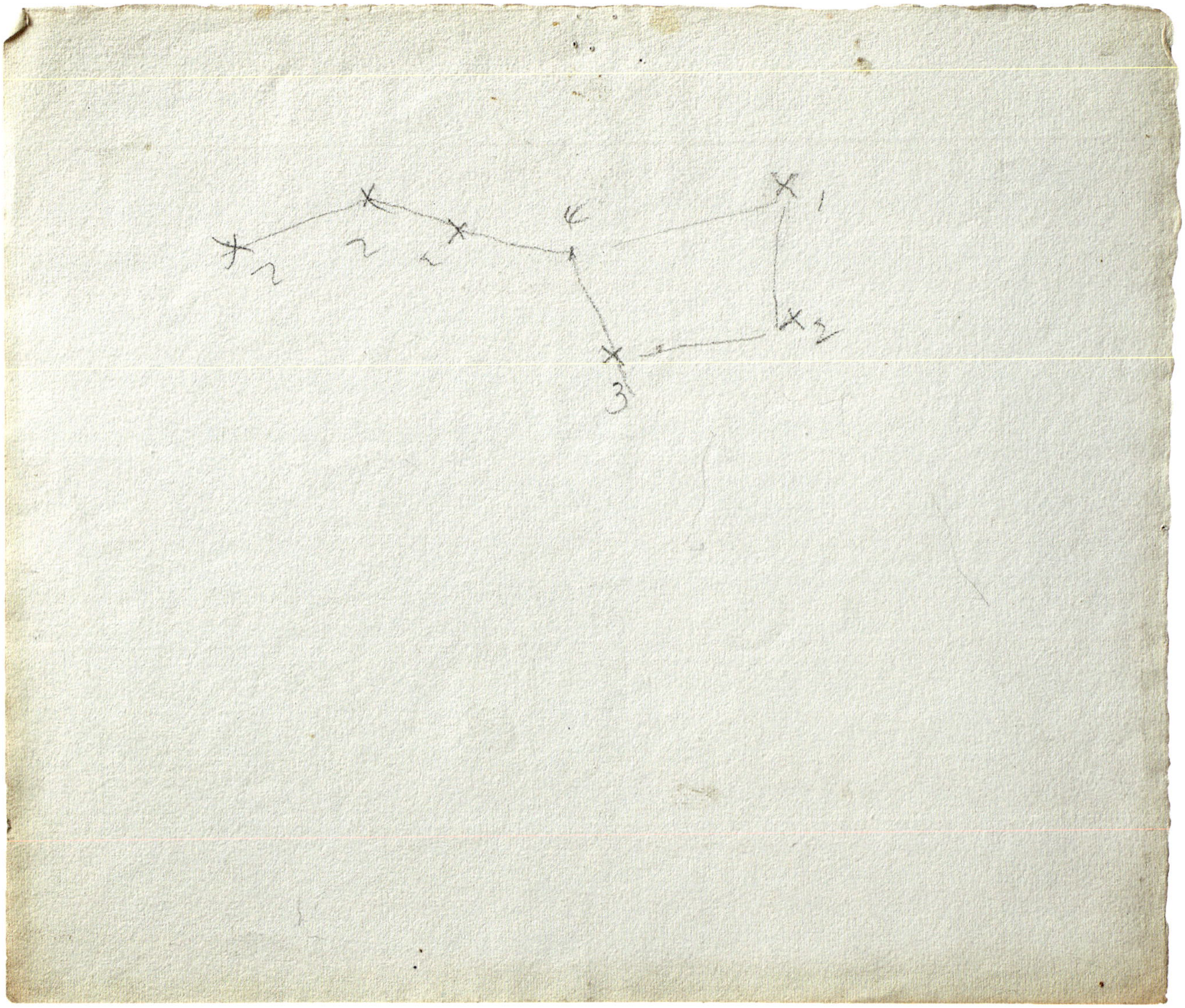

Untitled drawing
c. 1936, pencil on paper

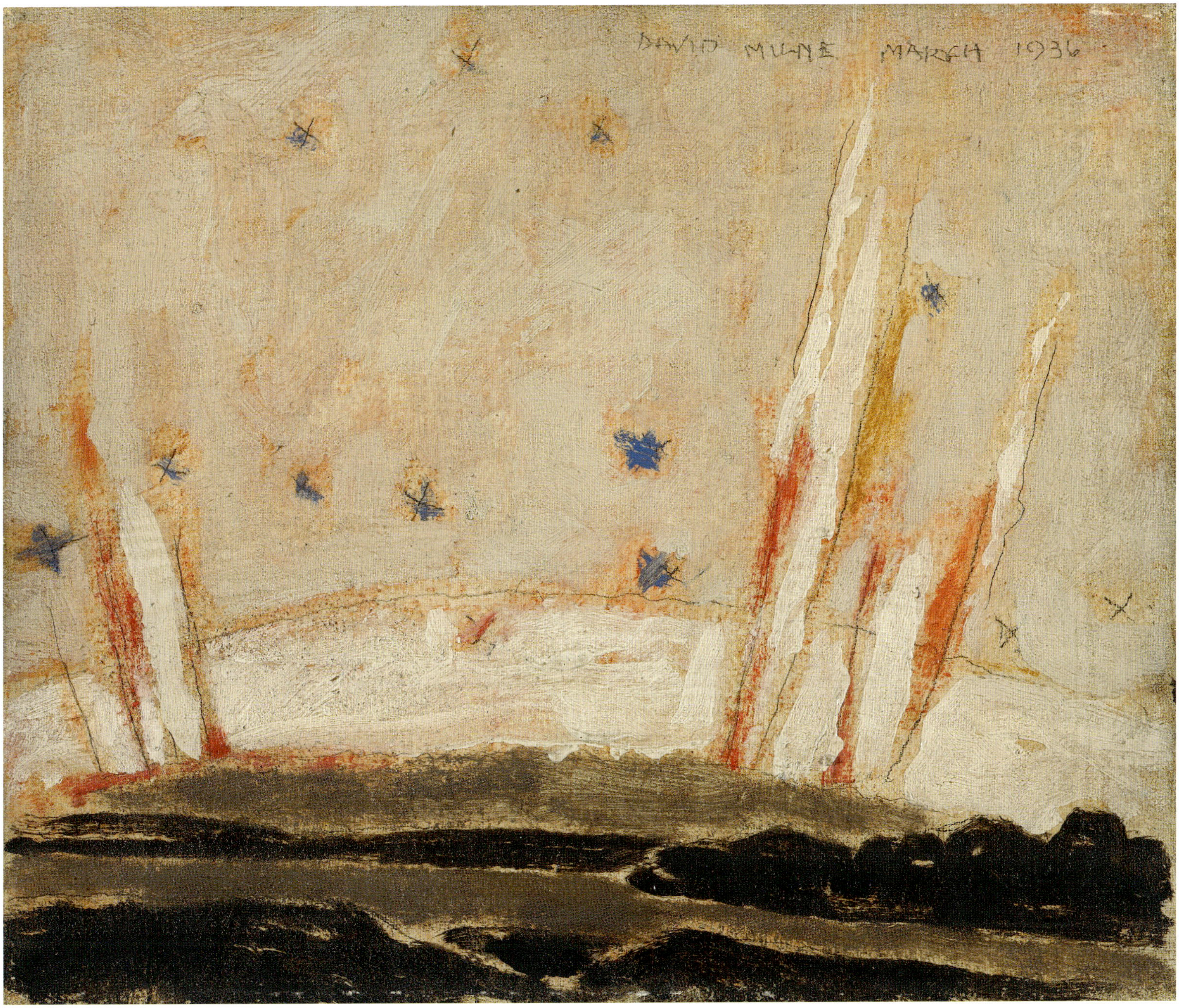

The Big Dipper
1936, oil on canvas

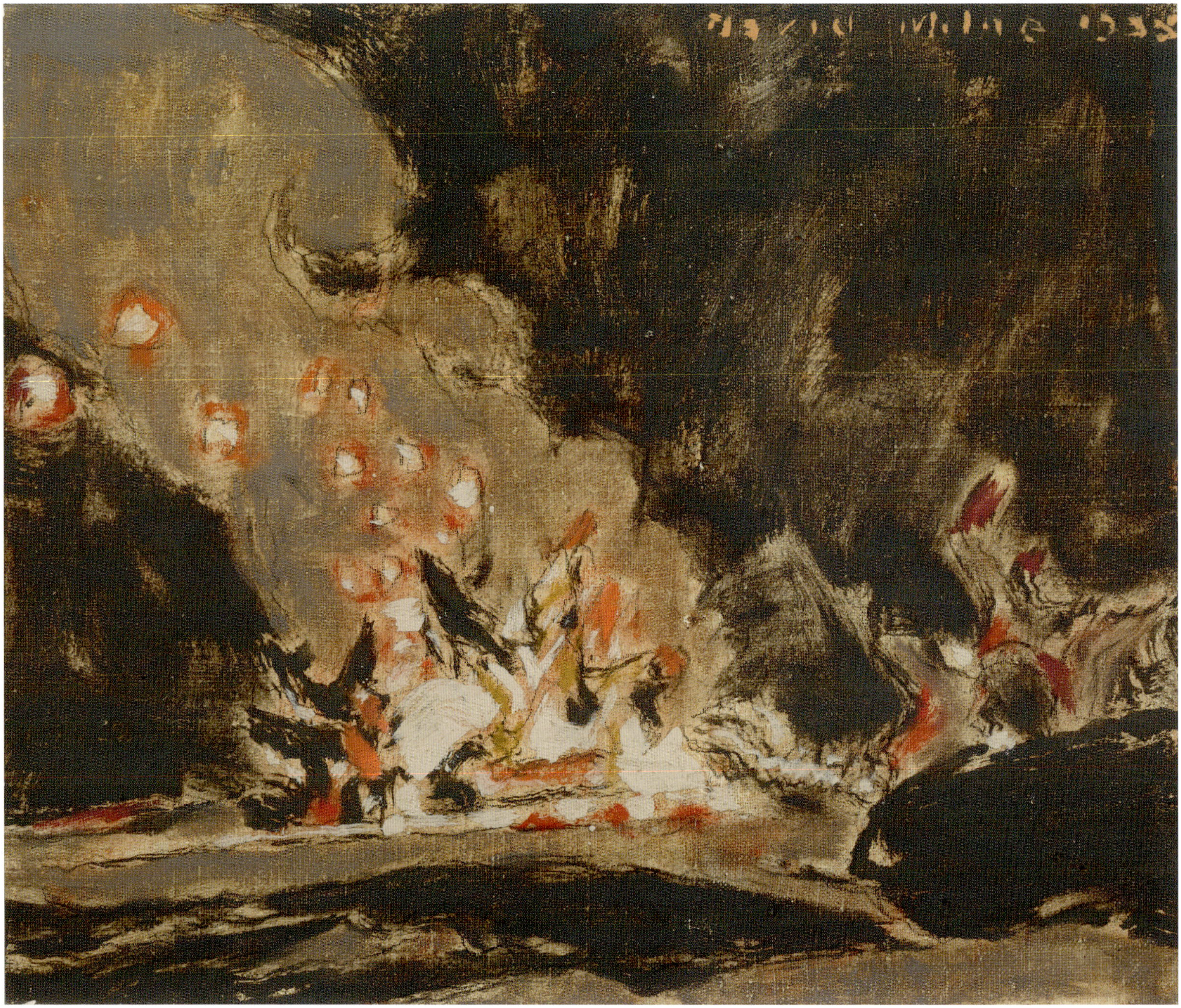

Smoke
1935, oil on canvas

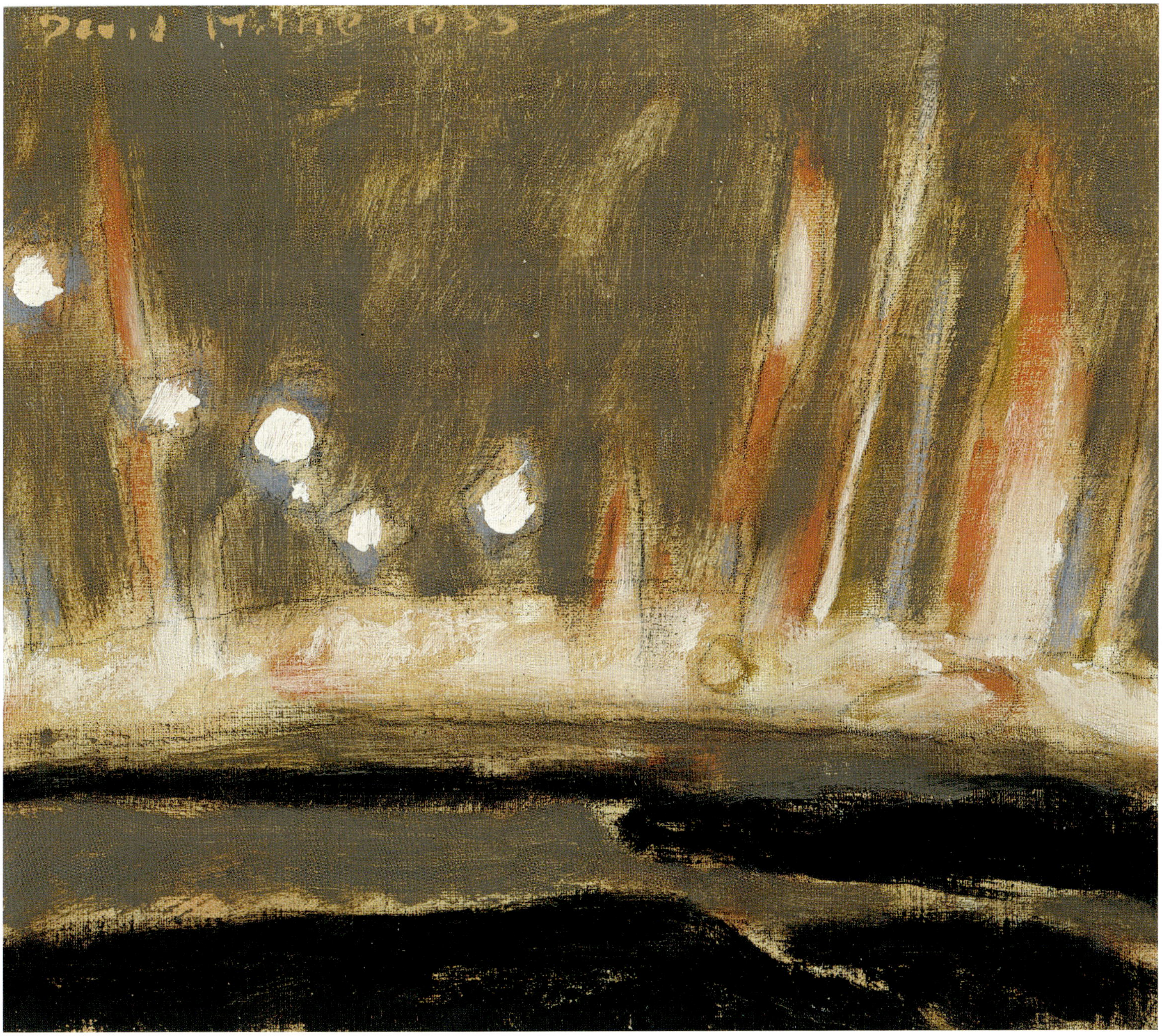

Northern Lights
1935, oil on canvas

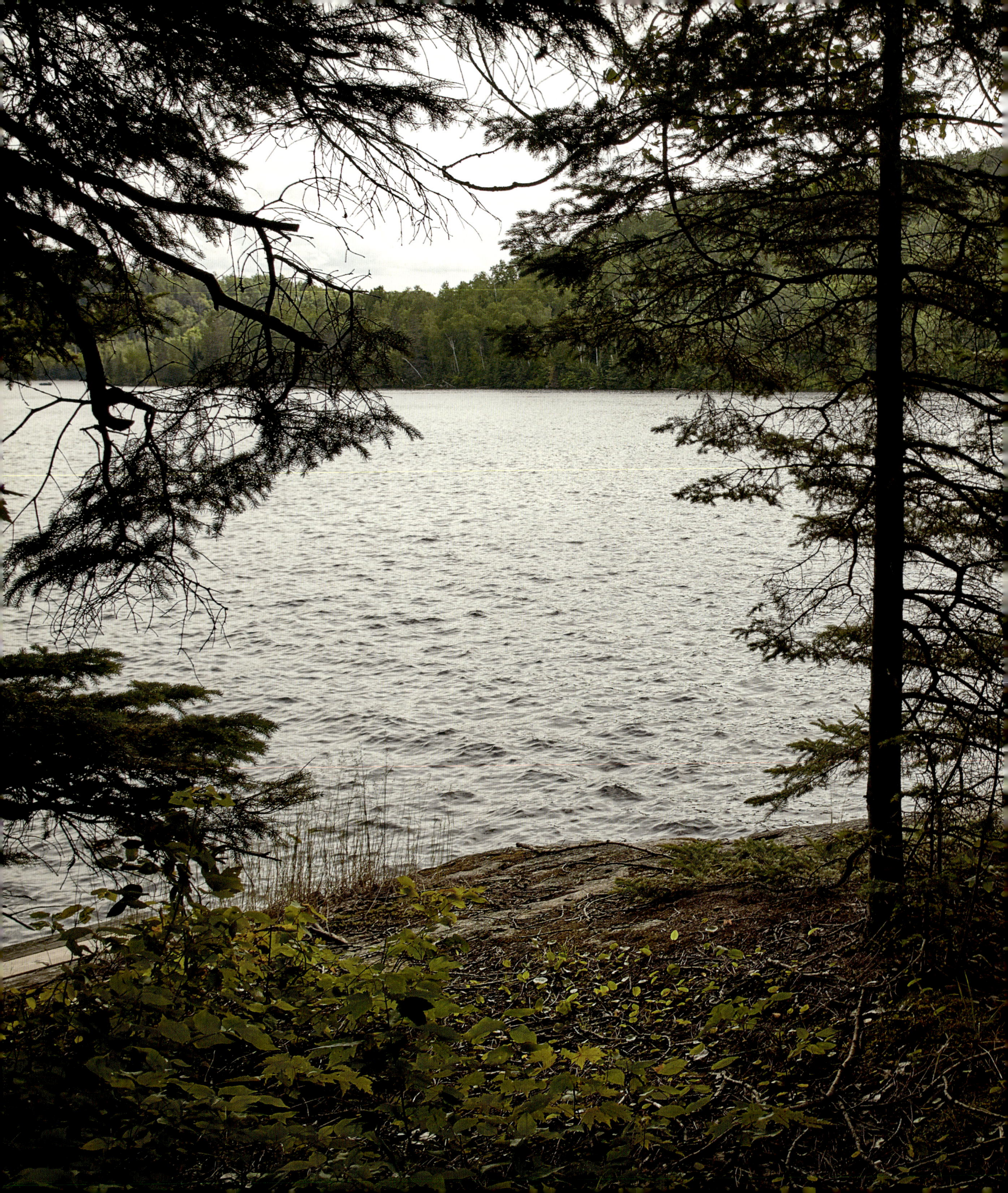

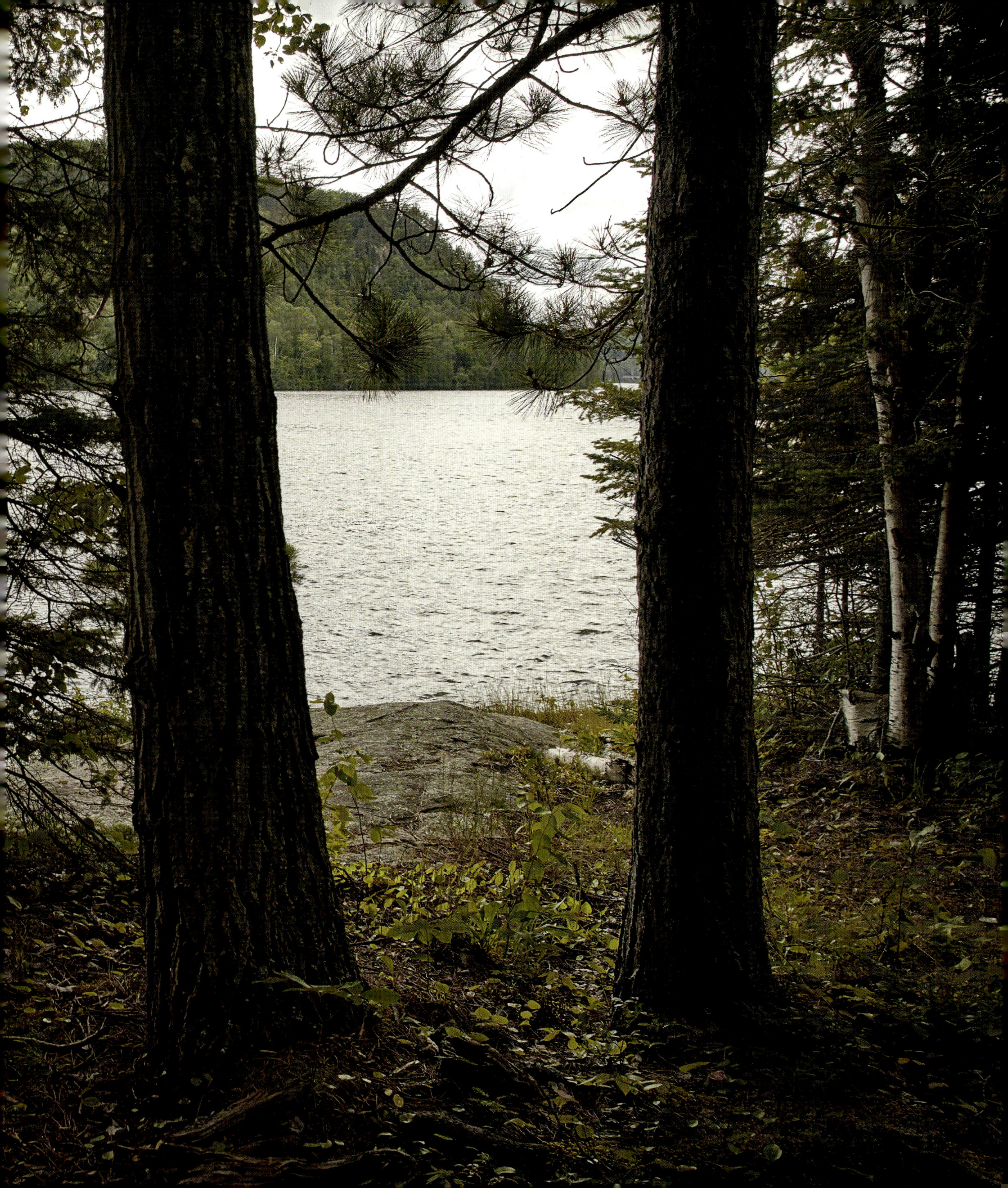

SCHOLARLY DEBTS AND PERSONAL THANKS

Readers in pursuit of a deeper knowledge of the art of David Milne will find the *Catalogue Raisonné of the Paintings* (1998) by David Milne Jr and David P. Silcox (with Elizabeth Driver and Liz Wylie) to be an invaluable resource. These two volumes are among the truly monumental accomplishments in Canadian art history. Silcox's earlier *Painting Place: The Life and Work of David B. Milne* (1996) is a brilliant work of compression and has likewise provided us with a firm platform on which to stand as we embarked on our explorations.

Other works help to fill in the full picture. John O'Brian's *David Milne and the Modern Tradition of Painting* (1983) is a brief but diamond-hard consideration of Milne's place in the history of art. His *David Milne: The New York Years, 1903–1916* (1981) is another invaluable source. Ian Thom's remarkable *David Milne* (1991), the multi-authored catalogue for his touring Milne exhibition of that year, is another key resource, as is Katharine Lochnan and her collaborator art historians' *David Milne Watercolours: 'Painting toward the Light'* (2005), the catalogue for the exhibition of the same name mounted at the Art Gallery of Ontario, Toronto, the British Museum, London, and the Metropolitan Museum of Art, New York. Gwendolyn Owens' earlier catalogue *The Watercolours of David Milne* (1984), which accompanied an exhibition touring from Cornell University to University of Vermont and University of Connecticut, has also played a role in spreading Milne's creative pollen in the United States. Finally, James King's *Inner Places: The Life of David Milne* (2016) is an approachable introduction to the artist's biography. As the reader will note, our catalogue for *David Milne: Modern Painting* has reunited many from this happy band of Milne scholars, most of whom have returned to look at him again at our invitation after decades of reflection and research, bringing fresh insights. We are deeply grateful for their camaraderie.

A decision was made early on in this project to focus on Milne's paintings, but his output in the medium of printmaking is likewise remarkable and worthy of study. In this regard, one could have no better guide than Rosemarie L. Tovell's *Reflections in a Quiet Pool: The Prints of David Milne* (1981), which provides extensive information on the prints but also sets these works authoritatively within the context of the wider career.

Milne's own collected writings have not yet been published, but we were privileged to have access to an edited version of the writings transcribed and collated by David Milne Jr and David P. Silcox in the course of their preparation of the catalogue raisonné. A multi-volume printout of this anthology has been placed at the E.P. Taylor Library and Archives at the Art Gallery of Ontario, in the Milne fonds, where it can be accessed by members of the public on request.

Readers can also find Milne's extraordinary account of his winter in the woods at Alander mountain (1920–1) in the August 1973 edition of *artscanada*, 'David Milne: A Document of Survival', which is devoted to his writing from this important period.

We are indebted to David Milne Jr for his willingness to read our manuscripts in proof and for such generous assistance in providing access to his own private archival holdings for both research purposes and for display in our exhibition. He has truly served as midwife in the birthing of this book at every stage, and we will be forever grateful for his deep knowledge and generosity of spirit.

Although they have been thanked elsewhere in this volume, I must draw attention to the glorious loans to this exhibition from the National Gallery of Canada, in Ottawa. The NGC's open-hearted response to our loan requests has made it possible for us to do our best. Special thanks to Katerina Atanassova, Anne Eschapasse and the NGC's director, Marc Mayer, for their solidarity in the mission to make Canadian art shine on the international stage.

Of the staff at the Art Gallery of Ontario's E.P. Taylor Library and Archives, there are not enough good things to say. The library at the AGO is a model of accessibility and cordiality, and particular thanks are due to Amy Marshall Furness, Rosamond Ivey, Special Collections Archivist and Head, and Donald Rance, Reference Librarian, Electronic Resources, for their endless patience as I sifted through their remarkable holdings.

Finally, in Toronto, thanks to Craig Boyko, whose photographs have brought this book to life, to John Geoghegan, who assisted me in locating a number of works in private hands, as did the art dealers Gisella Giacalone of the Mira Godard Gallery—representing the Milne estate for more than 40 years—Rod Green, Doug MacLean, Eric and Alan Klinkhoff, Alan Loch, Christopher Varley and the teams at Heffel Fine Art Auction House and Waddington's Auctioneers and Appraisers. Thanks also to Alison Reid for her gentle and insightful editorial fellowship. In London, my sincerest gratitude goes also to the wonderwomen of Dulwich—Clare Simpson, Phoebe Newman and Dana Mokaddem—and to Clare Martelli at Philip Wilson Publishers, copy-editor David Hawkins and art director Myfanwy Vernon-Hunt, for responding to Milne's art so deeply and going the extra mile.

Sarah Milroy

NOTES

The following abbreviations have been used:

AGO	Art Gallery of Ontario, Toronto
LAC	Library and Archives Canada, Ottawa
NGC	National Gallery of Canada, Ottawa
UTA	University of Toronto Archives

Dazzle and Kick: The Life of David Milne
Ian A.C. Dejardin

Some uncertainty exists about the year of David Milne's birth—8 January 1881 or 1882. Official documentation—a birth certificate, parish and early school records, even census data—vanished over the years, but the artist himself always used 1882, so Milne birthdate references in catalogues, books and scholarly articles have traditionally been to that year. Fairly recently, however, the Milne expert David P. Silcox uncovered fresh census information that seemed to affirm 1881 as the year of Milne's birth, a discovery that he published as 'A Postscript to the David Milne Biography and *Catalogue Raisonné of the Paintings*', in *The Journal of Canadian Art History* 36.2 (2015). But Milne family history uses the grave marker of the last-born sibling before David, a brother who died in infancy, as evidence of David's 1882 birthdate; there would not have been enough time for his mother to have brought another pregnancy to term by January 1881. Accordingly, we have settled on 8 January 1882 for *David Milne: Modern Painting*.

1 Milne letter to H.O. McCurry, April 1930, Milne fonds, AGO. 'Your Canadian art apparently, for now at least, went down in Canoe Lake. Tom Thomson still stands as the Canadian painter, harsh, brilliant, brittle, uncouth, not only most Canadian but most creative. How the few things of his stick in one's mind.'

2 Milne, 'Art Influences', an answer to a 1942 questionnaire from either *Canadian Art* or the National Gallery of Canada, Ottawa. Milne fonds, LAC. 'For a while they [Monet's pictures] influenced my painting, directly; perhaps they still do indirectly. I think it impossible for anyone to trace the influence by looking at my pictures.'

3 James Clarke in an interview with Blodwen Davies, 3 May 1961, Milne fonds, LAC. 'He was a great person for economy. He never used too much of anything. You can see that in his paintings ... economy of means was a characteristic of his whole being and his whole life.'

4 9 April 1919. Milne fonds, LAC.

5 David Milne, 'Notes for an Autobiography', K.M. [Kathleen Milne] typescript corrected by D.B.M., 13 April 1947, n.p., Milne fonds, AGO.

6 That selection of works has not subsequently been found, having been lost in transit between the London office and the Canadian War Museum.

7 David Milne, 'War Records' in 'Notes for an Autobiography', K.M. [Kathleen Milne] typescript corrected by D.B.M., 13 April 1947, Milne fonds, AGO.

A Mind of His Own
Sarah Milroy

1 David Milne, 'Touring on a Topographic Map', n.d., file 5-4, box 5, Milne fonds, AGO.

2 I say this while acknowledging that Milne expressed strong feelings about the nurturance of Canadian culture. In a letter to Alan Jarvis (19 October 1936, Milne fonds, AGO), for example, he endorsed the importance of the Canadian Broadcasting Corporation, saying that the overbearing presence of American radio

has prevented 'the growth of national feeling, splitting away from the mother country and the sister dominions, leading us to attempt to apply American solutions to Canadian problems and imposing on us American ideals, habits of thought, manners and language. With other things it is undermining Canadian independence. My own rather watery patriotism wouldn't carry me with Canada into the American Union, or even to a cutting loose from Empire—which I would consider merely a halfway step to the disappearance of Canada as a separate people.'

3 In a draft letter to Alice and Vincent Massey (20 August 1934, Milne fonds, AGO), Milne described his New York immersion thus: 'In the student years, Childe Hassam, Willard Metcalf, J. Alden Weir, Chas. H. Davis. The Ten and the French Impressionists were in the galleries. A little later, Luks, Bellows, Glackens ... All just the stirring of the wind before the storm. We heard rumblings of Cézanne, Van Gogh and Gauguin. Soon we were going to see thrilling little exhibitions of modernist painting and sculpture at Stieglitz's little cupboard of a gallery 291. Matisse, Picasso, Brancusi we missed none of them.' He added in a further draft: 'For the first time we saw courage and imagination bare, not sweetened by sentiment and smothered in technical skill.'

4 As Edward Steichen once stated, Stieglitz, with only a brief interruption for lunch, 'stood on the floor of the Galleries from ten o'clock in the morning until six or seven o'clock at night. He was always there, talking, talking, talking, talking in parables, arguing, explaining.' Richard Whelan, *Alfred Stieglitz: A Biography* (New York: Little, Brown, 1955), 260–1.

5 David P. Silcox, *Painting Place: The Life and Work of David B. Milne* (Toronto: University of Toronto Press, 1996), 386 n64.

6 Milne letter to H.O. McCurry, 28 March 1930, NGC.

7 David Milne, 'Notes for an Autobiography,' K.M. [Kathleen Milne] typescript corrected by D.B.M., 13 April 1947, Milne fonds, AGO.

8 John O'Brian wrote of this connection in *David Milne and the Modern Tradition of Painting* (Toronto: Coach House Press, 1983), 83–6.

9 Milne does not write of being influenced by Stieglitz's photographs, yet the melancholy tone of his earliest oil paintings of New York, such as *City Rain*, 1911–12, and *Waterfront*, 1911, seem to me to have as much to do with Stieglitz's moody cityscapes as they do with painterly precedent. Milne's exploration of patterning and high contrasts in his figure paintings and landscape studies in New York also suggest a kinship with Stieglitz's experiments, as well as an awareness of the Nabis artists. But influence is an infernally difficult matter to determine. As Milne wrote in his essay 'Pictures Have Beginning and Endings': 'A picture seen while walking past an open door might be grasped completely enough to be remembered for life—if it is a good enough picture.' Douglas Duncan typescript of the Milne essay, Milne fonds, AGO.

10 Milne letter to James Clarke, 3 October 1932, Milne fonds, LAC. In his 4 January notes from Alander mountain, winter 1920–1, he records '1 Vol Ruskin's Modern Painters' as his only reading material.

11 Milne letter to Graham McInnes, 15 June 1938, Milne fonds, LAC. It seems Milne admired particularly Fry's freedom of thought. To McInnes he wrote, 'About Roger Fry and his book, the most interesting thing, to me, is the evidence of his own development in the ten years or more in which the articles were written. Unfortunately in my book, the pieces are not in order, so I find some things hard to understand until I look up the date and realize that his point of view changed greatly—which is of course the very finest thing about him.'

12 Milne letter to James Clarke, 1 October 1920, Milne fonds, LAC.

13 Milne made a note of the Altamira cave paintings in a journal from his London sojourn, Milne Study Centre display, Art Gallery of Ontario, customarily housed in file 6-1, Milne fonds, AGO.

14 The highlight of Milne's visit to Toronto in 1930 was a talk on the Spanish master given by the British-born Canadian artist Bertram Brooker at the Art Gallery of Toronto (now AGO), noted in his letter to H.O. McCurry, *c.* April 1930, NGC.

15 Milne letter to H.O. McCurry, 17 March 1932, NGC. Milne wrote that the back of the canvas upon which the artist depicts himself working acts as a kind of visual pause for viewers, heightening

their connection to the more detailed areas of the painting. 'It is not a dazzle area because it is not violent', he wrote, 'it isn't a blow, it doesn't engage you in the picture quickly. It is rather a resting spot', a point of 'relief'. He uses this device in his own painting *Framed Etching (Lilies from the Bush)*, 1931 (p. 160).

16 Milne letter to James Clarke, 3 October 1932, Milne fonds, LAC. Milne paraphrased the legacy of Whistler thus: 'I have seen it put—"The less the apparent means in a picture the better the picture ..." The reason is simple. Anything in a picture that doesn't stir aesthetic feeling and takes the attention slows you up and so weakens the aesthetic quickening otherwise gained from it ... Anything that tempts or distracts you from the main motive is weakness.'

17 Milne letter to James Clarke, 23 January 1919, Milne fonds, LAC.

18 Milne letter to James Clarke, *c.* 28 February 1926, Milne fonds, LAC. 'Some time when you plan on having a lingering illness or get 30 days for turning Millerton's busy corner on three wheels lay in a couple of volumes of Marcel Proust. Absolutely bottomless! John Ruskin and Noah Webster were rough sketchers alongside Marcel Proust. He could write a thumping good volume, preface, introduction and notes, on your mental processes while going down stairs on a May morning at the Maple Shade inn.'

19 Kenneth Patchen, 'The Artist's Duty', *The Journal of Albion Moonlight* (New York: New Directions, 1941). I am indebted to Ihor Holubizky for alerting me to this poem, which he quotes in his essay 'David Milne, Dark Pool, Ti Magami, 1929', in *Picturing the Americas*, ed. Peter John Brownlee, Valéria Piccoli and Georgiana Uhlyarik (New Haven, CT: Yale University Press, 2016).

20 Milne Alander diary, 9 January 1921, box 5–3, Milne fonds, AGO.

21 Milne Alander diary, 1 December 1920, box 5–1, Milne fonds, AGO.

22 Milne Alander diary, 29 November 1920, box 5–1, Milne fonds, AGO.

23 Milne, 'Notes for an Autobiography'.

24 Milne, 'Notes for an Autobiography'.

25 Milne letter to James Clarke, 13 November 1927, Milne fonds, LAC.

26 In a draft letter to Maulsby Kimball dated 9 March 1931 (Milne fonds, AGO), Milne demarcates three types of experience that are simultaneously at play as he pursues the art of painting: the pleasing observation of nature, the search for the aesthetic kick, and the consciousness of memory that constantly plays below the surface of perception. 'And one set of thoughts doesn't seem to interfere with the others', he adds, noting wryly, 'One thing I do find very difficult though—to keep a pipe lit and paint.'

27 Milne letter to James Clarke, 26 April 1932, Milne fonds, LAC.

28 Milne, 'Pictures Have Beginnings and Endings'.

29 Writing to H.O. McCurry on 28 March 1930 (Milne fonds, LAC), in a mocking reference to the manly pursuits of the Group of Seven, Milne positioned himself as a wilful outsider in Canadian art, wittily noting, 'I am going to be quite fashionable this summer—joining the mountain painters. However, since the Rockies are getting so crowded, I am going to venture into the Toronto Range—which, as you no doubt know runs from somewhere up Yonge Street in the direction of Hamilton.' He would settle that year in the decidedly unheroic farming town of Palgrave, Ontario, just north of Toronto.

30 Milne letter to James Clarke, 3 April 1919, Milne fonds, LAC.

31 Milne, 'Notes for an Autobiography'.

32 This quotation comes from Douglas Duncan's 1945 typescript of Milne's essay titled 'The 1935 "Spring Fever" Picture', Milne fonds, AGO.

33 Milne letter to James Clarke, 30 September–1 October 1920, Milne fonds, LAC.

34 Milne letter of thanks to Alice Massey, 19 December 1934, UTA.

35 Even love, though, would not blunt his inclination to hold his own views. In a letter to Pavey of 3 May 1939 (Milne fonds, LAC), he banters: 'Still reading *Ulysses* doggedly. Once in a while I get a kick out of it, but this is pure realism, dream stuff, too loose not enough bones in it for me. T.S. Eliot puts form into much the same material.'

36 The work in question is *Snowy Hemlocks*, 1921 (p. 120), oil on canvas, Heffel Fine Art Auction House catalogue of sale, 26 November 2015.

37 Draft letter to the Right Honourable R.B. Bennett,

December 1932, Milne fonds, AGO; Milne letter to Graham McInnes, 16 February 1938, Milne fonds, LAC: 'A fine book, but one thing makes me sore. Here have I, with the greatest effort and expense, been forming some of these fine ideas, then Roger Fry steps in and says them first'; Milne letter to Kay and Carlson Mark and Kathleen Pavey, 27 November 1938, Milne fonds, AGO.

38 Milne, 'Notes for an Autobiography'; Milne letter to James Clarke, 7 November 1933, Milne fonds, LAC: 'P.S. Saw a wolf yesterday, very close. Neither of us appeared to be afraid'; Milne, 'Notes for an Autobiography'; Milne letter to Graham McInnes, 15 June 1938, Milne fonds, LAC.

39 Milne letter to Kathleen Pavey, 7 January 1939, Milne fonds, AGO.

40 Milne letter to James Clarke, 12 August 1924, Milne fonds, LAC.

41 'Peter Doig: Twenty Questions (extract) 2001', interview with Matthew Higgs et al., in Adrian Searle, Kitty Scott and Catherine Grenier, *Peter Doig* (London: Phaidon, 2007), 131: 'As regards David Milne, I'm very interested in his work, particularly in the way that he approaches the landscape, in the way that landscape is so reduced in his work. I like the distance that he is able to achieve from his subject while remaining quite specific at the same time. Stylistically, I also find his work quite extreme for the time that it was made. It is surprising that his work is not known more outside of Canada. I really like it when the reduction in his work becomes extreme: black mountains, black interiors, almost negatives of space.'

42 Wallace Stevens, 'The Snow Man', *The Collected Works of Wallace Stevens* (New York: Knopf, 1954).

'Plunging into the Sun': David Milne in New York City

Katerina Atanassova

1 David P. Silcox, *Painting Place: The Life and Work of David B. Milne* (Toronto: University of Toronto Press, 1996), 3.

2 Among many others, the American artist John Twachtman favoured square-shaped canvases. He was part of the Ten American Painters group who held annual exhibitions at the Montross Gallery, where Milne would have seen their work. Twachtman believed that patterns are best observed by the mind when they are seen in square shapes.

3 Robert W. Snyder and Rebecca Zurier, 'Picturing the City: Urban Vision and the Ashcan School,' in *Metropolitan Lives: The Ashcan School and Their New York*, ed. Rebecca Zurier et al. (Washington, DC: National Museum of American Art; New York: Norton, 1995), 152. John Sloan's *The Hairdresser's Window*, 1907, is in the collection of the Wadsworth Atheneum Museum of Art, Hartford, CT.

4 John O'Brian, *David Milne and the Modern Tradition of Painting* (Toronto: Coach House Press, 1983), 65.

5 Elizabeth Kilbourn, *Great Canadian Painting: A Century of Canadian Art* (Toronto: Canadian Centennial Publishing, 1966), 66.

6 Lora Carney, 'David Milne's New York', in *David Milne*, ed. Ian Thom (Vancouver: Vancouver Art Gallery and the McMichael Canadian Art Collection in association with Douglas and McIntyre, 1991), 41.

'The Mystery Thing': David Milne and Spirituality

Katharine Lochnan

1 *Paisley Advocate*, 14 June 1922.

2 David Milne, 'Aesthetic Agents,' unpublished essay, quoted in John O'Brian, *David Milne and the Modern Tradition of Painting* (Toronto: Coach House Press, 1983), 98.

3 David Milne, 'Notes for an Autobiography,' K.M. [Kathleen Milne] typescript corrected by D.B.M., 13 April 1947, Milne fonds, AGO.

4 At this time, the Presbyterian Church in Canada was engaged in a conversation about uniting with the Methodists, and the unionists from neigbouring St Andrew's joined Knox in 1873; the balance of its congregation was folded into Knox in 1891. In an email to Katharine Lochnan, 16 April 2017, Rev. William Kervin, Emmanuel College, University of Toronto, wrote: 'The unionists were the Protestant "evangelicals" of the time—

though that term means something specific in that context. They found in the prospects of union a greater good, while continuing Presbyterians feared for the loss of their Presbyterian identity.'
5 *Paisley Advocate*, 14 June 1922.
6 Stockton Kimball, 'Unpublished Notes', typescript, 9–18 September 1935, Milne fonds, AGO.
7 Milne, 'Notes for an Autobiography'.
8 Rebekah Smick, '"The Second Book of God": Protestant Mysticism', in *Mystical Landscapes: From Vincent van Gogh to Emily Carr*, ed. Katharine Lochnan et al. (Toronto: Art Gallery of Ontario and Prestel, 2016), 69–80.
9 Milne, 'Aesthetic Agents', 98.
10 Milne letter to Alan Jarvis, 2 May 1936, quoting John 3:1–5, Milne fonds, AGO.
11 Milne letter to Alan Jarvis, 2 May 1936, quoting Luke 10:38–42 and comparing the artist to Martha rather than Mary. Milne was particularly fond of the Gospel of Luke, the patron saint of artists, who was said to have been an artist and to have painted a portrait of the Virgin Mary.
12 James Clarke in an interview with Blodwen Davies, 3 May 1961, Milne fonds, LAC.
13 James Clarke interview with Davies.
14 Evelyn Underhill, *Mysticism: A Study in the Nature and Development of Man's Spiritual Consciousness* (London: Methuen, 1962 [1911]), 263.
15 David Milne, 'Art Influences', an answer to a 1942 questionnaire from either *Canadian Art* or the National Gallery of Canada, Ottawa. Milne fonds, LAC.
16 David Milne, 'Art: Monet', unpublished essay, *c.* 1945, Milne fonds, AGO.
17 Katharine Lochnan, '"Solitude and Silence": Contemplative Landscapes from Turner to Monet', in *Mystical Landscapes*, 156.
18 Roger Marx, 'Les "Nymphéas" de M. Claude Monet', *Gazette des Beaux-Arts*, Paris, 1909, republished in Roger Marx, *Maîtres d'hier et d'aujourd'hui* (Paris: Calmann-Lévy, 1914), 291. Trans. Dora Mark.
19 Milne, 'Aesthetic Agents', 99.
20 Robert D. Richardson Jr, 'Emerson and Nature', in *The Cambridge Companion to Ralph Waldo Emerson*, ed. Joel Port and Saundra Morris (Cambridge: Cambridge University Press, 1999), 103.
21 Ralph Waldo Emerson, 'The Poet', *Selections from Ralph Waldo Emerson: An Organic Anthology*, Stephen E. Whicher, ed. (Boston: Houghton Mifflin, 1957, repr. 1960), 227.
22 Clive Bell, 'The Metaphysical Hypothesis', *Art* (London: Chatto and Windus, 1928 [1914]), 54.
23 Bell, 'Art and Religion', *Art*, 81–2.
24 Bell, 'Art and Religion', 81–2.
25 Bell, 'Art and Religion', 77.
26 Bell, 'Art and Religion', 75.
27 Bell, 'Art and Religion', 93; he adds a caveat: 'What we may not say is, that art is the expression of any particular religion; for to do so is to confuse the religious spirit with the channels in which it has been made to flow.'
28 For information about the influence of Whistler, see Katharine Lochnan, 'Reflections on Turner, Whistler, Monet and Milne', in *David Milne Watercolours: 'Painting toward the Light',* Katharine Lochnan, ed. (Toronto: Art Gallery of Ontario with Douglas and McIntyre, 2005), 104–7.
29 Kimball, 'Unpublished Notes', 15.
30 Milne letter to Alice and Vincent Massey, 20 August 1934, Massey Papers, Massey College, UTA. He is referring to Isaiah 1:2, a passage regarding the Israelites: 'They shall beat their swords into plowshares, and their spears into pruning hooks.'
31 James Clarke interview with Davies.
32 Kimball, 'Unpublished Notes', 9.
33 Milne letter to Alice and Vincent Massey, 20 August 1934.
34 Milne, 'Notes for an Autobiography'.

Modern Catastrophe
Margaret MacMillan

1 David Milne, 'War Records', in 'Notes for an Autobiography', K.M. [Kathleen Milne] typescript corrected by D.B.M., 13 April 1947, Milne fonds, AGO.
2 Milne, 'War Records'.
3 Milne letter to James Clarke, June–July 1919, Milne fonds, LAC.
4 Milne letter to James Clarke, 26–8 June 1919, Milne fonds, LAC.
5 Milne, 'War Records'.

6 Milne, 'War Records'.
7 Milne, 'War Records'.
8 Milne, 'War Records'.

Five Stumps
Anne-Marie Ninacs

1 He says so to Blair Laing who sees 'mostly red tissue paper, boxes and string, a Christmas package' in *Christmas Morning*, 1937. David Milne interviewed by Blair Laing, CFRB Toronto, 16 January 1938.
2 Milne letter to James Clarke, 9 April 1919, MG30 D43 vol. 1, 0306–0317, Milne fonds, LAC.
3 Milne letter to James Clarke, 11 February 1921, MG30 D43 vol. 1, 0639–0643, Milne fonds, LAC.
4 Milne letter to James Clarke, 21–2 April 1921, MG30 D43 vol. 1, 0600–0611, Milne fonds, LAC.
5 David Milne, 'Art: Monet', 20 January 1947, Collections, miscellaneous curatorial files, Milne catalogues, NGC. Milne wrote more than once that he saw a series of three to six Haystacks by Claude Monet at Durand-Ruel Galleries shortly after arriving in New York in 1903, and that it was for him a breathtaking artistic encounter. Monet's art was highly visible in New York from 1903 to 1916, so Milne undeniably had repeated access to his paintings (including series of cliffs and views of the London Bridge), but it has been impossible for us to trace any series of Haystacks. According to the catalogue raisonné of Monet's oeuvre (Wildenstein, 1974), the 1907 exhibition at Durand-Ruel New York is the first one Milne could have visited, and it presented only one little bale of hay in *Prairie à Giverny*, 1890. The sole work from the Haystack series ever exhibited in New York during the time Milne lived there is *Meule*, *hiver*, *temps brumeux*, 1888–89, presented for the first time at Durand-Ruel in 1915, and again in 1916. Despite our research, and a snow-covered *Haystack* painted by Milne in February 1923 (p. 138), which seems to be a conscious homage to Monet, this discrepancy between the artist's memory (known to be quite reliable) and facts remains unresolved.
6 Milne letter to James Clarke, 30 September 1920, part ii, MG30 D43 vol. 1, 0475–0489, Milne fonds, LAC.
7 H.D. Thoreau, *Walden*, in *The Portable Thoreau* (New York: Penguin Books, 1975), 333, 344.
8 Milne letter to James Clarke, 11 February 1921, MG30 D43 vol. 1, 0639–0643, Milne fonds, LAC.
9 That is the feeling he derived from a similarly frugal and productive way of life in Palgrave. Milne letter to James Clarke, 14 August and 3 October 1932, MG30 D43 vol. 3, 1468–1492, Milne fonds, LAC.
10 From early on 'stumps of various heights' or 'stumps in the beaver pond' were also part of his lists of painting material. Milne letter to James Clarke, 7–8 August 1919, MG30 D43 vol. 1, 0419–0436; Milne letter to James Clarke, 26 June 1921, and after, 0586–0599, Milne fonds, LAC.
11 David Milne, 1934 sale list reproduced in David Milne Jr and David P. Silcox, *David B. Milne: Catalogue Raisonné of the Paintings*, vol. 2 (Toronto: University of Toronto Press, 1998), 532.
12 Despite what has often been written, Milne's aesthetic quickening seems to me to share little more than the wording with the idealist-essentialist 'aesthetic emotion' theorised by Clive Bell in *Art* (London: Chatto and Windus, 1928 [1914]). It has much deeper affinities with the thoroughly physical description of 'an experience' by his contemporary the pragmatist philosopher John Dewey in *Art as Experience* (New York: Putnam, 1934).
13 David Milne, 'In the 1880s', 'Notes for an Autobiography', K.M. [Kathleen Milne] typescript corrected by D.B.M., 13 April 1947, Milne fonds, AGO.
14 Milne, 'In the 1880s.'
15 Milne letter to James Clarke, 27 August 1926, MG30 D43, vol. 2, 1093–1102, Milne fonds, LAC.
16 Milne letter to James Clarke, 27 August 1926.
17 I agree with the observation made by Rosemarie L. Tovell in the catalogue *David Milne: Painting Place* (Ottawa: National Gallery of Canada, 1976), 26.

Milne's Great Indoors
Jane Urquhart

1 Milne letter to H.O. McCurry, November 1929, NGC.

Milne's Mineshafts: A Conversation
Edward Burtynsky and Sarah Milroy

1 Milne letter to H.O. McCurry, November 1929, NGC.

Motive for Metaphor
John O'Brian

This essay is for Kimberly Phillips, who prompted me to consider the matter of metaphor in David Milne's work. I am also indebted to papers presented by Margaret Werth, 'Matissean Poetics in the 1910s', and Alastair Wright, '*Le Bonheur de Vivre* and the Legacy of Symbolism', at the symposium *Matisse Today*, Barnes Foundation, Philadelphia, 14–15 October 2016. Thanks as well to Ryan Gauvin, my research assistant, for locating the information on flowers and flower wholesaling in Ontario, and to Gabriel Araujo and Brigitte Duchesne, Public Diplomacy Section at Canada House, London, who made the painting available for me to see.

1 See Alastair Wright, *Matisse and the Subject of Modernism* (Princeton, NJ: Princeton University Press, 2004), 79.
2 Milne letter to H.O. McCurry, 17 March 1932, published in David Milne Jr and David P. Silcox, *David Milne: Catalogue Raisonné of the Paintings*, vol. 2, 1929–53 (Toronto: University of Toronto Press, 1998), 506.
3 Milne letter to H.O. McCurry, 17 March 1932, 506. Milne makes no mention of the posy in the letter.
4 William Perkins Bull, *From Spring to Autumn: Favourite Wild Flowers Found in the Meadows and Copses of Ontario's Keystone County* (Toronto: Perkins Bull Foundation and George J. McLeod, 1937).
5 Kyle Neill, senior archivist at the Peel Art Gallery, Museum and Archives, considers it improbable that Palgrave had a flower shop but likely that the Palgrave General Store sold flowers. Email from Kyle Neill to Ryan Gauvin, 16 February 2017.
6 Wallace Stevens, 'The Motive for Metaphor', *The Collected Works of Wallace Stevens* (New York: Knopf, 1954), 288.
7 Milne draft letter to James Clarke, *c.* January 1926, Milne fonds, AGO. The relationship of Milne's work to that of Matisse is discussed in John O'Brian, *David Milne and the Modern Tradition of Painting* (Toronto: Coach House Press, 1983), 69–75.
8 David P. Silcox email to the author, 2 May 2017. A second painting by Milne, *Ground Contours* (*c.* 1930) in the Paris collection, was also stored in the broom closet.
9 Wright, *Matisse and the Subject of Modernism*, 79. See also John O'Brian, *Ruthless Hedonism: The American Reception of Matisse* (Chicago: University of Chicago Press, 1999), 113.
10 *Waterfall* was submitted to a juried exhibition of the Chicago Society of Etchers in 1930 and rejected. See David P. Silcox, *Painting Place: The Life and Work of David B. Milne* (Toronto: University of Toronto Press, 1996), 225.
11 Peel Art Gallery Museum + Archives, Ernest Alfred Parsons and William Perkins Bull fonds, PN2008_00777 and PN2010_00615.
12 Stevens, 'The Motive for Metaphor', 288. Northrop Frye analyses the poem in *The Educated Imagination and Other Writings on Critical Theory 1933–1963*, vol. 21, ed. Germaine Warkentin (Toronto: University of Toronto Press, 2006), 445–6.

A Radical Shift at Six Mile Lake
David P. Silcox

1 Quoted from Douglas Duncan's 1945 typed typescript of Milne's essay titled 'The 1935 "Spring Fever" Picture', Milne fonds, AGO.
2 Harold Town in conversation with the author, *c.* 1983, while screening colour slides of Milne's New York paintings.
3 Milne letter to James Clarke, 28 August 1935, Milne fonds, LAC.
4 Milne letter to James Clarke, 28 August 1935.

LIST OF WORKS

Works by David Milne

Ablain-Saint-Nazaire Church from Lorette Ridge Looking toward Souchez and Vimy, p. 101 [Not exhibited]
1919, watercolour over graphite on wove paper
35.4 x 50.6 cm
National Gallery of Canada, Ottawa
Transfer from the Canadian War Memorials, 1921
© The Estate of David Milne

Across the Still Lake, p. 176
1936, oil on canvas
31.3 x 36.3 cm
Art Gallery of Ontario, Toronto
Gift of Mrs. O.D. Vaughan, Toronto, 1986
86/91 © The Estate of David Milne

Alcove, pp. 21, 54 [Not Exhibited]
1914, oil on canvas
50.8 x 64 cm
National Gallery of Canada, Ottawa
Purchased 2007 with the Andrea and Charles Bronfman Canadian Art Fund © The Estate of David Milne

Ascension XX, p. 76 [Not Exhibited]
c. 1945, watercolour on paper
53.7 x 36.9 cm
Private Collection © The Estate of David Milne

Back of Clarke's House, p. 129
1923, oil on canvas
30.8 x 40.8 cm
Gift of the Founders, Robert and Signe McMichael
McMichael Canadian Art Collection 1966.16.27 © The Estate of David Milne

Beginning of Spring 1, p. 23 [Not Exhibited]
c. 1923, drybrush watercolour on paper
38.1 x 55.5 cm
Milne Family Collection © The Estate of David Milne

The Belfry, Hôtel de Ville, Arras, p. 108
1919, watercolour over graphite on wove paper
35.8 x 50.7 cm
National Gallery of Canada, Ottawa
Transfer from the Canadian War Memorials, 1921
© The Estate of David Milne

The Bend in the Arras-Lens Road above Vimy Village, p. 104 [Not Exhibited]
1919, watercolour over graphite on wove paper
35.3 x 50.7 cm
National Gallery of Canada, Ottawa
Transfer from the Canadian War Memorials, 1921 © The Estate of David Milne

The Big Dipper, p. 187
1936, oil on canvas
31.4 x 35.6 cm
National Gallery of Canada, Ottawa
© The Estate of David Milne

Billboards, p. 46
c. 1912, oil on canvas
51.2 x 56.5 cm
National Gallery of Canada, Ottawa
Gift of Douglas M. Duncan, Toronto, 1962
© The Estate of David Milne

Bishop's Pond (Reflections), p. 74
1916, watercolour over graphite on wove paper, with watercoloured wove paper overlay
44.2 x 54.2 cm
National Gallery of Canada, Ottawa
© The Estate of David Milne

Bishop's Pond in Sunlight, p. 126
1920, watercolour on paper
38.1 x 55.2 cm
Private Collection © The Estate of David Milne

Black, p. 59 [Not Exhibited]
1914, oil on canvas
51.9 x 62.1 cm
Gift of the Founders, Robert and Signe McMichael
McMichael Canadian Art Collection 1966.16.23
© The Estate of David Milne

The Black Couch, p. 56
1914, oil on canvas
50.8 x 55.3 cm
Private Collection
© The Estate of David Milne

Black Waterfall, p. 25 [Not Exhibited]
1921, oil on canvas, mounted on hardboard
48.5 x 56.3 cm
The Thomson Collection at the Art Gallery of Ontario, Toronto
2003/20 © The Estate of David Milne

Blue Lake, p. 185
1935, oil on canvas
41.3 x 51.5 cm
Art Gallery of Ontario, Toronto
Gift from the J.S. McLean Collection, by Canada Packers Inc., Toronto, 1990
89/893 © The Estate of David Milne

The Blue Rocker, p. 20 [Not Exhibited]
1914, oil on canvas
50.8 x 50.8 cm
Art Gallery of Ontario, Toronto
Anonymous gift in memory of J.S. McLean, Esquire, 1958
57/24 © The Estate of David Milne

Bomb Crater behind Vimy Station, p. 96 [Not Exhibited]
1919, watercolour over graphite on wove paper
25.4 x 35.4 cm
National Gallery of Canada, Ottawa
Transfer from the Canadian War Memorials, 1921
© The Estate of David Milne

Boston Corners, p. 72 [Not Exhibited]
1917–18, oil on canvas
51.2 x 66.4 cm
National Gallery of Canada, Ottawa
© The Estate of David Milne

The Boulder, pp. 30, 68
1916, oil on canvas
61.7 x 66.7 cm
Winnipeg Art Gallery
Acquired with the assistance of the Women's Committee and The Winnipeg Foundation, G-62-12 © The Estate of David Milne

Bramshott: Interior of the Wesleyan Hut, p. 82
1919, watercolour over graphite on wove paper
38.5 x 50.6 cm
National Gallery of Canada, Ottawa
Transfer from the Canadian War Memorials, 1921
© The Estate of David Milne

Bright Curtains, p. 57
1914, oil on canvas
45.8 x 40.7 cm
Collection of John and Helen O'Brian
© The Estate of David Milne

The Cathedral, Arras, p. 109
1919, watercolour over graphite on wove paper
70.6 x 50.4 cm
National Gallery of Canada, Ottawa
Transfer from the Canadian War Memorials, 1921
© The Estate of David Milne

City Rain, p. 19 [Not Exhibited]
1911–12, oil on canvas
46.4 x 38.7cm
Private Collection © The Estate of David Milne

Clouds over the Village, p. 169
1932, oil on canvas
45.8 x 55.9 cm
Private Collection © The Estate of David Milne

Cobalt Forms, p. 36 [Not Exhibited]
c. 1913, watercolour on paper on board
51.7 x 39.3 cm
Milne Family Collection © The Estate of David Milne

Columbus Monument, p. 52
1912, oil on canvas
50.8 x 45.7 cm
Milne Family Collection © The Estate of David Milne

Courcelette from the Cemetery, p. 110
1919, watercolour over graphite on wove paper
35.4 x 50.6 cm
National Gallery of Canada, Ottawa
Transfer from the Canadian War Memorials, 1921
© The Estate of David Milne

Doorway of the Painting House, p. 123 [Not Exhibited]
1921, watercolour over graphite on buff wove paper
40.9 x 40.9 cm
National Gallery of Canada, Ottawa
© The Estate of David Milne

Dreamland Tower, Coney Island, p. 41
1912, watercolour with bodycolour over black chalk on board
49 x 37.6 cm
Trustees of the British Museum © The Estate of David Milne

Drift on the Stump, p. 119
1921, oil on canvas
36 x 40 cm
Vancouver Art Gallery, Gift from the Douglas M. Duncan Collection, VAG 70.61 © The Estate of David Milne

Entrance to Cellar Shelter in Monchy-le-Preux, p. 88
1919, watercolour over graphite on wove paper
35.4 x 50.5 cm
National Gallery of Canada, Ottawa
Transfer from the Canadian War Memorials, 1921
© The Estate of David Milne

Fifth Avenue, Easter Sunday, p. 45
1912, watercolour on illustration board
56.6 x 43.2 cm
Private Collection © The Estate of David Milne

Figure on the Rocks, p. 65
1916, oil on canvas
50.5 x 61 cm
Private Collection, Toronto
© The Estate of David Milne

Flooded Prospect Shaft II, p. 153
1929, oil on canvas
46.2 x 55.6 cm
National Gallery of Canada, Ottawa
Vincent Massey Bequest, 1968
© The Estate of David Milne

Flour Bag, p. 170
1935, oil on canvas
30.5 x 35.6 cm
Private Collection © The Estate of David Milne

Flowers and Easel, p. 144
1929, oil on canvas
51.1 x 61.1 cm
Collection of Victoria University in the University of Toronto
© The Estate of David Milne

Flowers of the Maple, p. 167
1937, oil on canvas
30.7 x 35.9 cm
National Gallery of Canada, Ottawa
© The Estate of David Milne

42nd Street Library, p. 43
1913, watercolour on illustration board
42.9 x 36.5 cm
Milne Family Collection © The Estate of David Milne

Framed Etching (Lilies from the Bush), p. 160
1931, oil on canvas
66.4 x 71.7 cm
Collection of Global Affairs Canada, © The Estate of David Milne

From a German Gun-pit at Bailleul, East of Vimy, p. 91 [Not Exhibited]
1919, watercolour over graphite on wove paper
25.1 x 35.3 cm
National Gallery of Canada, Ottawa
Transfer from the Canadian War Memorials, 1921
© The Estate of David Milne

Gentle Snowfall, pp. 114–5
1919, oil on canvas
46 x 56.3 cm
National Gallery of Canada, Ottawa
Gift from the Douglas M. Duncan Collection, 1970 © The Estate of David Milne

German Pillbox at Messines, p. 98
1919, watercolour over graphite on wove paper
29.9 x 36 cm
National Gallery of Canada, Ottawa
Transfer from the Canadian War Memorials, 1921
© The Estate of David Milne

Gray Billboards, p. 51
c. 1912, oil on canvas
61 x 50.8 cm
Milne Family Collection
© The Estate of David Milne

Gray Pool, p. 154
1929, oil on canvas
51 x 61 cm
The Mendel Art Gallery Collection at Remai Modern. Gift of the Mendel family, 1965
© The Estate of David Milne

Haystack, p. 138 [Not Exhibited]
1923, oil on canvas
30.5 x 40.7 cm
Gift of the Founders, Robert and Signe McMichael
McMichael Canadian Art Collection
1966.16.26 © The Estate of David Milne

Heavy Snow, p. 32 [Not Exhibited]
1915, watercolour on paper
61 x 55.9
Milne Family Collection
© The Estate of David Milne

Interior with Paintings, p. 55
1914, oil on canvas
50.7 x 61 cm
Winnipeg Art Gallery
Acquired with the assistance of the Women's Committee and The Winnipeg Foundation, G-62-7 © The Estate of David Milne

Lanterns and Snowshoes (Interior of Tea-House), p. 130 [Not Exhibited]
1923, watercolour on paper
38.1 x 55 cm
Milne Family Collection
© The Estate of David Milne

Library Interior, p. 42
c. 1911–13, watercolour on paper
50.8 x 45.8 cm
Private Collection © The Estate of David Milne

Liévin, p. 92
1919, watercolour over graphite on wove paper
35.5 x 50.7 cm
National Gallery of Canada, Ottawa
Transfer from the Canadian War Memorials, 1921
© The Estate of David Milne

Lightning, p. 183
1936, oil on canvas
31.8 x 36.7 cm
MacKenzie Art Gallery, University of Regina Collection, gift from the Douglas M. Duncan Collection © The Estate of David Milne

Limestone Rocks, p. 67
1916, gouache and graphite on paper
39.1 x 55.3 cm
Winnipeg Art Gallery
Acquired with funds from The Winnipeg Foundation, G-68-38
© The Estate of David Milne

Looking towards Thélus and Thélus Wood from a Nissen Hut under the Nine Elms, p. 90 [Not Exhibited]
1919, watercolour over graphite on wove paper
35.4 x 50.5 cm
National Gallery of Canada, Ottawa
Transfer from the Canadian War Memorials, 1921
© The Estate of David Milne

Madonna and Child after Taddeo Gaddi's Madonna and Child Enthroned with Saints, p. 76 [Not Exhibited]
c. 1911–12, watercolour on illustration board
50.8 x 27.3 cm
Milne Family Collection © The Estate of David Milne

Moccassin Flower, p. 174
1935, oil on canvas
46.34 x 56 cm
Gift of David H.M. Vaughan and Lucinda Flemer Executors of the Estate of the Late L. Marguerite Vaughan
The Beaverbrook Art Gallery Fredericton, NB © The Estate of David Milne

Montreal Crater, Vimy Ridge, pp. 94–5
1919, watercolour over graphite on wove paper
35.3 x 101.3 cm
National Gallery of Canada, Ottawa
Transfer from the Canadian War Memorials, 1921
© The Estate of David Milne

Neuville-Saint-Vaast from the Poppy Fields, p. 111
1919, watercolour over graphite on wove paper
35.4 x 50.7 cm
National Gallery of Canada, Ottawa
Transfer from the Canadian War Memorials, 1921
© The Estate of David Milne

Northern Lights, p. 189
1935, oil on canvas
31 x 35.9 cm
Private Collection © The Estate of David Milne

Ollie Matson's House in Snow, p. 165
1932, oil on canvas
50.6 x 60.8 cm
National Gallery of Canada, Ottawa
Gift of Vincent Massey, 1936 © The Estate of David Milne

Ollie Matson's House Is Just a Square Red Cloud, p. 164
1931, oil on canvas
46.2 x 56 cm
National Gallery of Canada, Ottawa
Vincent Massey Bequest, 1968
© The Estate of David Milne

One Small Maple, p. 167
1936, oil on canvas
31.7 x 35.6 cm
Private Collection, Calgary
© The Estate of David Milne

Outlet of the Pond, Late Afternoon, p. 136
1926, oil on canvas
45.8 x 55.9 cm
Private Collection © The Estate of David Milne

Painting Place I, p. 124 [Not Exhibited]
1926, oil on canvas
40.7 x 50.8 cm
Collection of The Sobey Art Foundation
© The Estate of David Milne

Painting Place III, p. 157
1930, oil on canvas
51.3 x 66.4 cm
National Gallery of Canada, Ottawa
Vincent Massey Bequest, 1968
© The Estate of David Milne

Painting Place: Brown and Black, p. 124 [Not Exhibited]
c. 1926, oil on canvas
30.7 x 41 cm
Gift from the Douglas M. Duncan Collection
McMichael Canadian Art Collection
1981.41.1 © The Estate of David Milne

Passchendaele, Ruins of the Church at the End of the Road, p. 105
1919, watercolour over graphite on wove paper
35.4 x 50.5 cm
National Gallery of Canada, Ottawa
Transfer from the Canadian War Memorials, 1921
© The Estate of David Milne

Passing Car, p. 44
1913, oil on canvas
40.7 x 50.8 cm
Private Collection
© The Estate of David Milne

Path in the Woods, p. 117
1921, watercolour on paper
37.7 x 54.6 cm
Art Gallery of Ontario, Toronto
Gift from the J.S. McLean Collection, Toronto, 1969; donated by the Ontario Heritage Foundation, 1988. L69.43
© The Estate of David Milne

Pink Reflections, Bishop's Pond (Outlet of the Pond I), p. 127
1920, watercolour over graphite on wove paper
37.7 x 54.7 cm
National Gallery of Canada, Ottawa
Gift from the Douglas M. Duncan Collection, 1970
© The Estate of David Milne

Pond at Big Moose (Outlet of the Pond I), p. 133
1926, oil on canvas
41.6 x 51.5 cm
Carleton University Art Gallery, Ottawa, Canada: The Jack and Frances Barwick Collection © The Estate of David Milne

Prospect Hole, p. 155
1929, oil on canvas
50.9 x 61 cm
Winnipeg Art Gallery
Gift of the Women's Committee, G-60-3
© The Estate of David Milne

Raspberry Jam, p. 173
1936, oil on canvas
46 x 56.3 cm
National Gallery of Canada, Ottawa
Gift from the Douglas M. Duncan Collection, 1970
© The Estate of David Milne

Reader with Cat, p. 63
1916, oil on canvas
50.4 x 60.6 cm
Private Collection, Ontario © The Estate of David Milne

Red, p. 58
1914, oil on canvas
50.8 x 55.6 cm
Milne Family Collection
© The Estate of David Milne

Red Pool, Temagami, p. 148
1929, oil on canvas
50.8 x 61 cm
Private Collection, Toronto, Canada
© The Estate of David Milne

Reflected Forms, p. 79
1917, watercolour on paper
38.2 x 56.5 cm
Art Gallery of Greater Victoria
Women's Committee Cultural Fund
© The Estate of David Milne

Ripon: High Street, p. 83
1919, opaque watercolour over graphite on paper
50.8 x 35.6 cm
Art Gallery of Ontario, Toronto
Bequest of Mrs. J.P. Barwick (from the Douglas M. Duncan Collection), 1985
85/127 © The Estate of David Milne

The Road to Passchendaele, German Pillboxes on Each Side, p. 106-7
[Not Exhibited]
1919, watercolour over graphite on wove paper
35.4 x 50.5 cm
National Gallery of Canada, Ottawa
Transfer from the Canadian War Memorials, 1921
© The Estate of David Milne

Rock Flowers, p. 175
1935, oil on canvas
45.2 x 55.5 cm
Art Gallery of Greater Victoria
Bequest of Mrs. J.P. Barwick (from the Douglas M. Duncan Collection)
© The Estate of David Milne

Rock Forms, p. 69
1916, watercolour on paper
38.8 x 56.5 cm
Julia and Gilles Ouellette
© The Estate of David Milne

Rocks in Spring, p. 137
1922, oil on canvas
45.8 x 56.2 cm
Collection of the Winnipeg Art Gallery, G-54-4
© The Estate of David Milne

Ruined Furnace, p. 135
1921, watercolour on paper
38 x 51 cm
Private Collection
© The Estate of David Milne

Screened Road into Monchy-le-Preux, p. 93
1919, watercolour over graphite on wove paper
35.4 x 50.7 cm
National Gallery of Canada, Ottawa
Transfer from the Canadian War Memorials, 1921
© The Estate of David Milne

Setting Stars, p. 182
1935, oil on canvas
30.8 x 35.9 cm
Collection of Nancy and Ian Willson
© The Estate of David Milne

Shadows in the Woods, p. 116
1921, watercolour on paper
38.1 x 55.9 cm
Private Collection, Vancouver, B.C.
© The Estate of David Milne

Shattered Images in Thélus Cemetery, p. 103
1919, watercolour over graphite on wove paper
35.3 x 50.5 cm
National Gallery of Canada, Ottawa
Transfer from the Canadian War Memorials, 1921
© The Estate of David Milne

Shimmering Water, p. 40
1912, watercolour on illustration board
37.8 x 45.1 cm
Collection of Molly Anne and Bill Macdonald
© The Estate of David Milne

Shore Line, Six Mile Lake, p. 184
1936, oil on canvas
47.0 x 56.5 cm
Collection of the Vancouver Art Gallery, Gift from the Douglas M. Duncan Collection, VAG 70.62
© The Estate of David Milne

Side Door, Clarke's House, p. 128
c. 1923, oil on canvas
30.5 x 40.7 cm
Gift of the Founders, Robert and Signe McMichael
McMichael Canadian Art Collection
1976.25.2 © The Estate of David Milne

Skyscraper Pillbox at Messines, pp. 34, 99
1919, watercolour over graphite on wove paper
25.5 x 35.5 cm
National Gallery of Canada, Ottawa
Transfer from the Canadian War Memorials, 1921
© The Estate of David Milne

Smoke, p. 188
1935, oil on canvas
30.5 x 25.6 cm
Private Collection
© The Estate of David Milne

Snow Patches, pp. 22, 73
1917, oil on canvas
45.9 x 66.4 cm
Collection of Dr. W.B. Winter & J.W. Senyshyn, Nova Scotia, Canada
© The Estate of David Milne

Snowy Hemlocks, p. 18, p. 120 [Not Exhibited]
1921, oil on canvas
35.6 x 38.4cm
Private Collection
© The Estate of David Milne

Sparkle of Glass, pp. 139, 206–7
1926 or 1927, oil on canvas
41 x 51 cm
National Gallery of Canada, Ottawa
Vincent Massey Bequest, 1968
© The Estate of David Milne

Stream in the Woods, p. 26 [Not Exhibited]
1929, colour drypoint on wove paper
18.6 x 24.1 cm (top)
19.7 x 27.2 cm (bottom)
National Gallery of Canada, Ottawa
The Milne-Duncan Bequest, 1970
© The Estate of David Milne

Stump among the Saplings, p. 168
1932, oil on canvas
30.5 x 41.3 cm
Collection of Dr. W.B. Winter & J.W. Senyshyn, Nova Scotia, Canada
© The Estate of David Milne

Sumach, p. 172
1935, oil on canvas
48.5 x 55.9 cm
Private Collection © The Estate of David Milne

Summer Colours, p. 178
1936, oil over graphite on canvas
31 x 36.5 cm
McMichael Canadian Art Collection, Purchase 1993, 1993.4.2
© The Estate of David Milne

Summer Night, Saugerties, p. 62
1914, watercolour on paper
51.7 x 44.4 cm
Collection of Gordon and Janet Nixon
© The Estate of David Milne

Sunset beyond the Islands, p. 177
1936, oil on canvas
31 x 36 cm
Collection of The Sobey Art Foundation
© The Estate of David Milne

Tent in Temagami, p. 147
1929, oil on canvas
40.2 x 50 cm
Collection of the Tom Thomson Art Gallery, Owen Sound, Ontario. Bequest from the Douglas M. Duncan Collection, 1970.
© The Estate of David Milne

Thaw in the Woods, p. 125
1921, oil on canvas
34.9 x 45.7 cm
Private Collection, Ontario © The Estate of David Milne

'The Twins' Crater, Vimy Ridge, p. 97
1919, watercolour over graphite on wove paper
35.3 x 50.6 cm
National Gallery of Canada, Ottawa
Transfer from the Canadian War Memorials, 1921
© The Estate of David Milne

Trees in Spring, p. 71
c. 1917, oil on canvas
55.8 x 66.1 cm
National Gallery of Canada, Ottawa
Gift of Douglas M. Duncan, Toronto, 1968
© The Estate of David Milne

Verandah at Night II, p. 131 [Not Exhibited]
1923, oil on canvas
38.5 x 54.3 cm
Private Collection
© The Estate of David Milne

Water in a Jar, p. 171
1935, oil on canvas
30.5 x 35.6 cm
Private Collection © The Estate of David Milne

Water Lilies, p. 142
1928, oil on canvas
40.2 x 50.3 cm
Art Gallery of Greater Victoria
Gift of Mrs. H.A. Dyde, Edmonton
© The Estate of David Milne

The Waterfall, p. 64
1916, watercolour on paper
45.1 x 56.3 cm
Milne Family Collection
© The Estate of David Milne

Waterfall, p. 162
1930, colour drypoint on Japan paper
25.2 x 29.3 cm
National Gallery of Canada, Ottawa
The Milne-Duncan Bequest, 1970
© The Estate of David Milne

Waterlilies and the Sunday Paper (Water Lilies, Temagami), p. 143
1929, oil on canvas
51.4 x 62 cm
Gift of the Right Honourable Vincent Massey, 1947
Hart House Collection HH1947.003, University of Toronto, Toronto, Ontario, Canada © The Estate of David Milne

White Cloud, Boston Corners, p. 22
[Not Exhibited]
1918, oil on canvas
50.8 x 66 cm
Private Collection
© The Estate of David Milne

White, the Waterfall, pp. 25, 118
1921, oil on canvas
45.7 x 56 cm
National Gallery of Canada, Ottawa
© The Estate of David Milne

White Trees, p. 66
c. 1916, watercolour on paper
39.4 x 56.6 cm
Private Collection, Toronto
© The Estate of David Milne

White Trees in a Green Valley, p. 70
c. 1916, oil on canvas
50.7 x 60.9 cm
Collection of the Winnipeg Art Gallery
Acquired with the assistance of the Women's Committee and The Winnipeg Foundation, G-62-10 © The Estate of David Milne

White Waterlilies in a Prospector's Cabin, p. 156
1929, oil on canvas
50.6 x 62 cm
National Gallery of Canada, Ottawa
Vincent Massey Bequest, 1968
© The Estate of David Milne

Winter Shadow, p. 37 [Not Exhibited]
1912, watercolour on paper
35.5 x 45.7 cm
Milne Family Collection
© The Estate of David Milne

Wrecked Tanks outside Monchy-le-Preux, pp. 23, 89
1919, watercolour over graphite on wove paper
35.4 x 50.7 cm
National Gallery of Canada, Ottawa
Transfer from the Canadian War Memorials, 1921
© The Estate of David Milne

Yellow Billboards, p. 53
c. 1912, oil on canvas
45.8 x 55.9 cm
Private Collection, Toronto
© The Estate of David Milne

Zillebeke: Maple Copse and Observatory Ridge from Dormy House, p. 102
1919, watercolour over graphite on wove paper
35.4 x 50.5 cm
National Gallery of Canada, Ottawa
Transfer from the Canadian War Memorials, 1921
© The Estate of David Milne

Comparative Works (Not in Exhibition)

Edward Burtynsky, p. 150
Grasses, Bruce Peninsula, Ontario
1981, chromogenic print
Nicholas Metivier Gallery, Toronto

Edward Burtynsky, p. 152
Mines #13, Inco—Abandoned Mine Shaft, Crean Hill Mine, Sudbury, Ontario
1984, chromogenic print
Nicholas Metivier Gallery, Toronto

Peter Doig, p. 36
Windowpane
1993, oil on canvas
250 x 200 cm
Collection of Victoria and Warren Miro
© Peter Doig. All Rights Reserved, DACS 2018

Arthur Dove, p. 30
Silver Sun
1929, oil, metallic paint, and an unidentified material (possibly wax) on canvas
55.3 x 74.9 cm
Art Institute of Chicago

Paterson Ewen, p. 181
Lightning Storm
1971, acrylic and metal on carved linoleum on board
30.5 x 22.9cm
Private Collection © Mary Alison Handford

Marsden Hartley, p. 30
Smelt Brook Falls
1937, oil on board
71.1 x 58.1 cm
Saint Louis Art Museum
Eliza McMillan Trust 9:1939

Alexander Young Jackson, p. 34
A Copse, Evening
1918, oil on canvas
86.6 x 112.2 cm
Canadian War Museum, Ottawa

John Marin, p. 50
Woolworth Building, No. 31
1912, watercolour over graphite
47 x 39.8 cm
National Gallery of Art, Washington DC
Gift of Eugene and Agnes E. Meyer 1967.13.9.
© ARS, NY and DACS, London 2017

Henri Matisse, p. 21
The Red Studio
1911, oil on canvas
181 x 219.1 cm
The Museum of Modern Art, New York
Mrs. Simon Guggenheim Fund. Acc. n.: 8.1949.
© Succession H. Matisse/ DACS 2017

Claude Monet, p. 18
Haystack, End of Summer, Morning
1891, oil on canvas
60.5 × 100.8 cm
Musée d'Orsay, Paris

Claude Monet, p. 78
Water Lilies (Nymphéas)
1907, oil on canvas
92.1 × 81.2 cm
The Museum of Fine Arts, Houston,
Gift of Mrs. Harry C. Hanszen, 68.31

Claude Monet, p. 18
Wheatstacks, Snow Effect, Morning
1891, oil on canvas
64.8 x 99.7 cm
The J. Paul Getty Museum, Los Angeles

Georgia O'Keeffe, p. 30
Gray Tree, Lake George
1925, oil on canvas
91.4 x 76.2 cm
The Metropolitan Museum of Art
Alfred Stieglitz Collection, Bequest of Georgia O'Keeffe, 1986 (1987.377.2)
© The Metropolitan Museum of Art

Maurice Brazil Prendergast, p. 49
Central Park, New York
c. 1901, watercolour and pencil on paper
38.7 x 55.9 cm
Williams College Museum of Art, Williamstown, MA, USA: Gift of Mrs. Charles Prendergast in memory of Maurice and Charles Prendergast (67.13)

John Sloan, p. 49
The Hairdresser's Window
1907, oil on canvas
81.2 x 66 cm
The Ella Gallup Sumner and Mary Catlin Sumner Collection Fund, 1947.240
Wadsworth Atheneum © Estate of John Sloan. ARS, NY/ DACS, London 2017

Alfred Stieglitz, p. 32
From the Back Window, 291, Snow Covered Tree, Back Yard
1915, platinum print
24.4 x 19.1 cm
National Gallery of Art, Washington, DC, Alfred Stieglitz Collection

Tom Thomson, p. 18
Winter Thaw in the Woods
1917, oil on composite wood-pulp board
21.6 x 26.8 cm
The Thomson Collection at the Art Gallery of Ontario, Toronto
AGOID.69207

Édouard Vuillard, p. 20
Figures in an Interior
1896, oil on canvas
2.125 x 1.545 m
Petit Palais, Musée des Beaux-Arts de la Ville de Paris

James Abbott McNeill Whistler, p. 78
Nocturne: Blue and Silver—Chelsea
1871, oil paint on wood
50.2 x 60.8 cm
Tate: Bequeathed by Miss Rachel and Miss Jean Alexander, 1972

Photographs

David Milne, Self-portrait, Black Lake, Quebec, 1918, p. 16
(Milne Family Collection)

David Milne and his pupils, Walkerton, Ontario, p. 19
c. 1900-3
E.P.Taylor Library and Archives, Art Gallery of Ontario, Toronto, uncatalogued
(Milne Family Collection)

Life class at the Art Students League, p. 19
1906, unknown photographer
(Milne Family Collection)

David Milne in northern France, 1919, p. 23
E.P. Taylor Library and Archives, Art Gallery of Ontario, Toronto, uncatalogued
(Milne Family Collection)

David Milne near his Alander cabin, p. 24
c. 1920, unknown photographer
(Milne Family Collection)

David and Patsy Milne, Boston Corners, p. 24
1918, unknown photographer (Milne Family Collection)

David Milne at Six Mile Lake, p. 28
c. 1934, Photographed by Douglas Duncan
(Milne Family Collection)

Wurts Bros., p. 48
10–12 East 42nd Street
Gelatin silver print
Wurts Bros. (New York, N.Y.) / Museum of the City of New York. X2010.11.5466

Street scene, New York City, p. 49
c. 1909
E.P. Taylor Library and Archives, Art Gallery of Ontario, Toronto, uncatalogued
(Milne Family Collection)

David Milne at his Alander cabin, p. 122
1921, gelatin silver print
8.9 x 12.8 cm
Art Gallery of Ontario, Toronto

Dart's Lake, p. 132
1921, gelatin silver prints, David Milne (x4)
Portrait photos: 8.9 x 12.8 cm; landscape photos: 12.8 x 8.9 cm
Art Gallery of Ontario, Toronto

Charcoal furnace near Riga Lake, p. 134
1921, gelatin silver prints, David Milne (x2)
8.9 x 12.8 cm
Art Gallery of Ontario, Toronto

Dale Estate shipping room, Brampton, p. 163
c. 1910, gelatin silver print, unknown photographer
Region of Peel Archives, E.A. Parsons fonds, series 2 'Prints', sub-series 6

David Milne, Douglas Duncan and Alan Jarvis at Six Mile Lake, Ontario, p. 180
c. 1936, unknown photographer
(Milne Family Collection)

David Milne at Six Mile Lake, p. 208
Unknown photographer
c. 1933
(Milne Family Collection)

Archival Material

Mineral map of Canada, pp. 2–3
1925, Department of Mines, Ottawa
E.P. Taylor Library and Archives,
Art Gallery of Ontario, Toronto
Milne Family Gift, 2009

David Milne, p. 166
c. 1936, graphite on paper (x2)
18 x 23 cm
E.P. Taylor Library and Archives,
Art Gallery of Ontario, Toronto
Milne Family Gift, 2009

David Milne, p. 186
c. 1936, graphite on paper
18 x 23 cm
E.P. Taylor Library and Archives,
Art Gallery of Ontario, Toronto
Milne Family Gift, 2009

Notes from Alander cabin, 1 December 1920, p. 33
Recycled paper
E.P. Taylor Library and Archives,
Art Gallery of Ontario, Toronto
Milne Family Gift, 2009

Postcards, p. 84
Ruines d'Ypres: Maisons en ruines;
Ypres-Potisje. Puinen van het Kasteel;
Passchendaele. Puinen der Kerk en Kerkstraat
c. 1919, collotype prints (x3)
9 x 14 cm
Milne Family Collection

Postcards, p. 100
Messines. Puinen van het kasteel; Arras.
Guerre Européenne. Ce qu'il reste de la Tour
du Beffroi; Ypres 1919. Cathédrale et ancien
Évêché
c. 1919, collotype prints (x3)
9 x 14 cm
Milne Family Collection

PHOTOGRAPHIC CREDITS

All photography at Baptiste Lake, Ontario, 2017, by Craig Boyko, pp. 4–5, 10, 15, 190–1

Catalogue Entries

pp. 38 (bleed), 43, 44, 51–3, 58, 64–5, 69, 135, 148, 182, 188 Michael Cullen, Toronto
pp. 40, 56, 136 Frank Tancredi Photography, Toronto
p. 41 © The Trustees of the British Museum
pp. 42, 167 (bottom) Photo by John Dean
pp. 46, 54, 60 (bleed), 71–2, 74, 80 (bleed), 82,88–99, 101–11, 112 (bleed), 114–15, 118, 123, 127, 139, 140 (bleed), 153, 156, 157, 158 (bleed), 164–5, 167 (top), 173, 187, 206–7 Photo: NGC
pp. 55, 68 Photographer: Ernest Mayer
pp. 57, 126, 170 Rachel Topham Photography
pp. 59, 128, 129, 138, 178 McMichael Canadian Art Collection
pp. 67, 70, 137, 155 Photographer: Leif Norman
pp. 62 Courtesy Mira Godard Gallery
pp. 63, 66, 73, 120, 125, 168 Image courtesy of Heffel Fine Art Auction House
pp. 79, 142, 175 © Art Gallery of Greater Victoria
pp. 83, 117, 176, 185 Art Gallery of Ontario
pp. 84, 100, 132, 134, 166 (top & bottom), 171, 186 Craig Boyko
pp. 116, 172 Photograph courtesy Masters Gallery Ltd
pp. 119, 184 Trevor Mills, Vancouver Art Gallery
p. 133 Photography by Justin Wonnacott
p. 143 Toni Hafkenscheid
p. 154 © Remai Modern
p. 177 Sobey Art Foundation
p. 183 Don Hall, courtesy of the MacKenzie Art Gallery

Comparative Images

p. 14 Myfanwy Vernon-Hunt
pp. 18 (top left), 25 (top) The Thomson Collection at the Art Gallery of Ontario
p. 18 (top right) Digital image courtesy of the Getty's Open Content Program
p. 18 (bottom right) Photo © RMN-Grand Palais (Musée d'Orsay) / Hervé Lewandowski
pp. 18 (bottom left), 22 (top & bottom), 181 Image courtesy of Heffel Fine Art Auction House
p. 20 (top) Photo © RMN-Grand Palais / Agence Bulloz
p. 20 (bottom) Art Gallery of Ontario
p. 21 (left) © 2018. Digital image, The Museum of Modern Art, New York / Scala, Florence
pp. 21 (right), 23 (centre), 25 (bottom), 26 (top & bottom), 34 (bottom), 162 Photo: National Gallery of Canada
pp. 23 (bottom), 36 (right), 37 Courtesy of the Estate of David Milne and Mira Godard Gallery
p. 30 (top left) Image courtesy of Saint Louis Art Museum
p. 30 (top right) © 2018. Image copyright The Metropolitan Museum of Art / Art Resource / Scala, Florence
p. 30 (bottom left) © 2018. Digital image, The Art Institute of Chicago / Art Resource, NY / Scala, Florence
p. 30 (bottom right) Photographer: Ernest Mayer
pp. 32 (left), 50 © Board of Trustees, National Gallery of Art, Washington
p. 36 (left) Collection of Victoria and Warren Miro
p. 48 Museum of the City of New York
p. 49 (top right) Allen Phillips / Wadsworth Atheneum
p. 49 (bottom) © Williams College Museum of Art, Williamstown, MA. Petegorsky / Gipe photo
p. 78 (top) © Tate, London 2018
p. 78 (bottom) Photograph © The Museum of Fine Arts, Houston
p. 124 (top) McMichael Canadian Art Collection
p. 124 (bottom) Sobey Art Foundation
pp. 150, 152 Photo Edward Burtynsky, courtesy of Nicholas Metivier Gallery, Toronto
p. 163 © Peel Art Gallery Museum and Archives

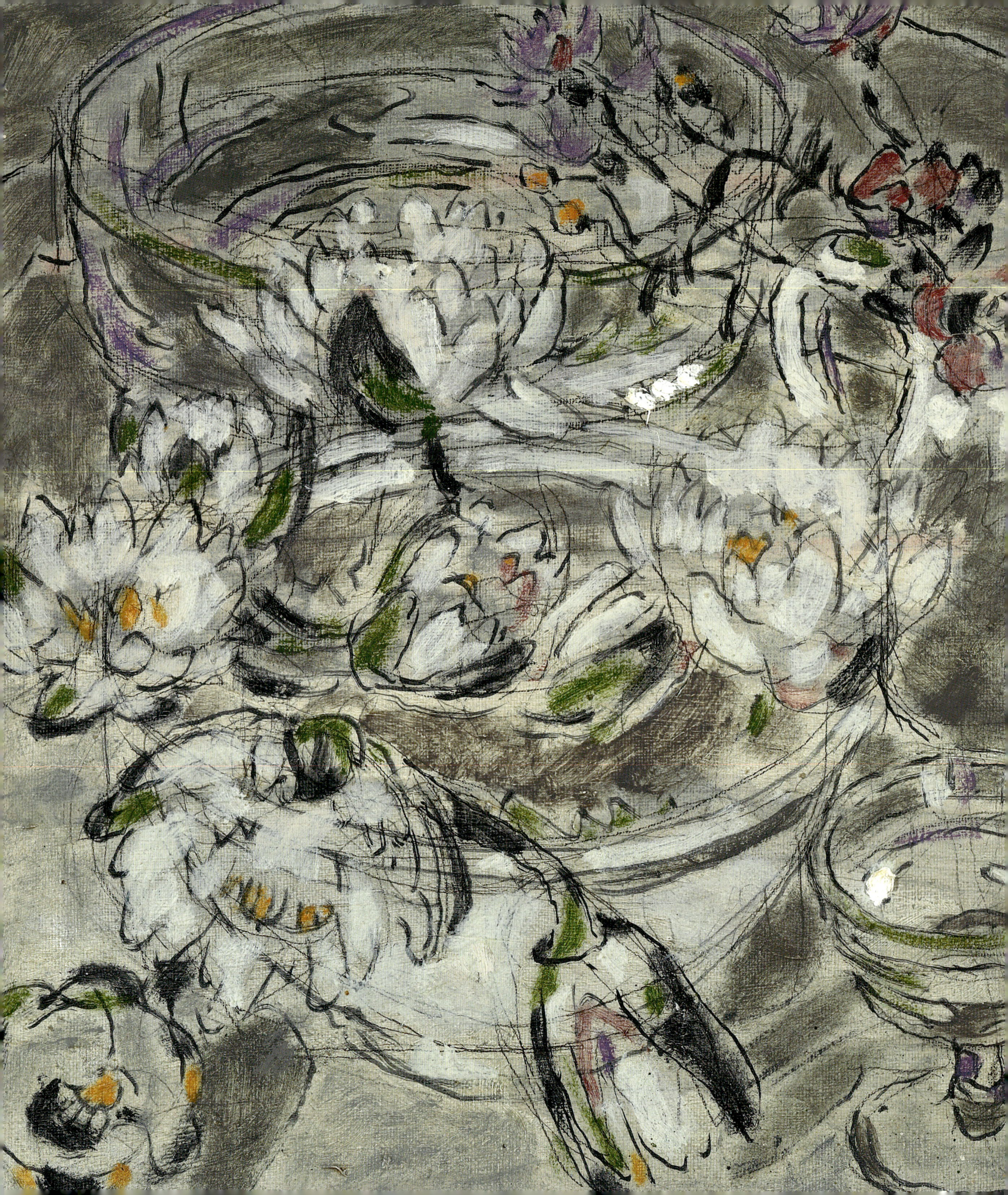

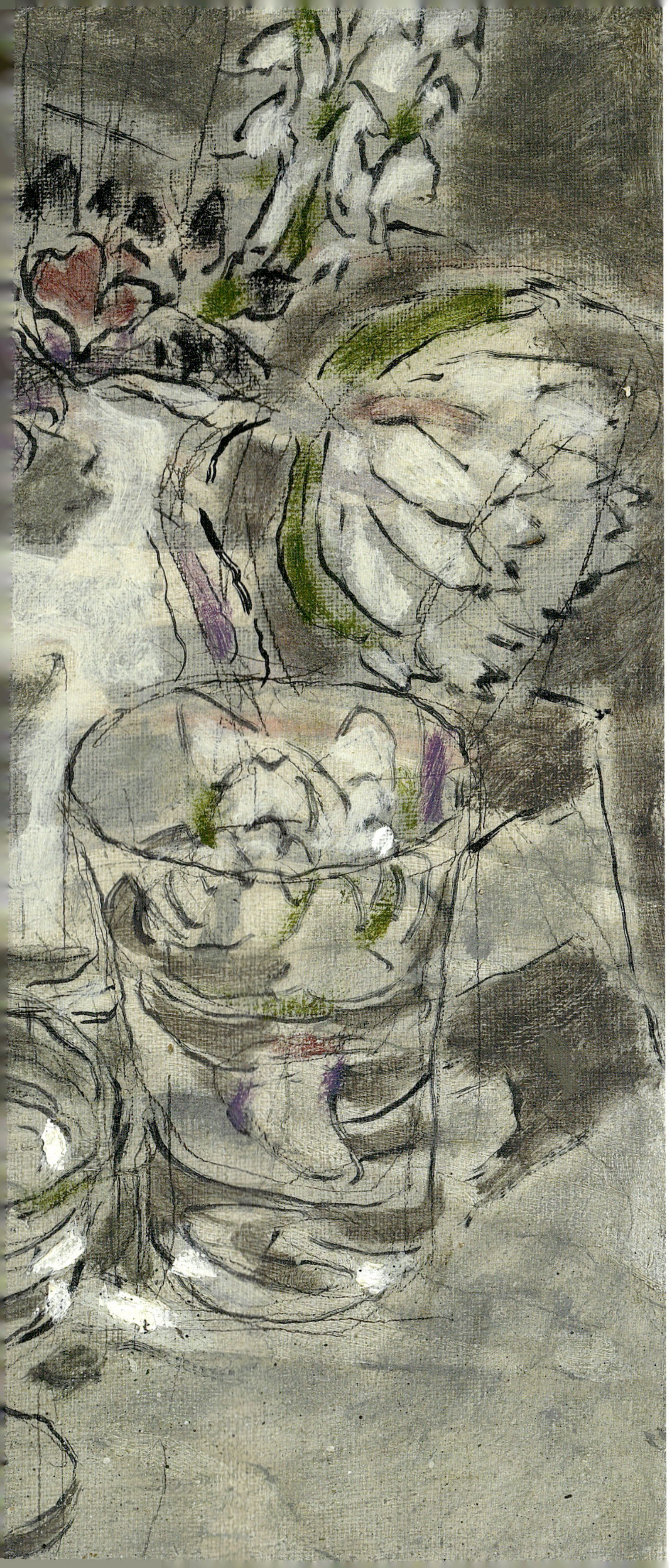

Who flies with the whirlwind is at rest

No one in France
could make such galaxies
of glass and water

intricate with flowers

All space came out in flowers
miraculous, erupting from a void or mouth

And every breath
a wind or sun, a season or delight
drew colour from the earth

as if a brush
stroked virgin canvas

D. G. Jones, from 'A Garland of Milne', 1977

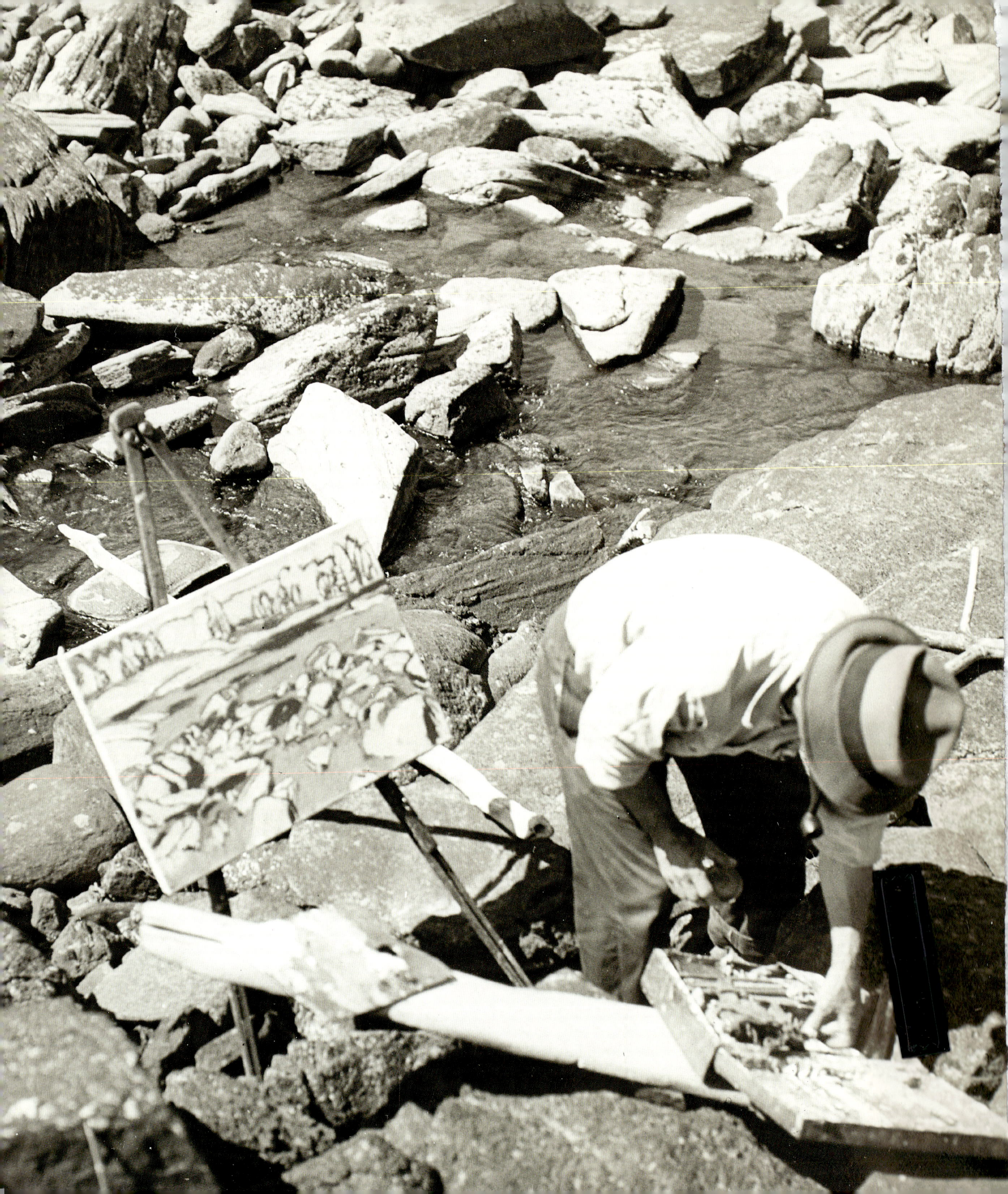